GORDON BROWN

GORDON BROWN
POWER WITH PURPOSE

James Macintyre

BLOOMSBURY PUBLISHING
LONDON · OXFORD · NEW YORK · NEW DELHI · SYDNEY

BLOOMSBURY PUBLISHING
Bloomsbury Publishing Plc
50 Bedford Square, London, WC1B 3DP, UK
Bloomsbury Publishing Ireland Limited,
29 Earlsfort Terrace, Dublin 2, D02 AY28, Ireland

BLOOMSBURY, BLOOMSBURY PUBLISHING and the Diana logo
are trademarks of Bloomsbury Publishing Plc

First published in Great Britain 2026

Copyright © James Macintyre, 2026

James Macintyre is identified as the author of this work in accordance
with the Copyright, Designs and Patents Act 1988

The excerpt on p.135 is taken from *Hack Attack* by Nick Davies, published by
Chatto & Windus. Copyright © Nick Davies 2014, 2025. Reprinted by permission of
The Random House Group Limited.

Every reasonable effort has been made to trace copyright holders of material reproduced
in this book, but if any have been inadvertently overlooked the publishers would be glad
to hear from them. For legal purposes, the Acknowledgements on p. 291 constitute
an extension of this copyright page

All rights reserved. No part of this publication may be: i) reproduced or transmitted
in any form, electronic or mechanical, including photocopying, recording or by means of
any information storage or retrieval system without prior permission in writing from the
publishers; or ii) used or reproduced in any way for the training, development or operation of
artificial intelligence (AI) technologies, including generative AI technologies. The rights holders
expressly reserve this publication from the text and data mining exception as per Article 4(3) of
the Digital Single Market Directive (EU) 2019/790

Bloomsbury Publishing Plc does not have any control over, or responsibility for, any third-
party websites referred to in this book. All internet addresses given in this book were correct
at the time of going to press. The author and publisher regret any inconvenience caused if
addresses have changed or sites have ceased to exist, but can accept no responsibility for any
such changes

A catalogue record for this book is available from the British Library

ISBN: HB: 978-1-5266-7341-1; eBook: 978-1-5266-7340-4

2 4 6 8 10 9 7 5 3 1

Typeset by Six Red Marbles India
Printed and bound in Great Britain by Clays Ltd, Elcograf S.p.A

To find out more about our authors and books visit www.bloomsbury.com
and sign up for our newsletters
For product-safety-related questions contact productsafety@bloomsbury.com

To Rachael

Contents

Prologue 1

PART ONE – THE MAKING OF GORDON BROWN (1951–97)

1. Son of the Manse 9
2. Edinburgh 20
3. Towards Westminster 29
4. Wilderness Years 43
5. Paying the Price 61
6. Turning Point 75
7. Truce 91

PART TWO – TREASURY (MAY 1997–JUNE 2007)

8. Revolution 103
9. The Euro Decision 111
10. Tragedy 121
11. Redistribution, Spending and Deregulation . . . 126
12. Iraq and International Development 141
13. Division, Consolidation and Transition . . 149

PART THREE – NUMBER TEN (JUNE 2007–MAY 2010)

14. Honeymoon and Hesitation 167
15. Saving the World 182
16. Fighting Chance 205

PART FOUR – MORAL LEADERSHIP (2010–)

17 After Downing Street: Referendum — 233
18 Charity Near and Far — 248
19 Joy in the Morning: Gordon Brown's Quiet Faith — 258
20 Supping with the Devil: Gordon Brown Versus the Murdoch Media — 268
21 Conclusion: Power for a Purpose — 281

Acknowledgements — 291
Notes — 294
Index — 309
Image Credits — 324

Prologue

Holed up in Downing Street on Tuesday 11 May 2010, Gordon Brown knew that, finally, the game was up. The general election five days earlier had resulted in a hung Parliament, triggering political turmoil and an end to an unprecedented thirteen consecutive years of Labour government. The votes were still being counted, but Brown had already admitted privately to his long-time aide Sue Nye that his time in office was almost over. Brown recognised then that the election result meant he could not stay on credibly as prime minister even if a Labour coalition with the Liberal Democrats were possible. He could, however, be the one who could broker it. In the best negotiating tradition, he wanted to keep that up his sleeve until the right moment. Brown and Nye had returned to the deserted room in Number 12 Downing Street that Brown had occupied for the last year of his time as prime minister, to find that their emails had been cut off and the furniture rearranged by the civil service. 'That is the brutality of the British electoral system,' says Nye.[1]

Four days previously, on the Friday morning, Brown had snatched a few hours of sleep upstairs and had come back down to the Number Ten offices re-energised. He and Nye heard the Liberal Democrat leader Nick Clegg's statement and knew that the Conservative leader David Cameron would speak in the next half-hour. Brown and the Labour peer Andrew Adonis, who had important Lib Dem connections, were working the phones. 'He was full-focus Gordon,' says Nye. Working with the switchboard at Number Ten, they managed to get as many cabinet colleagues as they could on the line before Brown spoke in Downing Street. He felt he had to explain as quickly as possible the constitutional situation: that the incumbent government remains in place until a majority government can be formed.

Over the weekend, Brown had remained motivated by trying to stop the Tories' austerity programme, for which, he believed, there was no mandate. After all, only 36 per cent of voters – let alone the wider electorate – had opted for the Conservatives. Critics in other parties accused him, during those days of paralysis, of squatting in Downing Street, determined to cling on to power. Even some Labour figures privately conceded that the party's performance, losing ninety-one seats and with just 29 per cent of the vote, made his apparent attempt to cling on to power look doomed.

By the Monday, though, Brown was ready to make the necessary sacrifice and announce he was standing aside as Labour leader in an attempt to retain for his party a chance of forming an alliance with the Lib Dems. There was a moment when the civil service could not decide on the propriety of using the Number Ten lectern for Brown's forthcoming statement. 'This was definitely uncharted waters,' says Nye. 'But in the nick of time we managed to find one that wasn't logoed so that Gordon had somewhere to put his notes.'

Brown then said in Downing Street: 'If it becomes clear that the national interest, which is stable and principled government, can be best served by forming a coalition between the Labour Party and the Liberal Democrats, then I believe I should discharge that duty to form that government which would, in my view, command a majority in the House of Commons in the Queen's speech and any other confidence votes.' But, he added, 'As leader of my party, I must accept that that is a judgment on me. I therefore intend to ask the Labour Party to set in train the processes needed for its own leadership election.' Brown walked back into Number Ten to spontaneous applause among staffers, including Peter Mandelson, who was in tears, along with several other aides. 'Thanks, but back to work, back to work,' Brown said.

The problem, however, was that Clegg, who now admits he was playing for time with Brown to wring more concessions out of the Tories – 'What did they expect us to do?'[2] – had been intent on going into government with the latter.

Come the Tuesday evening, Brown had effectively to resign again, this time finally, as prime minister, and make way for the new Tory-led coalition. In a sign of the multilayered relationships at the heart of New Labour, Brown now took aside Tony Blair's former director of communications Alastair Campbell, who had been fighting for a 'progressive alliance' with the Lib Dems, thanked him, and according to a source added graciously if crudely, 'You're a fucking genius, and don't let anyone tell you otherwise.' Brown was wearing a navy-blue tie behind the scenes and said, 'I can't go out in a blue tie.' The only person who had a red one on was Campbell, who lent it to Brown for his last public appearance as prime minister.

Brown emerged before the cameras, and said of his time in office: 'I have been privileged to learn much about the very best in human nature and a fair amount too about its frailties, including my own. Above all, it was a privilege to serve. And yes, I loved the job, not for its prestige, its titles and its ceremony – which I do not love at all ... And as I leave the second most important job I could ever hold, I cherish even more the first – as a husband and father.'

When Brown landed back in Scotland, his senior civil service foreign affairs adviser Tom Fletcher organised a phone call between him and the then US president, Barack Obama, in which Obama sounded in awe of Brown, the elder statesman. Fletcher recounts: 'And Obama just said [paraphrasing, about the 2008 financial crash], "Yeah, and no one else could have done it at that moment ... I know that people joked about how you save the world. But actually, Gordon, you know, you kind of did."'

Whatever Brown's achievements in office, however, 'nothing in his life became him like the leaving of it', to quote a line from Shakespeare's Scottish play. Brown's reputation has evolved for the better thanks to what he has done since.

And Brown knew about sacrifice. In 1994 he had stood aside for Blair in the Labour leadership struggle. At whatever cost to his future friendship with Blair, this was a personal sacrifice of primary political importance. Indeed, by preserving New Labour unity at this crucial stage, Brown had avoided the historic error made eighteen years earlier when Roy Jenkins, Denis Healey and Anthony Crosland, easily the brightest talents on the social democratic or right wing of the Labour Party, had forfeited the chance of one of them becoming prime minister by failing to agree among themselves which of them should be the leadership candidate when Harold Wilson resigned in 1976. Instead, all three had stood in the first ballot, thus helping to pave the way for James Callaghan's accession to the premiership. Giles Radice, the long-standing Labour MP who had been shadow education secretary under Neil Kinnock, and had long been preoccupied with the destructive impact of that split, swiftly wrote to Brown congratulating him for having ensured it was not repeated.

In his 2002 book *Friends and Rivals* about Crosland, Jenkins and Healey (all of whom had canvassed his support in that 1976 leadership election), Radice would contrast the two cases. Acknowledging 'the strong element of rivalry' within 'the strongest partnership in British politics' – that between Brown and Blair, a tension increased by Brown's ambition to succeed Blair – Radice pointed out that 'the remarkable fact about their relationship, which began when they were first elected as MPs in 1983, is that it survived the election of Blair as leader in 1994 and Brown's standing down in Blair's favour. It then went on to become the linchpin of the election of the New Labour government first elected in 1997 and re-elected by a landslide in 2001.'

When his friend Jimmy Carter died in December 2024, Brown wrote in a telling tribute to the former US president that his 'second act' – after leaving power – would prove more 'momentous' than his time in the Oval Office. Carter's presidency had been 'engulfed with problems', but he had gone on to devote decades to the promotion of democratic rights everywhere and his view 'that wealth and power mattered less than the opportunity to serve'.

It was hard not to infer that Brown saw Carter, whether consciously or not, as a role model. His own premiership had also been 'engulfed with problems'. Like Carter he failed to win a general election after one term. But like Carter, Brown, having lost office and after an understandable period of introspection and even depression at his home, emerged determined to make the most of his authority and freedom as a former leader to pursue the causes which had animated his original attraction to politics. The Gordon Brown story, in other words, does not end in 2010 any more than Carter's did in 1981.

This is one addition to a collection of books about Brown, his premiership and his place in New Labour, but one that seeks to reassess Brown's legacy, fifteen years after Labour last left office – and an aftermath which is still under way.

While this is not an 'authorised' biography, it draws on a series of face-to-face interviews with Brown in Scotland and London, alongside countless correspondence in which Brown was always responsive, papers, emails and details of phone calls, as well as permission for his friends to talk openly to me, and gives fresh angles on Brown's politics and his personality.

Brown is famously flawed. He is acutely aware of those flaws, both real and perceived. During his ten years as chancellor and his three as prime minister, he could be difficult, obstructive and needlessly suspicious, and he had many opponents, inside as well as outside of his party. But Brown, who pursued power for a purpose, is more than due a reappraisal. And talking to people away from Westminster, there appears to be a thirst for the kind of substance that Brown represents. So, what is the truth about him? What makes him tick? Where did he come from, and where is he going? Were he and Tony Blair really so different? What is his legacy? Where does he stand in the rankings of historical Labour figures? How will he be judged? And perhaps above all, what lessons are there from Brown's life for the current Labour Party, in government now, and beyond?

PART ONE

The Making of Gordon Brown (1951–97)

I

Son of the Manse

There's a hill just behind Gordon and Sarah Brown's Victorian family home above the Fife village of North Queensferry, with a panoramic view of the green and fertile county, where Gordon likes to walk two or even three times each day. The hill has no name, but it is the site of a battle four centuries ago between the Scottish and the English. Fife has been Brown's home for more than seventy years. He moved there three years after he was born at a nursing home in Giffnock, south-west of Glasgow, at 8.45 a.m. on 20 February 1951. Fife's proud industry and its beautiful coastline were the backdrops to his upbringing; its scent was that of linseed oil because of its linoleum industry, of which Kirkcaldy was the beating heart in the nineteenth and twentieth centuries. Its later industrial decline would help shape Brown's political outlook.

And, as Brown writes in an introduction to a book on Fife by him and his old friend, the writer Alistair Moffat: 'Fife has always been home.' Brown's political career meant he spent much time in London, of course, but when asked where home was, Brown would always reply that while he 'lived most of the time in London, I *stayed* in Fife'.[1] Fife is where his heart is. Before he died aged eighty-four, in 1998, Brown's father managed to trace his family's history back for almost 300 years, to the early 1700s, 'and almost all of it took place in Fife'.[2] He left Gordon and his brothers a family tree listing all their ancestors who had been born in Fife. Gordon's mother and father, and his and Sarah's daughter, Jennifer, are buried at Kingskettle, a Fife village with a population of little more than a thousand.

Gordon's parents – John, a Church of Scotland minister, and Elizabeth, who had been based at Whitehall during the Second World War – had met in Glasgow through church friends, the minister Murdo MacDonald and his wife Sadie, and married in July 1947. Elizabeth had been a sergeant in the Auxiliary Territorial Service and had gone on, thanks to her high IQ and achievements, to be an administrator assisting codebreakers passing information to and from Bletchley Park.

Her partnership with the Reverend John was strong, even if Elizabeth – known affectionately as Bunty – felt that she had been deprived of opportunities. By all accounts she found all the cooking and entertaining involved with being a minister's wife a slight strain and, less seriously, would smuggle sherry into the trifle served after the Sunday roast while the strictly teetotal John wasn't looking. She also made some 500 jars of marmalade every year. Their eldest son John recalls that his mother did 'an excellent job and she looked after us, but it couldn't have been easy with the pressure of it ... I don't think it was easy being a minister's wife.'[3] As Gordon and his brothers now recognise, Elizabeth was a woman who had known that she could have had greater opportunities, but had given them up for the sake of her family, partly because this was what was expected then. Gordon has repeatedly stressed that he has the greatest respect for women in the workplace today, exemplified by his own busy wife Sarah.

In October 1984, Maureen Brown, who was married to Reverend John's cousin Jack, wrote a letter which included a fine description of the relationship. 'I should like at this point to pay you and Bunty the compliment of acknowledging how good an example you have been, since my first knowing you, of a good "sparring relationship"! It is so healthy a thing, and so very helpful to the three sons, to see that kind of realistic process of normal good cheer/mutual support balancing along with grumbles against each other, a few complaints, some heartfelt arguments, etc., etc.'[4]

Gordon, as he quickly became known, was in fact originally named James, after one of the Apostles like his elder brother John and younger brother Andrew. But when family and friends started using the nickname 'Jimmy', Elizabeth objected, and when he was around two years old she switched the name to his middle one, Gordon, after her brother. 'She wasn't posh but she was quite particular,' says John of their mother.⁵ Brown still uses the initials 'JGB' in his private email account today.

The only 'real friction' between Elizabeth and the young Gordon was, according to Andrew, about the length of Gordon's hair, which his mother thought should be shorter. Brown's desire for lengthier locks was partly down to his shyness. 'In a way Gordon was trying to make a statement about himself with the longer hair, but he was also trying to hide himself as well,' Andrew explains.⁶

Gordon has said of his mother: 'She was very tall and very dignified. And she had wonderful hair, very thick, black hair. Sadly it went grey before she was forty which she didn't like. No one dyed their hair in those days, you had to leave it grey.'⁷ He added: 'I think my mother thought she hadn't had all the chances she could have had ... so she was adamant we should have the best chances possible. She was born the year World War I ended and was there as part of the World War II effort. She was the first person to come to London from our family to work.'

The Reverend Dr John Brown, whom Elizabeth described as 'my guiding light' through fifty-one years together, was born in October 1914 into a Fife farming family whose roots on the land there stretch back for almost two centuries, at Peattieshill Farm at Largo, one month after the outbreak of the First World War. Gordon's brother John recalls that his paternal grandfather was 'quite frugal' and would cook porridge for the week and two meals each day would be produced from the batch, so prudence ran in the family. John Senior was ordained and inducted at Dunoon St Cuthbert's in May 1939 before going on to Govan in 1943. Gordon remembers very little of the earliest years in Glasgow but his elder brother recalls going to nursery and riding on the city's subway.

The Reverend John found visiting families in overcrowded tenement accommodation in the city a formative experience for his ministry. He would strictly refrain from revealing his own politics even to his family, but his son John recalls him being 'quite dismayed' to learn from the radio that Hugh Gaitskell had lost the 1959 general election to Harold Macmillan's Tories, who won their third consecutive term. However, according to Andrew, their father would have voted Conservative on one or two occasions, and certainly locally, as he was close to Tory councillor congregants. Indeed, Uncle Gordon was a staunch Conservative businessman in Insch, who was particularly opposed to the Labour 'selective employment tax' that was introduced by Harold Wilson in 1966, and levied against employers that did not boost UK exports. Intriguingly then, Gordon did not grow up amid passionate conversations about politics.

Brown explains of his father's ministry today: 'I think when he came to Glasgow, he was very much influenced by the poverty all around because he came from a rural community. He came from a farming community, obviously not from an industrial community. And he went to Glasgow first as an assistant minister in the 1930s. And then he went to Dunoon as the war started, and ministers were not called up for the war. But they invited him back to Glasgow to become the full-time minister.'[8] The Govan parish in Glasgow where he ministered – and about which he frequently reminisced – included one of the world's biggest shipyards, which saw many highly skilled craftsmen building vessels that were sold internationally.

Back in Fife, when Gordon was three years old John became minister at Kirkcaldy St Brycedale's, a role he held for thirteen years when he was also chaplain to Kirkcaldy High School.

On the whole, Gordon and his brothers were given a safe, happy childhood in which they could express themselves and go on to explore interests such as writing and local and world affairs. They were not wealthy but they were financially secure, with Reverend John's minister's stipend of a few thousand pounds per year and Elizabeth's annual income of perhaps double that from her family's construction and timber business. It was not a political household but, with the help of elder brother John, Brown would himself become political – and Labour. Brother John was an admirer of Wilson, and felt the Conservatives looked exhausted in opposition during the 1960s. Though the boys' father was strictly non-partisan, he influenced the brothers with a strong social conscience developed by his faith and what he had seen at Govan in Glasgow.

Gordon recalls: 'In my memory my father still towers before me like a mountain. I am sure I always thought of him as far taller than the six feet he was. I seldom saw him in anything other than a suit – a trait he clearly passed on to me. His bespectacled face was normally smiling and gentle, but he did not need to say anything when he disapproved of my behaviour; his frown told me everything.'[9]

'He was a very fine man,' said Reverend Robert McLeish, minister at Insch. 'He was totally committed to the church and committed to the Third World. Even at the age of eighty-two, Gordon's father was out taking the collection round the doors for Christian Aid. For a man of his years to do that showed very great commitment indeed.'[10] Elizabeth was also committed to collecting house to house in the charity's annual spring Christian Aid Week.

After Glasgow, the Reverend John's next church would be at what became Gordon's home town (and later constituency after a boundary change) of Kirkcaldy in Fife. The church was two streets away from what was then one of the world's biggest linoleum factories.

The famous eighteenth-century economist Adam Smith loomed large as a backdrop to Gordon's upbringing and today his office organises talks and events in Smith's name. It was at Smith's home, just yards from John Brown's church, that he wrote *The Wealth of Nations* and *The Theory of Moral Sentiments*. In them he explained how the then new economy worked – with 'trade as the engine of growth, a global division of labour and comparative advantage for countries which produced the goods the world wanted', as Brown puts it.[11]

'Two hundred years on, the fate of the Kirkcaldy of my youth was still being determined by its economic position. The town was one of the very special close-knit industrial communities at the heart of our coal-mining industry. We literally walked on top of aeons of coal.' There had once been sixty-six pits in Fife, employing nearly a quarter of all adult men in the county, and as recently as the 1950s there were more than thirty pits. But then, Brown says, 'as cheaper energy sources were becoming increasingly available, Fife – and all of Britain – started to experience a catastrophic fall in mining employment. Hundreds of families were suddenly leaving Fife to find a new life in the diminishing number of minefields that were still thriving – in Yorkshire and the Midlands.'[12]

This change preceded the fight for jobs that would become the central economic issue in the area for the next fifty years, alongside the decline of the linoleum industry in the 1960s that hit the town hardest and led to further population decline. Meanwhile the last coal mine in the Fife region closed in 1988. The town's other mainstay, textiles, was also fading.

Kirkcaldy was frequently affected by storms and floods because of its exposure to the North Sea. In 1958, waves thirty feet high broke through the town's sea walls and poured into houses, with some forty families having to be evacuated. The young Gordon went with his father to see a few of the families who had to be moved out of their homes and he watched the Reverend John give each of them money to help them through. For decades afterwards, despite considerable investment in coastal defences, precautionary sandbags were stored on the esplanade.

Brown remembers to this day the announcement in 1963, when he was twelve, of the closure of Barry, Ostlere and Shepherd, the local linoleum factory. The massive factory, just beside Kirkcaldy's main rail station, and another set of linoleum factories to the north and east of the town, employed thousands 'whose jobs were about to vanish', Brown recalls. 'Some of the friends I made at school had to leave with their families for England so their fathers could find new work.'[13] These were practical consequences to which a child as curious and quietly sensitive as Brown could relate. So, even if Brown's father largely steered clear of politics, the young Gordon saw politics and economics in the raw, and the real-world impacts of the community's troubles.

Between Reverend John's church and the factory lay the Adam Smith Halls, all of which made the young Gordon and his school friends aware of a world beyond. The USA – a country with which he has long been enthralled – is as Gordon has pointed out blessed with a meritocracy that means any citizen can grow up to be president. But 'Britain is different'. He adds that while colleagues were ambitious in their teens, he was not at this stage: 'As I grew up it never occurred to me that I could or would become prime minister.'[14]

London was almost a foreign land, and Brown had visited it half a dozen times in the thirty-two years before he became an MP. Indeed, before he went to Edinburgh University, he had been to London only once, when his father's cousin Jack and his wife Maureen invited the Brown boys to spend Christmas 1964 in the capital. The couple entertained the boys by taking them to see a Royal Shakespeare Company production of *The Comedy of Errors* in the West End on Boxing Day,

Chelsea beating Blackpool 2–0 at Stamford Bridge on 28 December, and to Tottenham Court Road, where Gordon was focused on buying his first transistor radio by selling off his stamp collection to Stanley Gibbons, the famous philately dealer. He recalls that the party visited the Tower of London but not the Houses of Parliament. However, John insists that, as his diary from the time shows, they did, in fact, walk down Whitehall, past Downing Street and on to the Palace of Westminster. But John acknowledges that he was much more interested in that than Gordon.

At home, Gordon, John and Andrew found themselves mixing in a fairly open house of congregants, missionaries and other visitors. Once, while waiting for his parents to get home, Gordon himself inadvertently entertained a notorious local burglar who had tried his luck in the house. But on the whole, according to his elder brother, the introspective Gordon would slope off to another room with a book when visitors came to the house. 'He was quite shy,' says John.[15]

Gordon, who is indeed visibly shy in photos from his youth, probably disliked going to church because the family were seated in full view of the congregation, looking out at them and on show all the time. John recalls that their mother was conscious of what others at church thought of the family. Andrew adds in some hitherto unseen notes he took on Gordon's early years that their father remembered 'how he [Gordon] would always seek out the back row at any meeting he attended. He particularly [recounted] how he always took a back seat at the Sunday meetings of the youth fellowship at St Brycedale's.' The open-house nature of the manse may have instilled in Gordon a sense of self-sacrifice, an understanding that you can't always have what you want, a reluctance later in life to accept gifts and trappings in office. It may, too, have encouraged his decision with Sarah to invite a homeless person into their own North Queensferry home each Christmas for a few years.

During family discussions at the manse, congregants would be described formally as 'Mr ...' or 'Mrs ...', but the family had a strong rapport with members of the church. It was an unusual existence yet Gordon describes it as ordinary: 'A middle-class upbringing in middle Scotland in the middle of the century.' Brown remembers his disappointment when his father did not buy him the famous Subbuteo football game for Christmas. He recalls his desire for a pair of Adidas trainers, which he got himself when he left secondary school and earned his first pay packet from a summer labouring job. Family holidays were spent staying with relatives in Scotland, not in hotels or overseas. Their first car was bought in 1958 – a gift to the Reverend John from his own father – and a television arrived at the house in December 1959. Before that, the boys would regularly go next door to watch popular music shows. Gordon loved listening to music on his record player, too, especially the Beatles and the Rolling Stones.

Meanwhile, Gordon was a sporty child whose earliest memories are of running and playing outdoors in Kirkcaldy's many green spaces. At this point, he dreamed first of being a professional footballer and then of managing his beloved local team Raith Rovers, and eventually of owning a football club – an ambition he retains to this day. He would serve as president of the Raith Rovers supporters' club, promoting a 'progressive community policy' of outreach among schools, and raising funds, including from the Scottish author Ian Rankin who, after receiving a letter from Brown in 2005, sent a personal cheque for £5,000.[16] Brown still watches football live both in person and on TV or, when he's busy as he was in government, has matches recorded, insisting no one gives him a hint of the score so it remains a surprise. Friends and colleagues say he can put them to shame with an encyclopedic knowledge of their own teams.

The young Brown was football mad, and sold programmes at matches in exchange for free entry into Raith Rovers games. He was also junior champion of Kirkcaldy tennis club, to the pleasure of Elizabeth, who had been passionate about tennis in her youth.

Saturday evening was always a tense time in the Brown manse home because Reverend John would be writing his sermon at the eleventh hour. Effectively to bribe his boys and keep them quiet, he would visit the local newspaper seller and buy the papers for them, including the *Sporting Post* for Gordon, who enjoyed its weekly detective story. But mainly the boys would read the back pages, though they were frequently frustrated because these were the early editions due to the distance from Glasgow to Edinburgh, and the football results were usually only from half-time. The boys also liked buying the Sunday newspapers, with John favouring the *Sunday Express*. Their father objected, because the papers came out on the Sabbath. John used to argue they were printed on Saturday nights, but the minister would retort that they were bought on Sundays.

Gordon combined an exceptional attention to detail with an absent-mindedness. Andrew unusually took notes on the family even then. He wrote: 'Fifteen years old, Gordon was entered for the 400 yards sprint. He won the race against all comers from other schools, but was disqualified for wearing a jersey over his shirt which meant his ... number was hidden. Gordon was very upset about the incident. However, it is typical of his occasional absent mindedness ... His father [recalled] another occasion [when] his forgetfulness resulted in him leaving home for a school rugby match without his boots. Fortunately he was able to phone home and his father was able to bring them to him. When Rev John arrived, he found Gordon in his rugby strip, anxiously waiting with the other players and ready to play in his shoes if necessary.'

As well as being sporty, Gordon was clearly highly intelligent, and academic too, attending primary school from four and, after sitting his eleven-plus, secondary school at ten, and as a result did his O level exams at fourteen, his Highers – the Scottish equivalent of A levels – at fifteen, and, extraordinarily, went to university at sixteen, thanks to an unpopular 'E-stream' experiment in Kirkcaldy.

At the age of four, at the West Primary School, Gordon met Murray Elder, who was to become a friend for life. Elder would later lend Brown funds for a deposit to buy an Edinburgh flat. As Lord Elder, Murray was himself a central figure in Labour's period of electoral success in Scotland from the 1970s to the early 2000s, and through Brown would become close to John Smith and serve as his chief of staff. Elder once said of Brown: 'He doesn't work because he has to, he works because he works. Work is what Gordon does. He'd be like that whatever he was doing.'[17]

Kirkcaldy High School was among the finest in Scotland, and Gordon was by now mixing with pupils two years older than him and as he has said, 'it was tough adjusting'. For many of the thirty-six secondary-school students channelled into it, the 'E-stream' – with 'E' standing for 'experiment' – 'turned out to be a painful failure', Brown says. 'They were put under too much pressure.' Brown, along with Murray Elder, passed the experiment, unique to Kirkcaldy, which is why Brown would go on to Edinburgh University aged only sixteen.

In May 1967 Gordon wrote in a draft article that wasn't in the end published: 'I was a guinea pig, the victim of a totally ludicrous experiment in education … I watched as each year one or two of my friends would fall under the strain. I saw one girl who every now and then would disappear for a while with a nervous breakdown.'[18] In actuality, it was not unusual across Britain for pupils to be moved up a year, but Brown to this day specifically cites the Scottish Highers system as an example of iniquitous selection.

Gordon, like his brother John, became a firm supporter of Harold Wilson, who had talked of the 'white heat of the scientific revolution' and promised to clear the 'dead wood out of the boardroom' a few months before his victory in the 1964 general election. In one school debate, Gordon argued the case for the motion 'That the Smith regime in Rhodesia should be crushed'. Brown had followed not his more nuanced father – who would applaud both sides at a Raith Rovers game – but his politically tribal elder brother in believing that Labour was the best and ultimately the only vehicle for change, and that meant supporting its leader at the time. 'John was the catalyst,' says Andrew. 'John opened up the world to Gordon. The difference was that John was an extrovert but Gordon was an introvert and still is today despite what he went on to achieve.'[19] John was a modest but charismatic leader figure, and would later, as a university student, be seen by his friends as a future prime minister. Gordon has described John as 'much more dynamic and entrepreneurial than anyone I knew'.[20]

The brothers were not rivalrous but instead tended to encourage one another. John, three years older, was interested in journalism and influenced Gordon the cub reporter, who had his own first article published aged twelve in a church magazine called *Zeal*, edited by John. It was entitled 'Persecution' and was about the plight of the Jews who, Gordon wrote, had suffered 'unspeakable carnage' at the hands of the Nazis. He added that Israel was in 'a vulnerable position' and concluded that 'our debt to the Jews is very great'.

From the 1960s to the 1980s the Reverend Brown, who had learned Hebrew, visited Israel several times, representing the Church of Scotland and leading pilgrimages. Gordon, impressed by the reels of film his father brought back from the Holy Land, would remain a lifelong sympathiser with Israel. John also led Gordon into youth group activities at their father's church, including an exchange programme with Sweden run by John which Gordon participated in, called Operation Friendship.

The lack of competitiveness among the brothers was partly because John was a benevolent influence on Gordon and also because Andrew was considerably younger, having an eight-year age gap with John. 'I was sort of quite remote from them,' Andrew says of the boys' youth. 'It was John and Gordon that were much closer because they were relatively close together at school, even though they were three years apart.' Andrew modestly adds that he was 'never going to compete with Gordon because he had swept the board academically', and that 'doing well enough in the Highers to get to university was good enough for me'.

Despite condemning the 'ludicrous' experiment of advancing a year at the school, Brown has nonetheless praised his 'dedicated' headmaster, Robert Adam, and 'inspirational teachers whose names I still remember, like Sid Smith in English and Tom Dunn in History'. Dunn was a socialist and Labour supporter who also influenced the young Gordon. Aged fourteen, Brown sat seven O levels and passed them all. At fifteen, he secured the five A grades – in English, history, Latin, Greek and French – needed in Higher exams to be accepted for Edinburgh.

In May 1967, the *Scottish Daily Mail* reported, under the headline 'Gordon is top of the form at 16', that 'A minister's son is to begin studies at Edinburgh University next term a few months after his 16th birthday'. The university's principal, Professor Michael Swann, was quoted as saying: 'It is certainly most unusual. We do not usually accept students at 16 because we feel that they are too young.'

A prize scholar in the university's bursary competition, winning the then princely sum of £200, the sixteen-year-old Brown was excited when he took the train from Kirkcaldy to Edinburgh for the first time as a history student on a Tuesday in September 1967. 'The two communities were just 30 miles apart, but the Firth of Forth was also a boundary between the old and the new,' he has said. 'The Edinburgh of 1967 was about to cast off its Calvinist past and Edinburgh University become one of the centres of radical student protest.'[21]

As with the city, so with the man.

2
Edinburgh

Away from his Fife home, the teenage Gordon Brown was to develop rapidly from a reserved lad into the politically driven and charismatic campaigner of his adult life. Upon his arrival at Edinburgh, and sporting the free-flowing longer black hair that so dismayed his parents, he enjoyed the parties of freshers' week and visited a fair few of the city's hundreds of pubs with his fellow students.

Drugs passed him by completely but alcohol did not. Back then Brown mainly drank beer, albeit technically under age, though today he prefers sparkling beverages – prosecco, as well as fizzy water or Diet Coke (never tea or coffee) – and as a student he was quickly proving a popular, funny and sociable new entry into life in and around the university. The shy lad from Fife was able to fit in readily, despite his relative youth.

But a dramatic rugby incident in which Brown had been kicked in the head back in April 1967, during his last match of the school term, suddenly came back to haunt him before he was able to settle properly at university.

At fifteen, Brown had been playing for the school's first rugby team as a winger and then as a wing three-quarter. 'I had been knocked around for most of the season, though to my delight I scored the winning try in my first match,' he recalls. 'My speed – I had run in the Scottish schoolboy championships – did not compensate for my lack of weight.' Frequently Brown's side played Edinburgh schools, with opponents aged eighteen. 'In the last match of the season, we were playing our former pupils – some of them friends of mine – who wanted to teach us a lesson or two, by being overly physical during the first minutes of the match. I went down on the ball right at the start of play and then was surrounded and buried in a loose scrum. A boot landed on my head and I got up dazed, probably concussed. But since it was the first few minutes of the match I did not want to go off. Despite being more than a little hazy, I was so proud to be playing in this prestigious match that I just ploughed on. Afterwards, I thought nothing of it. Only gradually, during that summer term of 1967, did I start to sense a problem.'[1]

Now, in Edinburgh, 'I knew something was wrong, but I couldn't quite place what it was. It was like getting reflections from the sun in your eye all day.' Days into freshers' week, Brown was referred to an eye surgeon, who immediately diagnosed a retinal detachment. Brown was initially left with the impression that he was about to lose his left eye – to have it removed altogether. By the Sunday, he found himself in a bed alongside mainly elderly cataract patients, in what seemed to him one of the most ancient wards in Edinburgh's Royal Infirmary. He was ordered to lie flat for a few days before the operation. Then afterwards: 'Both my eyes were bandaged shut for what seemed to a 16-year-old an eternity – actually around a week or ten days – during which I had to lay flat again – no pillows allowed – to give the retina a chance to set itself back in place. I would be out of action for the whole of my first university term.'[2]

Some light relief came at 9 p.m. every evening when a trolley came round the ward, offering each patient a choice of Guinness, beer or wine which was open even to a sixteen-year-old. 'I knew the NHS was free,' recalls Brown, 'but I had not expected free beer.'

In January 1968, Brown returned to the hospital for a routine checkup and was told the retina was not in the right place. He was told he had to have another operation, but the prospect of it working was remote. The surgeon agreed that he could finish his third term and then spend the summer break in hospital. But in the autumn, Brown found himself suddenly back in hospital for a third operation, after the second one did not work. 'The surgeon said he and his colleagues would try one last time. Just before I went under a general anaesthetic he told me: "Okay, Gordon. We'll have a bash." 1968 was one of the most tumultuous years of the 20th century, but I saw very little of it.'

When the third operation did not work, Brown finally accepted that he was permanently blind in his left eye. To this day Brown types – with two fingers – his emails, speeches and letters in large, bold font – Arial 14 – or simply in block capitals. He uses a special contact lens which he jokes has served him well since the late 1960s. But his emails, sometimes dictated into a digital application, are frequently hard to decipher. And he is not the best with modern technology. Once, decades later, his civil service foreign affairs adviser Tom Fletcher was pleased in Brussels when Brown appeared to issue unusually fulsome praise as Fletcher showed him a policy paper on his BlackBerry, saying, 'That's good.' Brown then clarified: 'Not the document – the scroll function.'

Back at his hospital bed in Edinburgh, Brown planned an entry into an essay competition run by the *Scottish Daily Express*, in which entrants were asked to envisage Scotland in the year 2000. Brown, who wrote that 'By 2000, Scotland can, for the first time in history, have found her feet as a society which has bridged the gaps between rich and poor, young and old, intellectual and labourer', won first prize out of 900 entries in the adult category. He described the victory, which was announced in the paper in March 1969 and came with a prize of £200, as 'a great boost to my morale'.

Brown's spells in hospital had a major impact on him, and acted as the turning point when he decided to pursue politics. Lying on his back for months, blindfolded and with family and friends reading newspaper articles to him, he understandably became restless. But he also realised that his future did not lie in being a football manager, let alone in playing sport, though he continued to enjoy watching football. His brother John testifies that all that had happened before in his childhood – the deindustrialisation in Fife, the articles, the politics – came to a head in Gordon's mind. And he was in a hurry. 'That was the big change,' says John. 'The seeds of his social conscience had been sown.'[3]

Having returned to the university for his third year, Brown – who became editor of the campus paper *Student* in October 1969 – immediately found that the students were in a culture war with Edinburgh's city fathers. The students' union had previously passed a motion demanding that the seemingly radical rector, Malcolm Muggeridge, advocate free supply of the contraceptive pill by the university health service. Muggeridge refused. In January 1968,

Brown attended a service at St Giles's Cathedral when Muggeridge stood up and denounced the youthful generation that had elected him. He pronounced that the world was falling apart amid declining moral standards and ended his sermon dramatically by resigning.

It felt to Brown as if St Giles's had seen nothing like it since the Protestant Reformation was sparked by a woman named Jenny Geddes throwing a stool at the dean. Within months Edinburgh was the scene of protests. 'The city was awash with its own student counter-culture,' Brown recalls.

At Edinburgh, apartheid was the specific issue at the top of the students' agenda. Some of Brown's friends had been arrested when protesting against the visit of the Springbok rugby team to play against Scotland, on 6 December 1969. Following a sit-in at the university careers office calling for the university to sell its shares in South African companies, Brown and fellow student allies had found papers showing that the director of the careers office was a recruiting agent for MI6.

'When I was editor of Edinburgh's *Student* in 1969,' Brown says, 'I had a lengthy correspondence – and meetings – with the then rector, the well-known journalist Kenneth Allsop. Ken was angry that I had reported on a failed attempt of his to persuade the University Court to accept student representation. It would have been in the interests of what we both believed in, he said, to have held back and not given the impression students were losing the battle. This led to an impassioned dialogue between a teenage student editor and an experienced and highly respected media heavyweight on what were the responsibilities of the press.' Brown says he bore that conversation in mind when dealing with press regulation in later years while in office. But at the time, Brown clearly felt it was more important to run the story, while Allsop apparently felt doing so would lead the university authorities to not want to cave in.

In a special edition of the *Student* in December 1969 that sparked national headlines, Brown and his student allies exposed how the university had lied when it denied shareholdings in companies with interests in South Africa, after action taken by a whistleblower. 'Out of the blue, we had been handed a document which proved beyond doubt that the university held half a million pounds of investments in a range of corporations operating in South Africa including De Beers and Anglo-American. Far from divesting, the university had been amassing a bigger portfolio. After our special edition, "Sell the Shares" stickers and posters blanketed the university. A month later, the administration capitulated and sold the shares.'[4]

Brown also wrote in the 8 January 1970 issue of the *Student*: 'The demos [in December] against the South Africa team regardless of their political effect in South Africa have at least exposed the hypocrisy of a state which pays lip service to anti-racialist views but at the same time uses its instruments of coercion to protect the ambassadors of apartheid.' As we can see, having been free to explore the issues around him, and with his elder brother John's influence, Brown had developed over the course of little more than a year into a highly politically motivated and active student.

In June 1971, as Brown was preparing for his final year of studies, he was taking time out for a game of tennis when he realised he could not follow the ball because of his eye problems. Having already had three operations on his bad left eye, he now had one for another detached retina in his 'good' right eye, done by a young surgeon, Hector Chawla, who saved what was left of Brown's limited eyesight and with whom Brown remains friends to this day. Chawla had recently returned from a year in America and Brown was fortunate to benefit from his newly acquired technique. Born in Scotland, Chawla is the author of various books on the eye and a world expert on the retina. Brown credits Chawla with contributing to the success rate in reattaching retinas rising over a period of forty years from 20 per cent to 90 per cent.

In university but out of the classroom for much of his first two years, Brown was forced to renegotiate his planned studies. Remarkably, he got a BA arts degree at nineteen and then prepared for an MA degree in social and economic history. Brown kept in touch for years with some of his tutors, including Paul Addison, the prize-winning author of *The Road to 1945*. Brown missed some lectures due to his social life and embryonic political activities, and when he was awarded his first in history, the head of that department, Geoffrey Best, wrote to Brown about 'a splendid achievement and just the sort of thing to delight our hearts', adding: 'Absurd and reprehensible an admission though it may be, I am not sure I know what you look like. So I very much look forward to meeting you.'

Another history lecturer, Dr George Hammersley, wrote: 'I am sure you will continue to succeed in whatever you genuinely wish to do ... I have always thought of you as one of the most agreeable people I have had to deal with.'5 Brown had managed, despite barely turning up to lectures and tutorials, to gain a first at a time when such awards were rarely handed out, compared to today.

For a while, Brown thought his future lay in an academic life – in lecturing and research. 'But I had come alive politically,' he recalls. 'Shocked by the levels of unemployment and deprivation in my home town and across the central belt of Scotland, I felt something had to be done to address these injustices.' This was a significant turning point for Brown, who says of that time: 'I dreamed there could be no greater privilege than representing my home area in the House of Commons.'6

But before Brown's interests were primarily drawn to the Labour Party as the best vessel for change for the wider country, in 1972 he was elected the youngest-ever student rector, an advocate for student causes and voices, in the university's 112-year history, and held the post until 1975. There was a feeling on campus that it was time students wielded some power over the university's 'court' which was 'full of Edinburgh establishment types' according to brother John. Brown had been urged by many students to stand, and it was a route to early prominence. He had beaten the establishment candidate Sir Fred Catherwood, a Cambridge-educated captain of industry. The post had been held by five prime ministers: Gladstone, Rosebery, Lloyd George, Churchill and Baldwin. Yet Brown today regrets being rector. 'People pressed me to do it,' he says. 'It wasn't a good decision, to be honest, because I spent all my time dealing with internal university issues when I was more interested in fact in other issues outside.'7

While it is by all accounts true that Brown was 'pressed' by fellow students to run for the role, he clearly, by now, harboured ambitions and was in a hurry to make an impact after getting out of hospital. Brown got the position partly because he was highly popular on campus, where he stomped about with carrier bags full of papers, and it is claimed that at least 700 students had signed his nomination forms. In an early demonstration of Brown's ability to appeal across divides when he needs to, rival leftists pulled out of the race and the head of the Tory club, Rory McLeod, even signalled his support. The charismatic student Brown, with his long, wavy hair, was mobbed on campus by young women supporters in miniskirts – dubbed the 'Brown Sugars' – who had been given 'Gordon for me' T-shirts produced by Brown's campaign team. 'I am an idealist, a radical and a reformer,' Brown wrote in his manifesto. 'Society's problems today are not technical but social and moral ... There is no convincing argument against a student rector.'[8]

The student voters agreed. On 10 November, Brown won by a landslide against the businessman, gaining 2,264 votes to Sir Fred's 1,308. He was only the second student rector, after his one-time friend Jonathan Wills, who was heavily involved in the *Student*, and devised a cartoon series for it called 'Gaston' about life at the university. Gordon and his elder brother John are featured as the 'Beaverbrowns'. 'Lord Beaverbrown is of course John, Gordon's elder brother,' Wills explains. 'In the cartoon strip his little brother Boredom Beaverbrown, who is always seen earnestly typing copy, was somewhat in Lord Beaverbrown's shadow. Sheila McKechnie would become a well-known housing and women's rights campaigner and the head of Shelter. Now sadly deceased, she was too tall to fit in the frame of the cartoon so only her mini-kilted legs ever appeared.'

Wills went on to be Scotland correspondent for *The Times*. He was three years above Gordon at Edinburgh – and one year above John who was studying geography – and says today that the feeling then was that it was John who would go on to become prime minister. Wills broadly shared Gordon's centre-left, Labour politics up until the 2003 Iraq war, when he drifted towards the Scottish Nationalists. Now the two men share Christmas cards but are not otherwise in touch, though Wills, who comes across as slightly grudging towards Gordon, remains friends with John. Wills claims that if you are not politically aligned with Brown, 'you're out in the wilderness'. Many would disagree with this view. Wills adds that 'Murray Elder [Gordon's classmate and lifelong friend who would accompany Brown into high-level Labour politics] was Gordon's economic brain. You have to understand that Gordon is a historian, not an economist.'[9]

But although he now regrets the 'distraction' of being rector, Brown was in the words of one student contemporary 'a disrupter'. The university's own online account describes Brown's rectorship as 'perhaps the most eventful' ever. One area this applied to was the choice of the university's 'assessor', who analysed and recorded student achievements and upheld university rules. In 1973, Brown chose as his assessor Allan Drummond, who had previously been banned from attending court meetings due to his participation in a sit-in. An assessor in this context is a link between the rector and the student body. Seeing Brown's choice as a provocation, the 'court', a university governing body, voted to reject Drummond. Drummond took his case to the court of session, who ruled in his favour but laid down the conditions that Drummond refrain from disruptive activities or from inciting others to participate in them and that he maintain strict confidentiality on university court proceedings.

Upon becoming rector, a role with limited power but aimed at representing student interests, Brown immediately wrote to university officials, arguing that he must receive all minutes from the university court's committees because 'I must have all the business of the court on hand, in order to fulfil my function as chairman'. He listed seventeen committees whose minutes he wanted, including the Laboratory Technicians Committee, the Minor Buildings Sub-Committee and the Parking Sub-Committee. The university secretary, representing the university's alarmed officials, wrote back to Brown: 'What I want to avoid is the creation in the rector's office of another great accumulation of university papers which can be picked over by all sorts of other people as well as the rector.'

Brown eventually did receive the minutes, however, and described one set as 'inaccurate, biased and misleading'. He made 'very substantial corrections' to thirteen separate sections and demanded to see 'a full list of expenses and entertainment allowances paid to members of the University administration', adding: 'In this time of economy I believe it is vital that the University's finances must not only be properly managed but be seen to be so.' He stipulated that all spending over £250 should be approved by the court he chaired. Brown, who all his adult life has been surrounded by a chaotic mass of papers, soon requested an extra filing cabinet. This was declined by the university authorities.[10]

On the clash over Drummond and the university court, Brown has said intriguingly: 'I'm told that Prince Philip, then chancellor of the university and formally consulted on their proposal, sided with me. We will never know why, but perhaps it was because he had been lobbied by a friend of mine and one of his royal cousins, Margareta, the Crown Princess of Romania, who studied alongside me at Edinburgh.' It was rumoured that Brown was romantically linked to Princess Margareta, the god-daughter of Philip and eighty-first in line to the British throne. On that question, he confirms today with a smile: 'Well, it's true.'[11]

The couple were reportedly together, perhaps on and off, for five years. Little has been written about the relationship, but according to a rare 2007 interview feature on her in the *Telegraph*, 'Ever the fervent socialist … Brown is said to have grown increasingly uneasy about his girlfriend's royal lineage, immersing himself further in his obsession with politics. The Princess is once reported to have said: "I never stopped loving him, but one day it just didn't feel right. It was politics, politics, politics, and I needed nurturing." She now denies having made the comment, but it would be easy to imagine a modicum of truth in it. Like many young people, they drifted apart once their university days were behind them.'[12]

Brown was the second – and last – of the rectors (or advocates) who were students at the same time. The university establishment was not going to make what it saw as that mistake again, and reverted to a system without student rectors. Brown had been seen as a nuisance. But he had already made his mark. Now for the first time, and though he had mixed feelings about London's seat of power, the self-effacing future statesman was beginning to believe he could go all the way to the Commons benches – and beyond.

3
Towards Westminster

Once in the late 1970s, when Brown had been away from his flat in Marchmont, a mile south of Edinburgh's old town, on a research visit to London for his PhD, he came back to find the place had been burgled. A police officer told him it was 'totally ransacked' before Brown admitted that it was still in the state it had been left in. To this day, Brown is, in his wife Sarah's words, 'messy and noisy', but this masks – or perhaps helps to provide – a razor-sharp focus when it comes to his pursuit of politics.

Brown spent long hours dealing with internal university matters. He found this particularly frustrating during the two general elections in 1974 – the first amid the miners' strike. While also working on his PhD, Brown yearned to enter the fray – and the House of Commons.

During the February 1974 general election, Brown was working long hours on the 'minutiae' as rector while serving as a ward organiser for Robin Cook, who had graduated from Edinburgh in 1970 and whom Brown helped win the seat of Edinburgh Central with a majority of 961. It was the start of a long-running friendship turned feud and rivalry with Cook, which was only partially resolved months before Cook's untimely death in 2005.

The feud seems impossible to trace or explain fully. Cook recalled a rare encounter in the government years in his diaries, *The Point of Departure*, on 14 June 2001: 'At the end of Cabinet, Gordon asked for a word and we went next door to his room at Number 11. He was anxious that I should be aware that he had not known anything in advance of my dismissal [as foreign secretary], and I assured him that I was quite clear that nobody outside Sedgefield [Blair's constituency] had known. I added that maybe we had not seen enough of each other in the past four years, and we should do more now. I kept reading that we had fallen out, but I could never quite remember when this had happened, at which he laughed.'[1] Though Labour polled 220,000 fewer votes than the Tories that February 1974, the party managed to form the government in Britain's first hung Parliament since 1929.

Brown's PhD, which he turned into a book in 1986, was on the early twentieth-century Scottish 'common sense socialist' James Maxton, the chair of the Independent Labour Party (ILP) from 1926 to 1931 and from 1934 to 1939. The ILP was founded in 1893 at a conference in Bradford by a group of socialists, mainly from Scotland and the north of England, and encouraged by Keir Hardie, who would go on to found the Labour Party. Maxton, who served as MP for Bridgeton in Glasgow from 1922 until his death in 1946, was described by Winston Churchill as 'the greatest parliamentarian of his day'.

Brown's work originally started as a study of the explosive social and economic upheavals of post-1918 Europe, based on papers he found in Scottish libraries and vaults on what was happening in Britain at the time, and became a study of political, social and economic change in Scotland between 1918 and 1929.

The book takes us through the period, starting with the idealism and the passion after 1918, when Maxton became MP for Bridgeton, going to Westminster with other Scottish progressives. Brown was struck by the power of the words regarding the sorrows of the poor. They pledged they would always act in the interests of the people and resist the Westminster culture. Westminster would not change them; they would change Westminster. This was a moving statement that owed more to religion than to any secular ideology.

The book closes with the period of the 1930s, when they had become no more than a protest group, unable to change the direction of the country, and Aneurin Bevan's claim that by being over-dogmatic they had traded power for impotence. Hope and disappointment bookend the work. Maxton left Labour in 1932, though he was still chair of the ILP, and remained in the Commons until his death from cancer in 1946.

But though Maxton was a radical, it was his preference for change by wielding the levers of power over ideological purity in opposition that fascinated – and influenced – the young Gordon Brown:

> He had a credible programme which was vindicated in its essentials by the post-war Keynesian revolution. He brought to it vast personal appeal and brilliant rhetorical skills. Yet he and his ILP failed dismally.
>   One reason was that the economic crisis of the 1920s and '30s, far from increasing the possibility of radical change, diminished it. Though for the ultra-left the unemployed were an army already mobilised and simply waiting [for] the summons to attack, mass unemployment had not radicalised working people. The unemployed were demoralised and isolated by their poverty from those still in work, refugees within society rather than a force ready to attack it. MacDonald told the unemployed to wait and hope, further diminishing their political potential.
>   Between the frustrated incendiarism of the ultra-left and the time-serving passivity of MacDonald, Maxton offered a middle way.

Brown's biography of Maxton was not an uncritical book, arguing that Maxton's failure to implement a programme of socialist change to end mass unemployment foreshadowed the failure of an entire political generation. But as Brown recalls: '[The] real message of my book was that to hold to an ideological purity, at the cost of political impotence, served no one.'[2]

This surely reflected Brown's own position. He would expand on this approach to Labour politics in a 1997 speech to commemorate Anthony Crosland, the former Labour politician and author of *The Future of Socialism*. Brown said: 'There have been left-of-centre politicians who have espoused socialism but failed to meet the test of credibility. There have been those who have presented themselves as credible by abandoning socialism. The real challenge of left-of-centre politics is to be a socialist and at the same time credible.'[3]

In 1975, as the 24-year-old student rector, Brown produced another book, a collection of anti-nationalist, leftist essays he edited called *The Red Paper on Scotland*. As Lesley Orr has recalled: '[It was edited] by

Gordon Brown ... who could occasionally be seen stalking the campus in the vaguely Byronic manner appropriate for one who was courting a Romanian princess, the book was a symposium on the possibilities – and resources – for a socialist future in Scotland. What made this project stimulating and ground breaking was the manner in which it straddled the hot topic of nationalism (and the seemingly imminent prospect of a devolved Scottish Assembly).'[4] As Brown explained in the book: 'What this *Red Paper* seeks to do is to transcend that false and sterile antithesis which has been manufactured between the nationalism of the SNP and the anti-nationalism of the Unionist parties.' The context here was that the SNP seemed on a roll in 1974, with their share of the vote in Scotland going up from 21.9 per cent to 30.4 per cent, almost entirely at the expense of the Conservatives.

The *Red Paper* was as much about the benefits of democratic socialism as it was against nationalism. In the book, Brown, an admirer of the Italian Marxist philosopher Antonio Gramsci (1891–1937), went on to outline how the central political problem of the age was 'the sheer enormity of the gap between people's conditions of living and their legitimate aspirations'. That gap, he wrote, could be filled by the 'social forces of production', but they were curtailed by the free market. Meanwhile, it had become 'increasingly impossible to manage the economy both for private profit and the needs of society as a whole'. The answer was 'a massive and irreversible shift of power to working people' and 'a framework of free universal welfare services controlled by the people who use them'.[5]

Brown was showing himself to be a young man in a hurry, with ideas about how to make change and the confidence to put himself out there. In perhaps the most succinct summary of his position, he wrote in the *Red Paper*: 'Scottish socialists cannot support a strategy for independence which postpones the meeting of urgent social and economic needs until the day after independence. But neither can they give unconditional support to maintaining the integrity of the United Kingdom – and all that that entails – without any guarantee of radical social change.'

More practically, Brown had become chair of the Labour club at Edinburgh University in 1971, and had moved quickly to sever its ties with the International Marxist Group and the Trotskyist factions, showing the consistency of his mainstream Labour politics. 'I remember the very first time I was asked to stand as a Labour Party candidate,' Brown recalls. 'It was for a city council seat in the local elections in Edinburgh. The suggestion came from a trade union official. I was still a student and I replied honestly that I knew little about council funding and what were then rate support grants. "Look pal," he brusquely admonished me, "if we're going to win the seat you wouldn't be the candidate."'[6]

But by the second 1974 general election in October of that year, Brown's university friend Ian Levitt, later a researcher of Scottish social history, urged Brown to stand as a Labour candidate at the nomination conference in Edinburgh North. At the selection meeting, Brown gave a solid speech without notes, but he still lost out to a friend, Martin O'Neill. However, Brown helped Cook defend a slim majority in the election of October 1974, working to get the vote out in a central Edinburgh ward, Gorgie and Dalry. Cook increased his majority to nearly 4,000, bucking the trend towards the nationalists, who secured eleven out of seventy-one seats. Labour formed a precarious government with a majority of only three seats.

Brown was secretary of the Edinburgh South constituency when he was selected for it in September 1976. At this point Brown met Alistair Moffat, who was then running the Edinburgh Festival Fringe. As a Labour Party member, Moffat went along to his local meeting and found that Brown was their candidate. 'We got to know each other and I was variously vice chairman and chairman [of the local party branch] for a bit and so on and we campaigned together ... we spent a lot of days tramping the streets, giving people leaflets.'[7]

The night of the election in 1979 at 9 p.m., an hour before the polls closed, Moffat was driving Brown through the council estates in his Mini when they passed a pub called the Captain's Cabin and Moffat said, 'I bet half our votes are in there drinking beer.' So, with Brown slightly reluctant, they went in and saw Michael McGahey, the communist miners' leader, sitting with his friends. Moffat, who knew McGahey, went over and said, 'Look, Michael, I'm here with our candidate. Could you ask if everybody here has voted?' And McGahey banged his pint glass, stood on the table and shouted, 'Order! People have died for the privilege of voting. Now get out there and vote for the Labour candidate!' McGahey paused and said, 'What's his name?' And then shouted: 'George Brown!'

Whether this misnaming of the candidate was a joke on McGahey's part or a slip of the tongue, it's a moot point whether the electors of Edinburgh South would have been any keener to elect the famously volatile, sometimes drunken and quintessentially English former cabinet minister than the 28-year-old Scotsman who was Labour's candidate. In the event Brown lost to the Conservatives by 2,460, though his 34.3 per cent vote share was 6 per cent higher than it had been in 1974.

Earlier in the evening, Moffat remembered another constituent who probably hadn't voted, a Mrs Ferguson who lived nearby. They knocked on her front door but there was no response so Moffat led Brown round to the back garden where she was enjoying the evening sun in her slippers, and he told her to vote for Brown. 'Oh no, son,' she said. But Moffat was persistent, saying: 'Mrs Ferguson, you're in your eighties, do you think you'll get another chance?' Moffat affectionately describes himself and Brown at that time as 'bloody desperados'. But they offered to drive Mrs Ferguson to the polling booth, and their friendship and alliance was sealed for life.

Brown is 'the least materialistic person I've ever met', Moffat says. 'I mean, when we'd go to the pub, he either had no money at all, and I would pay for everything, which was fine, or he'd have money in all the pockets in his jacket. He would produce five-pound notes from his top pocket. And I can remember, you began to see people in the streets begging in the 1980s for the first time. Any time we ever passed anyone like that, Gordon would just give them all of his money, everything. He just does not care about possessions.' There's also a distinct lack of vanity. 'He may be the only person I've ever known who could put on a V-neck sweater backwards and the V is at the back because you don't care,' Moffat says. 'He always used to buy the same black slip-on shoes, because they required less work to get on. Because he didn't care.'[8]

In September 1979 Brown attended Labour's annual conference in Blackpool. There, although Neil Kinnock spoke against devolution, Brown invited five English Labour MPs and the brilliant anti-devolution Scottish MP for West Lothian, Tam Dalyell, to visit Scotland and witness the case for devolution. The MPs declined Brown's invitation, although Brown, a lifelong pursuer of devolution argued: 'Your opposition to devolution is born out of a complete misunderstanding of the mood in Scotland.'

Brown has always seen devolution, if properly implemented, as a tool with which to kill nationalism 'stone dead', as George Robertson – who that year won a by-election in Hamilton that Brown himself wanted to run for – mistakenly said it would. This would prove to be wrong. But for Brown, devolution deflected and pre-empted the nationalists. Many in politics, including senior Labour figures such as Dalyell and Robin Cook, opposed the fervour with which Brown consistently argued for devolution. Dalyell outlined the dangers in his prescient 1977 book *Devolution: The End of Britain?*, arguing that the problems of the poor in Glasgow are essentially the same as the problems of the poor in London, and predicted the emergence of an insoluble question in the wake of devolution: why should Scottish MPs continue to have a say over English affairs while English MPs lose their influence over Scottish governance? This conundrum became known as 'the West Lothian question', named after Dalyell's constituency. Around this time, Brown began to think seriously about the need for devolution instead of independence. Alongside the likes of Donald Dewar and the future leader John Smith, Brown was an early supporter of devolution, a position he has maintained to this day.

Meanwhile, some progressive, anti-borders unionists believed that devolution was 'the thin end of the wedge' to independence, and that George Robertson's claim was misguided. Tony Blair would later inherit John Smith's commitment to devolution, but some even in New Labour felt that the party should merely have strengthened the union by pursuing progressive policies more aligned with Scottish social democratic values while in office, without devolution, proving that Westminster could deliver for Scotland.

Brown saw Labour in power as the best way to defeat the idea that the nationalists were a progressive force. As he recalls, when Donald Dewar took on the nationalists in the Garscadden by-election of 1978, 'everyone thought he faced a steep uphill climb. I saw Garscadden as pivotal. If we could show that the SNP were not the progressive force they claimed to be, we could re-establish Labour in industrial Scotland. I enlisted as a foot soldier in the campaign and, after lecturing each day in Glasgow, I spent the evenings canvassing. Donald, with his masterful debating skills and indefatigable campaigning, won ... and forced the SNP onto the back foot.'

But the debate about devolution raged on, and it was decided that a referendum would be held in 1979. In the end, devolution was rejected. During the passage of the Scotland bill through Parliament, Labour had accepted an amendment that required the approval of 40 per cent of Scotland's electorate for it to pass, rather than a simple majority of votes cast. So, while the final result showed a narrow majority in favour – with 51.6 per cent supporting an Assembly, a majority of about 77,400 – only 32.9 per cent of the total electorate actually voted 'Yes'. The SNP then joined the Tories in a motion of 'no confidence' that brought down James Callaghan's Labour government. However, the SNP's rise was halted. Having grown in vote share through the 1970s, largely as a protest against the anti-nationalist Labour Party, they sank back in the 1980s as progressive voters united more behind Labour as the only realistic vessel to stop the Tories. Devolution would be largely irrelevant until the charismatic Alex Salmond first appeared on the Westminster scene as MP for Banff and Buchan in 1987. Salmond was a 'gradualist' who saw the long game of devolution as helpful to the nationalist cause.

It was against this backdrop that Brown took on the chair role of the Scottish Labour devolution committee. He threw himself into the task with his usual energy, and in the last seven days of February 1979 gave speeches at thirty meetings, a level of oratory to be echoed many years later in the independence referendum of 2014, as we shall see. Again, Moffat drove Brown around the country in his Mini.

Neil Kinnock remembers first meeting Brown in 1978 in Edinburgh and although, like Robin Cook, Kinnock was against devolution, the pair hit it off. Kinnock says today: 'We had a nice relationship, a couple of drinks, a meal, good chats. Even if we had an argument about devolution, it didn't get in the way of comradeship ... [Brown] was manifestly very bright ... And he was, for somebody in his twenties, an outstanding figure, though, when I arrived there first of all, I didn't know that about Gordon but it soon became evident that others were prepared to defer to him. And he was regarded as a small "l" leadership figure who I liked very much, because he had a great sense of humour and terrific insights. And he was very direct and honest. So I was delighted when he got the nomination [in 1979] and became the Member of Parliament in 1983 ... I mean, this guy is not just a politician. He's a bit of a poet among politicians and he can make audiences come alive.'⁹

The run-up to the 1979 general election, won by Margaret Thatcher, saw a divided Labour Party. The inward-looking hard left was proposing unilateral nuclear disarmament and withdrawal from the EEC (now the EU), as well as renationalisation, while Militant (a Trotskyist 'party within a party' that would control Liverpool City Council before being expelled by Neil Kinnock) were making inroads at a constituency level. The chancellor, Denis Healey, visited the Scottish Labour executive at which Brown defended Healey's economic record, but 'Sunny Jim' Callaghan's popularity was waning amid what became known as the 'winter of discontent' – a term coined by the *Sun* editor Larry Lamb – and there was a palpable mood for change after Callaghan's 5 per cent wage-increase limits and a series of private-sector and then public-sector strikes led by the trade unions. In September 1978, Ford car workers went on strike, demanding an increase of 17 per cent, breaking the income policy. This was followed by overtime bans for oil-tanker drivers and subsequent strikes in road haulage. Nationally coordinated strike action came in January 1979, resulting in images of piles of rubbish left in the streets with dustmen on strike, along with hospital cleaners and even picketing gravediggers.

Brown lost in Edinburgh South to the Tory aristocrat Michael Ancram, and reverted to working as a researcher for Scottish Television (STV) across the road in central Glasgow, where brother John had worked and where Brown covered major sporting events as well as current affairs.

At this time, Brown was also employed as a part-time tutor and lecturer at Glasgow College of Technology, which is now Glasgow Caledonian University, where he would shuffle into the spartan tutorial rooms with piles of papers stuffed into a plastic bag. Archie Dempster was a student there between October 1977 and May 1981, and Brown took his politics class in his first and fourth years. By today's standards these classes were very small – between seven and nine people – and Dempster had regular one-to-one tutorials with him in sociology and politics.

'He was very generous with his time and he taught you to value yourself, to take things seriously and to take yourself seriously,' Dempster says. Brown wore a long, dark leather coat with worn-out lining which Dempster puts down to it containing too many books. Brown was known at the college as 'the late Gordon Brown' because, commuting into Glasgow from Edinburgh, he would rarely be on time to start at 10 a.m. – more like ten past. 'He was very, very funny in private and he loved political gossip,' says Dempster. 'But he really reached out to people.'

It was also well known among the students that Brown would regularly borrow fivers from several of them in one day, 'usually' paying them back later. Brown smoked cigarettes at this stage, and at one point was the talk of the college after being spotted smoking a pipe in Glasgow city centre. 'I thought, oh, so you're going down the Harold Wilson route,' Dempster recalls. Occasionally, Brown would be seen emerging from a 'very smart' tiny black Fiat after getting lifts into Glasgow from Princess Margareta.

More seriously, Brown left a lasting impact on his students. 'Gordon has been a very influential figure to me since that time – foundational in many ways,' Dempster says. 'He has influenced how I have approached my professional life since in respect of employment choices.' Dempster had been an eleven-plus failure from a very poor background in industrial Lanarkshire who was later invited to carry out high-level research at Caltech (the California Institute of Technology) in Pasadena and acquired several degrees along the way. 'I attribute much of my motivation, application and approach to Gordon as both tutor and a role model. He exemplified hard work, application to a purpose, social engagement and a sustained and enduring commitment to social justice and the eradication of poverty. I watched, listened, hopefully learned, and tried to put those traits and ideals at the core of my own subsequent approach to professional and personal life.'

Though he still loved sport, and does to this day, Brown covering sports events for STV came about unexpectedly after a complaint was lodged in 1981 due to Brown working in current affairs and politics while exploring standing for Labour in Dunfermline in what would be the 1983 general election. The complaint was rumoured to be not from a Tory, but from Dick Douglas, the Labour MP for Dunfermline West, who later defected to the SNP.

To stop the complaint going to the Independent Broadcasting Authority, Brown, who had been working on current affairs documentaries on subjects ranging from hospital land sales to oil in

Scandinavia, was suddenly switched from politics to sport in the late summer of 1981, and sent to Spain for six weeks ahead of the 1982 World Cup on a fact-finding mission as a researcher.

After two weeks an excited Brown phoned his brother John and urged him to come out, so John flew to Madrid, where the pair saw Picasso's *Guernica*, the 1937 anti-war painting depicting the bombing of the Basque town of that name during the Spanish Civil War, which had just returned from New York. When John arrived at Gordon's hotel room he found papers all over both beds in the twin room. The brothers then went to see the city's chief of police together to find out about preparations for the impending tournament. 'As ever, he appeared disorganised, but he was in fact very methodical,' says John.[10]

At one point also in 1981, back in Glasgow, the two brothers found themselves in the same office at STV, where John worked in consumer affairs on the programme *What's Your Problem?*, with the STV newsletter publishing an article about the pair alongside a photo of them together.

Russell Galbraith, who at that time ran current affairs, news and sport at STV, remembers the young researcher as 'very serious, quite animated and with long, long hair' but above all Galbraith knew that the network had 'someone special' in their midst. Not everyone agreed. The managing director from 1963 to 1990, William 'Bill' Brown, was aware that he had 'ruffled feathers' among the great and good at Edinburgh University and when Brown left to go into Parliament, asked: 'Why did we employ this young man?' But Galbraith says Brown was 'extremely clever and hard-working' and recalls a long conversation about his future in Galbraith's office when Brown was 'absolutely determined' to go into elected Labour politics. Galbraith was sceptical, because Labour appeared to be 'unelectable' and he felt Brown had a great future in television management, but he did not try to dissuade the young man from eventually leaving STV.[11]

As well as STV and lecturing, Brown also plunged into working for the Edinburgh Festival Fringe programme with Alistair Moffat. Moffat's house in Edinburgh backs onto a tennis club, and around this time the pair hit the courts regularly. On one occasion in 1981 Brown was contacted via his office by ITN at Moffat's home during a game. Moffat lent him a shirt, tie and jacket but below the waist Brown was interviewed by ITN in his tennis shorts and trainers. Moffat, who had also worked for STV, instructed the crew to take a 'mid shot' and checked the shorts were out of view.

Brown's mind was never switched off from politics. Such were the divisions on the British centre left that on 26 March 1981 the new, breakaway Social Democratic Party (SDP) was formed by the former Labour moderates Roy Jenkins, David Owen, Shirley Williams and Bill Rodgers. Known as the 'Gang of Four', they issued the Limehouse Declaration as their statement of socially liberal intent. This came after Labour's commitments to unilateral nuclear disarmament and the EEC, as well as, at a local level, its apparent infiltration by the Militant tendency.

But there was never any question of Brown, who had been tribal towards his party since his teens, leaving Labour. It was always a case of Labour being the best and ultimately the only vehicle with which to change the country in a progressive way within the constraints of the adversarial parliamentary set-up and the 'first past the post' electoral system. Regarding Labour, you had to be 'in it to win it'. Brown firmly wanted to persuade the Labour Party to come round to his positions, rather than leave it. The same went for other future modernisers like Tony Blair of course, and Peter Mandelson, who was born into the Labour Party. Nor did Brown, who was in this sense a traditionalist, ever flirt with the Campaign for Nuclear Disarmament, unlike a young, more liberal Blair who would attend his Sedgefield selection in 1983 wearing a CND badge on his lapel.

Instead, Brown helped mark himself out as a Labour moderniser early on when he furiously denounced George Galloway on 14 November 1981, at the Scottish Executive Committee, with Michael Foot, the Labour leader at the time, present. Though leader, Foot presented as an amiable but shambolic man who was firmly from the left, similar, in some ways, to Jeremy Corbyn but more literary and humorous. An MP since 1945, Foot was an animated and highly intelligent character but not telegenic, and harshly nicknamed 'Worzel Gummidge' at Westminster. Galloway had criticised Foot for denying Tony Benn support for being elected to the shadow cabinet. Brown positioned himself squarely against the Bennites, who had criticised Healey for not supporting the party line on unilateral nuclear disarmament.

Brown declared that he disagreed 'completely' with Galloway's comments: 'We need to win the support of voters. Anything that prevents this and which puts the relationship between the party and the trade unions in jeopardy is not only needless but harmful.' Brown was by now lining himself up with the early emergence of the 'soft left' which would coalesce around Neil Kinnock as leader in 1983.

Brown had set his sights back on Fife when it came to a parliamentary seat. 'Friends in Fife were pushing for my selection as parliamentary candidate for the newly created constituency of Dunfermline East. Luck played its part. My selection as a candidate had nothing to do with me being a lecturer or working in television – it was about local connections, local people, local trade unions and local Labour party supporters.'[12]

The selection conference was chaired by David Stoddart, a retired mining engineer and prominent local trade unionist. Of the fifty-two votes cast, Brown won thirty-four in the first round. Brown asked Stoddart to be his agent. When Stoddart said he had not even voted for him, Brown replied that was an even better reason to pick him – 'if he was my agent, I told him, we could reunite the local party quickly. David was to be my agent over three general elections, and he became a close friend and invaluable adviser as we clocked up thousands of miles driving to and from the many towns and villages in the constituency.'[13]

Having attacked Scottish nationalists and Labour ideological purists, Brown also continued to target his principal opponents, the Conservatives, during the general election campaign. Some would claim Brown was scaremongering. On 3 June 1983 he held a press conference in Glasgow, accusing the Tory government of a 'Watergate-style cover-up' on social security. He told reporters that 'concerned civil servants' had informed him that Margaret Thatcher had personally ordered the destruction of internal government social security documents to prevent them being leaked during the campaign. 'The cover-up in Whitehall,' he said, 'is to hide the fact that under the Tory microscope are detailed plans for abolishing mortgage tax relief, abandoning the Wages Councils, ending the present system of child benefit and forcing everyone to take up private medical insurance – with charges for visits to the doctor under consideration.' And on 7 June he exposed another leaked document, this time an internal Coal Board paper showing that the mining industry in Scotland would shed 10,000 jobs over the next few years – one in three.

After a characteristically frantic round of campaigning, Brown won the seat, gaining 18,515 votes, and an overall majority of 11,300. Brown was sworn in as an MP on 21 June 1983. Labour had lost fifty-two seats amid one of its worst results on record. Aged thirty-two, the new parliamentary talent knew that there was much work to be done.

4
Wilderness Years

Michael Foot, a good man of integrity if not one cut out for leading a modern political party, had shepherded Labour to a defeat which saw the parliamentary party go down to 209 seats, the lowest number of Labour MPs since 1935. This was thanks to the SDP breakaway and its alliance with the Liberals taking a large share of the left-of-centre vote (25.4 per cent), even if they won only twenty-three seats, meaning Labour came close to third place in the national vote share, while the Tories under Margaret Thatcher had benefited from the broadly unifying Falklands conflict in April 1982 and romped home with a majority of 144. But the party did not help itself, not least with its manifesto, a collection of resolutions passed by members at the annual conference including unilateral nuclear disarmament, withdrawal from the European Economic Council and the renationalisation of a range of industries that were set for privatisation under the Tories.

Labour was being left languishing by a strident Thatcher, determined and indeed destined to wrench the British political consensus to the right.

Gordon Brown stood firmly on the side of what were becoming known as Labour's 'modernisers', and would back Neil Kinnock's battle to succeed Foot. In doing so, Brown would mark himself out even in this period as a potential future leader.

Although the Tory manifesto in 1979 had only promised to 'sell back to private ownership the recently nationalised aerospace and shipbuilding concerns', the Conservative government of 1979–83 privatised Amersham International, a spin-off from Britain's nuclear research industry which manufactured 'radiopharmaceutical' products, and half of Cable & Wireless. After the Tories were re-elected in 1983, they went on to privatise major utilities such as British Telecom (1984), British Aerospace and British Gas (both in 1986), and Rolls-Royce and British Airways (both in 1987).

The thirty-seven-page 1983 Labour manifesto, *A New Hope for Britain*, was famously described by Gerald Kaufman, the long-serving MP and former minister on Labour's right wing, as 'the longest suicide note in history'. Foot swiftly stood down, telling a meeting of the Parliamentary Labour Party, with characteristic wit, 'The show was excellent, but the audience was poor.' It was into this environment that Brown arrived in the Commons, a new MP in a party that appeared demoralised, out of touch and unpopular. Brown's belief, that the most important thing to do was to promote policies that people wanted to vote for, was about to be reinforced when he met up with a like-minded fellow new recruit.

According to Brown, he first met Tony Blair, who was thirty at the time, just before the 1983 general election, introduced by John Smith – then Labour MP for Monklands East and newly a QC – in the House of Commons bar. But within weeks of being elected, they ended up sharing a parliamentary office. Though different in personal style if barely so, in truth, in political outlook, they indisputably hit it off – and would remain close friends and allies for years to come. As Brown and Blair held discussions, they discovered they shared what Brown calls 'a fierce passion to see the party reform and recover'.

Blair had first been given an office with Dave Nellist, the Militant-supporting Labour MP for Coventry South East. Blair describes that as 'bizarre' and wanted to escape, and Brown too needed an office, having not yet been offered one. So, with Smith's help, they found one: a windowless room with erratic heating, hidden away off the committee-room corridors on the first floor. Initially, Brown was there more than Blair, who preferred working from home in north London when he could.

Blair lavishes praise on Brown. Contrary to conventional wisdom about a lingering mutual disdain, Blair says today:

> [We] became close immediately because it was clear to me he was head and shoulders above your ordinary politician. And this extraordinary intellect. I didn't really know much about politics.

I mean, I knew about political affairs, but I had no real idea about how to practise politics. And he obviously was very steeped in it. So I learned an enormous amount from him just by talking with him and by learning about the Labour Party. It's strange, really, but I was very much learning from him. [We] actually got along very well. We used to have fun together. Gordon, he has got his very serious side, but he can be immensely entertaining company.

It wasn't just a political friendship; it was a deep, personal friendship. [We] worked really closely together up until 1992 [the year when Smith succeeded Kinnock, with some already believing Blair would have been the better choice, and the *Sunday Times* magazine running a cover story about Blair headlined 'Labour's lost leader' on the day Smith won]. So there were nine years in which I guess I worked more closely with him than any other person. We would speak probably two or three times a day ... The best times we had were when we were thinking through the future of Labour in the late eighties, early nineties. And it was an incredibly productive partnership. [Brown] taught me an immense amount, taught me how to make a conference speech. And it was amazing how much I learned about politics. I was very much the junior partner really, throughout all of that.[1]

Despite Blair's evident excitement at learning from Brown, he would become deeply frustrated with the lack of progress in Labour between 1983 and 1986. The Labour Party's policies during this period did not significantly change on the important areas of Europe, economics and above all defence. Also, as we shall see, Thatcher was 'winning' at the miners' strike, and notwithstanding attempts to rein in Militant, Labour's troubles appeared to many as if they could be terminal.

With Tony Benn now out of Parliament having lost his seat in 1983, the two main rivals for the leadership at the autumn conference that year were Neil Kinnock, the Welsh former radical who was now increasingly a social democratic pragmatist representing what some in the party called the 'soft left', and Roy Hattersley, a former cabinet minister under James Callaghan who came from what was known as the party's 'old right'. Some of Brown's Scottish colleagues – John Smith, Donald Dewar and George Robertson – were supporting Hattersley. 'I was for Neil,' Brown recalls. 'While I liked and admired

Roy, Neil was one of the few MPs I knew well before I arrived in Westminster [from Kinnock's visits to Labour events in Scotland] and I felt he had the eloquence, charisma and pragmatism to inspire our recovery. Neil asked me to join his leadership campaign team. He had a wide range of supporters from Robin Cook, who ran the campaign, to the later UKIP MEP Robert Kilroy-Silk. I was the only new MP to be part of this team.'[2] Blair also backed Kinnock, who won 71.3 per cent of the vote for the leadership. Kinnock says today: 'Getting maximum support in the Parliamentary Labour Party generally was a matter of some importance. So youngsters that very quickly started to exert influence, like Gordon, were extremely valuable.'

Brown claims that Blair became so disillusioned with Labour's slow progress on its journey to electability, not to mention frustrated at his friends and contemporaries making more money in the City and elsewhere, that he had in 1986 wanted to quit politics and succeed Brian Walden as a TV presenter. The former Tory MP and *Times* writer Matthew Parris got the job.[3] Blair does not remember this but admits he was 'certainly frustrated' with the state of the Labour Party and with politics.[4]

For his first few months as an MP Brown stayed with friends, including Murray Elder, when in the capital as, unlike many parliamentarians, he did not have a London property. Much of the week – usually Thursdays to Tuesdays – would be spent back in Scotland anyway, and he can't recall a full weekend between 1983 and 1997 spent in London. 'This was a blessing in disguise,' he says. Most new MPs focus on the Westminster and London scene. But as Brown says: 'I got to know the constituency inside and out. I built up enduring friendships. And away from Westminster I learned more about what we needed to do as a party to win back the country's trust.'[5] A close friend of Brown's reflects today that while Brown was gaining perspective on what the country needed by spending more time away from Westminster, Blair was building up a political and media network of support at Westminster and in London which would later stand him in good stead for becoming leader.

Robin Cook, whom Brown had helped get elected ten years earlier, advised Brown on his maiden speech and also on the frequency with which he should intervene in the Commons: once a month was about right. Brown decided to make his maiden speech during a debate on social security. In his constituency more people were out of work than were employed in manufacturing industries, and one in seven was dependent on means-tested benefits. Brown vowed to raise their plight every month while the jobless figures remained so high. The Tory employment secretary Norman Tebbit had pointed in 1981 to his father who hadn't rioted but had got on his bike until he found a job, and the minister for social security on the day Brown spoke was the ultra-right-wing former headmaster Rhodes Boyson, who liked to blame poverty and unemployment on people's laziness, claiming that there were plenty of potential jobs as window cleaners.

Maiden speeches are by tradition supposed to be funny, and the window cleaners notion provided a good joke from Brown, who said he now understood what the Conservatives meant by ladders of opportunity. Brown finished the speech with a question: 'In 1948 the welfare state was created to take the shame out of need. Is that principle to be overthrown by an ever-increasing set of government assaults on the poor that are devoid of all logic, bereft of all morality and vindictive even beyond monetarism?' Brown, who disdains many of the conventions in Parliament, recalled later: 'As is usual practice in the House of Commons, the response was to praise the speech and fail to answer the question.'[6]

Even at this early stage in his political career, Brown took more of an interest in the ideological currents of the Tory Party than many others in Labour. Now he made the Conservatives' drift to the right under Margaret Thatcher a personal theme throughout Thatcher's second term. The MP wrote articles for the newspapers about jobs, social security and the NHS, and in February 1984, for example, he exposed a government plan to pilot a scheme in Cowdenbeath to force 18- to 25-year-olds to accept any low-paid job on offer or lose their benefits.

Brown had quickly learned how important it was to maintain good relations with civil servant 'sources' – often trade union contacts, whom he perhaps spent more time courting than he did ingratiating himself with fellow Labour MPs – and one of those passed on to him the details of the government's 1985 welfare reforms. He recalled: 'I used the computer printout to show that seven million people would lose out. While we could not reverse the policy in the face of an overwhelming Conservative majority, we did manage to water it down.'[7]

In November 1984 Kinnock, recognising that the MP for Dunfermline East was one of the stars of Labour's newcomers, made his first frontbench offer to Brown, with the role of Scottish spokesman under Donald Dewar. Brown declined on the grounds that he was still a new MP and for now he could learn more on the backbenches. Kinnock responded by saying he would have done exactly the same in Brown's position. The two men were getting on well. Kinnock says today: 'I knew the next time that I made any significant changes, he was going to get an economic job, which was an absolute natural thing.'[8]

The backdrop to the British political scene became the year-long miners' strike in 1984–85, a pivotal episode in Thatcher's premiership, with the miners under Arthur Scargill being called by the electricians' union leader Eric Hammond 'lions led by donkeys'. Thatcher had vowed to defeat them. The police were instructed to back working miners, helping them to cross picket lines, while they clamped down violently on striking miners, and this approach would cause lingering bitterness between those on either side of the strike. What an elderly Harold Macmillan in the upper house called 'the best men in the world – the miners – who beat the Kaiser's army and beat Hitler's army', endured, along with their families, police brutality and harassment, poverty, hunger and a lack of fuel. The families – especially the women – fought back, raising funds and protesting. But their efforts ended in failure.

'Scargill turned the dispute into a political strike personalised around himself,' Brown recalled. 'I had spoken with him once or twice at meetings in Fife before the crisis. I noticed that when he was before an audience he talked only about himself. A settlement was possible in the summer of 1984. But because of Scargill, the strike dragged on for a further nine months through a bitter and cold winter.'[9] Ultimately, Scargill made a catastrophic error by failing to grant the miners a vote on the strike, as miners' leaders had done with success in 1974. As Brown puts it, 'deprived of legitimacy, the miners lost the battle for public opinion'.[10] The situation was agonising for Kinnock, who was sympathetic to the miners and wanted them to prevail over Thatcher, but knew that his Militant hard-left opponent Scargill was wrong not to allow a vote.

Technically, Brown was an honorary member of the National Union of Mineworkers (NUM), as the National Union of Scottish

Mineworkers was incorporated into the NUM (Scottish area) in 1944. To be resident in Fife at that time must have had an impact on him. In his constituency, there were now no pits thanks to deindustrialisation, but a number of people living there worked elsewhere in mines, also across Clackmannanshire and the Lothians.

'There were ten strike centres locally and most Fridays I visited them to give whatever financial help I could,' Brown said. 'There was grinding hardship such that I had never seen before.'[11] Nationally, the Department for Social Security slashed the only benefit payment for miners' children and their mothers by £15 a week.

Amid splits and lasting bitterness, the will of the miners was ground down if not broken. On the day the strike ended, on 3 March 1985, Brown addressed the miners in Cowdenbeath. He pledged that he and his colleagues would continue to fight in Parliament for justice – including regarding welfare – for striking miners and their families. Within a few days, nearly 300 Scottish miners were dismissed by the National Coal Board, many of whom had been arrested while picketing a company moving coal through Brown's constituency during the strike.

Brown was a member of the select committee of MPs on employment, and he persuaded the chairman, Ron Leighton, to organise hearings into the dismissals. The committee summoned the head of the National Coal Board, Ian MacGregor, and Brown was ready. The MP asked MacGregor why he had not given the dismissed miners a right of appeal as had been outlined in their terms of employment. MacGregor made excuses over the chaos and unusual circumstances of the strike. Brown then asked how many miners had been fired during the strike and how many since the end of the strike. Most had been dismissed afterwards. MacGregor was then made to concede that there was no reason why the sacked miners could not have been allowed their right of appeal.

The National Coal Board was forced to back down and all the miners but one retained their jobs. Brown tried hard to persuade the odd man out to accept the deal, but the former miner expected a big cash settlement for unfair dismissal and not even his union could convince him to return. 'Though I disagreed with Scargill, I stood with the miners,' Brown has said. 'I am proud of their decision to make me an honorary member of the Scottish Mineworkers' Union.

To this day, I proudly display in my home the plaques and lamps that were given to me after that harrowing time.'[12]

The cold winter of 1984 was formative for Brown in other ways, too. While it was a disaster for miners and their families, Brown now proposed that low-income households be awarded an automatic payment to help with crippling fuel bills.

Brown's contacts in the civil service continued to help him make headlines, as when he obtained a leaked internal government document showing that the defence secretary, Michael Heseltine, was planning to close the Rosyth Naval Base and to privatise the dockyard. Brown gave a three-hour speech in the committee stage of the bill as he and his parliamentary allies attempted to delay it from going back to the Commons for its third reading. It was a filibuster, and Brown read out every statistic he could get hold of about ship-repair protocols around the world – even in landlocked states. The government pressed ahead with the privatisation at Rosyth and in other areas.

By now Brown's younger brother Andrew had taken a break from his TV work as a BBC Scotland researcher to help out in the parliamentary office, which he would do for longer than initially planned. Gordon persuaded Andrew to work for him in the Commons shortly after he had done some – paid – archive research in London and Scotland on Gordon's Maxton book. From 1984 to just after the 1987 general election, the two men shared a one-bedroom flat in the Barbican, with Andrew sleeping in the dining area, after driving a truck down from Gordon's Edinburgh flat with his old sofas and chairs.

They observed the Tories' rightward shift and what they saw as the government's indifference towards the industrial regions. They discovered that in order to secure regional funding from the European Community, the government had to submit honest accounts of the state of each area, and by publishing extracts they demonstrated the need for more support for the depressed areas. Andrew worked by copying and pasting and using a Xerox machine to post findings to the regional media. 'Photocopying was difficult then,' Andrew says. 'We literally mailed things out to regional newspapers all around the country. What it meant was that Gordon was getting calls from all around the regions to do interviews, and getting a tremendous amount of publicity.'[13]

Andrew also prepared research, including a timeline of events for John Smith on Michael Heseltine's role in the Westland row with Margaret Thatcher between 1985 and 1986 over the future of Britain's last helicopter manufacturers, with Thatcher favouring an American merger over a European takeover. Andrew quickly learned always to have backup documents of anything he had prepared for Gordon in case his brother lost them, which was frequently the case. 'I enjoyed that [period],' he says. 'It was fascinating, and it was very good for me, because I was at a bit of a loose end as to what I was going to do, where I was going to go, and it also brought me in touch with London.' Andrew lives today in a Westminster apartment which Gordon uses for London visits and meetings.

In November 1985, John Smith, the shadow trade and industry secretary, asked Brown to join his team. Brown accepted his first shadow ministerial role and set about travelling around England and Wales on a mission, as he put it, to reach 'beyond traditional Labour supporters and draw in the business community'.[14] Brown worked closely for the first time with John Prescott who, Brown said, 'proved to be the most energetic and consistent advocate of economic devolution'. Prescott was a working-class former steward in the Merchant Navy who had failed the divisive eleven-plus and gone on to be a significant figure in the trade union and Labour movements. Like Brown, Prescott, an MP for Hull East since 1970, had become a moderniser, siding with the 'soft left' and even the 'right' of the party on some issues such as disarmament, and would be crucial in dragging the unions onside with major party voting reforms to dilute the influence of the hard left. The two men bonded while making the case for regional development agencies, which Prescott would later introduce in government.

Meanwhile the party leader, Neil Kinnock, marked himself out as a key Labour moderniser in the most memorable speech at a British party conference in recent times when, addressing the party and the nation in Bournemouth on 11 October 1985, he heralded the beginning of the expulsion of the hard-left 'militant tendency' with a flourish of his undoubtedly brilliant oratory:

> I'll tell you what happens with impossible promises. You start with far-fetched resolutions. They are then pickled into a rigid dogma, a

code, and you go through the years sticking to that, out-dated, misplaced, irrelevant to the real needs, and you end up in the grotesque chaos of a Labour council, a Labour council, hiring taxis to scuttle round a city handing out redundancy notices to its own workers.

I am telling you, no matter how entertaining, how fulfilling to short-term egos – I tell you and you'll listen, I'm telling you that you can't play politics with people's jobs and with people's services or with their homes.

'I joined Neil's fight to expel militant from the party,' says Brown, who was present at the sensational speech. The Kinnockites faced down the Trotskyist faction, named after their newspaper *Militant*, which had formed in 1964. There is no questioning the significance of that moment. Famous within the party and witnessed too by the wider electorate, the speech – and the reaction, including Eric Heffer, the hard-left MP for Liverpool Walton, walking out of the hall – embodied the heavy lifting done by Kinnock when it comes to an already changed party inherited by the architects of New Labour: Blair, Brown and Mandelson. Kinnock recalls: 'Obviously it was classic denunciation. And it was necessary. I would have done it in '84. But of course, that would have been in the middle of a miners' strike, and nobody would have been listening. Anyone who did would have rejected it. And I wasn't worried about losing votes or anything at that stage. It was [about] making an effective impression on the mind.'[15]

The context for this intervention was that Thatcher was breaking the post-war consensus of British politics, and in the process breaking the strong influence of the trade unions, with new laws restricting their powers, and with widespread media support as 'middle England' voters felt more able to make money and run businesses more freely. Kinnock was persuading his party, meanwhile, to accept the 'right to buy' council houses, another popular policy, as well as continued membership of the European Council. Brown stood firmly behind such policies, which fitted with his belief that Labour had to be attractive to the wider electorate and ultimately be in power in order to effect change.

Sue Nye, Brown's long-time aide, was sitting on the stage behind Kinnock for the speech. 'When Neil became leader he knew that his job was to take the party on its first steps of modernisation after two defeats,' she says.

There were still many in the party who thought it was the failure to win support for the programme and not the programme itself that was the problem, with many blaming the media and poor organisation. Two things stopped the process of modernisation beginning as quickly as he wanted – the miners' strike and Militant. But in 1985 Neil wanted to give a speech that showed the direction he felt the party had to go if we were ever to be electable. He said that elections were won in years before not in the weeks of an election campaign. That was the moment that modernisation began. It was also the speech that took Militant head-on. Divisions killed the party's electoral efforts in the 1980s. Those were [on] Militant, defence and an acceptance of the market economy. We would never have won the election in 1997 without the hard work Neil put in to change Labour so that we could change Britain.[16]

By 'modernisation', Nye is referring to the shift away from Militant and Trotskyism and the Bennite wing of Labour, and towards compromising with the British electorate, monetarism and, yes, the Thatcher consensus.

The general election campaign of 1987 was the first in which Mandelson, now the party's director of communications, played a key role, running it along with Bryan Gould. Mandelson, a former London Weekend Television producer and the grandson of the former Labour cabinet minister Herbert Morrison, had got the job in a testing interview panel discussion, after Kinnock's chief of staff, Charles Clarke, had persuaded him to apply. Mandelson already knew Brown from Labour circles and political television, but the pair would become intensely close in the years that followed up until 1994. By 1988, according to Mandelson's biographer, 'Mandelson had ... identified Brown and Blair as the stars of the future, with Brown the leading figure of the two.'[17]

Brown and Blair, obviously bright, articulate and energetic, were both forging a reputation as powerful speakers, and shared Mandelson's outlook (namely that Labour had to drop its more unpopular and 'old left' views) and were supportive of Kinnock, promoting the changes in policy on defence (against unilateral nuclear disarmament), Europe (continued membership of the council), tax (scrapping commitments to tax the wealthy more) and more. Brown, however, frequently instigated media appearances, with leaks, press releases, surveys and more.

As Mandelson has said of the period, Brown was 'a non-stop media machine, and therefore tremendous for the press office, absolutely tremendous'.[18]

The Mandelson dynamic mattered partly because he was in a powerful position to bring promising frontbenchers forward and give them a higher profile, given he was the party's communications director, looking for people to put on television. One friend of Mandelson's today says that the communications chief 'made' Brown in terms of his prominence in the Labour Party, promoting him and 'excluding others'. Brown and Mandelson would develop a love-hate relationship which underwent extraordinary cycles of closeness and distance. But their closeness at this stage was not merely personal: it was intensely political. They were 'modernisers' in that they shared a belief that the party needed to change to be elected on key issues like Europe, the economy and unilateralism; and they were Kinnockites in that they believed Kinnock shared this view, even if they sometimes felt he wasn't moving fast enough. They were not dissidents in the sense some on the 'soft left' were, like Margaret Beckett on defence, Gould on Europe and Smith on the economy.

In June 1985 Brown decided to stand for the shadow cabinet, which in the Labour Party back then was elected by MPs. With the help of his friend Nick Brown, the Newcastle MP and the cunning manipulator of parliamentary votes who would later be chief whip, Brown received eighty-eight votes, coming joint eleventh on the ballot. Brown – the only member of the '83 intake to be elected to the top team – with some justification describes that outcome as 'a decent enough result for someone standing for the first time'. Blair would not be voted onto the shadow cabinet until 1988, when he became shadow secretary of state for energy. Brown had been re-elected onto the shadow cabinet in 1987, and topped the poll in 1988.

Brown played what he describes as a 'small' role in the 1987 campaign. He brushes aside the conventional wisdom of the time – 'Labour won the campaign, but lost the election' – saying: 'If you do not get the policy fundamentals right, no amount of good political presentation – from red roses to new anthems – can make up the difference ... [The manifesto] did not do enough to answer the concerns voters had about Labour's position on defence, taxation and economic management.'[19]

In other words, despite the work that Kinnock had put in visibly to change the party, not to mention the modern, disciplined media relations forged by Mandelson, Brown believed that the party was in fact doing too little to compromise with the electorate on the big issues. 'It was this election that taught me and my colleagues that we still had a long way to go to establish our economic credibility as a party of government.'[20]

He described the one national press conference which he took part in with Blair: 'All the coverage Labour might have received from my employment initiatives was swept away by a comment Tony made alleging that Mrs Thatcher's policies on private rented housing were the result of "an unchecked and unbalanced mind".' Michael Brunson, ITN's political editor, asked if Blair was suggesting that the prime minister had psychiatric problems. '[The] press reported his comment as a desperate gambit by an increasingly desperate party,' Brown said and, not for the first time describing his big-brother-type role over Blair, he added: 'Tony was despondent as he got pilloried; I told him these things happened and it would pass.'[21]

In Scotland, Labour made gains – nine MPs and a 7 per cent higher vote share – and Brown's own majority in Dunfermline East was doubled to nearly 20,000. Across the UK, however, Labour won only twenty extra seats, and the Tories still held a parliamentary majority of more than a hundred. 'Labour – now destined to be out of power for a dozen years – had to change even more radically if we were ever again to return to government,' Brown said.[22]

He now decided it was his mission to go about helping to make Labour a mass-membership party by recruiting many of the UK's 5.5 million members of trade unions affiliated to Labour. Brown (and others) wanted to do this in order to create an 'army' of party members on the ground able to take on the Conservatives and Liberals and enhance Labour's ability to win elections. In Brown's own constituency, membership more than doubled in the late 1980s, partly because of Brown's profile and active nature. By 1993, there was a similar story in Blair's Sedgefield constituency. The local success acted as a precursor to Brown and Blair's drive to make the national party a mass-member one going into the 1990s. Brown was influenced in his mass-membership mission by British political scientists including Patrick Seyd, a former Labour member in the early 1980s, and

Paul Whiteley. Brown says today: 'We raised our own constituency from four hundred to around 1,500, but the party did not do enough to become a mass-membership party as I wanted.'[23]

Soon after the 1987 general election in the shadow cabinet reshuffle, Kinnock appointed Brown as shadow chief secretary to the Treasury under John Smith, who was the new shadow chancellor. Here, Brown would join Kinnock in doing some significant 'heavy lifting' when it came to changing the party. As Kinnock explains, Brown helped 'in terms of shifting the party finally, away from the idea that in opposition we could promise to spend endlessly, ignoring the reality ... I realised that in modern politics, it was important for people to be able to make a connection between what they were paying in their taxes and what they were getting as a consequence of that expenditure.'[24]

The economy under the Tories was growing and the governing party was able to deliver tax cuts while also maintaining spending levels, even as spending as a share of the economy fell. Brown himself said: 'I spent the next year thinking through how to modernise Labour's approach in the area that had become our Achilles heel – taxing-and-spending. None doubted our willingness to spend money, but too many doubted our capacity to spend prudently. I argued that we had to become wise spenders rather than big spenders. John Smith, also keen to transform Labour, developed a mantra, repeated over and over, of a Labour party committed to economic stability.'[25]

In the late 1980s, Brown and Smith were up against Tory ministerial heavyweights in Nigel Lawson as chancellor and John Major, whom Brown described as a 'rising star', as chief secretary. The backdrop for Labour was more division, as the left fought back and Tony Benn, who returned to the Commons in a 1984 by-election, challenged Kinnock for the leadership. Benn was himself a charismatic aristocrat, a fine orator who had renounced his family peerage and claimed to represent the working classes. 'Bennism' stood for the traditional hard left: anti-European, pacifist, in favour of radical constitutional reform including the abolition of the House of Lords, and uncompromising with the electorate when it came to high tax and spending.

Kinnock, the party reformer, won the internal battle by a landslide, but in November 1988, just a month after the leadership contest, Labour lost to the SNP at a by-election in one of Labour's safest Scottish seats: Govan, in the heart of 'red' Clydeside where Brown's father had ministered. Nonetheless, Brown sensed Tory weakness – and yet another rightward shift for that party – when Lawson in the Budget of 1988 dramatically reduced the top rate of income tax from 60p to 40p. 'On the spot, I concluded that Lawson had handed us a weapon that could eventually help us get back into power,' he would claim later.[26] 'As I pointed out at the time, 95 per cent of the British people would gain nothing; in one swoop, he had handed out billions to the wealthiest people in the country.' As Brown said: 'no Budget this century has given so much to so few'. To be fair to Lawson and to criticise Brown, the latter declined to change this tax rate through his entire time as chancellor and would only move the rate up to 45 per cent while prime minister and with his own chancellor, Alistair Darling.

The following day, Lawson audaciously reduced interest rates, claiming that inflation was under control and his policies were working successfully. This planted the seed in Brown's mind to create independence for the Bank of England almost a decade later. 'It was this kind of cynical ploy – the Chancellor pronouncing favourably on his own economics and rewarding himself with an interest rate cut – that was discrediting the conduct of monetary policy. In my own mind, I started to question Treasury control of interest rates and remarked to John Smith that there could be a case for Bank of England independence.'[27] More generally, Brown was right to see this as a turning point. Lawson's tax cuts followed by his interest rate cuts helped fuel an unsustainable housing boom which would eventually bring recession.

Problems with John Smith's health would, not for the last time, provide another turning point for Brown personally in October 1988. On the Saturday after Labour's annual party conference, where Brown had sensed Smith was unwell, Smith went to see his GP with a severe headache. The GP sent him to hospital, and when a cardiogram failed to identify any problems, Smith returned to his Edinburgh home. The following day, while dressing, he suffered a heart attack. Smith was now instructed to take several months off, cut out alcohol and lose weight. With Parliament returning in a few days, Bryan Gould, the trade and industry spokesman, was the next senior person with an economics portfolio and the obvious stand-in. But to Brown's surprise, Kinnock asked him to step up temporarily as shadow chancellor. Brown recalls: 'Throughout the next three months, I kept in close touch with John, visiting him frequently, but trying not to overburden him and simply get on with the job in hand.'[28]

Kinnock says that 'within minutes of hearing' about Smith's heart attack, he asked Brown to step up into the shadow chancellor role 'because we had an important debate in the Commons the following Monday ... I called Gordon, asked him if he'd do the debate, and without any hesitation he said Yes. And of course, he was stunningly brilliant. I mean, Gordon had been recognised as a great Commons performer before in any case, rightly because he was outstandingly good, but then, that he took that debate on with a couple of days' notice in an emergency to rescue his friend, was just outstanding. It shone a light on his capabilities.'[29]

The economy had now become the main national story, and Brown did indeed electrify the Commons with his performance across the despatch box from Lawson. Brown boomed on about rising inflation, debt and unemployment, and concluded: 'Historians will be interested to know what special powers the chancellor has over the prime minister that she should witness these appalling errors and then describe them as brilliant, wonderful and marvellous. The Right Honourable gentleman was wrong about inflation, about interest rates, about imports, about savings, about trade deficits and about the money supply, and his response is to tell us that what we need is self-discipline – not from him, but from everyone else who borrows and spends. These problems could have been averted if the chancellor had practised some self-discipline himself.'

Brown, aged thirty-seven, was hailed as a new Labour star by the press, and his elevation, his acclaimed performance – also during the autumn statement – and the dominance of economic affairs led him to top the poll in the shadow cabinet elections in November 1988. 'I remember when he stood in for John Smith, when John was ill, and did a really brilliant job,' Blair says. 'I mean, he was extraordinary at the despatch box during that time.'[30] Seeing how effective Brown was at skewering the Tories had perhaps reassured the wider parliamentary party of his traditional Labour credentials and meant they wanted to back an effective parliamentary performer on top of his brief, even if they still harboured misgivings about his modernising agenda regarding spending.

Smith returned to his role as shadow chancellor in February 1989. At this point Brown decided again to focus on the Tories' drift to the right with a book called *Where There is Greed*. Brown regrets this. 'I missed a chance: while it was important to reveal what was wrong with the Tories' policies, I should have done more to define New Labour, set out a detailed agenda for change and provide a stronger intellectual framework for the modernisation movement within the party.'[31]

In private, Brown had begun to clash with Kinnock over several policy areas, including devolution and wider constitutional reform, and the need as Brown saw it to focus relentlessly on the economy. But the 1989 annual conference marked the completion of the Kinnock policy review process. By now the party had abandoned what Brown describes as its 'three most unpopular policies of our decade out of power – unilateral nuclear disarmament, old-style nationalisation and high taxation. Thanks to his leadership, Neil's new policies were approved with relatively little dissent and they would form the basis of the 1992 election manifesto.'[32]

Kinnock promoted Brown again in November 1989, this time to shadow trade and industry secretary. Brown's vision in the role was to make the case for a 'modern industrial strategy' for Britain, but first he had to address the party's continuing – and unpopular – commitment to renationalising telecommunications. As Brown explains, 'privatisation was all but irreversible because of the fast-changing nature of the industry and the fact that so many millions had already bought shares in the privatised companies. By now, I was thinking of an alternative policy which would secure benefits for the country through regulation without the expense of renationalisation: in due course this was to lead to my proposal for a windfall tax on the privatised utilities to fund a welfare-to-work agenda.'[33]

Michael Gove, who went on to work for *The Times* before becoming a senior cabinet minister in successive Conservative administrations from 2010 to 2024, worked as a researcher and occasional presenter on STV at this stage, having been hired by Brown's elder brother. He recalls Gordon Brown at the time:

> Because he was a hegemonic figure in Scottish politics there, and indeed, John's brother, it would sometimes be the case, or often be the case, that I would interview him … in the sense of him coming down to College Green for a clip or two for a TV news broadcast. I got to know him because I was a young journalist, essentially taking

news clips. And the things that I remember were, he was always polite and considerate, and always in a hurry.

He would peer into the camera before recording, just to make sure that the unruly lock of his fringe was in place. And the other thing is that long before they invented the soundbite, he'd mastered the ability of providing a quote of just the right length for the evening news on the subject under discussion. So there was already a sort of discipline or professionalism about him, but also he had a ration of small talk. The other people whom I used to regularly interview – or clip, more accurately – at the time include Ian Laing, Malcolm Rifkind and Donald Dewar. Dewar was the most garrulous and the person who was the most obviously engaging. But there was never anything other than, as I say, politeness and professionalism from Gordon Brown.[34]

Margaret Thatcher's government would implode dramatically over the following two years, not least because of the infamously regressive poll tax, first introduced in Scotland. Lawson resigned as chancellor over economic policy, especially the exchange rate, and following criticism from a government economic adviser, Alan Walters, with whom Thatcher sided. The pro-European Geoffrey Howe also quit as deputy prime minister after repeated humiliations from Thatcher, and quietly savaged her in his devastating resignation speech from the backbenches. On Thatcher's approach to Europe, Howe said in the Commons: 'It is rather like sending your opening batsmen to the crease only for them to find, the moment the first balls are bowled, that their bats have been broken before the game by the team captain.'

Michael Heseltine, who had resigned from government in 1986, stood for the leadership in 1990 and gained enough votes to persuade Thatcher to stand down. But then in the ensuing Tory contest the mild-mannered former foreign secretary and chancellor John Major emerged through the middle as leader and prime minister, offering a fresh start for the Conservatives. As Brown has said about the demise of Thatcher and its impact on the opposition party, Major's 'shift to the centre and his rags-to-riches story ... created a new set of challenges for which Labour was less prepared'.[35]

5
Paying the Price

Douglas Alexander, who would go on to run election campaigns for and serve in the cabinets of Tony Blair and Gordon Brown, was in his early twenties when he first met the latter. A fellow Scot and a fellow son of the manse, Alexander was continuing postgraduate studies in 1989 at Edinburgh where he had chaired the Labour club. One of Alexander's tutors, Paul Addison, who had supervised Brown's PhD, informed him that Brown had an opening for a researcher.

At the Scottish Labour conference at Dunoon in the spring of 1990, Brown told him later to visit his flat at Marchmont in Edinburgh, the one the police had wrongly believed was 'ransacked'. Alexander turned up to find Brown watching football in a chaotic room full of piles of books lining the walls from the floor to the ceiling. The pair watched the rest of the game together before Brown climbed a precarious ladder to pick off various books that would help Alexander complete his finals. There was no job interview. Instead, like many to whom Brown takes a fondness, Alexander went away with a cardboard box packed with books. A few weeks later in July 1990, he started work for Brown in the House of Commons, and would become an important link-man between Brown and Blair.

At the turn of the decade, Brown retained his friendship with and older brother role to Blair, who had himself won 77 votes in the 1987 shadow cabinet elections. And in 1991, the pair made a lengthy trip to Australia in which they toured eight cities and met the Australian Labor prime minister Bob Hawke and treasurer Paul Keating.

On the long plane journey out, Brown and Blair took out a blank sheet of paper and tried to set down from first principles what a modern social democracy would look like. Both were in no doubt that they needed to back markets, competition and the role of the private sector, which they genuinely saw as essential too, in achieving economic growth, and that they also had to change from a 'tax-and-spend party'. The domestic party context was that Neil Kinnock had long battled against those who had opposed nuclear weapons, council house sales and public–private partnerships to rebuild the infrastructure. Overseas, the Berlin Wall had fallen in November 1989 and the Soviet Union would follow, finally collapsing in December 1991.

Brown and Blair had done much thinking when it came to markets, the economy and fiscal policy, against the backdrop of Thatcherism. They both recognised that there were market failures. Though effective for creating financial prosperity, the markets did little or nothing to tackle inequality. And, they believed, only government could help get the balance right between the public and private sectors, and end the stand-off between the two. 'In future, public spending had to be judged not by how much we spent, but by what it achieved,' Brown has said. 'On all of this, Tony and I agreed and we were to follow through these ideas in party policy reforms a year or two later.'[1]

However, the seeds of tension were planted in different areas. 'Where we found it more difficult to agree was on what to do about poverty and inequality. Both of us favoured promoting opportunity and felt that equality of opportunity was a goal that no one was yet delivering. But on equality I think it is fair to say that I gave more emphasis to prosecuting a war on poverty and addressing inequalities of income and wealth.'[2]

However, a look at Brown's speeches between 1992 and 1994 especially shows that he firmly believed and argued that the correct socialist position was to have economic stability before addressing inequality: prudence, in other words, for a purpose. The speeches, which drew criticism from the left, demonstrate the gradual taming of Brown, the turning of the sense of moral outrage about inequality in his earlier years to political pragmatism. Ultimately, then, Brown's lifelong belief that Labour had to be in contention for power in order to bring about changes that affect people's lives, and his conviction that you had to have economic stability before addressing inequality and the circumstances of the poorer in society, prevailed. He held this position in Parliament in his own right, as he had done before he came to Westminster, but it was doubtless reinforced by the positions taken by his friend Tony Blair.

Brown by now had one significant policy difference with Kinnock too, arguing firmly that Labour should fight the 1992 general election on the economy. With unemployment rising sharply, the recession was biting and higher mortgages were driving negative equity. 'At last, I believed, we could successfully attack the Conservatives for their mismanagement of the economy and credibly position Labour as the party of economic competence,' he recalled. 'None of this, I am afraid, happened.'[3] He says today: 'I wasn't really central to the 1992 general election.'[4]

Unlike many in Labour at the time, Brown was privately convinced the party would lose in 1992. His old friend Alistair Moffat recounts asking Brown about the likelihood of Labour winning and Brown merely shaking his head.[5] 'The expected Labour breakthrough never happened,' Brown has said. 'Why? Because we failed to stress the one issue that mattered most to the country. In Britain, too, as with Bill Clinton's successful Presidential campaign in 1992, it should have been a version of "it's the economy, stupid" – as I argued, "jobs and the economy first".'[6]

Instead, for reasons Brown says he understood, Kinnock focused Labour on looking fresh and dynamic by ridding the party of extremists and advocating constitutional reform, including planning to introduce proportional representation, which Brown still says to this day was a mistake.

Labour – and Brown especially – had worked hard since 1987 to counter attempts by the Tories, ramped up in the run-up to the 1992 general election, to claim that Labour was the party of tax and spend. As shadow chief secretary to the Treasury, Brown had introduced an important system, which was not always popular among Labour MPs, in which every spending commitment had to be vetted to make sure it fitted in with the party's new approach and fiscal discipline. Smith had backed the idea.

But a few days before the start of the campaign, Labour was, in Brown's words, 'caught out' by Norman Lamont's pre-election Budget. Lamont dramatically introduced a new and lower 20p tax rate which took 4 million lower-paid workers out of the 25p tax band. Brown adds: 'The ingenuity of the Lamont plan was that in effect Labour now favoured higher taxes on the low paid than the Conservatives did: our plans cut far less ice than the Lamont proposal.'[7]

Smith did focus on the economy, but probably with the wrong argument. He wanted to fight back, and six days into the campaign launched a 'shadow budget' in which he tried to argue that increased tax would result in gains that would appeal to the electorate: rising pensions, increased child benefit, more for the NHS. But the result was – perhaps predictably – a bombardment of claims from the Tories that Labour was profligate with its spending. In retrospect, the 'shadow budget' was to prove a key turning point in the election campaign. Brown says that for months he had argued with both Smith and Kinnock – who was worried about Smith's tax plans – that the party should be focused on 'jobs and the economy', not tax rises. 'The Conservatives, I said, were finally vulnerable on the economy,' he wrote.[8]

Kinnock today says that he, too, was opposed to Smith's approach and the 'shadow budget'.

> John made what I consider still, and did then, to be a critical error about policy announcement and delivery. I held very firmly to the idea that even though our fiscal policies would have a disadvantage on a minuscule minority – less than 5 per cent of income earners – they ought to be presented and explained for months, and that it couldn't adequately be done in the weeks of a general election campaign.
>
> John took an entirely different view. Hence his complete insistence on the shadow budget. And I just thought we were leaving it too late. The problem was, I couldn't afford to have a dispute with John because even a private dispute would have been public within two minutes. And obviously, he was held in high regard in the party and publicly and to have a bust-up with John would have risked my credibility and the party's standing ... So that was my view of affairs. John's was divergent. I was always glad to have Gordon's support, but he wasn't going to have a big bust-up with John, partly because of justifiable personal regard.[9]

Brown remained frustrated during the campaign, and his requests to do national events highlighting unemployment were sometimes, he claims, dismissed. In a stunt worthy of the Liberal Democrats, who are better known for such election gimmicks, Brown did unveil a clock showing a job was being lost every seven seconds, but other than that he was largely consigned to touring the regions.

Meanwhile, the Tories plastered the country with two posters: 'THE PRICE OF LABOUR: £1,250 A YEAR FOR EVERY FAMILY' and 'LABOUR'S DOUBLE WHAMMY: MORE TAXES, HIGHER PRICES'. Brown concedes that, though crude, these attacks were 'effective'. 'Despite all our work, Labour was less trusted on tax than a Conservative Party that had recently tried and failed to impose a poll tax and had already more than doubled VAT. I was frustrated: the Tories had made the shadow budget and tax-and-spend the issue.'[10]

The prime minister, John Major, rounded off the campaign giving symbolic plain-speaking speeches on a simple soapbox. This contrasted with Labour, whose leadership appeared to get a collective rush of blood to the head and held an American-style triumphalist rally in Sheffield that has become as infamous in party terms as Kinnock's expulsion of Militant seven years earlier was celebrated. Kinnock – alongside many others – was convinced Labour was going to win, with Roy Hattersley saying as much publicly, and Kinnock returned the love from the hall and shouted, 'We're all right! We're all right! We're all right!' This was portrayed by a largely hostile media as outrageous complacency.

By chance, on election night, John Brown was producing the coverage from Scotland and linked his brother into a discussion with the Conservative Kenneth Clarke and the Liberal Democrat Alan Beith. As the panel were about to begin debating, the programme dramatically switched to the count at the marginal seat in Basildon, where Labour had achieved only a 1 per cent swing and the Conservatives had held the seat. Brown recalls: 'It was a bellwether outcome. As the camera returned to me, I dutifully retreated to the standard holding line that it was "still too early to say". But my worst fears had been confirmed.'[11]

As Blair would keep pointing out to anyone who would listen, Labour had secured a lower percentage share of the national vote – 34.5 per cent – than its 37.8 per cent in the 1979 defeat.[12] So, although their share of the vote was up by 3.6 per cent on 1987 and they gained forty-two seats to take them up to 271 (the most at an election since 1974), Kinnock, after nine years as leader, stood down. He tried to push Bryan Gould as his successor, including to Brown who politely declined to support him, but the competent and respectable John Smith was the obvious replacement.

Despite their differences on constitutional reform, including diametrically opposed views on devolution, Brown is full of praise in the round for Kinnock. 'For nearly a decade, with courage and unstinting determination, Neil had taken the party into the modern world,' he wrote. 'He had confronted Militant entryism, transformed our policies from defence to the economy, and given the party back a belief in itself.'[13] Both Brown and Blair thought it was urgent now to build upon what Kinnock had achieved on party reform and change.

It was in 1992 that Blair himself would argue – as later the ultra-Blairites retrospectively would claim too – that Brown had had his chance to stand for the leadership, in an attempt to justify Blair beating Brown to it two years later. But that was never going to happen. Smith was not only seen as the natural successor to Kinnock, but he was by now a close friend and mentor to Brown. Brown says he pushed Smith to go further and faster on party modernisation and had disagreed with him over tax, but: 'I had no doubt that he had the strength, ability and desire to take on John Major and win the next election.'[14]

Brown travelled to see Blair in his Sedgefield constituency the day after the 1992 general election defeat, on a mission to thrash out a further policy modernisation agenda as opposed to that of constitutional reform and proportional representation. Here, with Peter Mandelson present too and amid policy talks in which Brown was seen as the senior of the three men, Blair suggested Brown should run. 'I'm not sure Tony was serious when he said to me in his living room that I should stand for leader – and I did not take it seriously,' Brown recalls.[15]

This is almost certainly true, though Blair explains today: 'It was a very difficult thing, because we were both close to John. John had been a kind of mentor to both of us ... I'd spent many a convivial evening with John and those evenings were long. And I had a great respect and liking for John. But I did feel that we needed a complete renewal, and I thought that John would be a really good, capable leader because he was a great advocate and, you know, a smart, capable man, but I didn't feel he would modernise the Labour Party in the way I felt it needed it.

What I said to Gordon was, if you go for it I'll support you and I'm happy to speak with John about it. Not out of any disrespect for John but just because I felt this was ... but it would have been a difficult thing; difficult because Gordon was close to John; difficult because, you know, to have ended up having a fight between the two would have been problematic. I mean, it would have been difficult. I think, in the end, it's possible that Gordon would have won actually. But it would have been quite personally distressing. Because he would have taken on someone whom we both really liked, so it was a conversation for a time.[16]

Blair meanwhile wanted to stand for the elected and influential position of deputy leader. Brown offered to support him, but warned that he did not stand much chance up against Margaret Beckett and John Prescott, both of whom were running. Nick Brown, who was also there in Sedgefield, issued the same warning, adding that Blair could not win the trade union vote, which made up a third of the electoral college. However, the group agreed that an endorsement by Smith would greatly help Blair among MPs and Brown agreed to call Smith to ask. 'But when I put Tony's case to him, John was unequivocal in his response. He did not want him to stand and preferred Margaret,' Brown says.[17] So in 1992, for all its changes, Labour had not yet moved on far enough to fully embrace Blair and Brown, and were still dominated by an old guard. Only a shocking tragedy two years later would jolt the party into taking the generational leap.

Meanwhile, Smith himself swiftly became the favourite to become leader, backed by a majority of all three groups of the college: the unions, MPs and party members. His one challenger, Bryan Gould, gained only 9 per cent of the overall vote, and Smith's choice of Beckett decisively won the deputy leadership over Prescott.

On the day that Smith became leader – 18 July 1992 – the *Sunday Times* magazine featured an interview with Tony Blair, his photo with the headline 'Lost leader' on the front cover. It would upset Brown and even embarrass Blair, whose aide, Anji Hunter, tried to get it removed from the cover at the last minute because of the awkward timing. One friend of Brown's claims that Blair was courting the influential Murdoch press back then, though there is no evidence for this. The right-wing Murdoch outlets would go on to torment Brown, as a powerful and opinionated centre-left Scot, when he emerged fully in frontline politics.

Brown and Blair polled first and second respectively in the subsequent shadow cabinet elections. Labour's frontbench was strengthened by new talent, including Harriet Harman, David Blunkett and Mo Mowlam, as a generational shift gained pace. Brown was unsurprisingly named shadow chancellor, while Blair surprised Brown by pushing to be made shadow home secretary, which would enable him to reshape Labour's approach to law and order. Brown had expected Blair to be shadow trade and industry spokesman but saw the merits of his fellow moderniser being at shadow home and encouraged Smith to make the appointment, which the leader did.

In July 1992, Brown delivered the annual lecture for the centre-left Tribune group, outlining his own case for policy modernisation in order to win the next general election. He argued that Labour's priorities were out of date and out of sync with those of the electorate. He pointed out that Labour's constitution was written in 1918 and needed to change. The implication was that Clause IV in the constitution – the commitment, however theoretical, to nationalisation of the major industries, which Blair would later abolish – should be scrapped.

In a significant breakthrough for the modernisers, ahead of the 1993 annual party conference both Brown and Blair were elected onto the party's national executive committee for the first time, after it had long been dominated by the left and the likes of Tony Benn. At the same time, Smith, albeit somewhat reluctantly at first, took up the cause of 'one member, one vote' (OMOV) for parliamentary selection and was backed by Brown, Blair and Prescott in doing so. Smith ran into trouble with the unions and especially John Edmonds, the GMB general secretary, but as he told Brown he was so determined to push the internal though important party reform through that if necessary he would make it an issue of confidence in his leadership, which he would put to a vote. It mattered because OMOV helped make Labour look more democratic, and at the same time meant a weakening of disproportionate union power when it came to Labour selections.

At the conference, Smith's chief of staff Murray Elder, Brown's close friend since primary school, produced figures showing they were going to lose on the issue. But the modernisers then came up with what Brown calls a 'masterstroke', which was to hand the task of making the final appeal to John Prescott, seen as a Labour traditionalist rival to Smith. 'A trade union negotiator to his fingertips, John Prescott could assure them that Labour had no intention of breaking its links with the unions,' wrote Brown.[18] In a speech that is famous within the party if not beyond, Prescott declared that Smith had put his 'head on the block' over the issue and that the unions should trust and back him. Smith won the vote by a mere 3 per cent.

With party constitutional reform under way, albeit headed by a relatively reluctant Smith, Brown for his part focused on changing Labour's economic agenda. He persuaded Smith to ditch the 'shadow budget' he had pushed under Kinnock, and in a symbolic move announced publicly that the party had got it wrong. When one Labour MP asked why he had scrapped commitments to higher taxes, there came a classically blunt Brown answer: 'Because we didn't win the election.'

In 'Campaign for Recovery', a paper with a double meaning about country and party, Brown, in what would become one of his trademark policies, set out the case for a one-off levy on the excess profits of the privatised utilities. Unlike many other transient Labour policies of recent times, it lasted, and would be implemented five years later as the windfall tax to finance the New Deal for unemployed workers. Brown also attacked what he called the 'undeserving rich' – the privatised utility bosses, tax avoiders and 'something for nothing' executives. It was a difficult policy for the Tories to oppose, and Brown was careful to distinguish between 'those who made money because of the monopoly that they enjoyed – who had to pay more – and those who did well competing successfully in a harshly competitive marketplace'.[19]

In a pivotal piece of modernisation heavy lifting meanwhile, Brown annoyed some shadow cabinet colleagues by cracking down on unfunded spending commitments. It was time to get serious about preparing for government, and Brown describes it as 'a long, hard fight'. This level of discipline enforced by him came at a cost. 'I suspect because of my uncompromising stand on tax-and-spend, I never did as well again in shadow cabinet elections as I had in 1992,' he correctly recalls. 'I think it is fair to say that I was the reformer who at that time felt the most heat from within the party. My hard-line stance on public expenditure provoked continuing divisions.'[20]

At the same time, Blair was developing a modern home-affairs policy agenda. It is true that Brown helped him by coming up with the famous New Labour slogan 'Tough on crime, tough on the causes of crime', and as Brown says: 'I was working hand-in-hand with Tony. We seemed to be of one mind and at times we could each anticipate what the other was thinking. It was almost as if we still shared the same office ... For the first time for years we had a position on law-and-order around which the whole party could unite, and this rewriting of Labour's approach, focusing both on the victims of crime and the causes of crime, rightly earned him great plaudits.'[21]

Blair's profile began to increase rapidly thanks to powerful Commons speeches, regular media appearances, and the national focus on law and order following the murder of the Merseyside toddler James Bulger by two ten-year-old boys in February 1993. As Blair's popularity grew inside the party and beyond, Brown suffered political collateral damage with the collapse in September 1992 of the European Exchange Rate Mechanism (ERM), British membership of which Brown and Smith had subscribed to despite objections from some in the shadow cabinet such as Robin Cook. Smith and Brown knew that to oppose ERM membership would have resulted in speculation against the pound sterling and allowed the Tories to accuse Labour of being the party of 'devaluation'. As another author outlines, fiscal prudence and the ERM crash both damaged Brown's standing within Labour: 'He had bravely delivered an unpalatable message to the party, that the days of tax and spend were over. Both stances had cost him support; to the very extent that he had been serving the interests of his party, he had not been serving his own.'[22]

As a whole, however, Labour was making progress in the polls, and when 'Black Wednesday' – with its collapse in the value of the pound sterling – came on 16 September 1992, and the Tories abruptly withdrew the country from the ERM, Smith delivered a blistering performance against John Major in his first Commons speech as leader, branding Major as 'the devalued prime minister of a devalued government'. This may have been shameless given Smith's and Brown's previous support for the ERM, but it worked.

It was a turning point for the worse for a severely weakened Tory government, and Brown now seized the opportunity to build on his economic changes – and his team. He brought in his long-time aide

Sue Nye, who had at a very young age run James Callaghan's office before doing the same for Michael Foot and Neil Kinnock. Nye (now a baroness) was a major asset to Brown for the decades in which she worked for him, and a cool-headed analyser of the Labour and political scene. 'Sue came to work with me after Neil stepped down as leader,' he recalls. 'Her loyalty was beyond any call of duty; and her knowledge of the Labour Party, broader and deeper than anyone I know.'[23] Nye would remain the head of Brown's political office until 2010.

Nye herself says:

When John became leader in 1992 he was only fifty-four and at the height of his career. There was no question that he would be leader for a long time and would fight the next election. So when I went to work for Gordon it was to do with carrying on the modernisation process that had begun with Neil. John and Gordon had known each other for many years through Scottish politics and he was certainly a mentor to Gordon. Although there was true respect and friendship, it didn't mean that there was total agreement on what needed to be done in the party. John continued the path of change with abolishing the trade union block vote with the introduction of 'one member one vote' in 1993 but Gordon certainly felt that more needed to be done.

I had known Gordon since my days working for Michael Foot and he had been chair of the Scottish Labour Party. There was a particularly awful meeting of the Scottish Executive and Michael which Gordon later said convinced him that the party had to change. There had also been some talk at the time that Gordon might come and work in some capacity in Michael's office to help with that change. But I didn't really get to know him or Tony well until Neil gave them junior positions in the frontbench teams.

Both men had been elected in 1983, but, says Nye, 'Because of Gordon's long involvement in all levels of the party, it was inevitable that he was seen as more senior in terms of his understanding of the deep-rooted problems the party faced.' When Nye started working for Brown, he had an office in the shadow cabinet corridor in 1 Parliament Street. He was at one end and Blair was at the other. Nye told me: 'Anji [Hunter, Blair's aide] and I had lunch or coffee most days and if we lost either of them they could usually be found in the other's office. That was a time of talking, talking, talking ... it was a time of great debates about the future.'[24]

Brown took advice, too, from Nye's husband, the economist Gavyn Davies, who would later help guide him during the financial crash that would hit under his own premiership. Brown was also consulting with a young Ed Balls, then a leader writer for the *Financial Times*, whom Brown describes as 'probably the most gifted economic thinker of his generation'.[25] Balls had come to the *FT* via Harvard in 1990 and says he 'didn't really have any contact with Labour people before the 1992 election' except, he recalls, speaking to Tony Blair about the minimum wage once while writing an *FT* editorial.[26]

Balls got more involved after the 1992 general election when Geoff Mulgan launched the Labour modernising group Progress. Balls was asked to go and see Blair and Brown, and published his Fabian pamphlet in autumn 1992. The editor of the *FT*, Richard Lambert, gave Balls permission to talk to the shadow chancellor, and the bright young economist ended up working with Brown on policy papers and speeches in 1993. 'I would come down and we would just talk about economics and economic policy,' says Balls. '[Brown] was voraciously reading. I would be continually finding him things to read and connecting it with people to talk to. It's part of the way he is that he wanted to have that immersion ... So it was mutually intellectually facilitating: he taught me how to use history to understand economics, and I taught him how to use economics to make history.'

Brown first asked Balls to come across the divide between journalism and politics and work for him in 1993, but Balls initially resisted, saying he could continue to 'support' Brown from his position at the paper.

> I was a leader writer. They gave me a column. I was travelling around the world. It was great. And then it got to a crunch point in the autumn of 1993 [and] Gordon ... was being quite persistent. So he would have weeks where he wouldn't mention it, and then weeks where he was very on it, and then I applied to be the Africa correspondent for the *FT* ... I'd been to Africa a lot of times for the *FT*, it would have meant being based out in Nairobi for eighteen

months. I said I wanted to write the economic story of Africa for the *FT* ... And then the editor said to me it wasn't a priority ... I could go to Tokyo or Washington, but they didn't want me to go to Africa. And I think in that moment, I thought, well, actually, in that case, that's it. So then I told them I was going to resign and go work for Gordon.

Balls worked his notice period, and in January 1994 he went across, at a time when, because of his fiscal position within the party, 'Gordon was under a lot of pressure internally, politically'.

But, says Balls, 'I always wanted to work for Labour and the Treasury ... And if Tony Blair had been the shadow chancellor, and Tony Blair had said to me, come and be my economic person at the time, I would have said Yes – I don't think I was particularly choosing between Tony Blair and Gordon Brown; but it was Gordon and he was the one.'

As well as Balls, Brown appointed Charlie Whelan, the press officer who came from the Amalgamated Engineering Union. After helping the party leadership over 'one member, one vote', Whelan came on the recommendation of Peter Mandelson, who had won the seat of Hartlepool in 1992. Whelan was smart but could be a ruthless party infighter, as Mandelson himself would later discover to his cost.

Infinitely less of a bruiser was the young Ed Miliband, whose talents Brown had spotted when he worked for Harriet Harman. Brown hired Miliband, a social democrat who would focus on anti-poverty policies and monitor the Tories. The team that was to form Brown's trusted inner circle for a decade or more was beginning to take shape.

In January 1993, the two leading Labour Atlanticists, Brown and Blair, who admired America and especially felt they had much to learn from the 'New Democrats' there, flew to Washington DC to meet with key figures in President-elect Clinton's team including Larry Summers, Robert Reich and Paul Begala. The Democrats explained to Brown and Blair that they had made their party electable again for the first time since Jimmy Carter's victory in 1976, by placing the economy at the centre of campaigning, by appealing to 'Middle America', and by stressing responsibilities as well as rights in an echo of John F. Kennedy's inaugural speech as president, which told people to 'ask not what your country can do for you; ask what you can do for your country'. Clinton had done much to rid his party of a perceived devotion to tax for its own sake, as well as overcome the notion that the Democrats were soft on crime.

However, the Washington trip infuriated John Smith. While Brown and Blair were away, the leader called Mandelson into his office and expressed his anger. 'All this Clintonisation business, it's just upsetting everyone,' Smith said. 'Stop boat-rocking with all this talk of change and modernisation. It will just divide the party. If we remain united, we'll win. Do just shut up.'[27] But Brown unashamedly felt the trip was well worth making. It strengthened his resolve to modernise economic policy and to win the argument for change within the party as well as in the country.

In September 1993 he published *How We Can Conquer Unemployment*, which outlined the case for a 'New Deal' to tackle youth and long-term unemployment, and *Fair is Efficient*, which argued that greater equality was the prerequisite for economic efficiency. The idea that prosperity had to be bought at the cost of fairness was a false choice, Brown thought. However, in January 1994 he faced criticism over his broader economic strategy when the left of the parliamentary party demanded 'a clear socialist commitment' to higher spending and taxes. The Campaign Group of Labour MPs tabled a Commons motion warning the shadow chancellor that 'massive public investment' and higher taxes would be needed to fulfil Labour's pledges for full employment, improved public services and the regeneration of industry. This came after Brown rejected a plan by David Blunkett, the frontbench health spokesperson, to raise NHS spending with a specific new tax aimed for health.[28]

And as Brown says, 'Such was the conflict between the traditionalists and modernisers within Labour that Tony and I were barraged with criticism even for visiting Washington … The attacks only served to bring Tony and me closer together – just before events would begin to drive us apart.'[29]

6

Turning Point

Just after 9 a.m. on Thursday 12 May 1994, Gordon Brown received a phone call from his old school friend Murray Elder, John Smith's chief of staff. Brown had been up early as usual that morning, preparing for Treasury questions in Parliament against Kenneth Clarke.[1] The previous evening Brown had watched Smith deliver a speech during a fundraising dinner at the Park Lane Hotel in central London, in which the Labour leader had said, 'An opportunity to serve our country – that is all we ask.' Brown felt that Smith had done well but looked tired, and says they exchanged a look in which Smith appeared to indicate he'd managed to get through it – just.

Now Elder, who was himself calling from hospital with his own heart problems, told Brown that Smith was gravely ill after a second heart attack and had been rushed to St Bartholomew's Hospital in the City of London. A few minutes later, Elder called Brown again to tell him that the medics had not been able to resuscitate Smith and that the Labour leader had died. Elder added that the news would not be announced for two hours while Smith's wife Elizabeth and others could inform and bring together the family, including his three daughters, Sarah, Jane and Catherine.[2] It was an event that would be a turning point for Brown, the Labour Party and the country.

After a stunned Brown hung up, it felt natural immediately to call Tony Blair, who was in Aberdeen campaigning in the European elections. Brown, described by his brother Andrew as 'an open book', claims that 'within a few minutes' Blair was on his way back to confer with Alastair Campbell – then a journalist with the *Today* newspaper – 'and others'.[3] In fact Campbell heard that Smith was in hospital from

Hillary Coffman – a former Labour special adviser, who called him when he was being driven across London to work – and not from Blair.

It is true that at around 9.10 a.m. Blair phoned Peter Mandelson from Dyce Airport in Aberdeen. Blair merely told Mandelson at this stage that something extremely serious had happened.[4] Mandelson reflected later that he felt Blair already knew Smith had died but had been asked not to say anything for now.[5] Mandelson now called Brown at his London base at Great Smith Street, Westminster, to arrange to meet later that day, though the meeting would be cut short by the arrival of Nick Brown, a long-time close ally to whom his namesake wanted to talk privately. Mandelson has claimed he was effectively forced to leave the flat.

That morning Brown also called his young on–off researcher Douglas Alexander in tears, asking for his help writing obituaries for Smith for the *Daily Record* and the *Independent*. Alexander, who was at his flat in Edinburgh, went to Waterstones in George Street to buy a copy of a Smith biography.[6] Meanwhile, as Sue Nye recalls,

> It was a huge and terrible shock ... When I heard the news, I immediately went to Gordon's flat. Donald Dewar – another great friend – was there and although they were still coming to terms with the news, they also had to find words to write obituaries. Gordon also had Treasury questions that afternoon and we then tried to get the Speaker to let him pay a tribute at the beginning ... It was hard for the whole of the Labour movement to come to terms with John's tragic death, but Gordon also had to deal with the very human emotion of losing a friend, a mentor and someone who was hugely important in his life. He obviously knew Elizabeth and the girls and knew how dreadful it was for them to lose a husband and father.[7]

Brown, though beyond doubt deep in grief, did already have his eye on the succession. 'I believed that I was the best candidate to take over from John,' he admits frankly. 'As Murray Elder reminded me at the time, John had told him that he shared that view. And I assumed Tony would support me.' Sue Nye – along with Blair himself – rightly sees no shame in Brown's ambition. 'Top politicians want top jobs – there is no disgrace in that,' she says. 'Gordon had spent his whole political life thinking and writing and talking about solutions to the enormous problems facing the country he loved and of course he would want the opportunity to put that into practice. But there was never any question of them standing against each other and our soundings were showing that Gordon would win but at what cost?'

Blair, meanwhile, was being urged to stand by a very wide range of party figures, from Charles Clarke, Kinnock's closest lieutenant, to Chris Mullin on the left. They reflected a growing feeling in Westminster that he would be a new and fresh face to present to the voters, while Brown, for all his rhetorical skills and intellectual heft, represented continuity with the Kinnock and Smith years.

The night after Smith's death, Brown phoned his brother Andrew, who had already gone to bed, asking him to come round to the Westminster flat. Charlie Whelan, Brown's press officer, was there with the first editions of the newspapers and, according to Andrew's hitherto unseen diary, 'it was clear there was huge media hype behind Blair … That evening GB was shaken by what he saw as Tony's deceit. "Years of campaigning have been blotted out" because of the Blair bandwagon, he said.'[8]

With Andrew's reference to 'years of campaigning', Brown clearly felt keenly that he had been the senior partner, as Blair acknowledges he had been, until at least 1992. Now suddenly Blair, who had been portrayed by the *Sunday Times* in 1992 as Labour's 'lost leader', appeared ahead of the pack, including in the Murdoch press. Brown feels today that, in retrospect, Blair had worked the London media scene, and that the Murdoch stable had moved against him, even then.

Other names were soon in the frame as Labour's traumatised ranks tried to look to the future, including Margaret Beckett, who served as acting leader after Smith's death, John Prescott, who'd stood in 1992, and centre-leftist Robin Cook. But all the attention – both in the media and within the party – soon focused on the ambitions of Blair and Brown, each of whom were convinced they were best suited to lead Labour out of its demoralising cycle of electoral defeat.

Kinnock saw the two clear frontrunners – 'the reformers' in his words – in the immediate aftermath of Smith's death. Alastair

Campbell says Kinnock was 'desperately torn' about which of the pair to support. Kinnock himself says:

> In the days after that, I spoke to both Gordon and Tony separately and together, because either by accident or design, they had offices within a couple of yards, literally, of my office, in Parliament Street. And so it was always easy for them to drift in or me to drift into their offices. I spoke to them separately, and I said: 'You two have got to decide who runs. If you both run, that's fine, but it would be better for the movement if it is only one of you. Because whoever it is, whichever one of you it is, you will win and it's very good if there haven't been great divisions and antagonisms. And it can also be that the result can be evident very quickly, even a long time before it's announced ... Only you two can decide, don't listen to anybody else'... He and Tony were very close, as they have been since day one. And there was [previously] no sense of rivalry between them at all. None whatsoever. Tony had his job to do. Gordon had his job to do, they cooperated on so many things. And, I mean, they were the reformers.[9]

When Brown and Blair eventually met face-to-face on Sunday 15 May in Edinburgh where they paid their respects to Smith's wife Elizabeth, suddenly there was rivalry – and tension. At this point, when Elizabeth Smith got Brown alone, she told him that her late husband would have wanted Brown to be leader. And Andrew Brown's diary from the period, seen by this author in full for the first time, recounts that 'She, like Murray Elder, hints to GB that he was John's choice. "It's up to you now," she tells GB as he leaves.' A moment of light relief came when Brown locked himself in the bathroom at the house of a friend of Blair's, the property developer Nick Ryden, in Merchiston. Brown had to make calls from his brick-like mobile phone to communicate with the outside world.

But what followed was, for Brown at least, more Greek tragedy than comedy, with Blair doing all he could to persuade Brown not to run. Blair almost charmed Andrew Brown who had picked him up from the Smith home and wrote in his diary at the time: 'It had been years since I had chatted to him for more than passing pleasantries. But immediately we talked at ease. With a pinch of salt, I hear his eulogy to GB. He's the "greatest political mind the Labour Party has had", he says – and TB "couldn't do it without GB". "I love him to bits."'

At Brown's North Queensferry home, Blair stressed that were he to become leader, he would give Brown control over economic and social policy. As they worked on precise wording dividing up their roles, there was an argument over the word 'guaranteed' and whether it applied to Brown's role, not only to the chancellorship in a future Labour government, but also to a whole range of economic policies. At one point Mandelson, who was presiding over the dispute and various copies of the wording from his constituency base in Hartlepool, found his fax machine had broken down because of all the action. But eventually a formula was agreed, and it was reported accurately in a *Times* column the following morning by the authoritative commentator Peter Riddell, who wrote that the agreement had 'guaranteed Mr Brown that [his] fairness agenda, broadening employment opportunities and improving training and skills, will be the centrepiece of Labour's economic and social programme'.

And it was at this point, claims Brown – not at the famous Islington Granita restaurant encounter on 31 May when Blair, Brown and briefly Balls met to discuss the leadership – that Blair also said he would stand down in his second term of office. Blair told Brown that this was a family choice that he had already made. 'He wanted to be free from day-to-day politics to be with his children in their teens – the time of life when parents are most needed. It was a promise he repeated on several occasions,' Brown recalls.[10]

In his diary Andrew Brown – who today says that Blair appealed to his brother's sense of 'altruism' in trying to persuade him not to run[11] – recounts taking Blair back to the airport:

> He showed the desperation of his position when he reveals that GB could win if he stood. What he doubted was not that – but whether GB could win the general election. It's the trump card to play – especially against GB who believes above all else that, after four defeats, nothing should come in the way of Labour winning the election. TB also talks about how all of this has come 'too soon' for his young children. Only aged 10, 8 and 6 years old, he's worried about the prospect of media attention on them. Talks about how if

he goes for the leadership now, he would want to spend time with them later before they're too old – perhaps in five years' time.

That would seem to imply Blair standing down in around 1999 – a highly unlikely prospect. But Brown also claims that Blair had been thinking of other reasons why Brown should not run. According to Brown, Blair now added two reasons why he should be leader at the next election, as opposed to Brown. 'I was Scottish, he said, and I was unmarried. We could not, he said, have two leaders in a row from Scotland. I reminded him that he too was Scottish: born in Scotland of a father raised in Glasgow, and also educated at a school in Edinburgh. The only difference seemed to me [to be] that people knew I was Scottish and assumed he was not.'[12]

Brown goes on: 'The "being single" charge was more insidious. At least one or two of Tony's adherents went out of their way to imply to the press that they knew more about me than the public did.' In conversations with colleagues, according to Brown, some MPs were persuaded to raise questions or cast aspersions about his private life. 'In the dark world of rumours and counter-rumours that swirl around Westminster, people believed what they wanted to believe and what suited their purposes. This was echoed in a low moment for the BBC two years later, when I was interviewed for *Desert Island Discs*, and the presenter Sue Lawley insinuated that being unmarried meant I was gay. I was not. But the insinuation was born of prejudice: that somehow there was something wrong with being gay. The allegations were as untrue as they were unworthy, but during these years damage was done.'[13]

However, Kinnock says: 'I always thought of Gordon as one of my successors. Because he had all the kit. The only thing he didn't have, at that stage, was a wife' – still deemed necessary for a major party leader amid ongoing prejudice in the traditional Westminster world. 'But I never had any doubt that would come ... He isn't that sort of fawning, seeking-to-impress-ladies kind of guy, but he did have lots of women who adored him, some in a sort of fan club way. I knew lovely excellent women who would melt if Gordon was coming into my office. They really did think Gordon was the Tom Jones of politics, you know. And he was so completely lacking in any presumption that that added to his charm. And it was totally unconscious. So I knew there would be a wife at some stage.'[14] Kinnock may have been agonising between the two, and though Blair led across the party, Brown did have his firm backers, too, including the highly respected future first minister of Scotland who served as shadow social security secretary under Smith, Donald Dewar.

Brown, who was not ready to concede, may or may not be correct in his view that he would or *could* have secured the majority of Labour MPs as well as the membership and trade unions had he stood quickly and decisively in 1994. But either way, Mandelson outlined the case against him running in a letter faxed to Brown on 16 May, including the question of whether Brown commanded enough 'southern appeal'.[15] By this point the relationship between Brown and Mandelson – once so close – was beginning to turn poisonous as the former started to suspect that Mandelson and Blair were edging him out of the leadership stakes. In the letter, which Andrew Brown says 'infuriated' his brother, Mandelson wrote:

> I thought I should give you my best view of the situation from the media standpoint ... Nobody is saying you are not capable/appropriate as leader, merely that the timing is bad for you or you have vocal enemies or that you have presentational difficulties ... If Tony felt he had to stand and you did too, what would be the consequences? I think you both, and our cause and the party, would be hugely damaged. It would be a gift to our enemies. Because you would be appearing to come in as the second runner, you would be blamed for creating the split. I think the media would attack you and that your standing in the party would suffer.
>
> The only way to overcome this media resistance to you is to mount a massive and sustained briefing which concentrated on your political skills, ability to unite and manage all sides of the party, dominance in the House, blend of party transition and modernising agenda. I have not encountered much difficulty selling this so far but to be effective it would have to be greatly escalated, begun immediately, and I am afraid, only done by explicitly weakening Tony's position ...
>
> Ultimately the card the media are playing for Tony is his 'southern appeal'. He doesn't need to point it out or build it up: it is there firmly in their minds and it is linked to their (and our) overriding question, is Labour serious about conquering the south? My fear is

that drift is harming you ... You have either to escalate rapidly ... or you need to implement a strategy to exit with enhanced position, strength and respect. Will you let me know your wishes?

Blair today reiterates the Mandelson sentiment about the huge risk of a Blair and Brown division at this stage. He says: 'I felt it was going to be quite disruptive if [Gordon] had to win by distancing himself from the modernisation of the Labour Party, which would have been his way probably to win. And that would have been a traditional versus moderniser battle in which he wasn't really traditional. Therefore, it wouldn't have suited him long term. And I was convinced it was better that we did it by agreement.'[16] Blair also agrees with Mandelson about the 'southern appeal' point. 'I think the reason people turned to me rather than him when John died was partly because we'd had the two years of a Scottish leader and the party felt that this problem was basically an English problem. And even though I am actually Scottish ... it seemed more natural.'

On Friday 20 May, Brown attended John Smith's funeral at Cluny Parish Church in Edinburgh along with Blair and many in the Labour movement. Dewar, Smith's closest friend, gave an emotional but at times funny eulogy, saying Smith could 'start a party in an empty room'. After the service, Blair sought to meet again with Brown, who told Sue Nye to delay.

Deeply suspicious about Mandelson's fax, Brown at this point continued to campaign – both for himself to become leader and in the European elections. On the Sunday after Smith's funeral, Brown gave a speech paying tribute to him at the Welsh Labour Party conference in Swansea. It had been decided by the party that campaigning for the European elections had to go ahead. Smith had been due to give the leader's speech at the Welsh Labour Party conference and Brown was asked to give it in his place. Sue Nye says: 'Gordon asked me to go down in advance to talk to people to reassure them that the modernisation would never be put in jeopardy by there being two candidates on the modernising ticket. I stayed the night with Neil and Glenys in their home in Pontllanfraith and we spent most of the night debating the way forward. The message from Gordon was clear. He had spent the 1980s in Scotland seeing at first hand the devastating effects of Thatcherism in Scotland and his overwhelming priority was to defeat the Tories and put in its place a fairer and more equal society and nothing would get in the way of that.'[17]

Brown used the opportunity in Wales to set out in his words 'a vision of a party awash with ideas, vibrant with dynamism and purpose, that would reform the welfare state and appeal beyond our heartlands'. He admits: 'It did not make the impact with the media that I had hoped for,' adding, 'I had an agreement with Tony that we would not attack each other's speeches, but a briefing went around that I had made my speech to appeal to what an unidentified briefer termed – without a hint of irony – "forces of darkness" within the party. The phrase appeared prominently in the next day's *Times*. There was evidently a campaign underway to characterise me not just as unelectable but anti-reform too.'[18] Brown regards that briefing as critical, and representative of an early stitch-up between the Blairites and the Murdoch titles.

In the days that followed, Brown attended a memorial service for Smith in the latter's Lanarkshire constituency and then criss-crossed the country – playing a full part in the European election campaign – during which he had a further meeting with Blair. 'But my mind was already made up. I would accept his assurances. He would give me control of economic and social policy and would stand down during a second term. Unwilling to see the party divided in a way that would endanger the prospects for reform, in the days leading up to 30 May I informed those closest to me of my intention not to stand.'[19]

The Granita encounter in London on 31 May, at which Ed Balls was initially and briefly present, became a mere formality. 'I always smile when commentators write that we hammered out a deal in the restaurant,' says Brown. The exaggerated significance of the Granita dinner has been enhanced by its television portrayals, especially Channel 4's *The Deal* and the media's desire to find one dramatic, defining moment that secured a deal, when the truth is more complicated and messy.

What is under dispute is the element of the agreement over when Blair would step aside for Brown to be Labour leader and prime minister. Brown, who believes Blair said he would step aside after ten years *as leader*, says: 'Long into the future, the focus of the 1994 leadership race would wrongly remain on what was said at Granita. The restaurant did not survive; and ultimately neither did our agreement.'[20]

Sue Nye recalls this tense period:

In the days leading up to Gordon's decision not to stand, there were many, many meetings – in my house, in Tony's house, in Gordon's house, in flats in Scotland after John's funeral and then of course in a restaurant in Islington. Obviously in all those meetings there were discussions about the future – who should stand but also on what the future direction of policy should be. [Brown] wanted assurances over policies that he cared about and he wanted the freedom and the room to control the policy agenda in those areas – the fairness agenda if you like – that he most cared about.

He also got an assurance that Tony only wanted to serve for two terms [as prime minister] for personal as well as political reasons. He came straight back from that last meeting in Granita to meet us in the restaurant at 4 Millbank and told us that he would make the announcement that he would not be standing the next day and that privately Tony had said he would only serve two terms. Now, none of us were at that dinner but Gordon was adamant about what had been agreed. The next day the form of words was agreed and the announcement was made – there was a piece of paper that I faxed to Peter [Mandelson].[21]

From what Sue Nye says, there remains a slight difference even within the Brown camp as to whether Blair had agreed to stand down after ten years as leader, or after ten years (two terms) as prime minister.

Brown himself reflects today: 'I am certainly not in politics to get titles or particular offices. I felt that I had something to offer.' In other words, there is absolutely no doubt that Brown wanted, if not expected, the leadership after Smith. In many ways his whole life up to this point had been building towards it. 'I had tried to modernise Labour's economic and social policy. I was quite unpopular at that time because I had been very tough on the fiscal position and I'd been tough actually on devaluation ... So I was unpopular for that and I was unpopular because of the tough fiscal position, which we had to do because we couldn't get into another position where we were spending where we couldn't show where the money was to come from. So I had to accept that that was the case but equally I was happy to work with Tony and try and get things done.'[22]

There remains in the Brown camp a sense that Blair should not have stood for the leadership in 1994, that Brown was the senior man (which he was) and that he could have won, even across all three sections of the party. That may or may not be true, though it would have caused an almighty fight within the ascendant modernising wing of Labour. But to give him due credit, despite his dismay and even anger, he did go on to adapt to the new reality of Blair's leadership that he had not, rightly or wrongly, previously envisaged. He then did all he could, through a sense of duty instilled in him from childhood as well as tribal loyalty, to help ensure New Labour's electability.

But as Blair quickly forged ahead as the clear favourite to succeed Smith, it is surely true that Brown resented his younger friend, whose support he expected. And it may be true, too, that Brown blamed Mandelson, then an MP and informal media adviser to both men, for supposedly betraying Brown by allegedly switching sides to support Blair. Brown claims to this day that he was sitting in the House of Commons grieving and trying to do justice to Smith in an obituary for the *Independent*, which is no doubt true as well. But he was also canvassing support among MPs and his brother took time out of television work to help his campaign.

Nonetheless, Mandelson certainly sent Brown what the latter saw as a duplicitous message outlining why Blair would be more popular in the country, especially in England, than Brown, which cannot have been easy reading for the senior man of the three. Brown's press aide Charlie Whelan would exact revenge against Mandelson four years later, as we shall see. Whelan's ways were the dark arts many assume take place at Westminster, and they would continue under Brown's later spin doctor Damian McBride.

Mandelson told a 2021 BBC documentary, *Blair and Brown*, that Blair was more 'New' and Brown was more 'Labour'. But Ed Balls counters Mandelson:

> To say that Gordon Brown was Labour but not new is entirely diminishing to Gordon. And to say Blair was new but not Labour is entirely diminishing to Tony Blair. Tony Blair was not somebody who was an advertising slogan or a construct. He was somebody who was wanting to win a big argument about the future and social values in the same way that Bill Clinton was trying to do – that's

what the 'third way' was all about. There were things that Tony Blair could do ... which were not things Gordon would do as well as Tony Blair, but the shaping of an economic policy which Gordon could deliver in new times, successfully, incredibly – a Labour alternative – that's why they are both quintessentially New Labour together. Because if it hadn't been for Gordon, there wouldn't have been New Labour. I don't think anybody else could have succeeded as chancellor in doing what Tony wanted, other than Gordon in that time.[23]

In 1994, to some extent a myth was built up around Brown, by his outriders if not by him, that he was betrayed, a myth that was used to justify some destabilising behaviour by Brown's camp towards Blair and his own allies over many years. Even Blair's departure in 2007 can be sourced back to the events of 1994.

But some Blairite outriders have in turn perpetuated several myths of their own around John Smith's death. Brown would never have run against his old ally, and this seems to be a post-hoc legend to justify Blair's overtaking of Brown as a potential leader. A few also argue life would have been easier for all concerned subsequently had he stood against Blair – and lost. But for Brown, that would have involved an unthinkable breach in party unity. Either way these events sowed the seeds of a troublesome relationship between Blair and Brown – and even more between their allies and lieutenants – after Labour took office in 1997. As Neil Kinnock says: 'These highly significant and very talented fellas attracted tribes. And tribes always go to war. And I think a hell of a lot of the trouble that was experienced after the turn in the century derived more from the retainers than from the principals.'

Ultra-Blairites say that in his death Smith enhanced Labour's relationship with the British public in a way that he had failed to do in his life while leader. However, the national opinion polls tell a slightly different story. Through 1993 and the first four months of 1994, Labour was consistently scoring well above 45 per cent in the polls. Smith to some extent failed to compromise with the wider electorate by accommodating the trade unions and the parliamentary left. But he was a mentally sharp, witty heavyweight and occasionally an intimidating opponent for John Major, whose credibility was battered by Tory infighting and the UK's chaotic departure from the ERM on Black Wednesday.

The likelihood is that Smith – despite being a slower moderniser than Brown and Blair – would have become prime minister had he lived. And Brown too almost certainly would have won the 1997 general election, though perhaps he might have won with a smaller majority.

On the issue of whether Brown should have run against Blair, Kinnock says: 'In retrospect if there had been a contest between them, I really don't know which one would have won because I think that Gordon's standing among the unions was probably stronger than Tony's and Tony wouldn't have had a giant lead in the constituencies. And I think they would have been about even stevens in the Parliamentary Labour Party.'[24] This may be sentimental, given Blair was leading in all sections of the party.

Nonetheless, on 1 June at 3.30 p.m., Brown made a formal announcement that he was not running to the Press Association. It was a characteristically self-sacrificial move. Yet in his memoir Brown claims that even at this stage, there was serious tension between him and Blair. 'Originally, we planned to be photographed in public to affirm the strong partnership Tony had talked of. The plan was to walk between Westminster and Lambeth Bridge on the pathway overlooking the Houses of Parliament. But immediately after I published my statement, Tony's team changed tack.'

Andrew Brown's diary states:

> The whole episode was nearly a disaster. Tony had agreed to a photocall immediately after the statement was issued ... But Tony's aides got cold feet. After GB had issued his press release withdrawing, TB threatened to break his agreement and not take part in a photocall. His advisors were suggesting that – even with no interviews by either TB or GB – he would be in danger of breaking Shadow Cabinet rules on not making any pronouncements on the leadership question until after the European Campaign. I suspected even worse than that. Without the photocall – particularly in TV terms – GB would have looked like a loser – and it would have been interpreted that way. After at least five phone calls between the two offices, Tony eventually succumbed to a photocall which took place much later

than planned – at about 4.45. The pictures themselves showed Tony looking very uncomfortable – and hardly acknowledging GB.

That night, Brown had dinner at 4 Millbank with his then girlfriend and future wife Sarah Macaulay, Sue Nye, Charlie Whelan and Ed Balls – 'in what amounted to a wake', according to his brother Andrew. And though Andrew's wife Clare joined the group, he said in his diary: 'I opted out, not wanting to take part in a post-mortem.'

Balls gives unique insight into how Brown was feeling after pulling out of the race.

> I think Gordon found it very hard. This was not his plan, and he knew that he had probably missed his moment. That's how he would have thought about it, and that he was always going to be the number two, and he conceded ... accepted leadership going to Tony Blair and I think he found that, for very many months, really hard. Of course, it didn't actually turn out that way, because he then became prime minister, but that's not how he would have been thinking of it then ... His mindset was, given that I am pulling out, and the leadership is going to Tony Blair, what do I need [to do] in order to be a successful chancellor? And that was what the deal was about. He wasn't sitting there thinking, you know, it's okay, because in ten years' time, I'll get my moment. Yes, he was absolutely thinking, what do I need to do to stay in the game? How do I make my mark, and how do I proceed? That was much more immediate. I think it was for him just a very big blow, because it was not how he had thought about it in the previous decade.[25]

'[What] I regretted is that the understanding we had was never properly honoured,' Brown says today.[26] He confirms that a rumour that the agreement was that Blair would stand down after around ten years as leader – so 2004 and not 2007 – is correct. And he accepts that he was pushing for Blair to go before the 2005 general election. Of course, politicians say what they need to in order to secure their position at the time, and Brown was perhaps naive to have latched on to this.

'The deal was about partnership in 1994 to 1997 and in government, and about Gordon leading on economics and social policy,' Balls says. 'And that was the agreed briefing which we gave to the newspapers.'

On the question of Blair saying he would step down after ten years as leader, so in 2004, Balls says: 'I don't want to contradict Gordon, but I can't confirm it ... it may have been what Tony Blair said, but he shouldn't have said it, and it may have been what Gordon believed, and he probably shouldn't. They weren't in a position in 1994 to reach an agreement about the transition ten years on.'[27]

Later, Blair declined Brown's offer to run Blair's leadership campaign, apparently preferring to exclude his old mentor after the tensions. Jack Straw, who would be Blair's first home secretary, ran the campaign because 'I was from neither his nor Gordon's camp'.[28] Straw reflects: 'There was only going to be room for one at the very top of the party. You could see them eyeing each other.'[29] Brown recalls: '[While] I helped write his leadership speeches, I was frozen out of the campaign.' Andrew Brown's diary from the period states at its conclusion that 'GB was bitter about what happened – and annoyed about the circumstances surrounding the photocall. But, now it was time for planning a future course.'

On 21 July, Blair gained 57 per cent of the overall vote against his two opponents who were largely laying down a marker: John Prescott – who would be elected deputy leader – on 24.1 per cent, and Margaret Beckett – who also stood for the deputy leadership – on 19.9 per cent. But Blair was not without his critics. Even Prescott had said in June 1994: 'I have quite fundamental disagreements with Tony Blair.' And on the other side of the party, Tony Benn said, after Blair became leader: 'I think the truth is that the Labour Party isn't believed any more because people suspect it will say anything to get votes.' But as the respected academic John Gray has written: 'Tony Blair came to power aiming to break the hold of the right on power and open up a new path to modernity for Britain.'[30]

Relations between Blair – whom Andrew Brown described in his diary as Gordon's 'student' – and Brown, meanwhile, would never be the same again. They could and would still work brilliantly together, but there was nonetheless a corrosive trust problem which perhaps still remains to this day. As Sue Nye says: 'Although Gordon and Tony continued talking and working together after [Brown] had pulled out and before Tony became leader, our team weren't involved at all. I think we all thought that once it had been decided who was going to run it would be a joint enterprise. That didn't really happen and the two teams at that point could have worked together and developed a better relationship from the start and some of the misunderstandings that came later might have been avoided.'[31]

When I approached Tony Blair for an interview for this book, he agreed on the condition that Gordon Brown was happy for him to speak. When I asked Brown about that, he replied, 'I don't think you'll get a balanced account.' As it happens Blair lavished Brown with praise – 'an astonishingly high-quality intellect' – and described himself as 'the junior partner' for ten years during the run-up to 1994, one who could not have gone on to serve three terms were it not for Brown's constant presence in government.[32] Brown's response had perhaps been a sign of an occasionally needless suspicion towards his perceived opponents. It is a dynamic born out of the Labour leadership crisis in May 1994, when Blair stopped being the 'junior partner'.

'We used to have fun together,' Blair told me. 'I mean, Gordon, he has got his very serious side, but he can be immensely entertaining company.'[33] Brown says today: 'Well, [Blair] was entitled to run of course if he wanted to, but it was stupid to think that two of us could run so he essentially tried to gazump me.'[34]

In conclusion on the leadership, then: as Balls makes clear, Brown found the result difficult to accept and process, not least because of his confidence that he was best placed to succeed Smith, and there remains a lingering distrust to this day, towards Blair himself, as well as Mandelson. Brown's critics accuse him of brooding on the past and of harbouring grudges spanning decades.

There is a case for saying Blair could have given way to the more senior partner, and that had he done so, Labour would have governed in a way that was a marginally more authentic reflection of the party's roots, including the trade union movement.

But with Brown having wrested control of economic and social policy, and serving as the ideological engine behind New Labour, and with Blair as the brilliant front man who would one day stand aside for Brown to be leader and prime minister, in the end the best outcome emerged for the party and the country.

7
Truce

When they worked well together in their respective positions, the partnership of Tony Blair and Gordon Brown was perhaps the most successful in British politics since the Second World War. Although the seeds of tension between the two camps had been sown in the days following John Smith's death, Brown was determined to make a mark once in power, as would be shown by the dramatic moves that would come out of the Treasury in the opening days of their government.

Alastair Campbell says that, although there were some days when it was 'like wading through shit … when Tony and Gordon were getting on, and I don't mean as friends but I mean on the same agenda, delivering the same stuff, focused on what was happening, they were amazing'. The same applied to being on message: 'When Peter [Mandelson] and I were getting on, on the kind of strategy side and all that, I'm going to work some days thinking, this is like Barcelona versus Accrington Stanley. That is a great feeling.'[1]

Sue Nye and Blair's aide Anji Hunter, who would stay at Nye's London home once or twice a week, were relatively relaxed about the two men shouting at one another because, as they saw it, this was creative tension helping to develop New Labour policy in the absence of proper Tory opposition.

Blair concurs with this analysis. 'First of all, we could speak completely frankly with each other. So, you know, as time went on in government, it became rougher at points but certainly, in that first period, it was an important interaction that we would have because we would get to the heart of an issue and be able to debate it in a very frank way with each other. And he has an astonishingly high-quality intellect. So I never really objected to having the debate.'[2]

At times during this period and even later, then, the pair revived the spirit of that partnership from the 1980s, when Brown accepts that he and Blair worked 'extraordinarily well together' and 'hand in hand'. Others intimately involved in the tensions, too, agree that Brown was crucial to the cause.

As Alastair Campbell points out today, 'I am not anti-Gordon. I was anti-him being anti-TB on those occasions when they should have worked together. But I have a lot of time for him and always did.' The Brown–Campbell relationship is a complicated one that epitomises the multilayered nuances of relations at the heart of New Labour. As a Labour-supporting journalist on the *Daily Mirror*, Campbell recognised Brown as an 'obvious talent' in the 1980s, and used to help him craft his thoughts into columns for the *Daily Record*, the *Mirror*'s Scottish sister paper. Campbell's friend and Keir Starmer biographer Tom Baldwin has long called Campbell 'Mr Loyalty' – and Campbell's first loyalty aside from his family and closest friends is to the Labour Party, including its leadership, albeit apart from that of Jeremy Corbyn.

But Brown remains slightly suspicious of Campbell, whom he feels was opposed to him from before Smith's death, and towards whom he appears to hold residual resentment over Campbell's appearance on BBC's *Newsnight* on the night of Smith's death declaring that Blair would be the next leader. When Campbell, by then a frequently sought-after broadcaster, was invited to go on the programme, he stipulated that he would pay 'straight tributes' and not get into the 'TB–GB thing'. He did not set out to back Blair, but he had sensed the mood earlier in the day walking round the Commons 'a bit kind of dazed', bumping into various people including the Labour MP Jack Cunningham – who actually confirmed to Campbell that Smith had died – and the centre-leftist unionist Scot Brian Wilson. In the evening, at the end of the interview, Campbell was asked who would be leader and he ended up predicting that Blair would win the leadership.

'I do think Gordon still has at the back of his mind a feeling that there was some kind of plan,' Campbell says today. 'And it really wasn't like that.' Campbell recognises that Brown is a titan of the Labour movement and a uniquely substantial political figure. And

Brown would repeatedly call on Campbell for help in later years, at one point calling him 'a fucking genius' according to a well-placed source.

However, a week after Blair's election as leader, Brown and Balls visited his home in Islington, where already a key argument about fiscal policy took place. 'We were in for a shock,' Brown recalls. 'Sitting in the garden lapping up the sun on a very bright morning, we were both surprised when he announced that Labour must rule out forever any rise in the top rate of tax. I agreed that we should rule out a rise in the basic rate – indeed we were considering a lower band, a 10p rate – but I said I didn't know how we could meet our promises unless we left open, for the time being at least, the possibility of a top-rate increase on very high incomes. I said we had to do in-depth work on the costing of our programmes – for example, the needs of the NHS – before we made such a unilateral move. He was adamant: no party he led would ever raise the top rate of tax.'[3]

Brown concedes this was good electioneering – but also a hostage to fortune. 'By putting a pledge never to raise the top rate at the centre of our modernisation, we did prove that we had changed, but it was not in the national interest to rule out the possibility of even a modest change in the top rate for the highest earners. It was a fateful decision which implied we could do far too little than I had hoped about the needs of our public services and the rising inequality in our country.'[4]

New Labour in government would struggle adequately to fund the NHS and education, Brown feared. As well as a 1997 windfall tax on privatised utilities such as BAA (British Airports Authority) and British Telecom, along with various energy and water companies, Brown would raise national insurance for high earners.

Brown today sees the ruling-out of raising the top rate by Blair as a breach of their agreement that he was in charge of economic and fiscal policy. Despite this considerable policy difference, Blair did allow Brown to be in overall charge of strategy for the forthcoming general election, while Mandelson and Philip Gould were responsible for day-to-day campaign planning.

But Brown and Mandelson had by now cemented their feud. At Chewton Glen, a five-star hotel in Hampshire, early in September 1994, less than two months after Blair became party leader, key New Labour thinkers gathered in secrecy to discuss the challenges ahead. On the evening before the brainstorming session, Blair, Brown and Mandelson dined together, discussing how the party would now be organised. Brown had arrived with various proposals for changes in personnel – including the installation of a former television producer and later minister Michael Wills, who described Brown and Mandelson as like 'two scorpions in a bottle', as deputy general secretary at Labour's headquarters in Walworth Road, south London. Blair was not keen. Brown was dismayed to find that Mandelson, who would have supported Brown a year previously, was urging caution.

After Blair went to bed, Brown and Mandelson stayed up for a nightcap, and Brown asked Mandelson why he had failed to back him, arguing that if they were both in agreement, Blair would always take their advice. Mandelson said that his loyalty to Brown was not in question, but that he was not going to conspire to outmanoeuvre Blair. At which point, a source close to Mandelson has said, Brown replied: 'Choose for yourself' [between the Blair and Brown camps] – or words to that effect.

Although Brown presided over morning party leadership strategy meetings, with Blair present alongside a handful of key ministers and advisers, to discuss Labour's approach to political developments, he was kept in the dark over Blair's hugely symbolic plan to abolish Clause IV of the party's constitution, its blanket commitment to nationalisation. In its place, Blair would present a new text to a special conference at Easter 1995, which read, in part: 'The Labour party is a democratic socialist party. It believes that by the strength of our common endeavour we achieve more than we achieve alone, so as to create for each of us the means to realise our true potential and for all of us a community in which power, wealth and opportunity are in the hands of the many, not the few, where the rights we enjoy reflect the duties we owe, and where we live together, freely, in a spirit of solidarity, tolerance and respect.'

The move, dismissed by Ken Livingstone on the party's left as 'a giant waste of time', was the first attempt to change the party's constitution since the 1950s and, though it only merits two sentences in Brown's memoirs, it appears in retrospect along with many other factors to have helped, in symbolic terms at least, seal the deal between Blair's opposition party and the electorate.

Brown, meanwhile, had been focusing on opposing the government's attempts to raise VAT on fuel, which went against its own manifesto of 1992. The Tories had already raised VAT from 15 per cent to 17.5 per cent in 1991, and Brown would win a major victory – very unusual from the opposition in the Commons on economic policy – which would be a personal triumph. A young researcher, Chris Leslie, who would later become an MP and even shadow chancellor for a period, went through each Tory-held seat and found quotes from the MPs backing up the Conservatives' pledge not to raise VAT. An amendment to stop the second VAT increase was passed by 319 to 311 in December 1994. The chancellor, Kenneth Clarke, compounded the problem for the Tories when he declared that the Conservative Party would stick to manifesto promises but not necessarily to speeches made on a 'wet night in Dudley'.

In May 1995, amid a series of speeches about the economy devised by Brown, with Ed Miliband and Ed Balls, focusing on higher growth and lower unemployment, the shadow chancellor issued an important intervention. Brown and Balls had by now been discussing the idea of Bank of England independence and, under the title 'Labour's Macroeconomic Stability', Brown now stated that a Labour government would only borrow to invest, and set out the principles that could form the basis of the move.

At the end of that month, Brown argued the case for using public-private partnerships (PPPs) – controversial then, given Labour's only recently abandoned commitment to nationalisation – to rebuild Britain's infrastructure, schools and hospitals. Brown supported the mobilisation of private money to build hospitals, but he drew the line at privatising services run by the NHS. The case against PPP, sometimes referred to as the government's 'fiscal credit card', also conveniently took spending off the balance sheets and stacked up long-term costs for the future, though they worked well for most of Brown's chancellorship.

In the following months, the outrageous behaviour of the privatised utilities' bosses became a national story and the term 'fat cats' was commonly used to describe those who ran the companies on excessive profits devised in the boardrooms, such as Cedric Brown, the chief executive of British Gas, who had awarded himself a 900 per cent pay increase during the ten years British Gas had been in private hands. As Labour ramped up their campaign, Cedric Brown doubled his salary while cutting 25,000 jobs, and he was by no means the worst in the utilities boardrooms.

Meanwhile, as if to help explicitly link such excesses to the Tories, several former cabinet ministers had joined the boards of the very companies they had privatised. Brown read out their names at the annual conference in autumn 1995. Norman Tebbit now sat on the board of British Telecom, which he had privatised. Peter Walker had done the same with British Gas. David Young was on the board of Cable & Wireless, which he had privatised. Norman Fowler did likewise with National Freight, and so on. In total, as Brown pointed out, there were sixteen Tory ministers and MPs with well-paid directorships or consultancies linked to the utilities.

Brown and his team now thrashed out plans in secret, at the home of Brown's friend and adviser Geoffrey Robinson, for a windfall tax which Brown believed could raise at least £5 billion. 'Then out of the blue Tony told me that he wanted to exempt British Telecom from the windfall tax because of a separate arrangement he was negotiating with BT's Chairman, Iain Vallance,' Brown recalls.[5] It would be another Blair–Brown dispute. Blair outlined the proposal whereby the company would get a broadcasting licence if it provided free internet links to schools, hospitals, libraries and other public buildings. Brown agreed that widening access to the internet was good in principle, 'but I told him that if one company was arbitrarily exempted from the windfall tax, even for the best of reasons, our whole plan would be struck down and, without a consistent justification for our actions, we would be accused of discriminating against individual companies'.[6]

But Blair persisted, and in January 1997 asked Brown to scrap the windfall tax proposal altogether. Brown refused and told Blair that he would resign over the issue. Of course Blair could not afford such a major loss so close to the general election, but that March Brown was lobbied directly by Iain Vallance to drop the idea. 'I bluntly told him no,' says Brown. 'Iain was a decent man who would later become a Liberal Democrat peer, but his glib comment that the hardship of running BT justified his salary – "I would quite like a job as a junior doctor in the NHS. It might be quite relaxing," he said – enhanced my confidence that this was a public debate we would win.'[7]

BT staff briefed the media that they might take the new Labour government to the European Court. But Vallance knew the game was up and sent a note to Brown at the Treasury on his first day as chancellor, saying: 'I write to offer my warmest congratulations on your confirmation as Chancellor, and in what overwhelming circumstances. The tectonic plates have moved, in no small part due to your rigour on matters financial and economic. We are, of course, very aware that Labour has a clear mandate for the windfall levy and I know from our conversation ... that we fall within the scope of the tax.' Brown thanked him for the magnanimity of his approach.[8]

Meanwhile, an upsetting moment for Brown's mother Elizabeth came in an early attack on the family from the Murdoch stable in November 1996, when the Tory journalist Andrew Pierce, then a gossip columnist for *The Times*, made mischief by phoning her after Gordon had given an interview marking a speech to the Confederation of British Industry (CBI), in which he claimed that because of her, business was in his blood. On the front page and under the headline 'Parents deny Brown's business roots', the story asserted that Brown had used his parents' 'high powered business careers to counter charges that he lacked entrepreneurial experience'. Brown told the Press Association in an interview to coincide with his speech that Elizabeth had been a director of a company of builders and timber merchants for forty years. He said: 'Indeed she was probably, at the stage she became a company director, one of a small number of women who were company directors.'

Pierce called the Browns' home in Insch, Aberdeenshire, and – according to John Brown – exaggerated what Gordon had said. She was quoted as responding: 'It's all a bit embarrassing. I was not a working director at all. It was a small family firm. I was not very important. I merely performed some light administrative duties when I was there, which was far from all the time. I went away when I got married. I would hardly have called myself a businesswoman.'

John complained on behalf of the family to *The Times* as well as the other papers which followed up the story, including the *Daily Express*. Replying to a letter from John, David Hopkinson, the assistant managing editor of *The Times*, conceded privately: 'I think that, with hindsight, the headline was perhaps a little insensitive, and I hope you and your mother will accept our apologies for that; I am sorry also if she found the report itself upsetting.'⁹ John confirms today that his modest and deeply private mother was 'really, really upset' by the episode.¹⁰

In early 1997 Brown decided on a final flourish to counter ongoing claims from the Tories that Labour remained the party of tax and spend: he wanted to rule out an income tax rise for the whole Parliament and stick to Tory spending plans for two years. Brown briefed the shadow cabinet except John Prescott, who was staying with Chris Patten, the governor of Hong Kong, where Brown did not want a fax to be sent in case it leaked. He was set to give a speech outlining the joint move, but with Brown's approval Charlie Whelan had tipped off James Naughtie, the Radio 4 *Today* programme presenter, who was on the following morning, with Whelan pointing Naughtie towards a question about tax.

The story that Monday across several newspapers was the freeze in spending, but now when Naughtie asked the question, Brown said: 'I will be making commitments for a Parliament, and the basic rate and the top rate of tax will remain unchanged.' Naughtie responded with some incredulity: 'For the lifetime of a Parliament ... that's a very important announcement.' The episode shows that, as Ed Balls argues, at this stage there was not so great a difference between Brown and Blair, who had insisted on not raising the top rate of tax. It also shows Brown enjoyed the 'stunts' involved in political theatre, and was determined to make the most of presenting the card he did have, being tough on tax.

In the 1997 general election campaign, there was no leaders' debate but there was one between chancellor and shadow chancellor, and Clarke, usually a fine and lively debater, was not on top form on the day, put on the defensive by a confident Brown's references to the VAT hike and repeated claims that it was the Tories who could not be trusted on tax. Brown was seen by commentators to have won the debate. Further, by refusing to oppose privatisation, Brown showed the party really was New Labour. He had won an internal dispute among senior Labour figures over whether to resist or at least frustrate Tory rail privatisation, with Brown and Clare Short on the one hand, refusing, prevailing over an alliance between Prescott and the Scottish Labour stalwart Brian Wilson on the other. 'We failed but we were right,' Wilson wrote upon Prescott's death in November 2024.¹¹

For all of Blair's campaigning brilliance, the New Labour agenda would not have stacked up if Brown's economic policies had been more vulnerable to criticism, and his various policy interventions meant that few feared voting for Labour in the way they would have done previously. Not for the first or last time, despite the internal tensions, they were showing themselves to be the outstanding partnership in modern politics.

New Labour also had timing on its side with a jaded Tory government testing the patience of voters with its feuding – in contrast to a revived Labour opposition presenting a broadly united and unthreatening face to the nation. There were seemingly endless media allegations of Tory sleaze, such as the so-called 'cash for questions' for Conservative MPs, including Jonathan Aitken, and the corrosive feuding over Europe, instigated by those whom Major called anti-European 'bastards' within his own party. All the while Blair, at forty-four, and Brown, at forty-six, looked fresh against an exhausted Tory government which had apparently run out of ideas after eighteen years in government.

And it is undeniable that while Brown's fiscal 'prudence for a purpose' came at a personal cost and undermined support for him within Labour in 1994, it helped the party immeasurably when facing the country in 1997 – and it would help Brown once again when he came to office ten years later.

In many ways, Brown managed to put aside the bitterness he felt after Blair emerged as leader after John Smith's death. He knuckled down and helped prepare for the crucial 1997 general election. He thought creatively about how to make his mark on the Treasury in what would be the longest, most powerful and coherent chancellorship since the Second World War.

There is no doubt he brooded, and with some justification perhaps, although Blair as front man and Brown as chancellor was almost certainly the right result in the end. True, he was at times angry, and ministers recount that he bit his nails to the quick while Blair was speaking in cabinet meetings. But he delivered.

In other words, though Brown may still feel gazumped even today, in 1994 he recognised that sometimes in politics, as in life, you have to make a sacrifice to move forward.

PART TWO

Treasury (May 1997–June 2007)

8

Revolution

Gordon Brown was fired up and ready for action. New Labour had gone into the general election campaign maintaining record poll leads and all but certain of victory. Its lead was defended like that of a football team 5–0 up at half-time. During the campaign no more spectacular goals were sought. Instead, mistakes were avoided. The party's manifesto, 'New Labour – new life for Britain' launched in July 1996, was modest if not timid. Its five pledges were: reduction of class sizes; fast-track punishment for young offenders; reduction of NHS waiting lists; a commitment to low inflation; and, in Brown's remit, proposals to take 250,000 young people off benefits and into work. Brown's announcement that he would not raise the top rate of income tax had defused the Tories' plans to claim there was another Labour 'tax bombshell' coming.

Journalists were given more access to the party than before and a new campaign headquarters was established at Millbank Tower on the north bank of the River Thames next to Parliament. There, Peter Mandelson ran a tightly disciplined media machine and a 'rapid rebuttal unit' using a new £500,000 computer system, presenting policies that reflected John Prescott's mantra of 'traditional values in a modern setting'. Prescott was commissioned to tour sixty-five key marginals across 10,000 miles on his 'Prescott Express' bus. Brown was also a key front man alongside Blair. To the extent that Blair, Brown, Prescott and Mandelson had been rivals, they pulled together with lethal effectiveness, while John Major appeared to embark on a farewell tour of the UK.

With Labour still scarred by the experience of an unexpected Tory victory in 1992, Blair repeatedly warned there must be 'no complacency'. The Liberal Democrat grandee and former Labour minister Roy Jenkins had described Blair's task as 'like a man carrying a priceless Ming vase across a highly polished floor'. Brown helped to ensure there was no significant slip-up as New Labour clinched a landslide victory on a scale beyond the most optimistic hopes of its leading figures.

During the early hours of Friday 2 May 1997, Brown flew down from Scotland to London with Robin Cook, whom he had helped become an MP for Edinburgh Central in 1974. The two intellectual giants of Scottish Labour had once been friends – indeed they co-authored a book, *Poverty and Deprivation in Scotland: The Real Divide*, in 1983 – but had later fallen out over policy as well as personality. Brown disagreed with Cook's continued support for proportional representation and his opposition to devolution, which he believed to be the thin end of the wedge to independence, while Brown, as we have seen, always thought it crucial for preventing independence and boosting Scotland's distinct pursuit of social justice and success. Today Brown merely says of Cook that they were 'Friends at the beginning; friends at the end'.

Now, though, the pair made their way by car to the Royal Festival Hall on the south bank of the Thames to join the party's post-election celebrations, with Brown congratulating supporters individually for their work, using his characteristic phrase 'Thank you, for what you do'. With Cook grinning and clapping to the tune of the D:Ream song 'Things Can Only Get Better', a thoughtful Brown combed his hair with his hand while Tony Blair told the Union flag-waving crowds to loud cheers, 'A new dawn has broken – has it not?'

The atmosphere was electric. But Brown did not stay long. Armed with the knowledge that he was about to oversee a major overhaul of macroeconomic policy, he went to bed for a few hours' rest. For Brown, the real work was about to begin, though he would not formally be confirmed as chancellor by Blair until later that day.

Brown – flanked by Ed Balls and Charlie Whelan – was eventually applauded into the Treasury with great enthusiasm by officials on the ground floor and lining the balconies on the upper levels of the building. 'Opening the doors, a huge roar of cheers and applause greeted us,' Balls says. 'It made the hairs on the back of my neck stand up, and still does when I think about it today.'[1]

Brown had become the first Labour Chancellor of the Exchequer since Denis Healey left office following Labour's election defeat to Margaret Thatcher in May 1979. Most officials present had served only under Conservative chancellors – and now the anticipation among civil servants about working under a chancellor who would take the reins of the department in a new era was genuine. Brown had inherited a Treasury implicated in Britain's post-war economic failures: it was responsible for the 1949 and 1967 devaluations, the IMF crisis of 1976, the monetarist experiment under Thatcher and – five years before Brown entered office – Britain's departure from the ERM on 'Black Wednesday'.

Brown came in with a plan to embark on a revolution in monetary policy and make the Bank of England operationally independent, removing the power of the Treasury to set interest rates. In his memoir, Blair says he too had considered the move. But Bank of England independence had long been in Brown's mind. In the early 1990s, he had spoken to his friend and the husband of Sue Nye, the economist Gavyn Davies, about the case for it. But it was in 1995 that as shadow chancellor Brown began a detailed analysis of the operation of independent central banks. This would constrain politicians, who would no longer be able to manipulate interest rates for political reasons, and provide a huge boost for market credibility and confidence. The Bank of England would focus purely on using interest rates to keep inflation low and stable, and this in turn, in theory at least, would mean that businesses could feel more confident that interest rates were no longer going to be set with an eye to political gain.

According to Brown, for too long in Britain political considerations had dominated economic decision-making. The argument that appealed to Brown was that independence meant that Britain was thinking long-term and rejecting the short-term expedience that had led Nigel Lawson to cut interest rates to 7.5 per cent – seen as low back then – while the economy was overheating in 1988, helping to cause a recession, only to raise them again less than three weeks later. Lawson had cut interest rates because he believed the economy was slowing down to a more sustainable position, but months later he would have to double interest rates when the economy was running its biggest ever balance of payments deficit. The rates peaked at 15 per cent in October 1989. Lawson was trying to be too clever, partly trying to shadow the Deutschmark in a belief that monetary policy could balance the economy; Brown's idea, to simplify the remit and to focus on simply using interest rates to control inflation, was better than trying to use rates to control the balance of trade, the exchange rate, inflation and the balance of the economy.

In 1995 Balls had developed a detailed plan that built on the ideas contained in his 1992 Fabian Society pamphlet 'Euro-Monetarism: Why Britain Was Ensnared and How it Should Escape', written in the wake of the UK's suspension from the ERM.[2] The idea, also, was that Bank independence would help secure Labour's credibility with the markets, where there were nerves about a loosening of fiscal policy.

Brown's original aim was to make the Bank of England independent at some point in the first term. He only confirmed to Balls on the Monday before the general election his intention to do this early and with immediate effect. Soon after he arrived at the Treasury on the Friday following the general election, Brown indicated to officials, to their surprise, that he wanted to make the announcement after the bank holiday Monday.

'We talked about it from 1992 onwards, although I don't think in 1992 I thought Gordon was signing up to it,' Balls says today. 'In the 1993 policy document, we talked about Bank of England reform and a monetary policy committee ... [and] ending boom and bust, all that. I then did a paper for a policy meeting we had with Tony Blair and his people down in Hampshire.' Within that paper, about which Balls had consulted Brown at some length beforehand, there was a call for the Bank of England to be independent with a Monetary Policy Committee of nine, an inflation target and fiscal rules. 'Our phrase was we'd make a decision based upon the track record of the Bank's performance with our reforms,' says Balls.

'And so sometimes we would talk about, was it the right thing to do? How would it work, politically? Can we make it work? What are the downsides? We talked about it a lot in the autumn of 1996 ... What was happening at that time, which goes back to the history point, is that the Ken Clarke–Eddie George [the governor of the Bank of England] relationship had become quite difficult, having this monthly meeting. Minutes were being published. Eddie George was calling for rate rises, which Ken Clarke was refusing to do.' On the Monday evening of the week of the general election, Brown said to Balls that he'd been thinking about it, and if they were going to move on this, they should go into the Treasury and move very quickly.

'And I think that he was very worried about getting into a wrong dynamic with the governor. He didn't want to repeat the Wilson–Lord Cromer [tense relationship] in the 1960s. He didn't want to be in a position where, having had the first monthly meeting with the governor, having an argument with the governor, that independence would then be a concession. And I think he also realised, if we're going to do this, which I'd be pushing the whole time, the immediate impact of doing it would be very big.' Brown then said they should tell the Bank on Friday. 'I said "Great", and off we went. But I don't think I knew that was going to happen until that Monday, one of those moments where he just said, "I've thought really hard about this, you've been going on at me, and this is what we should do."'

Blair was not in on the decision, according to Balls. 'I don't think there'd been any recent conversation with Tony Blair about doing it or anything like that. But he was supportive.'[3] On election day, though, Blair had had a long discussion with Peter Mandelson at Blair's constituency home in Sedgefield and had that morning asked Mandelson for a note on Bank of England independence, which Mandelson's friend and the then Number Ten special adviser Roger Liddle had written in longhand and sent to Blair. Liddle listed the advantages of the move: it would be a powerful signal that Labour was serious about economic stability; it would reassure the markets, jittery about Brown's plan to tighten the fiscal rules in his first Budget in July 1997; it would shift responsibility of an unwelcome rise in interest rates to the Bank; and it would pre-empt criticism from 'old Labour' if done swiftly. As a result of the note, Mandelson backed Brown to Blair.

However, it is also the case that Bank independence was included as a proposal in Liddle and Mandelson's 1996 book *The Blair Revolution*. Brown had been sent a draft of the book and had called Mandelson demanding that the section was taken out as it was his surprise plan. Blair had been open to the idea but had wanted to be sure via his own advisers.

On the Saturday, Brown met with Blair at the latter's home in Islington. Also there was Blair's new economic adviser, Moira Wallace, a Treasury civil servant, who would later become permanent secretary in the Department of Energy and Climate Change under Brown as prime minister.[4] Wallace urged a more cautious approach, perhaps influenced by Robin Butler, the cabinet secretary and head of the home civil service. Her view was that the 'proper procedure' should be followed, with papers and a full discussion among ministers before going ahead. For Brown, though, time was of the essence – moving quickly to operational independence was a key part of his ongoing determination to cement Labour's economic credibility. Ultimately, Blair agreed with Brown, closing the meeting with a simple 'Fine'.[5]

Brown then returned to the Treasury, whereupon he was met with similar arguments for caution by the permanent secretary, Sir Terry Burns. Balls had been talking to the Treasury in the week of the general election and Burns had predicted, unlike many, that the incoming Labour government was going to move in this direction two days beforehand. On the eve of the 1997 general election, Burns approached a young and upcoming official, Tom Scholar – who would himself become permanent secretary to the Treasury from 2016 to 2022 – to prepare a paper on Bank of England independence for the following day. The paper was to be ready for the new chancellor at 5 p.m. on the Friday evening. This and Balls's own paper were the basis of discussions on the Friday evening before Brown met with Blair on the Saturday.[6]

In turn it formed the outline of the letter that would later be delivered to the governor of the Bank of England, Eddie George, announcing the move. During Brown's first days in office, there was a series of 'rolling meetings', not just dealing with Bank of England independence, but also welfare-to-work, the windfall tax and the Budget – only some of which had been in Labour's manifesto. There was a feeling within the Treasury that Brown and his team distrusted officials. This perhaps resulted from a lack of communication prior to May 1997 – and from the perspective of officials, this made it difficult to know how to conduct business. However, the Treasury began to thrive off Brown's own relentless energy, embodied by his early-morning starts, and his and his team's creativity.

The decision to go for operational independence was met with near-universal joy in Threadneedle Street, home of the Bank of England. Prior to the 1997 general election, Eddie George, known as 'Steady Eddie', initiated meetings with the opposition by asking Clarke for permission to speak with Brown to discuss Labour's plans for the Bank – a request that was accepted. At the meetings with Brown, who was usually accompanied by Balls, discussion focused on the shape of an independent Bank of England: George never discussed the timing of Bank independence, though he anticipated that this would occur midway through the first parliamentary term.[7]

Andrew Bailey, who was George's private secretary and was to become governor in 2020, recalled in 2022: 'Eddie, of course, was very supportive of the decision – and the famous letter now sits in the Bank of England's museum. Though I confess it is not in mint condition, as for a number of weeks after Gordon handed it over, it went around in my briefcase.'

A blow for the Bank was the transfer of banking supervision, the regulation of financial institutions to ensure their stability, which had been its long-standing responsibility. Brown believed that the Bank of England should not be seen as a creature of the City, and decided to pull responsibility for banking supervision into one institution: what would become the Financial Services Authority (FSA). Brown approached the Bank of England's deputy governor, Howard Davies, to establish the FSA.

Davies asked Brown, 'What do you have in mind?' to which the new chancellor replied with his characteristic blunt-speaking style: 'I have in mind that you go and sort it out.' When setting up the FSA, Davies took with him 450 officials from the Bank of England. He established a small committee to deal with the FSA's structure and most of the people transferred from the Bank to the FSA were eventually content with their new positions.[8] But Eddie George was opposed to the move and had for some reason been assured by Terry Burns that there would be no transfer of financial responsibility – something Brown had never agreed to. George told the press he had considered resigning but he did not follow through on the threat.

Some of the press did not immediately understand the scale of the change when the decision was revealed on the Tuesday. Brown announced an interest-rate rise and for some minutes they thought this was the biggest story. Eventually Brown's statement about operational independence was processed by the media – and hugely well received. In advance, Brown had phoned cabinet ministers to tell them of the decision and he also called some of his predecessors as chancellor. Kenneth Clarke – who was by then standing for the Tory leadership – was firmly opposed on the grounds that the step removed fiscal decisions from democratic accountability. However, Nigel Lawson was strongly in favour: his book *Memoirs of a Tory Radical* outlines his views on the Bank of England and advocates the concept of its operational independence in order to enhance market credibility. In a 1988 minute to Margaret Thatcher, Lawson had proposed that an independent central bank would 'assume sole responsibility for the operation of monetary policy, with a statutory duty to protect and maintain the value of the currency'.

Alastair Campbell popped over to the Treasury at this point for a 'pre-meeting' on Bank independence to find Treasury officials looking a bit 'shell-shocked', but Brown himself – who was firing off questions and then answering them – much more relaxed than he had been towards the end of the general election campaign. He had, Campbell felt, taken to the Treasury 'like a duck to water' and was pleased by the positive press reaction to the move, though Campbell felt there was too much coverage of the fact that it had been Ed Balls's idea. He recalls in his diary how Brown was in 'better form' during this period and more 'engaged' with Blair and Number Ten.

The Bank of England independence move by Brown – which was unusually kept secret by his camp under strict orders from the chancellor – proved a spectacular and lasting success. The innovation helped to keep inflation – which had been the biggest problem for successive governments over the previous forty years – at or below target for the next ten years. Brown had envisaged this, and wanted not only to relinquish control for the political message it sent out, but also to take it away from future chancellors after years of 'boom and bust' under the Conservatives. For Brown, then, the advantages of the move were both that the new Labour government would gain credit with the financial markets for ceding control over interest rates, and that the Treasury would be able to focus on Britain's long-term problems.

9

The Euro Decision

Britain joined what was then known as the European Economic Community in 1973, which was controversial enough, with some on the Tory right and Labour leftists like Tony Benn opposed. Indeed, it remained a topic of concern such that Labour had pledged to leave in its 1983 manifesto. The Maastricht Treaty of 1992 brought the member nations closer together, and meant the organisation was officially renamed the European Union (EU). But the next stage of 'ever closer union', the creation of the European single currency, known as the euro, was even more contentious. It was finally adopted into the global financial markets on 1 January 1999 (though it was first used in Madrid on 16 December 1995), resulting in a fresh debate in Britain, as well as other European nations, about the extent and desirability of integration. Labour had seen from the opposition benches how the European issue tore John Major's government apart over Maastricht.

While the intention of monetary union had recurred among European leaders since the late 1960s, it was given fresh impetus by the establishment of the single market in January 1993, which allowed the free movement of goods, services, capital and people across the EU's internal borders. The strong advocates of a single currency within Europe – who were opposed by Thatcher – had argued persuasively that it would help to complete the single market. Just as the single traveller across Europe would not lose out by changing money at each border, so, and more importantly, businesses would no longer face 'transaction costs' by having to navigate varying exchange rates. Those annual transactions had been estimated at costing between 20 and 25 billion euros a year across Europe. At the same time, they argued, it would lead to greater price transparency, furthering competition, lower prices, economic stability growth and jobs.

But to the dismay of many British politicians, European leaders also wanted to establish the euro for reasons, primarily, of further *political* integration. As Sirkka Hämäläinen, a member of the executive board of the European Central Bank, said in a key speech at the meeting of the Institut International d'Études Bancaires on 21 May 1999 in Helsinki: 'First, we should not forget that the idea of introducing a single currency was originally motivated by the overall political arguments that an increased integration of the European countries would reduce the risk of war and crises on the continent. Through the establishment of common institutions, political conflicts could be avoided or, at least, resolved through discussion and compromise, rather than by resorting to force. Hence, at a general level, the introduction of a single currency in the euro area is an important symbol for political and social integration in Europe which should serve as a catalyst for further co-ordination and integration also in other policy areas.'

But this more political impact of the Economic and Monetary Union (EMU), launched in 1992, was just what made it a more radioactive issue for those most concerned about the potential loss of national sovereignty entailed by further European integration. The issue had never been far from the surface in the 1997 election. Ken Clarke, who favoured euro entry, had persuaded John Major not to rule out joining the single currency over the next Parliament, threatening to resign if he did. Labour, for its part, matched this by also refusing to rule it out, while committing, like the Tories, to a referendum before any final decision was taken.

Once Labour came to power, however, it was clear that this holding position could not be sustained and that a decision would have to be made. In fact, the stance among those at the top of Labour fluctuated and developed through the summer of 1997. From being relatively open to the idea, Brown would eventually adopt the position that the time was not ripe for British entry, while Robin Cook, who had been negative about the single currency, warmed considerably towards it as foreign secretary. As the EU embarked on its apparent drive towards political and monetary union, Tony Blair was, in theory at least, mostly in favour of taking the emotive step of ditching the pound – a move that would be a hard sell to a country with deep reserves of

'Euroscepticism', especially given the opposition of press barons like Rupert Murdoch.

Brown and those around him have always insisted keeping Britain out of the euro was based on genuine policy objections. He had been badly burnt by his support for British membership of the ERM and didn't want a repeat. His emphasis on the economic dangers of euro entry would precipitate a clash with Blair, though Balls now claims that Blair never really wanted to join. However, one pro-European former Blair aide says that Blair was 'very upset by the Eurosceptic dance' performed by Brown and Balls. 'To be fair to Tony, he never pretended, even to Rupert Murdoch, that he was anything other than pro-European,' the aide makes clear.

But although Brown would be portrayed by some in the media as the more Eurosceptic of the two, he is actually a lifelong pro-European. One Blairite Labour figure who held conversations with him in the 1980s said that Brown 'saw pro-Europeanism as fundamental to the modernisation of the Labour Party', which Kinnock had first achieved by reversing Labour's opposition to the EEC.

On the euro, government policy as it evolved over 1997 was that British entry into stage 3 of the EMU – involving the pooling of monetary sovereignty and the adoption of the single currency – would depend on the UK meeting, first, the convergence criteria set down in the 1992 Maastricht Treaty which established the EU in February 1992. These were: price stability, sustainable public finances, exchange rate stability and long-term interest rates.

But another requirement was the fulfilment of five new economic 'tests', set and judged by the UK government. These tests, reportedly written in the back of a New York taxi by Balls, and unveiled by Brown shortly afterwards in a February 1997 speech he made as shadow chancellor to the American-European Community Association, were whether: 'i) the business cycles and economic structures of the UK and eurozone were compatible, so that the eurozone interest rate could be permanently adopted by Britain; ii) there was sufficient "flexibility in the system" to deal with (undefined) problems that might arise within the eurozone; iii) membership would encourage business to make long-term decisions to invest in Britain; iv) membership would enhance the competitive position of the country's financial services industry; and v) membership would, overall, "promote higher growth, stability and a lasting increase in jobs" in the UK.' These economic conditions would inevitably make any decision to adopt the euro on merely political grounds more difficult.

Nevertheless, according to Blair, Brown was initially keener on euro entry. Brown would claim later that it had been the prime minister who was 'resisting'. That was probably true. It was Blair, after all, who had decided to write a pre-election article in the *Sun* saying he 'loved' the pound. Brown would also recount that he had advised against Labour tying its hands by committing to a referendum before euro entry. Balls too alleges that Blair was never truly in favour. 'Tony was a politician who was skilled at playing to his audience. It's not a criticism. So, I never thought Tony Blair wanted to join the euro. I think he'd have been appalled at the idea of joining the euro if we had proposed it. But he wanted to be a leader in Europe. And maybe he didn't ever think that was possible if he was seen as an anti-euro. So I think it was hugely in his interests … to say, "Well, you know, of course, it is what I want, but it's very difficult for me because of Gordon, Ed Balls" … As for the idea that Gordon had a less cooperative relationship with Tony Blair because I got to Gordon: I know why he might say that, because rather than criticise Gordon, it's the easier thing to say. But it's actually garbage. I never persuaded Gordon of these things. It was a much more common endeavour between us.'

The Blairites emphatically deny that Blair did not want to join the euro. One says he was 'boxed in' by Brown over the issue. The reality appears to be that Brown and Blair criss-crossed and wavered in their views, partly on principle and partly and naturally influenced by how they would benefit politically. While Brown was initially enthusiastic, he retreated into scepticism later; and Blair, having been more sceptical, became keener in due course.

Brown did recognise the potential advantages of British euro membership – it could increase trade with Europe and increase national income. At a meeting in the Treasury on Sunday 4 May 1997, just three days after polling day, Brown made clear that he did not want 'at this stage' to rule out the UK joining the euro in 1999. The minutes show that the chancellor described how he aimed to 'shift public opinion towards a more balanced and less Europhobic position … This debate would be of benefit whatever the eventual decision on whether to join [the euro] in the first wave.' And on 15 July 1997, at a meeting with Balls and trade union leaders including John Monks, the minutes show that Brown 'explained that he planned to publish lots more information to stimulate the debate on the European single currency'.

Brown had been advised by Nigel Wicks, his second permanent secretary, that Hans Tietmeyer, then head of the Bundesbank, the central bank in Germany (where public opinion was still against the single currency), had privately floated the idea that the British should consider pressing for a two-year delay. But Brown was reluctant to take that line. His argument was that a delay would 'choke off the debate that he was hoping to get going'.[1]

For now at any rate, Brown decided to stimulate such a debate in an abridged version of a paper written by the Labour peer David Currie, which even-handedly set out the case for and against British euro entry. But Currie's admirably neutral paper, complete with a foreword by the chancellor, did not damp down speculation about what the government actually intended to do about the single currency – and when. Some journalists were sporadically briefed by allies of the chancellor into the early autumn that he was planning euro entry.

It was widely assumed – but denied by the Treasury – that such an ally had been the source of a front-page report by the *Financial Times*'s political editor Robert Peston on 26 September, which said the government was more positive about euro entry than it had hitherto been. The story, which produced an appreciable though temporary fall in the value of the pound as markets adjusted to the prospect of euro entry, quoted one unnamed minister as saying: 'It is now clear that we must indicate our willingness to be in there.' This was followed on 14 October by a story by the *Independent*'s political editor Tony Bevins suggesting, in effect, that the Treasury was trying to bounce Blair into early euro entry.

This evidence of disarray, which may have emanated less from Brown and Blair themselves than from zealous lieutenants of each, initially, if unintentionally, led only to more confusion. Brown saw immediately that the government's credibility was threatened by such uncertainty, rather as the Conservatives had been by their persistent comments that they would join the ERM 'when the time is right'. Brown secured Blair's agreement that an announcement would be needed before the end of the year and then decided, as he told Blair, that he would grant an interview – or at least release an exclusive statement – to *The Times*'s Philip Webster to end the speculation.

The problem which then occurred was over the statement – agreed between Charlie Whelan and Alastair Campbell – in which Campbell had actually toned down some of the more generally pro-European language. On top of that, the headline, 'Brown Rules out Single Currency in the Lifetime of this Parliament', went further than Webster's article and further still than Blair had expected.

Although Blair had known of Brown's initiative with *The Times*, he had not known exactly what and how this was going to be delivered. As the story broke, Blair, who had been tied up at Chequers in a meeting with another cabinet minister, was sufficiently alarmed to find out what was happening. Unable to track down either Brown, who was at a constituency surgery, or Campbell, he reached Whelan and the conversation went, as recorded by Campbell in his diaries: 'TB asked if we had ruled out EMU this parliament. Yes, said Charlie. "Is not that what you want?" No, it is not said TB. "Oh" said Charlie.'[2] For all Blair's apparent early scepticism about joining the euro in practice, he certainly wanted to keep the option open.

All this would not be worth recounting if it did not contain the seeds of an explosive clash between Blair and Brown almost six years later. For at least as much as it was about whether Britain was going to enter the single currency, it was about how a decision not to do it *now* was to be presented not only to the British public and to the largely pro-European big business constituency but also to Britain's European partners. Blair insists that his disagreements with Brown were not over actual euro entry, but because 'Gordon was expressing himself negatively on the euro'. While acknowledging that he was 'in principle' in favour of joining on the political grounds that it was 'better to be ... full players in Europe's economic decision-making', Blair says in his memoirs that it was fundamentally an 'economic proposition' and could only be justified on economic grounds. 'If the economics had changed I would have gone for it. They didn't.'

This chimes with Balls's claim that Blair never really wanted to be in the euro, of course. Nevertheless, both Balls and Blair are probably underestimating in hindsight what at times was Blair's eagerness to join even if the economic criteria were at best ambiguous. But there was also the issue of how a postponement of any decision to enter the single currency should be presented if the British government was to keep its pro-European credentials intact and at least keep its options open.³

Certainly the pressure, especially but not only from business, to keep his options open that Brown would now have to withstand, proved as intense as the jingoistic right-wing media pressure to stay out of the euro. On the Monday after the *Times* story, Brown had the embarrassment of opening a new trading system at the London Stock Exchange as the screen behind him turned red, reflecting the markets' reaction to all this disarray and confusion on euro entry. But he was adamant that if Britain could not join on 1 January 1999 – the planned single currency launch date – it would be impossible to do so in 2001 in the run-up to the next general election.

It was now obvious that a statement to Parliament would be needed, and initially Blair wanted to make it himself – finally yielding to Brown's insistence that it was a Treasury matter and the statement should be made by the chancellor. Eventually it was agreed that the statement should make clear it was unlikely to happen in the course of the Parliament, but adding what was little more than a fig leaf as a qualification: 'barring some fundamental or unforeseen change in economic circumstances'. This would allow Blair's pro-euro aides to spin the 27 October statement as keeping their options open; but this hardly changed the stark reality – that Britain would not be holding a referendum on euro entry in the first Labour Parliament.

The Treasury papers show that before Brown's statement on 27 October the pleas from business – and from John Monks – were heartfelt. On 22 October, Currie, a key Labour figure liaising with business and the City, shed his public neutrality and wrote a private 'Dear Gordon' letter saying: 'Like other colleagues in the party I am deeply concerned that we are putting ourselves into a box from which it will be electorally difficult to escape.' He added: 'Britain must join EMU in the long term because of the economic benefits and because of the economic and political costs of isolation in Europe.'

Currie's reference to 'other colleagues in the party' was correct – Robin Cook was far from alone in being in favour of euro entry: the Labour peer David Simon, the former businessman and a minister in the department of trade and industry under Blair, was also for it. But now it would be the turn of business leaders – along with Monks – to apply pressure at a series of back-to-back meetings three days before Brown's statement. The Bank of England governor, to whom Brown confided the general thrust of the statement, warmly welcomed the fact that it would end the 'uncertainty' over euro entry. But Christopher Haskins, the Labour peer who had headed Northern Foods; Niall Fitzgerald, the chairman and CEO of Unilever; Colin Marshall, the chairman of British Airways; and Adair Turner, the director general of the CBI, had all registered their concerns. The meetings were separate, but the line was similar in each case: that they understood that Brown was ruling out joining the euro at its start but appealed to him to keep the options open for 2001. Brown nevertheless held firm.

The approach of both Brown and Blair could be said to have been more about tactics than principles. Brown was wary of joining in the run-up to a general election, and some around him wanted to take control of the decision away from Blair. In turn, Blair – conscious of the political problems of trying to sell to voters the idea of scrapping the pound – wanted to be more vague, despite the damage to business confidence. While it is true that, in the end, Blair was more in favour, as a liberal pro-European, than Brown, there was little high politics involved on either side, with even the Brown camp's opposition being based on economics rather than political vision.

If anything, after the euro came into being in 1999, Brown became more entrenched in his scepticism over the single currency. Despite the Conservatives under William Hague making a pledge to 'save the pound' the centrepiece of their campaign, it was never in any great danger of being replaced. Labour won another landslide in 2001, with a 166-seat majority, and the party's number of seats dropped only from 418 to 412. Between December 1999 and December 2002, the euro traded below the US dollar. It would later pick up, but during that period it was far from a triumph, which reduced any need to adopt the new currency. Meanwhile, the British economy continued to grow and did not seem to suffer from staying outside of the euro.

Although seemingly settled, the issue later exploded into a bitter and highly personal argument between prime minister and chancellor on 2 April 2003, after Treasury civil servants and Balls had completed an assessment of the five tests. It culminated in a tense Blair, no doubt distracted by the build-up to the Iraq war, demanding that Brown 'consider your position' as the chancellor; he then turned and made his way from Number Ten to the flat at Number Eleven. 'I didn't know how much longer I would be there,' Brown recalled, 'but I was not prepared to give way on a decision that could inflict damage on the British economy.' Balls is perhaps exaggerating the extent to which Blair was not really in favour of the euro. The prime minister had by now decided that entry would be part of his premiership's pro-European, progressive and liberal legacy, while Brown at this point wanted to give clear guidance that they would not be adopting the euro.

On 9 June 2003, Brown delivered the verdict to the Commons in a half-hour statement with Blair by his side. Brown claimed his position was 'in the British economic interest' after the assessment found that four of the five tests had failed. The only one that was met came in the financial services industry – the City – while convergence, flexibility, employment and investment tests were all given a 'no' or 'not yet' label. Michael Howard, then Tory shadow chancellor, responded to Brown by saying that the five tests had originally been written in October 1997 'on the back of an envelope, in the back of a taxi, to fix the damage done by the chancellor's spin doctor in the back of the Red Lion pub'. He added: 'It was a four-pint briefing that led to a five-point plan that's just given us a six-year run-around.'

That day, Blair hit the phones and spoke to international leaders – including the French president, Jacques Chirac, and prime minister, Jean-Pierre Raffarin; the German chancellor, Gerhard Schröder; the Irish taoiseach, Bertie Ahern; and the Spanish prime minister, José María Aznar – seeking to reassure them that Britain might yet join the euro following a referendum. But it never did. Brown remains proud of the decision today. This is despite the fact that if we had joined the euro, Britain might not have left the European Union in 2016, a move which Brown vehemently opposed. But again, Brown and Balls insist that for economic reasons staying out of the euro was the right call.

Intriguingly, Balls himself says that one major area frequently forgotten in the debate about New Labour's record is its failure to win the pro-European argument, which, he implies, helped lead to Brexit in 2016. 'We didn't win the argument for Britain and Europe. We didn't join the euro, which was the right decision. But we were thriving in Europe, and we didn't really win the big political argument ... Neither Tony nor Gordon really addressed it. They took it a bit for granted. If anything, they sort of sometimes slipped into the old default British governing view, which is, you [do] a bit of short-term politics when you went to summits and so on.'[4]

10

Tragedy

Away from Westminster, on New Year's Day in 2000, Brown proposed (without a ring to hand) to the former public relations executive Sarah Jane Macaulay, during a walk on a remote, windswept Fife beach.

The couple had been seeing one another since 1994, just after the momentous events surrounding John Smith's death. Sarah has recalled one of their first dates, on 18 June that year. It was during the World Cup football tournament and Sarah was working in high-level public relations. She had spent part of her early life in Tanzania in East Africa, before attending school in north London and then studying psychology at Bristol University. 'We'd been in contact through work, he phoned me up and said would I like to meet for supper?' she told Matt Forde at the Edinburgh Festival in 2024. 'We went and had dinner and for about an hour and a half we had the most amazing time, we were talking and then he started looking at his watch. Then I realised it was the Ireland v Italy game that night. He'd obviously worked out we'd have dinner then he would be back in time for the match. I've got brothers so I could see the signs so I said "why don't we finish this dinner another night" and off he whizzed to go and watch the match.'[1]

Sarah is an impressive, attractive and highly intelligent woman, an ambitious charity leader who guards her family's private life closely. Her serenity has helped shape the more well-balanced man Brown is today. She has always been fully behind her husband both personally and politically, and has several times come to his rescue, as we shall see, even if she occasionally comes across as very slightly detached from his relentless political schedule. For his part, Gordon was rescued in the wider sense from a single life without children, and a love affair with only the Labour Party, politics, current affairs and history. He has gained a hinterland that seemed impossible before 1994. The couple's ongoing feelings for one another are in no doubt.

Seven months after the proposal they were married in North Queensferry, where they now live and work together, running the Office of Gordon and Sarah Brown from the top floor of their house, and where Sarah focuses her charity campaigning work on maternal and premature birth health and expanding educational opportunities.

That work is the legacy of personal tragedy. For it was on 7 January 2002 that Gordon and Sarah Brown were struck by a devastating loss that was to affect their whole outlook on life.

After being overjoyed when Sarah became pregnant in the summer of 2001, a year after they married, their first-born child, Jennifer Jane Brown, was delivered by emergency Caesarean section at the Forth Park Hospital in Kirkcaldy on Friday 28 December 2001. She died ten days later in the couple's arms. Jennifer weighed just 2lb 4oz when she was born seven weeks premature, and she had already suffered a brain haemorrhage.

Gordon describes the impact of the tragedy to me: 'You can imagine the sheer joy and happiness as she came into the world with me present at a difficult Caesarean section birth. But this turned into previously unimaginable pain. The joy of her being born turned into the grief and then a blanket of sadness that never really leaves you. We sat with Jennifer at her hospital bed for most of these ten days and for some of the last few days stayed overnight in the hospital. By day four, when the extent of her brain haemorrhage had been diagnosed, we were told that all hope was gone and were fully aware that she had no chance of survival.'

The doctor 'told us gently that there was absolutely no hope whatsoever; all we could do was sit with her – which we did for twenty-four hours a day, sleeping at the hospital – as gradually the life support she had was withdrawn. Even then we did not realise how short the time we would have with her was. Although we knew she would not live, we hoped that maybe she had more days.'

The couple took the step of getting their sick baby baptised on the ward. 'Her beautiful face still unaffected, untouched by the scale of the tragedy that had befallen her. Sarah and I took our vows as parents to do everything to bring her up "in the nurture and admonition of the Lord",' Brown recalls. 'The baptism was not for us just a comfort or a ritual: it was a recognition that every single life, even the shortest one, had a purpose and every person is irreplaceable.'[2]

The Saturday, Sunday and Monday were 'essentially a vigil', Brown has said. 'We spent Jennifer's last nights taking it in turns to be at her bedside and sleeping next door in a room set aside for the parents of critically ill children. There was nursing help to ensure Jennifer had no pain or suffering. We were with her all Monday afternoon as her life ebbed away.'

Tahir Mahmood, the consultant obstetrician who delivered the baby, said a routine scan revealed she was suffering from intra-uterine growth restriction, a condition which occurs in 10 per cent of pregnancies and causes the child to have an irregular heart rate. Brown, who is still tearful today when discussing Jennifer, was understandably very depressed by the death of his first-born daughter, and could not listen to music for a year afterwards. 'Life seemed empty,' he has said. 'Westminster was the last place I wanted to be.'[3]

Needing something to do, he helped his brother John write the eulogy for Jennifer's funeral. Brown says he was personally grateful to the *Daily Mail*'s editor, Paul Dacre, and his wife Kathy and the editor of the *Daily Mirror*, Piers Morgan, 'who came to the aid of Sarah and me in the days when Jennifer was critically ill and dying'. He adds: 'Following some intrusive and unfair reporting of her condition, they helped secure a period of restraint when it came to reporting on her death. For that we remain grateful to this day.' Some comfort came with the birth of their sons, John in October 2003 and Fraser in July 2006.

In February 2010, as prime minister and weeks before the general election, Brown gave an interview to Piers Morgan on ITV, with Sarah wiping away tears from her place in the studio audience, as Brown paid tribute to his wife's bravery. 'Our partnership is so strong possibly because of these events we've had, we've had to respond to [them] together,' he said. 'But for a mother having borne a child … having had an emergency operation, producing milk for that child and then to see that child go, it's … I mean my admiration and respect and love for Sarah just grew and grew.'

Speaking to ITV News in March 2017, Sarah Brown said: 'It's always going to be painful and it's always a huge part of you. She's our precious little girl who lives in our hearts. I received over 13,000 letters and replied to everyone who gave me an address.' She described this effort as a 'healing task'. Sarah went on to help to establish the Jennifer Brown Research Laboratory at the University of Edinburgh, as part of Theirworld, the charity she helps lead – which is a longitudinal study looking at the causes and consequences of prematurity. The couple wanted to help 'prevent what we had suffered', and between them they continue to raise £1 million per year for the laboratory.

The Browns rarely discuss their family, but in an interview with the lifestyle magazine *HouseBeautiful* in 2015, the year Brown left Parliament, he talked about his sons, who live entirely private lives. He said: 'Before I had children I always thought I'd want them to succeed, do well and study hard. But when you have your boys, you realise you just want them to be happy. I would add to that – I'd also want them to know and understand what our values are and then take them forward and do things their way.'

Sarah also talked about the influence of her mother Pauline, saying: 'When I was growing up, Mum was a strong role model as a feminist, working mum and somebody who had gone back to a career after having children. She trained as a teacher, then a headteacher and has a PhD in social anthropology. Whatever glass ceiling exists, my mother's always pushing it higher. My mum's home in Dorset has always been a base where I can come and take stock. All the family spent time there last summer. When I come and see Mum I do a lot of sleeping and not a lot else! … My home life with Gordon and the boys in Scotland is similar in some ways to my childhood. It's busy and we all have our own activities, but the heart of my house is the kitchen table, just like Mum's. You never know whom you're going to find around that table.'[4]

But as Sarah wrote in June 2022:

> Losing our first child Jennifer after she was only here in this world for ten days was the most painful moment imaginable. Aside from the profound loss, what was so tormenting was not knowing why she hadn't survived. She was born suddenly and early, at 33 weeks, but the pregnancy had seemed healthy. My husband, Gordon, and

I desperately wanted to understand what had happened but doctors couldn't offer us an answer. In 2002, the problems that cause premature birth and its often devastating consequences were often under-researched or even ignored. Amid our grief, the response from the public was overwhelming. [What] struck me was how many people, particularly women, shared their own stories of similar loss in their families. Our sadness and sense of loss prompted a search for the answers we desperately needed ... Surely we could start to change things. I felt determined that something should come out of all this unhappiness.[5]

11

Redistribution, Spending and Deregulation

Brown's chancellorship is conventionally – and accurately – remembered for its period of economic growth. It was the longest on record, though the economy had been growing for some eighteen months before May 1997 under the Tory chancellor Kenneth Clarke. Brown and the government benefited from the major advantage of a benign economic inheritance when Labour came to power. But his ability to sustain that was exceptional and resulted from his policies.

It is little coincidence that the Labour government enjoyed four years of sustained popularity – helped by the demoralised state of the Tories after their huge election defeat – during its first spell in office. The UK's economic performance after 1997 was relatively good compared to that of other major industrialised countries, with a GDP per capita growth rate of 1.42 per cent annually between 1997 and 2010, which was better than that of Germany (1.26 per cent), the US (1.22 per cent), France (1.04 per cent), Japan (0.52 per cent) and Italy (0.22 per cent).

Brown's time at the helm was also known for its stability, fiscal 'prudence for a purpose' and reducing the national debt. His target was to keep the debt under 40 per cent of GDP, which he succeeded in doing, before it was abandoned in the financial crisis of 2008–9. However, because considerable amounts of spending were through public-private partnerships, using private-sector cash for national projects, he faced criticism of 'cooking the books' as the costs were spread out over years.

Brown's early years at the Treasury were marked not just by giving the Bank of England its independence but also by adhering to his 'golden rule': borrowing only for investment over the economic cycle, though some investment was through PPP, and ensuring that the national debt remained low and stable.

In his first budget in July 1997, Brown introduced the landmark New Deal, a series of programmes to reduce unemployment through training, support and job opportunities. He says today it was one of the most fulfilling policies he has ever implemented. The New Deal aimed to help 400,000 people without jobs, nearly 100,000 of whom had been receiving unemployment benefits for more than a year. Brown also introduced a windfall tax on the privatised utilities to raise £5.2 billion for the New Deal, which was rolled out in April 1998. The number of those employed would rise by 3 million while Brown was chancellor, from 26.5 million to 29.6 million. The Institute for Fiscal Studies (IFS) says that the chances of young people finding a job rose by 20 per cent, though this may have come from economic growth as well as policy.

He can also be credited with considerable redistribution of wealth during his time as chancellor, even if he may not at the time have been keen to reveal this. Robert Peston recounts how Brown confronted him in March 1999, saying: 'Why did you write that the Budget would be "seriously redistributive"?' The term was credited in Peston's story to 'a government member' and Brown demanded to know who Peston had been talking to. Peston quotes Brown as telling him: 'It was profoundly unhelpful.'[1]

By 2002 Brown was less reluctant to acknowledge his redistributive goals, at least within the privacy of cabinet. Expressing his own frustration at how reluctant the government was to admit to helping the poor, Robin Cook recalled telling the cabinet on 8 March 2002: 'The truth is Gordon is outstandingly and clearly the most redistributionist Labour chancellor in history. He has taken millions of children and pensioners out of poverty. Yet the paradox is that when I talk proudly of what we've done for the poor, inside I feel vaguely uneasy as if I've somehow gone off message.' He continued: 'When I was finished Gordon gave a beaming smile and said, "Thank you very much". Part of Gordon's tragedy is that he is an old believer in redistribution, but stuck within a Blairite ideology which only allows him to do it by stealth. The result must be a constant frustration of not getting credit for the enormous amount he has achieved.'[2]

Yet Balls in recent years has accepted and indeed made a virtue of such a level of redistribution under the Brown regime at the Treasury, even if some of it was by stealth. He told the BBC documentary *Blair and Brown: The New Labour Revolution* that their government was 'the most redistributive since 1945'. This was done in a number of ways, including the introduction of the first ever national minimum wage in 1999, record levels of spending on public services from 2000, and the introduction and then the expansion of tax credits, especially the working tax credit and the child tax credit, designed to support low-income working families and – a passion of Brown's to this day – reduce child poverty, on which he also placed effective targets.

However, the gap between the poorest and the richest grew during this time, reflecting, perhaps, Peter Mandelson's declaration in October 1998, first reported in the *Financial Times*, that he was 'intensely relaxed about people getting filthy rich as long as they pay their taxes'. Inequality fluctuated during the 1990s and 2000s, but by 2007–8, the Gini coefficient, a measure of income inequality, had climbed to 0.36. In other words, while many were helped out of poverty during this time, those at the top of the income scale also managed to improve their wealth even more, hence all these changes both reduced poverty and increased inequality.

To tackle child poverty and inequality, Brown announced in July 1998 an initial £540 million of funding for the Sure Start programmes to help deprived children early on in life. He pledged to deliver 250 local Sure Start centres and a visit from an outreach worker for every mother in Sure Start areas, amid evidence that some children were falling behind before they started school. The IFS has reported that Sure Start, which was inspired partly by the older US initiative Head Start, reduced the number of people attending hospitals, and therefore saved the NHS millions of pounds.

A 2024 IFS study, funded by the Nuffield Foundation, found that children from low-income families who lived near a centre performed up to three grades better at their GCSEs than those who lived further away. The study used postcodes from when children were five years old to determine roughly how close the nearest centre was, before focusing on the GCSE results of those children eleven years later, and found 'big improvements' in the performance of those living near a centre, especially those from low-income backgrounds. Spending on the landmark Sure Start policy would be increased by 17 per cent in 2004, after Brown had pledged in 2003 to create a centre in 'every community' according to 'the levels of deprivation within their areas'. At the peak of the programme in 2010, there were 3,600 Sure Start centres in England, enough to ensure they were available in almost every community.

The story of Brown's chancellorship is partly one of patience: he waited until after the two-year period, in which he stuck to Tory spending plans for the sake of New Labour's credibility, to begin spending and redistribution in earnest. When he came to office in 1997, 27 per cent of children lived in households whose income was less than 60 per cent of the national median, while at the 2010 general election, that proportion had fallen to 18 per cent.

During his first term as chancellor, in 1999, Brown introduced the working families' tax credit, the first in a number of tax credits aimed at helping the poor, low-paid and vulnerable – a means-tested benefit that could be claimed by working individuals, childless couples and working families with dependent children. The benefit, which became the working tax credit in April 2003, was responsible for reducing the number of children living in poverty in the UK from 3 million in 1998 to 1.6 million in 2010.

A 2013 report by the IFS showed that the extra money provided by Brown and Blair – an £18 billion annual increase in spending on benefits for families with children and an £11 billion annual increase in benefits for pensioners – was vital in bringing down poverty rates between 1997 and 2010. The report stated: 'Our modelling suggests child and pensioner poverty would either have stayed the same or risen, rather than fall substantially, had there not been these big spending increases.'[3] It went on: 'Labour had very clear objectives to reduce poverty amongst families with children and pensioners, and accorded these objectives high priority ... However, it is much less clear that Labour took a strong view on the appropriate level of inequality within the top half of the income distribution.'

Child poverty, which Brown describes as 'an obscenity', had doubled under the Tories by 1997. Brown says that it was the devastation caused by poverty and unemployment in Fife in the 1960s that made tackling it a lifelong ambition for him.

He pursued the introduction of a relatively progressive tax system, increasing the tax burden on higher earners while providing relief to lower- and middle-income households, leading eventually to the introduction of the 50p top rate of tax while he was prime minister, following Blair's refusal to do so. But as chancellor, Brown did reduce the starting rate from 20 per cent pre-1997 on the first £4,100 of earnings, to 10 per cent in 1999 on incomes between £4,335 and £5,835, before much later abolishing the starting rate in his final year at the Treasury in 2007. He also reduced the basic rate from 23 per cent pre-1997 to 22 per cent in 2000 and 20 per cent in 2007.

In April 2008, Brown would admit he had made 'two mistakes' over the abolition of the 10p starting rate to fund a cut in the basic rate of income from 22p in the pound to 20p in the pound, in his final 2007 Budget. He told the *Today* programme: 'I'll be honest about it. We did not cover as well as we should that group of low-paid workers and low-income people who don't get the working income tax credits. And we were not able to help the 60- to 64-year-olds who do not get higher pensioner tax allowance.' At the same time he introduced pension credits to provide additional income to low-income pensioners, ensuring a minimum-income guarantee.

Balls says now that New Labour was indeed the most redistributive post-war government in terms of 'what we did with the tax system'. He says that they did with tax credits – which were increased year on year – what they were unable to do with tax rates. 'One of the things which we had pushed Tony Blair quite hard on in the autumn of '96 up to '97 is whether we should increase the top rate of tax.'

The government redistributed more radically than any government since the Second World War, Balls says, through a combination of the minimum wage, tax credits and also pension credit, as a way of using tax revenues and tax expenditure to increase substantially the incomes of the bottom half of the income distribution. Then you add in public services, 'and in my mind, the expansion of NHS spending is a big act of redistribution, because it's for all'.[4] As Balls points out, 'That [is a] more overt act of distribution than I think any government had done since 1945.' In other words, while tax rates – especially top rates – broadly stayed the same, other changes at the bottom of the scale did have a considerable impact.

Tom Clark, a distinguished economist, author and journalist, and formerly a special adviser under Brown at the Treasury, explains what the thinking was on the inside when it came to redistribution: 'I remember an experienced official in the Department for Work and Pensions [DWP] saying, "If you want to get Gordon to sign off on something it's a good idea to stick a chart on the front showing the big gain going to the poorest 10 per cent." That's a bit of a caricature, of course, but there was a lot in it. When the times got tough he was a redistributive politician ... for much of his term in the Treasury, when the economy was strong, he was in the fortunate position to be a "distributive" rather than a redistributive chancellor, with considerable freedom to spread the fruits of growth as he saw fit. And he chose, to a remarkable extent, to concentrate them on banishing the worst of Britain's poverty problem as he understood it.'[5]

Most of the 'distribution' came through twin drives to eliminate child and pensioner poverty. The latter was ultimately the more successful in terms of results: the share of pensioners beneath the poverty line was cut in half. This was a historic achievement, Clark points out. 'Since the days of the [1601] poor law ... the words "elderly" and "impoverished" were as good as synonymous, but by the time Brown left office a pensioner was no more likely to be poor than anyone else. This remarkable advance was made easier than it might have been because this was progress that went with the tide: the pensioners of this era had far better workplace pensions than the cohorts that had gone before.'

By contrast, child poverty – where even more political effort was expended – proved harder to shift, 'because the underlying drift of society was less supportive', says Clark. There were, for example, many more lone parents than a generation before, and at least when New Labour arrived in power the vast majority of them were not in work. Progress was made on employment, 'but the options available were often not great, and the new minimum wage back then remained low. Against that backdrop, to have ultimately got – depending on the measure – around a million children out of poverty was another remarkable feat. Some worried that the focus on "children" and "pensioners" was in some way akin to restricting attention to the "deserving poor". But in these years ... around four poor households in every five contained either a child or a pensioner, so this wasn't so far from a general war on poverty.'

Clark explains that with both child and pensioner poverty, the most important tools by far were sharp increases in means-tested benefits. 'But steeped in Labour history and keenly aware of bitter lingering memories of the interwar means-test, Brown was desperate that his transfers should not be thought of this way.'

He fought 'tooth and nail' to get money into the new family tax credits in particular, Clark testifies. Although Blair had originally given a speech about ending child poverty 'in a generation', it was Brown who converted these words into so-called 'public service agreements' – that is, self-binding redistributive efforts. Ahead of nearly every Budget or autumn statement, Brown 'would face down Blair's demand to put the largesse to attractive alternative uses, such as easing the council tax or further boosting NHS spending', Clark says:

> A couple of times I sat in the Number Ten den when these arguments were playing out, Brown bulldozing over the Blair objections – punchily articulated by the PM's private secretary Jeremy Heywood – about how expensive the poverty commitment was. Once I heard Blair himself concede of the child poverty pledge: 'Yes, it was one of those [speechwriter] Peter Hyman specials: you read it out, sounds great, then you think "shit, that sounds expensive".' Brown, by contrast, raised the resources with, in [post-war Labour chancellor] Hugh Dalton's phrase, 'a song in his heart'. As Labour is back in government it's very important that Labour people don't assume that action on poverty happens automatically because their lot is back in power: last time it happened because Labour had a chancellor who was hell-bent that it should.

Brown is often seen as a high-spending chancellor. But, intriguingly, he was also conservative when it came to elements of what could be called 'social spending', because of his desire to concentrate resources where they were most sorely needed. Widows' benefits, for example, were cut, and 'he'd air impatience with teachers with bad backs spending years on the sick, and he was sceptical about Adair Turner's [2002] pensions commission, which Blair had used as a device to ramp up the universal pension which he had come to judge as politically necessary'. Brown was initially resistant to Blair's aim of increasing universal pensions. New Labour had made what Tony Blair now regards as one of the government's biggest mistakes when the basic state pension was increased by inflation – what Blair has called a 'derisory' rise of just 75p a week, which led to criticism from both sides of the argument: those arguing for more and those arguing for less. Some in Labour were keen to blame the Thatcher administration for breaking the link between pensions and earnings, and Labour did eventually restore the earnings link, which would become the 'triple lock'.

Clark concedes there are elements to criticise in Brown's economic record. These include 'the ease with which it proved possible completely to unwind the Brown settlement for families. The right balance between targeted and universal support is inevitably fraught, and Gordon was aware of the delicacy – boosting universal child benefit and introducing universal winter fuel payments for pensioners. He also extended his tax credits far further up the income spectrum than traditional means-tested benefits ever did.'

Clark concludes: 'Brown created a welfare state that coped well with the economic tsunami that hit Britain in 2008: remember, the foodbanks didn't come under him, only later under austerity. If he hadn't have been there, New Labour might have been more like Bill Clinton's New Democrats, who banked everything on their economic boom and connived with the political right in cutting holes in the safety net, ultimately with the socially ruinous results for poverty seen in the Great Recession. Brown showed terrific application to the anti-poverty cause in power, and has, as a campaigner since leaving office, shown remarkable continuing dedication to the cause.'[6]

Also little known is that early in his time as chancellor, Brown became chairman of the Interim Committee of the International Monetary Fund – enabling him to oversee reform of key international institutions, further the cause of global South debt alleviation and build the international contacts that enabled Britain to lead the world through the global financial crisis that would later engulf – and arguably make – his premiership.

This didn't stop the generally partisan readers of the *Daily Telegraph* in May 2024 voting Brown as the worst chancellor of the past three decades – ahead of even the Liz Truss ally Kwasi Kwarteng. This was partly because of Brown's role in selling Britain's gold reserves. Between 1999 and 2002, the Treasury sold 401 tonnes of gold – out of its 715-tonne holding – at an average price of $275 an ounce, generating about $3.5 billion during the period. Some economists claim that the gold was sold at the bottom of the market – in 2011 the price reached more than $1,900 an ounce, and in May 2005 it stood at more than $3,000 – and the Bank of England is said to have opposed the move.[7]

But his poor rating among *Telegraph* readers was also because of perceptions over the financial crash of 2008–9. The right's achievement, particularly in the 2010 election, would be to persuade many voters that the measures Brown took swiftly, after allegedly failing to 'fix the roof while the sun was shining', were because of his irresponsible desire to spend rather than because of a crisis in the global banking system triggered in the US.

Brown's hard-won reputation for fiscal responsibility made it possible eventually to raise national insurance to pay for improvements in the health service without significant opposition. He skilfully used an inquiry by the economist Derek Wanless to prepare the ground for several years and come up with the recommendations he wanted. The subsequent *employees*' (as opposed to recent employers') national insurance rise – of 1 per cent – announced in April 2002 was, perhaps, the only popular levy hike, and it was pivotal in providing long-term funding for the NHS, with health spending rising by 43 per cent.

But in another sign of major tensions at the top, Brown was furious that the prime minister, and not he, had announced the move, and reportedly told him, 'You stole my fucking Budget' after Blair announced the £12 billion NHS boost on BBC1's *Breakfast With Frost*.

Spending on the NHS at the end of the two-year spell in 1998–9 was 4.6 per cent of GDP (having remained under 5 per cent since the 1940s), and by the end of 2009–10 it had risen to 7.5 per cent. It was still at 7.3 per cent in 2019–20, just before the Covid crisis, showing how even the Tories had accepted the changes to spending levels brought in by Brown.

Incidentally, the *Sun* was critical of Brown's spending on the NHS, despite its popularity. It wrote attacks including: 'Taxer Brown', 'Chancellor's cure for the NHS is a massive gamble – using our money' and 'If Gordon returns to tax and spend and hikes taxes, we will be gunning for him'. The *Sun*, Rupert Murdoch's tabloid, was in fact already 'gunning' for Brown, whom it saw as a powerful centre-left Scot, quite different from Blair, who went well out of his way to court the Murdoch stable, as we shall see.

Nonetheless, Brown was, at this stage, far from immune from courting the *Sun* and the Murdoch press more broadly himself, and as the investigative journalist Nick Davies outlines in his book *Hack Attack* on the Murdoch-led phone hacking scandal, this tax episode 'evidently panicked Brown, who contacted the *Sun* and agreed to rearrange his diary so that he could go to their office that day in order to try to make peace'. With Balls, Brown sat down with the *Sun*'s political editor, Trevor Kavanagh, for an interview which, 'according to one of those present, rapidly became a negotiation about policy', Davies reports. 'Kavanagh insisted that Brown should accept the advice in that morning's *Sun* for the NHS to start buying in services from private medical businesses.' At the end of the tense encounter, Brown agreed that the NHS would receive not one penny of extra funding unless it agreed to 'reforms' and 'modernisation'. As Davies concludes: 'The language was coded, but the meaning was clear: private health companies would be allowed into the NHS.' Brown denies there was any hint at NHS privatisation at the meeting.

Michael Gove, the former cabinet minister who is now editor of the right-wing *Spectator*, says: 'My critique would be spending was too high for too long, because [Brown] wanted to come in on the crest of a wave ... The other thing is that while the public service agreements that Brown put in place were a highly effective way of driving change across government, on the one hand, he was perfectly willing to work with the private sector through PPP and PFI [private finance initiative].'[8]

On PPP, Brown's determination to push through a £30 billion public-private partnership to refurbish the London Underground was widely criticised as a waste of taxpayers' money. It was also firmly opposed by the London mayor, Ken Livingstone, whom Brown intensely disliked. The PPP scheme was devised by Brown and Treasury aides alongside the consultants PricewaterhouseCoopers. PPP and PFI were controversial, not only in the eyes of the left who saw it as the thin end of the wedge to privatisation, but also more broadly, as any company that needed to borrow money had to do so at a higher cost than the government would have been able to, so it was immediately a more expensive way to borrow. The advantage for Brown was that it did not count as government borrowing, because it was the companies who paid for the debt, but they then passed on that cost. Other concerns included transparency, and questions about the quality of assets returned to the public sector at the end of contracts.

Balls has a nuanced but of course more positive overall analysis of the period economically. 'I think that we established monetary and fiscal credibility by the early actions in 1997 and sustained that all the way through the ten years until the financial crisis.' He also points to '[our] reputation for low inflation and prudence, while substantially increasing public spending or public services and putting in place redistribution to tackle child and pensioner poverty, which had a huge impact. By the time you get to 2005 ... you have this huge increase in spending on the health service, financed by the national insurance rise for which we don't pay a political price because the trust we had won allowed us to go further ... Every left government in the previous decades had only raised taxes when they failed and [needed to] make up a gap. We went out and said, we want to do more. We want to raise taxes to do more.' It is undeniable that the fiscal prudence did allow for rising public services spending, and indeed redistribution, until the 2008 financial crash. Further, there were no recessions during those ten years between 1997 and 2007, partly thanks to the stewardship of an independent Bank of England.

As Balls says, 'The economy grew strongly in those ten years, and that was throwing up resources.' Nonetheless, after 2001, the ability of the economy to continue to produce tax revenues from growth diminished somewhat, 'so it was more of a struggle'. Plus: 'there is the [question of] did we do enough to really tackle weaknesses in growth and living standards in some places. I don't think we did.' Balls also laments the lack of action on the increasingly topical and urgent issue of housing, saying 'in particular, we didn't do enough' on that area.[9]

Some critics, coming at spending from the left, claim that Brown's record on poverty was not so cemented into the British politics of the age that it became a consensus which the Tories under David Cameron and his chancellor George Osborne could not change. Perhaps this was impossible; perhaps the Conservatives were always going to pursue that ideological agenda and portray Brown's record on poverty as helping 'scroungers'. But Winston Churchill and Harold

Macmillan had not tried to challenge the post-war great welfare state reforms of the 1945–51 government, with Macmillan's council housing programme even building on them. On the other hand, this is, arguably, largely about perception: the real cuts that the Tories made were often on defence, the Home Office and in local government.

Balls refutes the idea that New Labour economic reforms did not become consensual.

> The only things which last in politics are the things which become consensual, and when they become consensual, sometimes the politics goes out of them ... So central bank independence, a choice for the UK, the introduction of the minimum wage and tax credits, the national insurance tax rise in 2002 – to put the National Health Service on that funding trajectory. Those are big landmark policy innovations which Gordon drove, which have stood the test of time and become consensual. And in that sense, I think there's a parallel with Margaret Thatcher, in that there were things which were contested and things she got wrong, and when she left, there was a debate about her legacy. But when you think about the Thatcher settlement, there's parts of that which have lasted, endured and become consensual. And the same is true for Gordon.

Some Westminster observers say that Thatcher's most significant political achievement was forcing Labour to change fundamentally, abandon its hard-left approach and adopt what could be called a Thatcherite agreement around fiscal policy, privatisation and even industrial policy. Despite the Tory pursuit of austerity under David Cameron and his chancellor George Osborne, the same could be said of Brown's legacy, when it comes to the subsequent spending on the NHS especially.

Of the true significance behind that slogan 'prudence for a purpose', Balls says:

> I think that in the history of Labour, and you could say this of left-of-centre governments around the world, in France and Germany, in America as well, that often a view has been taken that the only way for a left-of-centre government to succeed is by prioritising stability and economic retrenchment ... We said you didn't have to

be remembered as the guy who implemented tax rises and spending cuts, because that version of austerity was the only way to succeed ... The phrase we always had was 'prudence for a purpose', and it was the prudence that unlocked the purpose, and it was doing those difficult things on the economy which allowed you to have the longest sustained rise in NHS spending, and actually to win the public trust for a tax rise, not because you'd screwed the economy up and have to close the deficit. And it allowed us to spend money to reduce child poverty into the millions in that part of the Labour government. And those were kind of landmark Labour achievements, a purpose made possible by the prudence.

The Democrat strategist and friend of Brown's Bob Shrum stresses the significance of the national insurance rise to pay for the NHS, and says more broadly of Brown's period at the Treasury: 'I'm not an expert on British history, although I know probably more of it than most Americans, and I would suspect that he's the most significant Chancellor of the Exchequer that this country has had, at least in modern times. He's a reformer, but he was also someone who really made the economy work and made it work much better.'[10]

The 1997 general election manifesto made no commitment to undo any of the 1980s deregulation of the City. Brown and Blair introduced a 'business manifesto' entitled 'Equipping Britain for the Future'. At its launch, Blair told his specially invited City audience that they would be the 'entrepreneurs' champions'. The City made substantial contributions to the Treasury coffers through which Brown could increase funding for public services, especially from 2001 onwards with a radical shift away from the limited public spending he had committed to in Labour's first two years of office. Corporate receipts from the financial services industry accounted for up to 25 per cent of revenue into the Exchequer. But in retrospect it could be argued that Brown relied too much on financial services and did not do enough to rebuild the manufacturing base, one that Brown had seen decline at close quarters, in Fife, and elsewhere, throughout his life.

There is no doubt that Brown and Balls had – after a Faustian pact with the City of London, and, to be fair, to ensure a flow of tax revenues from financial services to go on public expenditure – fostered a regulatory regime with too light a touch when it came to the commercial banks. Ed Miliband has long conceded this failure of New Labour to friends privately.[11] And Balls himself admitted when he was shadow chancellor under Miliband in 2011 that 'regulation wasn't tough enough' during this period. 'All around the world the banks behaved irresponsibly, but regulation wasn't tough enough. We were part of that. I'm sorry for that mistake, I deeply, deeply regret it.'[12]

At his annual Mansion House speech to the City, Brown may have broken tradition by not wearing a bow tie, but he fulfilled the Tory tradition of lavishing praise on his audience. 'The City of London has established itself as one of the world's greatest financial centres for over three hundred years,' he said in 1997.[13]

Though Balls regrets the lack of regulation, he points out that the atmosphere at the time was for the opposite. He outlines the context, including that the Bank of England itself had 'a rather chequered history on bank regulation ... And there was a whole plethora of overlapping different bodies, which were essentially ... self-regulatory ... We wanted to make changes on the regulation side alongside bank independence. And we set off on this long process to what became the Financial Services and Markets Bill, which established [in October 1997] the FSA ... And in that whole debate about unifying statutory regulation, the whole critique of what we were doing was that we were regulating too much.'

Addressing a conference in New Hampshire in 2011, Brown also admitted he made a 'big mistake' over the handling of financial regulation. 'We set up the FSA believing the problem would come from the failure of an individual institution ... We didn't understand just how entangled things were.' Brown added that he had to 'accept responsibility' but that he was not the only one who had made mistakes. This led the Conservative Party deputy chairman Michael Fallon to say: 'These are the first words of contrition Gordon Brown has uttered in his entire political career.'

Speaking at the Institute for New Economic Thinking in Bretton Woods in April 2011, Brown added that he had come under 'relentless pressure' from the City not to over-regulate. He said: 'We know in retrospect what we missed.'[14]

Balls transferred from being an adviser to being an MP in 2005, and when he was swiftly appointed as a Treasury minister in April 2006, he was tasked by Brown to try to improve the government's relationship with the banks and the City, which by this point was 'pretty bad', Balls says. 'Gordon was not popular because he was seen as being too heavy-handed and regulatory.' The Tories at the time joined in with the criticism that Brown was 'too heavy-handed'. Some leftists at the time argued they were all wrong, and we now know they were.

With the wisdom of hindsight, Brown and his team, in common with economic ministries around the world, allowed the interconnected banking sector to become exposed to global shocks, while light-touch regulation gave the green light to extreme risk-taking and the sale of complex products such as subprime mortgages. The resulting international financial crisis that was to explode under Brown's premiership a decade after he entered the Treasury – and his handling of it – came to define his entire political record.

12

Iraq and International Development

Although Gordon Brown's focus during this period was on the domestic economy and doing what he could to help make people better off, increasingly foreign affairs began to play a major role, none more so than the 2003 invasion of Iraq, but also his desire to boost international development. Seven years after John Smith's death, 2001 would prove a different kind of turning point in Labour, and indeed in Tony Blair's premiership and in British history, as public opinion shifted over terrorism and war. No one could have predicted how radically 11 September 2001 would shape the legacy of the prime minister, whose decision apparently to back America whatever it did in response placed him at odds with most of the membership of his own party and even seriously jeopardised his erstwhile popularity with the nation.

In the build-up to the Iraq war, it was portrayed by the US government, if not by that of the UK, perversely, as a reaction to 11 September 2001, which had nothing to do with Iraq. On 9/11, the majority of the terrorists who flew planes into the Twin Towers in New York and the Pentagon in Washington DC were actually from Saudi Arabia, an ally country of both the US and the UK. Some had reportedly trained in Afghanistan, from where Osama bin Laden was leading the al-Qaeda Islamist terrorist organisation.

US administration officials under George W. Bush, especially Dick Cheney and Donald Rumsfeld, tried hard to link 9/11 with Iraq, whose regime under Saddam they wanted a pretext to remove. That pretext became that they possessed 'weapons of mass destruction' (WMD), which both the US and UK governments and intelligence services claimed were being developed by Saddam. The brutal dictator had gassed the Kurds, and killed 'his own people' as Blair repeatedly said. But he did not have the WMD that were claimed, and his government was in no way linked to 9/11.

Alastair Campbell was involved in redrafting an intelligence dossier on Iraq with the head of MI6, John Scarlett, emphasising the alleged threat from Iraq, including to Britain, which became known in the media as the 'dodgy dossier'. It resulted in one headline, in the *Evening Standard*, suggesting Saddam's missiles were '45 MINUTES FROM ATTACK'. In reality, Blair probably favoured regime change anyway, as shown by the memo from Blair's foreign policy adviser David Manning as early as 14 March 2002 – a year before the invasion – written after a dinner with Condoleezza Rice, George W. Bush's national security adviser.

'We spent a long time at dinner on Iraq,' Manning wrote. 'It is clear that Bush is grateful for your support and has registered that you are getting flak. I said that you would not budge in your support for regime change but you had to manage a press, a parliament and a public opinion that was very different than anything in the States.'[1] And it's hard to imagine Brown himself going against the Americans, though he might not have committed British troops, as Blair did, and as Harold Wilson declined to do despite great pressure from the Americans while supporting the Vietnam war in principle, in 1967.

Brown now regrets backing the Iraq war, though he claims he was largely left out of its planning. He takes the position of Blair's ally David Miliband, that had he known then what he knows now about the lack of weapons of mass destruction, then he would have opposed military action. Brown even implies that had Robin Cook and he been speaking, Brown might even have followed him to the backbenches – which could have stopped the war or at the very least Britain's involvement in it.

Despite working together in cabinet meetings, Brown and Cook were not speaking after their falling-out many years earlier, well before their brief rapprochement during the flight from Edinburgh to London on the night of the 1997 general election. On 9 March 2003, Clare Short called Blair 'reckless' for his apparent determination to involve British troops in Iraq, and threatened to resign as international development secretary in the event of war without a second UN resolution – a key reason that led to Cook's resignation, on 17 March. But Blair persuaded Short to stay, arguing that she could make a difference to the peace process. He deployed James Wolfensohn, the president of the World Bank, to phone Short and tell her to remain in government. Short eventually resigned on 12 May that year, blaming the invasion's aftermath. Brown, Short's political mentor through that period, is said to have been aware of both stages of her staggered move to quit. 'She told me of her doubts about the war,' Brown confirms today.[2]

Short says:

> In the run-up to the Iraq war, Gordon and Tony were estranged. Gordon said nothing at the cabinet meetings – mind you, hardly anyone spoke. After the first meetings when people felt free to give an opinion, discussion halted. My interventions on 'just war theory' and so on, were not welcome. On a few occasions Gordon invited me for coffee immediately after the cabinet meeting. I would talk about my worries and doubts about Iraq and he would talk about his doubts about proposed changes to hospitals [market reforms and foundation trusts]. Then John Prescott brought Tony and Gordon together and Gordon was active in the cabinet and beside Tony with his strategy of claiming – falsely – that [Jacques] Chirac had said he would not back any [UN] Security Council resolution. Gordon did ring me up one weekend when I was coming close to resignation and asked me what I would say in my speech. I think he was calculating fairly carefully. His instincts are very pro-American (and pro-Israeli). The tragedy is, as I reflect on it, that if Robin, Gordon and I had stood firm against backing the invasion of Iraq, Tony would not have been able to do it.[3]

Brown seems to agree with this. He now says ruefully that Cook did not consult him over his sensational resignation. Perhaps Brown just might have joined him, despite being perhaps the biggest pro-America 'Atlanticist' in the Labour Party?

> Robin did not approach me to say, you know, 'I've got a sense that there are no weapons.' I mean, he said it publicly but he never talked to me privately about it and he made his own decisions and obviously I had no evidence to believe that we were being told false

information, so I kept [saying] we wanted to see the documentation. I then met the head of MI6 [Richard Dearlove] and asked him, because I was worried that the information we had was not correct. But I didn't have the information to go on to be sure.

No, Robin had been in front of us and Robin had a clearer view. So, you know, he felt very strongly that there were no weapons. And I did not have that evidence ... I met a lot of people during that period of time. I met a lot of religious leaders who were very worried about the war, and I understood their misgivings. But I had to go on the basis that I was being given this information. I had no way of contradicting it. And every time I asked for confirmation, I was being told ... that there were these weapons ... But I was misled like everybody else and I did ask lots of questions ... and I didn't get the correct answers.

One senior former minister says that Brown did, in fact, privately believe the Iraq war was a mistake at the time. He claims that Brown could easily have 'moved against' Blair on the issue – and brought him down – with his supporters in the House of Commons voting against the invasion, but that Brown refrained from doing so simply for the cynical reason that he did not want to take over in the circumstances of a massive breach in relations with the US. He believes that had Brown been prime minister himself at the time, he would not have committed British troops.

But Brown insists that he was 'cut out' of a close inner circle around Blair on the issue, including unelected advisers led by Campbell, and intelligence chiefs, as well as the likes of the defence secretary Geoff Hoon, and that when he consulted the head of MI6 he was categorically assured there were weapons of mass destruction in Iraq. To be fair to Blair, he had no obvious reason to bring his chancellor into such discussions, though he might have done as the key partner in New Labour. Blair says today: 'He would have backed it and did back it ... He was supportive of it at the time, and also, I think, supported particularly the fact that we had to stick with America.'[4]

Meanwhile in Afghanistan, which the US and UK had also attacked after 9/11, 212,191 people died, including 457 British troops. The Iraq invasion – which was more controversial because of the issue of terrorist training in Afghanistan – was broadly supported by the media and even the public until it became clear there were no WMD. On 15 February 2003, the BBC reported that a million people protested, though police put the figure at more like 750,000. Nonetheless, a month and three days later on 18 March, amid high tension, the House of Commons voted for Britain to join the war by 412 votes to 149. Gordon Brown was among those who voted in favour.

Britain under Blair did 'stick with America' and from 20 March to 1 May, it took part in the invasion which the US called 'shock and awe'. According to a 2010 assessment by John Sloboda, the director of Iraq Body Count, some 7,500 civilians were killed in the invasion along with 179 British armed forces personnel.

Brown puts the situation like this:

Look, on Iraq, I got us out by negotiating us out by 2009. [In June 2009, as all remaining British troops withdrew from Iraq, Brown would tell the Commons he was ordering an inquiry into the 2003 invasion of Iraq led by Blair and Bush, perhaps reflecting his own regret over backing the war.] That was three years before America ... All I can know is that I took British troops out of Iraq as quickly as I could ... It took time because of the danger to British lives.

I could have made an almighty row about it [in 2003] and broken with America, said where they had got it all wrong and we'd have ended up with a fight with America, that I didn't think was going to be the best way forward for Britain. So in a way I was admitting that there was a problem about us being in Iraq by trying to get us out quickly and we did get out, but I didn't want it to become a central dividing line between ourselves and the rest of the allies. That was my judgement. But remember Labour lost votes in 2005 to the Liberals because of Iraq, and that is one of the reasons we didn't win in 2010 as well, that we never got lots of these votes back.[5]

Nonetheless, though he was careful not to go on the record frequently in favour of what he knew was a controversial area, Brown did back the war, and he told the Labour conference in September 2003: 'It is right to back our leader Tony Blair in his efforts today to bring security and reconstruction to Iraq.' During that same speech in Bournemouth, Brown began to set out his stall as the next leader, appealing to the party faithful and ending the speech to prolonged applause with: 'This Labour Party – best when we are boldest, best when we are united, best when we are Labour.'

While there was a huge financial cost in Iraq in the aftermath of the invasion, there was a political cost for Blair, due to the widespread public opposition to the war. At the 2005 general election, Labour still won but its majority went from 167 seats to 66. The Lib Dems gained 11 seats, and the Conservatives won an extra 33. Blair's grip as New Labour's most electorally appealing asset was finally slipping, which had obvious implications for Brown, who was by now thinking seriously about taking over as Labour leader and as prime minister. Robin Cook, incidentally, was saying by 2004 that Brown would easily walk a leadership contest against Blair.

Elsewhere internationally, Brown pursued his passion of development. In a move that was a far cry from today's politics, Brown tripled the aid budget. He also negotiated on the world stage to cancel the debts of the world's poorest nations, playing a key leadership role in the international Jubilee 2000 campaign. The campaign built on the Great Jubilee celebration in the Catholic Church to pressure governments and international organisations such as the World Bank and IMF to help relieve debts owed by the most impoverished countries. It ultimately led to the cancellation of over $100 billion in debt.

Brown was personally committed to action on this after being lobbied by charities in the international development sector, such as Oxfam and Christian Aid. Despite the challenges of opposition from the right, including a largely hostile media, though in an easier climate than today's, an announcement of a $23 billion debt relief package crowned a stunningly successful campaign fought by Jubilee 2000 for several years. As the *Guardian* said in an editorial in September 1999: 'The deal, though not all that was wanted, represents a major new commitment on the part of the industrialised countries to tackle deepening global economic inequality. The campaign could never have succeeded without the personal support of Gordon Brown – whose drive on this issue owes something to his mother and late father, both Jubilee 2000 activists. The chancellor took a bold gamble before the Cologne G7 summit in June, announcing the British £171m contribution in an attempt to conjure comparable largesse from other countries. The tactic appeared at first to have failed when world leaders declined to match their rhetoric with cash, but in the end it paid off.'[6]

The debt relief cause so close to Brown's heart since he was a boy, when his parents would fundraise for Christian Aid, came to a head again at the G8 summit in 2005, held at the Gleneagles Hotel in Auchterarder, Scotland, and hosted by Blair. The summit coincided with the 7/7 bombings on the transport network in London, to where Blair returned. Brown forced an agreement to support the world's poorest countries and tackle climate change. At the pre-meeting hosted by Brown in London before the summit, it was agreed that $40 billion of debt owed to the World Bank and IMF by the eighteen most indebted countries would be written off.

The move was highly popular among international development activists, and the Make Poverty History grassroots movement staged many demonstrations in favour of action. In the largest in Scottish history, more than 200,000 people marched in Edinburgh on 2 July that year. Meanwhile the singer Bob Geldof organised concerts in each of the G8 member states, also on 2 July, as well as a concert in Edinburgh on 6 July. In London, a concert featured Annie Lennox, Sting, the Who and a re-formed Pink Floyd.

Kevin Watkins, the former chief executive of Save the Children, worked with Brown from early in the Labour government. 'When people look back at the debt reduction story, they tend to overlook just how difficult it was,' he says. Oxfam had been conducting research and campaigning on Africa's debt for several years, wringing a few concessions out of Kenneth Clarke in particular. However, the UK, IMF, World Bank and G7 saw the problem first and foremost as a liquidity crisis, not one of solvency. 'The argument was essentially that a bit more growth through market liberalisation and a big cut in fiscal deficits would resolve the debt issue,' says Watkins. 'Gordon basically demolished that approach on day one. I can vividly remember doing a presentation to him at the Treasury, getting flak from his civil servants, and him essentially endorsing the case for a major debt reduction. HIPC [heavily indebted poor countries] had around $100bn in debt written off. It released huge amounts of finance that went into schools, health clinics and clean water, and so on. There is absolutely no way it would have happened without Gordon. He led from the front in bulldozing Germany, France, the US, Japan et al. to recognise the problem and act – and he fundamentally shifted the positions of the World Bank and IMF.'[7]

Watkins also reveals a Brown tactic, the likes of which we will see again: 'We would occasionally get messages indicating that the Treasury – in other words Gordon – would like to receive a petition and demands for more action ahead of G7 meetings, which he would then use with G7 finance ministers to point out the groundswell of public opinion.'

Watkins goes on: 'For me what was striking was his mastery of the technical detail and his ability to translate hard-nosed analysis into an effective political strategy ... There is a sense in which New Labour fundamentally shifted the UK's standing on international development – and set a big part of the global agenda through more poverty-focused approaches.' If Margaret Thatcher's greatest impact was in setting the parameters of political debate for over a decade after she left office, 'part of Gordon's legacy was in shifting approaches to aid, driving multilateral solutions to global problems ... which locked the UK into a progressive international agenda. The fact that Cameron was so heavily engaged in the SDGs [sustainable development goals] and the "leave no one behind" agenda is one illustration, though [Brown] was very adept at pushing people behind it in the UK.'

Brown had shown by now that he wanted to spread his wings beyond the UK, having an impact on the global stage, which would prove very important for the global financial crash in 2008. Brown had taken his first tentative steps in international politics in 1999–2000, before taking a backward step in 2003 over Iraq, and then moving more forcefully in this area in 2005, which meant he was better prepared for what lay ahead. And like his friend Jimmy Carter, Brown would much later return to the international development agenda which helped fuel his passion for politics in the first place.

13

Division, Consolidation and Transition

Gordon Brown's achievement of running the Treasury for a decade is unprecedented in modern British history, underlining the relative political and economic stability of the majority of the New Labour years.

He was the longest-serving Chancellor of the Exchequer since William Gladstone (who occupied the post four times between 1852 and 1882) and he held the office for the longest continuous period since Nicholas Vansittart two centuries previously. Some say that the post of home secretary is the one that always ends in failure. But Brown likes to joke, 'There are only two types of chancellors: those that fail and those who get out in time.'

Brown could not be seen by many objective historians to have failed at the Treasury. Indeed, he was rated as the most successful post-war chancellor in an Ipsos poll of nearly 300 academics belonging to the Political Studies Association in November 2006. They rated Brown's period at the Treasury as 7.9 out of 10, with his nearest rivals being Kenneth Clarke (Brown's Tory predecessor as chancellor, between 1993 and 1997) and Stafford Cripps (the Labour chancellor between 1947 and 1950), both rated as 6.1 out of 10. Brown was ranked as the most successful chancellor on providing economic stability, working independently from the prime minister and leaving a lasting legacy on Britain's economy.[1] Yet despite these achievements and this legacy, in 2004 Tony Blair, amid personal tensions between the two, tried to remove Brown from his position as chancellor, and if he couldn't do that he was going to limit his powers dramatically and those of the Treasury.

Relations between the two men – once seen as politically joined at the hip – had reached a nadir. The bitterness and the outright hostility displayed by their teams of outriders deeply scarred the final years of Blair's premiership and Brown's chancellorship. Some Blair allies still believe that, in retrospect, he should have moved Brown out of the Treasury after the second landslide election victory, his moment of peak political power.

Brown says today: 'I think the position with Tony really changed more after 2001. I think he began ... he thought he didn't need somebody like me.'[2] Blair denies this and, although he did try to make Brown foreign secretary, says he could not have served three terms without Brown at the heart of the cabinet as chancellor. Despite Blair and Brown both favouring significant increases to public-service spending, a key difference between them was that Brown used Treasury targets while Blair preferred a shake-up within the services themselves, including in the NHS.

The New Labour founders had worked well together in the first parliamentary term, delivering Bank of England independence and beginning to spend more on health and education. But the NHS became the focal point – perhaps an excuse – to exacerbate tensions on both sides which were perhaps more realistically, given their similar political outlook, about tensions over the leadership and handover question. The government was planning to increase spending massively here, but Blair also wanted to reform it and open it up to more private enterprise, something Brown decided to oppose.

In a kind of proxy war with Blair, Brown battled with Alan Milburn, the Blairite health secretary from 1999 to 2003, who would come back under Keir Starmer in July 2024 to advise the new government on health reforms. Brown fought against the Blairite drive for foundation hospitals and foundation trusts. A foundation trust remains an NHS organisation but gives greater input to patients and staff to have more of a say about the way in which services are provided. Foundation trust status was awarded to hospitals that had showed they demonstrated the highest clinical standards, quality leadership and a great record of patient responsiveness and safety. However, foundation hospitals were the cause of many arguments within the party, including at the Labour conference in autumn 2003 in Bournemouth where the general secretary of Unison, Dave Prentis, condemned the plans as 'ill-conceived'. This echoes some of what happened in education, with Blair supporting more independence from local authority control to give greater parental choice and an opportunity for improvements in schools.

Brown once also remonstrated with Alastair Campbell about the Blair-led health reforms, arguing that Campbell, surely, did not share the politics behind them.[3] As Brown has said: 'Where the private sector can add to, not undermine, NHS capacity and challenge current practices by introducing innovative working methods, it has a proper role to play – as it always has – in the NHS. But it must not be able … to exploit private power to the detriment of … equity.'[4]

Balls claims that the policy differences were not, in the end, so real. He scoffs at the idea that Blair was in favour of even stealthy privatisation in the NHS, in another indication that the Blair–Brown rows over policy were basically fake to suit both camps in their symbiotic battles. 'When it came to the crunch, he agreed with us, not with Alan Milburn, much to Alan Milburn's anger.' Balls adds that Blair was seeking to look 'radical'. Of the row about the limits to markets in health, Balls naturally lays the blame at the Blairites' door. 'The reason why it became a big sore was because the outriders around Tony, people like Alan Milburn and [the transport secretary] Stephen Byers, went out to find a dividing line with Gordon on reform,' he claims. 'We were always for reform. What we wanted was to have a conversation about good reforms and bad reforms, and we weren't going to be in favour of bad reforms. Very rarely did Tony ever say he disagreed with us. Actually, he knew that it was a bit [of] rubbish, really. So he would play along with the idea of me being the problem. In politics, there's always people who end up becoming the lightning rods.' Mandelson, of course, would play the same role for Blair.

However, Milburn today fundamentally disagrees. He says the policy differences were real, and blames Brown, and Brown's people, for the 'dividing line' approach, suggesting that it was partly driven by the chancellor's political ambition.

> As ever with Gordon, it's complex. There were perfectly legitimate policy differences, on choice, competition, foundation trusts, and some of those were appropriately legitimate concerns, but they were obviously amplified into a political narrative. I think he wanted to

pick a fight, to exemplify the dividing line with me and by extension with Tony. And I think part of that was political; part of that was personal. He obviously thought I was going to run against him or something, when Tony went, for leader. So his personal ambition and policy differences were together in one, and obviously that came to a head around the whole reform agenda. He put himself on the anti-reform end of the spectrum ... It became a drag anchor on progress, a drag anchor on change and a drag anchor on the modernisation of public services. And frankly it weighted the government down with an ongoing political row, sapping energy, time and resources out of the very thing that we were elected to do, which was to try to modernise Britain, because that essentially was the Blair mission. It was a huge inhibitor of the progress that we needed to make. The government could have achieved so much more. Unfortunately, the dividing line overpowered the shared mission.[5]

Milburn and Brown had previously got on well when Milburn was chief secretary to the Treasury in 1998–9. But when he became secretary of state for health, 'obviously we were just locked into an extremely difficult political relationship, and obviously a much more difficult personal relationship between us. We were often in ferocious arguments, with briefings taking place.' By briefings, Milburn is referring to leaks and damaging accounts to the press.

Robin Cook recalled how when Brown was presenting the Wanless review to the Commons in November 2001, 'the House was bemused at the chancellor of the exchequer metamorphosing into the health secretary. Any other chancellor would have referred to the report briefly and announced that his right honourable friend the health secretary will be making a statement on it tomorrow. If Gordon would only be satisfied with being our best chancellor for half a century he would have fewer problems and a lot more personal satisfaction.'[6]

The rows between Brown and Blair from 2001, then, were frequently about health reforms, but they were also about education, and specifically making students pay tuition fees, which Brown opposed. Everyone in government knew that more money had to be found for universities, and that the ordinary taxpayer who might not have benefited from higher education should not pay the bill. The argument was between those who backed fees, including Blair, and those who backed a graduate tax, including Brown. One Downing Street political aide at the time recalls Brown being visibly 'fired up about fees after delivering a lecture to Tony on the subject'.[7]

Some Blairites claim that Brown opposed fees partly, at least, to ingratiate himself with the left. But to be fair to Brown, he and Nick Brown, the unofficial whip of pro-Brown MPs, were credited with saving the Blair premiership at one point during a vote over top-up fees on 27 January 2004. Brown spoke personally to three of the key rebels that night, making the argument that they had to vote with the Labour government. Charles Clarke told *Channel 4 News* that night, referring to Brown: 'He wasn't pushing for particular changes in the wording of the bill. What he was pushing for, and which I agreed, was further close consideration of the picture, particularly of entrance into the professions and the situation of people on low and middle incomes and how we could deal with that.'[8]

Top-up fees were additional charges students incurred when pursuing a higher education qualification after completing a lower-level qualification, to obtain a full undergraduate degree, subsidised by loans for poorer students. The vote which Nick Brown unofficially whipped came on the day before Blair had to defend himself in the wake of the conclusions of the Hutton Inquiry into the death of the Iraq weapons inspector Dr David Kelly. After a six-hour debate, the government won the vote by a tiny margin of just five, with 316 voting for the bill and 311 against. Whether this row was really about higher education, or because of the impending inquiry, the chancellor and his camp had twisted the arms of at least three MPs and ensured the bill was passed. Brown preferred a graduate tax, but pulled together for the sake of the party. It is an example of Brown coming to Blair's aid, and the two men working alongside one another when it really mattered, at a time when this was happening less frequently.

As we have seen, Brown believed Blair had indicated he would leave office after ten years as Labour leader, not as prime minister – meaning 2004, not 2007. This led Brown famously to say to Blair in 2004, according to a briefing by the Brown camp to the author Robert Peston, 'There is nothing that you could ever say to me now that I could ever believe.' To be fair to Blair – who denies Brown said this – he would have had more pressing matters worrying him than an agreement apparently made some ten years earlier, and, in retrospect, that such an agreement was made when there was no way of knowing what events would shape and shake his premiership, or even if he would have one, was questionable.

But by early 2003, according to one former political adviser in Number Ten, Blair allegedly believed that Iraq could be his 'Falklands' – a reference to the 1982 conflict that is seen as having benefited Margaret Thatcher in the 1983 general election – and off the back of it he would be riding high in the polls, and therefore strong enough to remove Brown from the Treasury.[9] Even the deputy prime minister John Prescott, who hated the press and normally played down talk of tensions, gave an interview to *The Times* in 2004, confirming there had been a 'pretty serious breakdown in relations' between Blair and Brown. This was largely about Blair stepping down, but other policy issues had become tension points too, as Brown presented himself to the party and occasionally to the Labour-supporting media as more 'real' Labour.

At a particularly tense meeting of the Parliamentary Labour Party, on 10 January 2005, as the former Labour MP Chris Mullin recalls in his diaries, 'Gordon and [Blair] were given a bollocking the likes of which I have never previously witnessed over the damaging revelations in the weekend press about their rift.' Clive Soley kicked off, talking of 'anger and frustration' at the feuding and rebuking the so-called 'anonymous' briefers. He warned that they weren't as anonymous as they might think, and if they didn't stop Soley would name them. Angela Eagle called for discipline at the top and warned the party could yet lose the next general election. Blair replied, 'I hear what you say ... we all have, and we will act on it.'[10]

Despite his central role in the government's agenda, Brown initially found himself sidelined in planning for the 2005 general election campaign, which was to be fought against a much more difficult backdrop than the 1997 and 2001 contests because of the chaotic aftermath of the Iraq war, which had not proved to be the electoral boost Blair had hoped for.

Balls says that what was 'very bruising for Gordon' was that he got 'thrown out [of 2005 election planning] in the autumn of 2004'. Alan Milburn was put in place by Blair to run the forthcoming general election campaign, in an attempt to control general election strategy which Brown had been heavily involved with in 1997 and 2001. This proved another difficult time for Milburn, who says, 'I must have had

"MUG" written across my forehead in capital letters,' and for the Blair government. Milburn claims that Brown 'went on strike' and 'downed tools', refusing to campaign properly and help with strategy. This was 'a very destructive thing to do'. Milburn points out 'we sort of pulled through in the end and won for a third time, but I hope in retrospect that [Brown] and the people around him would accept it wasn't his finest hour'.

The general election campaign planning without Brown was, by Easter of 2005, 'going really badly', according to Balls. 'They need Gordon. Alastair Campbell and Philip Gould rang me to say, can we put the band back together? Essentially Milburn gets pushed aside for Gordon. I do the first press conference. I was a candidate – a candidate! – and I did the first press conference of the election campaign with Alan Milburn. The reason I did it was Alan Milburn says to Gordon, if you're taking charge, get Ed Balls into the press conference with me, and Gordon says, "Okay then," and I end up in the middle of it, but it was slightly odd.' It was indeed bizarre that neither Blair nor Brown fronted the first press conference.

To rebut reports of tensions between the party's top two men, Labour's spin doctors staged an awkward photo call in Kent when Blair bought an ice cream for Brown from an ice-cream van, but few were fooled by the show of forced camaraderie. By this stage Tony Blair was no longer the electoral asset that reached out to the voters of 'Middle England'; his credibility had been badly battered by the Iraq invasion and the Hutton Inquiry into accusations that the government exaggerated the case for war.

After the general election on 5 May, Brown did fight off an attempt by Blair in the 10 May reshuffle to sack him as chancellor and move him to the Foreign Office. But in the end, Blair hesitated and decided against the plan to break up the Treasury, which Ed Balls dismisses as 'mad'. Blair had tried to clip Brown's wings by keeping him at the Treasury but in a reduced role, and failed. Now he failed to move him to the Foreign Office which, while one of the great offices of state and a crucial one, would have stripped Brown of all his domestic power that had been wrestled over in 1994.

In the immediate aftermath of the Iraq victory, Blair felt powerful enough to try to ease out Brown from his role. When he failed to do that, Brown hit back and began to put pressure on Blair to do as he had promised and resign. It soured the partnership between the two men until Blair eventually did step down – because of pressure from Brown and Brown's allies, who also exploited policy divisions and media and public hostility over Iraq and related foreign affairs.

There is no doubt Blair felt harassed by his old friend. He describes Brown thus in his memoir: 'Political calculation, yes. Political feelings, no. Analytical intelligence, absolutely. Emotional intelligence, zero.'[11] However, today of this period he says: 'Now, when things came later and we actually did have a policy disagreement around some of the reform programme, that was more difficult ... because we had two views about this. [But] I always say to my own people, if we had fought, and he had gone out of the government, I'm not sure we would have got three terms. Because I think there would have been a rupture inside the government. Especially post-Iraq, it would have really destabilised the government. And as it was, we contained the debate and the argument, whatever disagreements within the tent. But I think had he gone out, it would have been problematic and quite brutal in the end without necessarily being at all productive for the country or the party.'[12]

Blair continues:

> What I used to say to people is he can't be blamed for wanting the top job and I point out he's a very bright guy and he's got a lot of political ambition. He's been chancellor for ten years. I mean, it would be odd if he didn't want it. I never resented it at all. Actually, the only thing I think that was ever difficult between us in that latest stage was the policy disagreement, because I was always of the view that New Labour had to carry on to the next level of 'New'. I think he and others, both Eds [Balls and Miliband], felt that we were going too far, but that's a policy disagreement. It's not an ignoble ambition to be prime minister. Why shouldn't he have it? So I was always completely understanding of that. The question was, what would he do when he got there? But you know, that he should be entitled to that ambition I never had any difficulty with at all.

Despite the arguments with Blair, Brown continued to exert unparalleled power over domestic policy – often in the face of opposition from Number Ten and occasionally within his own department. As chancellor, Brown was master of almost all he surveyed. Michael Gove, who became an MP in 2005, recalls being 'in awe' of Brown when he first arrived in the chamber and saw him at the despatch box. 'One of the things is that he has a physically powerful, potentially intimidating presence, and he had both a mastery of his brief and also an operation with parliamentary private secretaries behind him and notes on everyone who might intervene. So you were slightly, not awestruck, but almost in awe of his ability to focus and discharge the matter in hand with almost brutal efficiency.'

Gove remembers one debate when Labour appeared in trouble 'and we thought that we could exploit it ... George [Osborne] made an absolutely good speech, and then Gordon just destroyed him, not in a cruel sense, but it was just the case that Gordon had internalised the argument that he needed to make. And yes, there were notes in front of him, but it was a bravura performance ... There's a driven quality to the way in which he operates and works, which means that he was the superlative standout figure [but] he also had a flip side of certain insecurity.'[13]

Wider political change was also in the air in 2005. The Conservatives were undergoing a generational shift as they elected as leader, succeeding Michael Howard, the relatively unknown David Cameron, a great admirer of Blair's political skills. The Liberal Democrats under Charles Kennedy had just amassed the highest number of seats in their history, benefiting from the growing mistrust in Blair and the sense that the New Labour project was looking jaded.

Balls recounts how events were moving now towards Blair's departure: 'There was this rolling conversation in which Alastair [Campbell] and Philip [Gould] wanted Tony essentially to say he will stand down for Gordon in the next Parliament.' Blair at one point told Campbell and Gould that his closest advisers had clearly come 'to tell me to fuck off'.[14] But, Balls continues, 'none of us thought that was a good idea, because you knew it made Tony a lame duck. In the end, Tony doesn't have any of it. We're going to have a stable and orderly transition, which was my phrase to Phil Webster [of *The Times*], Tony and Gordon have agreed on a stable orderly transition. And then we set off on this long dance, which is, when's it going to happen? This is continual. They keep coming up with all sorts of things which have to be done first.'[15]

Alastair Campbell, in turn, explains what his position was to Blair and Brown during the talks before the 2005 general election: 'The fact is, if we're going into this campaign with an absolute focus on the economy, you're going to stick together? Well, if you are, then this is going to have to be a joint campaign.' Campbell points out that the policy differences between Blair and Brown were, in reality, minimal. 'There were some people close to Tony who felt, we've really got to make this look different, sound different ... More than that, I think, there were some people around Gordon who felt we have to emphasise the differences rather than the similarities. I've never really bought the idea of the six of one and a half-dozen [of] the other.'[16] Campbell believes, in other words, that people around Brown behaved worse than those around Blair. However, Campbell's point about the need to 'look different, sound different' concurs with the thesis of Balls from the other side of the Blair–Brown divide.

Charlie Whelan fits into a pattern of certain individual Brown employees who were clever masters of the dark arts. It was Whelan who leaked details of Budgets and other spending announcements to the press – the *Sun* and the *Mail* as well as the *Financial Times* and the BBC – against conventions at the Treasury but in a style which became absolutely standard among Brown's Tory successors as chancellor. And it was Whelan who more spectacularly brought down Peter Mandelson from his position of trade and industry secretary in 1998, four years after the bitter fallout from John Smith's death, by leaking to his friend, the anti-Mandelson writer Paul Routledge, details of a private £370,000 home loan given to Mandelson by the wealthy businessman, Brown supporter and fellow MP Geoffrey Robinson.

Whelan has now admitted being the source behind the leak, though he claims Routledge was going to remove reference to the loan in his impending hostile biography of Mandelson but couldn't because his manuscript was discovered by two *Guardian* journalists in the House of Commons press gallery.[17] 'Yes, I was the source, but Paul was going to take it out,' Whelan told *The Times* in a 2022 interview. 'Had [the *Guardian* reporters] not done that, it would never have seen the light of day.'[18] Whelan, who is described as charming by friends but was a hugely divisive figure among political reporters excluded from his inner circle, did not respond to an approach to speak for this book.

Having discussed it with Brown, it does seem that he himself did not know about the Whelan home-loan leak. 'I wouldn't do that to Mandelson or anyone else,' Brown says. Presumably there was a feeling that it was best for Brown to have plausible deniability. Though as Campbell reflects: 'I have massive respect for Gordon, but you do have to take responsibility for the people who work for you.'

Blair remains relaxed about past tensions with Brown. According to one former Downing Street aide, Blair would describe 'in a matter-of-fact way' privately how Brown was using the *Mail* and the right-wing media to attack people from the right on the one hand, and the *Guardian* to go after Blair from the left on public service reform and tuition fees on the other.[19] But Blair says today of the briefings against him: 'I never really saw any of it, but people would say to me they were briefing the papers and all the rest of it ... I always used to say to people, the thing is, I'm speaking to Gordon the whole time so I don't really care what was in the media, because I'm talking with him.'[20]

By all accounts, Balls was distinctly rude to Blair at the meetings. When I ask Balls about that, he says: 'There's this continual thing going on where, if Gordon doesn't announce he's in favour of this tough thing on anti-terror, or this tough thing on defence, the Murdoch papers will never support him. And we're all to go and see Tony as part of this process. There were a couple of lunches in Number 11 with me and Ed [Miliband] and Gordon and Tony and Philip and Alastair Campbell, the people who put it back together in 2005, and it's undoubtedly true that at some of those meetings, Ed and I said, "Tony, we want to make this really cooperative, but you know, you've got to get on with it."' Balls, a bright but precocious young MP, was telling his leader here to resign and make way for his mentor, Brown. 'And I do think that Tony was very angry as a sitting leader of the Labour Party to be told by these young punks like me that he should get on with it. So when you say to me, I've been rude to the prime minister in that moment, probably, but not in a nasty way or antagonistic way. It was more like, "Come on, let's get it over with".'

On Thursday 7 September 2006, during a visit to the Quintin Kynaston School in St John's Wood, north London, Blair announced in a filmed statement to the Press Association that he would stand down within a year. Brown and his press officer Damian McBride had not been told about this plan. 'I'm not going to set a precise date now,' said Blair, looking relaxed and smiling slightly. 'I don't think that's right. I will do that at a future date, and I will do that in the interests of the country.' Demonstrating that his hand had been forced by months of pressure from the Brown camp and others on the party's left, Blair continued: 'I would have preferred to do this in my own way – but the next party conference in the next couple of weeks will be my last party conference as party leader.'[21]

Tensions had been running high that year at all levels of the party – including the cabinet – over Blair's prolonged support for Israel's war with Lebanon, and events were brought to a head by renewed plotting against the prime minister.

In what became known as the 'curry house conspiracy' to remove Blair and install Brown at Number Ten, Tom Watson, a Brown ally and a defence minister at the time, and three fellow West Midlands MPs – Siôn Simon, David Wright and Khalid Mahmood – met at a Wolverhampton Indian restaurant on 31 August to plan a letter calling on Blair to stand down. Watson was rumoured to have met with Brown on the eve of the gathering. Watson and his wife were indeed holidaying in Scotland prior to the restaurant gathering and they went to see Brown in Fife. But Blair's departure was not discussed according to a friend of Brown's, who points out that it was the *Sunday Times*, the Murdoch-owned outlet that frequently pursued Brown stories, which somehow caught word of the alleged 'plot'.

The letter, signed by seventeen MPs, which said it was in the interests of the party and the country for Blair to step aside, was leaked to the press, and Blair publicly described Watson as 'disloyal, discourteous and wrong', adding that he would have removed Watson from his post had Watson not resigned after the leak. Benjamin Wegg-Prosser, the former special adviser to Peter Mandelson who was now the director of Number Ten's strategic communications unit, later reflected that the Blair camp's reaction to the rebel letters had been 'remarkably naive, coordinated through random email chains, conference calls and impromptu meetings' while the Brown operation was running a 'more disciplined war room'.[22]

Blair's circle was deeply dejected. They knew the end was coming – and they blamed Brown and his aide Damian McBride. On 8 September, the day after Blair's St John's Wood statement, Wegg-Prosser emailed

Blair's aide Anji Hunter, saying: 'I am shattered. I did my best – taking orders from our friend in Brussels [Mandelson, then an EU trade commissioner] and my own instincts. Key points impossible to have proper negotiations cos every time they agreed something they leaked it to the papers. GB kept demanding TB's endorsement yet at the same time told that he had to leave office immediately cos the public hate him – weird or what.'

Blair's team had tried to reveal that Brown was behind the coup. And in a sign of the extent of ongoing tensions at the top, McBride had brazenly emailed David Hill, a Number Ten media official, saying: 'Gents, I am still getting calls from lobby ... saying they have written up today's story as Number 10 accuses Brown of plotting coup, and saying that far from knocking that down tonight – their Number 10 contacts have been reaffirming it. This is not what the PM told GB would happen, Can you explain? Damian.' To which Blair's chief of staff Jonathan Powell wrote: 'I hope you don't reply to any of this ridiculous person's ridiculous emails.'

Watson's departure was swiftly followed by the resignations from government positions of six other signatories. These preceded Blair's St John's Wood announcement, which came at just after 3 p.m. An hour earlier, Brown had broken his silence, telling reporters: 'I want to make it absolutely clear today that when I met the prime minister yesterday, I said to him, as I have said on many occasions to him and I repeat today, that it is for him to make the decision.' And in a reference to the 1994 'deal', Brown added boldly: 'I said also to him, and I make clear again today, that I will support him in the decisions he makes, that this cannot and should not be about private arrangements but what is in the best interests of our party and, most of all, the best interests of our country.'[23]

'I think it's important for the Labour Party to understand that it's the public that comes first and it's the country that matters, and we can't treat the country as an irrelevant bystander in a matter as important as who their prime minister should be,' Blair said. 'The first thing I'd like to do is to apologise actually on behalf of the Labour Party for the last week which, with everything that's going on and in the world, has not been our finest hour, to be frank.'

At the Trimdon Labour club in Blair's Sedgefield constituency, on 10 May 2007, Blair did announce he was stepping down after ten years as prime minister and thirteen years as the Labour leader. In September 2024, Blair told the *Observer*: 'I would have stayed if I could have, is the truth. But it was impossible by then.'[24]

Blair had always known, even if it was sometimes in the back of his mind – especially during the preoccupation with the Iraq war – that however unfair he now saw it to be, he would have to fulfil his promise to stand down in favour of Brown. Indeed he would have to back him. Blair would be only fifty-four when he resigned as prime minister, in many ways in his prime, and he would resent it, or at least be dismayed by the events that led up to it. Blair today tells friends that he is 'a fan' of Brown and, at least publicly, talks about him with grace. But to Blair's camp, it seemed wildly absurd that he should be ousted. Friends of Blair say that, as was clear in 1994, he has the natural touch when it comes to the voters. One says that Brown understands the British electorate too, but 'only if their views are shown on a chart'. From Brown's point of view, Blair broke his promise to stand aside, and this of course came after Blair had also 'gazumped' him back in 1994.

Either way, on 10 May 2007, in a seventeen-minute speech at Trimdon that moved those present, Blair said the judgement on record was 'for you, the people, to make' and, in an apparent reference to Iraq, he apologised for 'the times I have fallen short'. However, he concluded: 'Hand on heart, I did what I thought was right. I may have been wrong – that's your call. But I did what I thought was right for our country ... This country is a blessed country. The British are special. The world knows it, we know it, this is the greatest country on earth.'

In Washington, President George W. Bush led global tributes, saying Blair was a 'remarkable person. And I consider him a good friend ... When Tony Blair tells you something – as we say in Texas – you can take it to the bank. He's a political figure capable of thinking over the horizon. He's a long-term thinker.'

Back home, Brown, who had led tributes to Blair at that morning's cabinet meeting where Blair had made it clear he was going, said: 'I think I spoke for millions of people when I said to the cabinet today that Tony Blair's achievements are unique, unprecedented and enduring ... At all times he tried to do the right thing.'[25]

Six days later, on 16 May, Brown secured the backing of enough MPs to ensure he would not face a contest to become the next Labour leader and prime minister. Brown had 313 nominations, leading to his only challenger, John McDonnell – who would later serve as shadow chancellor under Jeremy Corbyn – to concede because he could not gain the required forty-five MP nominations. McDonnell described the outcome as 'a blow to democracy'. On 17 May, Brown and his team were travelling back to London on a train from a campaign visit. 'We were having a glass of wine as it was my birthday,' Sue Nye says, 'when I got a call from party headquarters ... and he [Brown] was the uncontested leader. So we raised a toast.'[26]

After the party's nomination procedure closed, Brown gave a brief speech before the media in the City of London, joking that it was 'almost embarrassing to have so much support'. He said that 'the conversation with our country is just beginning' and promised a 'different type of politics', with 'open and honest dialogue'. Asked about Iraq, Brown said, 'We cannot deny there was a big division in public opinion,' but pointed to reduced British troop presence there, the withdrawal from three provinces, and obligations to the UN and a democratically elected Iraqi government. Pressed to praise Bush, Brown said merely that the relationship between a British prime minister and a US president 'must be a very strong one'. For his part, Bush from the White House called Brown 'a good fellow'.

Addressing the British people, Brown said: 'To those who feel that the political system doesn't listen and doesn't care, to those who somehow feel powerless and have lost faith, to those who feel Westminster is a distant place and politics all too often a spectator sport, I will strive to earn your trust – to earn your trust not just in foreign policy, but in our schools and our hospitals and our public services and to respond to your concerns.' Referring back to his roots, he said: 'As a teenager, I chose this party because of its values – values I grew up with and knew.'

According to the Labour Party's rules, Brown was anointed at a special leadership conference in Manchester on 24 June, with Harriet Harman elected as his deputy, but had to wait until 27 June to become prime minister after Blair gave his resignation to the Queen.[27] At that special conference, finally relieved of some of his frustration, Brown heaped praise on Blair, saying: 'All of us will remember his leadership – his leadership has made Britain stronger, more tolerant, more prosperous and fairer. And let us never forget his towering presence in the international community, his work on Africa, climate change, his work to win the Olympics for Britain, and the skills and determination he brought to securing peace in Northern Ireland. Tony Blair's achievements are unprecedented, historic and enduring.'

But looking ahead, in comments that annoyed some Blairites, Brown said: 'Don't let anyone tell you the choice at the next election will be change with other parties and no change with Labour. Because when I take office on Wednesday I will, as our party has always done, heed and lead the call of change.'[28]

After ten years as chancellor, with a broader role than many who had gone before him, Gordon Brown had delivered a strong and growing economy, and made numerous changes to help build a better Britain. Amid record spending on the NHS and other public services, pensioner poverty was on the wane, and Brown had made good on his lifelong passion of tackling child poverty: he was on the way to halving it.

After so long as the second-most-important man in government, albeit with a legacy that meant he was already one of the most consequential and successful political figures of his time, Brown finally now had his chance to show how he could bring his formidable talents to the top job. He showed every sign of making the most of the challenge. But even before the onset of the financial crash, he was to find that the premiership presented new challenges that threatened to overwhelm him.

PART THREE

Number Ten (June 2007–May 2010)

14

Honeymoon and Hesitation

On the morning that Gordon Brown, at fifty-six, became prime minister – Wednesday 27 June 2007 – he started it with a final one-to-one meeting with the outgoing premier Tony Blair. The mood was calm after some three years of arguing on and off over what Brown saw as Blair's promise to leave after ten years as party leader. Blair was busy preparing for his last session of Prime Minister's Questions (PMQs) and Brown was thinking about his first speech, without notes, when he would be the new prime minister in a few hours, standing outside Number Ten. Later that year, just before Christmas, Blair would call Brown and tell him that people want 'a leader, not a workaholic'.[1] But that day Blair offered little advice. 'There was no big discussion,' says Brown.[2]

After Blair's final PMQs at noon, where he was given a standing ovation by MPs from both sides of the House instigated by the Tory leader David Cameron, Blair told the Commons, 'I wish everyone, friend or foe, well, and that is that, the end.' Brown returned to the Treasury and had a modest lunch in the staff canteen. He then wanted to rehearse his speech for outside Number Ten, as ever with his long-time closest aide Sue Nye. Nye recounts: 'There was an area in Downing Street that was set aside for demonstrators and we didn't know how vocal they would be. So we ended up in the bizarre situation where his press secretary [Damian McBride] and I pretended to be demonstrators trying to shout him down.'[3] Nye's jeers were more polite than those of McBride, who shouted things like 'blood on your hands' and 'murderer' and 'Scottish git'.[4]

After that, Brown thanked the staff in his private office, and when he left that room, he found that civil servants had come out to line the landings of the Treasury building. Blair, meanwhile, was resigning to the Queen at Buckingham Palace just after 1 p.m. At 1.30 p.m., Brown left the Treasury, with his wife Sarah, for his own first personal audience. Her eleventh prime minister, Brown was with the Queen for the best part of an hour, from 1.51 p.m. to 2.48 p.m. 'She was very well informed,' Brown says. 'She wanted to talk more about the Commonwealth. She was interested to hear of events and well up on them. She watched television and so sometimes was ahead of me in knowing what was going on. It was a change from my Budget representations each year – then she was interested in [talking about] the horse-racing industry.'[5]

Outside Number Ten, with Sarah standing slightly behind him, he announced before the media pack: 'This will be a new government with new priorities ... And at all times I will be strong in purpose, steadfast in will, resolute in action in the service of what matters to the British people, meeting the concerns and aspirations of our whole country.' Proposing to lead a government of 'all the talents', he said his 'mission' was to provide 'the best of chances for everyone'. He quoted the motto of Kirkcaldy High School, his alma mater: 'I will try my utmost.' Brown added: 'This is my promise to all of the people of Britain. And now let the work of change begin.' Brown turned to walk into Number Ten, pausing briefly for photographs with Sarah, to find inside that the staff, who had earlier clapped out Blair, were there to greet him. There was a happy surprise when he got to the end of the line, as Sarah had arranged for their sons, John and Fraser, to be there to give him a hug.

Sue Nye recalls: 'I remembered how it had felt in 1979 when Jim Callaghan had left and then Margaret Thatcher had arrived. The same lining of the halls to bid farewell to Jim and then the clapping in of the new prime minister. There was a mixture of emotions – sadness but also excitement. Gordon completely understood that the Number Ten staff, who had worked for many years for Tony and his family, would be sad on his departure. So I got the staff together in the Pillared Room and Gordon's first act was to thank them for the work they had done and for the welcome they had given his family. He ended by joking that there weren't many days in anyone's life that you met the

Gordon (right) with older brother John (centre) and parents, John and Elizabeth. Gordon has said of his mother, 'She was very tall and very dignified' and of his father: 'In my memory [he] still towers before me like a mountain.'

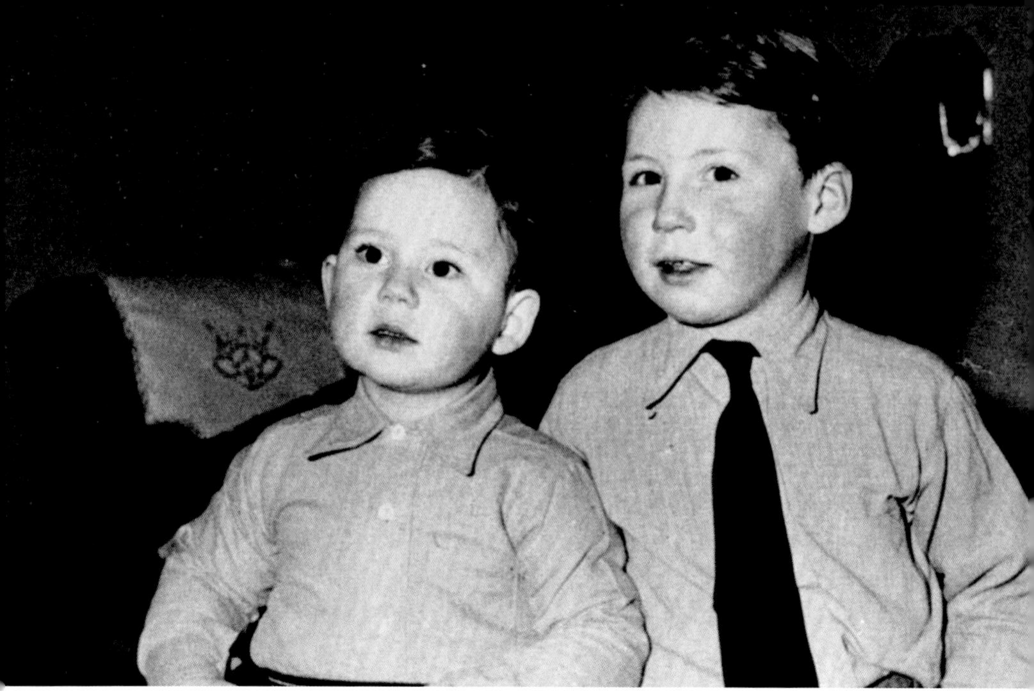

Gordon (left), with older brother John in 1953. Gordon would follow John into Labour politics and to Edinburgh University, where some saw John as a future prime minister.

Gordon aged six, in 1957. He and his brothers were given a safe, happy childhood.

Gordon (left) with younger brother Andrew in 1959. Many years later, Andrew would work closely with Gordon in parliament.

Brown, the student radical in 1972. A disrupter against the university establishment, he was the second – and last – student allowed to be elected to the position.

Brown, graduating alongside his father, the Rev John Brown. Brown gained a first in history despite rarely turning up for tutorials. The department head wrote to him saying: 'I am not sure I know what you look like.'

Brown working as a journalist for Scottish Television in Glasgow before he was elected to parliament in 1983. He covered major sporting events as well as current affairs.

Brown playing tennis, one of several sports he loves. It was while on court in 1971 that he realised an old rugby eye injury had come back to haunt him.

Brown with reforming Labour leader Neil Kinnock in 1989. Kinnock today says Brown 'has all the kit'.

Brown with Ed Balls, whom Brown describes as 'probably the most gifted economic thinker of his generation'.

Brown with Tony Blair (right), Margaret Beckett, and John Smith (left). Smith was a mentor to Brown, who in turn was the senior partner to fellow 'moderniser' Blair – until Smith's death in 1994.

Brown with Tony Blair and advisers including, from left to right, Ed Balls, Peter Mandelson, Charlie Whelan and Alastair Campbell.

Brown shuns the traditional white tie at his Mansion House speech in the City as chancellor.

Brown with Blair celebrating their landslide election victory in 1997. Brown was soon to unveil his surprise move to make the Bank of England independent.

Brown with Blair in government. Despite acute tensions, when the pair worked well together they were perhaps the most successful partnership in British politics since the Second World War.

Brown with on-off friend and fellow Scottish Labour intellectual Robin Cook. Today Brown says, 'Robin Cook was right and I was wrong' over the 2003 invasion of Iraq.

Brown with Tony Blair and deputy prime minister John Prescott (left) in 2006, a year before Brown finally became prime minister.

Brown at Raith Rovers. As a boy he dreamed of playing for and managing his beloved football team. He would later settle for being president of its supporters club.

Brown returning to Kirkcaldy High School, whose motto he quoted upon entering Number 10: 'I will try my utmost.'

Gordon and Sarah Brown with their baby son John, in 2003 while Brown was chancellor. Their first child, Jennifer, had tragically died days after being born in 2002.

Brown with Sarah in Downing Street on becoming prime minister in 2007. A charity leader in her own right, she often provided critical support in difficult times.

Brown in Iraq. As prime minister, he would withdraw all British troops from that country by 2009.

Brown with world leaders whom he would rally to work together during the 2008 financial crash. 'Gordon has a plan,' said Barack Obama.

Brown alongside his very different Italian counterpart Silvio Berlusconi, with whom he had a bizarre encounter in 2009.

Brown emerging from Number 10 to call a general election on 6 April 2010 for the following month.

Brown during a televised debate with the Conservative leader David Cameron (centre) and Liberal Democrat leader Nick Clegg (left) in 2010.

Brown addresses Citizens UK on 4 May 2010, in the most electrifying speech of the campaign – too late to help him stay in power.

Brown with Sarah and Ed Balls at a classroom during the dogged 2010 campaign.

Brown's encounter with Rochdale voter Gillian Duffy on 28 April 2010. Moments later, he would be caught on air describing her as a 'sort of bigoted woman'.

Brown resigns as prime minister with Sarah looking on.

Gordon Brown's last moments in Downing Street, with Sarah, their boys Fraser and John, and various advisers and ministers.

Brown gives the eve-of-referendum speech at the Maryhill Community Centre in Glasgow on 17 September 2014. The speech was credited with tilting Scottish voters towards staying in the UK.

Brown greets supporters after his Maryhill speech against independence.

Brown speaking against Brexit in 2016. He was passionately opposed but reluctant to appear on the same platform as David Cameron.

Brown with Sarah at the Leveson inquiry into media intrusion prompted by the phone hacking scandal, in June 2012. Brown remains committed to taking on the Murdoch media empire to this day.

Brown with brothers John (left) and Andrew (right). The three were never competitive and remain very close.

Brown at the United Nations, where he has served as special envoy for global education since 2012.

Queen, became prime minister, spoke to the president of the United States and then get told to put the kids to bed.'[6]

Brown now had to make a cabinet reshuffle. Having decided that he wanted to avoid the modern trend for drama, with the media speculating on every coming and going in Downing Street, he made phone calls to ministers and whips at his House of Commons office. Only when it was finalised did the new cabinet members get the chance to go up the street to be formally appointed. 'I had worked on a seating plan with the civil service for the first Cabinet meeting – a very fraught task – which took place that Thursday afternoon,' Sue Nye says. 'As the meeting started, Gordon remarked that it was strange to see Alistair [Darling] sitting in the chair he had sat in for so long.' Brown agonised over making Ed Balls chancellor, but it was seen as 'a step too far'.[7]

However, Balls now says that he was at one point in the frame to be chancellor. In the months leading up to Brown becoming prime minister, the pair talked a lot about how the government would be structured. 'And there was a fundamental frustration for Gordon, which is he really wanted to pick up the Treasury operation and move it to Number Ten.' But Balls and Ed Miliband felt they 'needed to kind of have our own chance'. Balls adds: 'That's not a disloyal [to Brown] thing. But Gordon was continually trying to think, is there a way to use senior positions, the Cabinet Office, or a joint chief secretary, Cabinet Office minister? And I was always very sceptical about that, because we'd resisted Tony Blair wanting to mess around with the chief secretary and Cabinet Office. I had said that I wanted to go and do a department.'

Brown did tell Balls that he was to be chancellor when Brown was officially elected leader and crowned at the party conference at Manchester. Balls recalls:

> He pulls me into the [conference centre] kitchens [and says] 'I need to have a conversation'. And he said to me, 'I've thought really hard about [this] and I'm going to be bold, and I'm going to make you chancellor and David Miliband foreign secretary. And you need to think now about who you want to be your chief secretary, and what's your plan. It's going to be hard. That's what I'm going to do.' And I said, 'Well, I've always thought this is not a great idea,

because I think it's quite sudden, soon, but if that's what you've decided, that's your call.

So I then spent Sunday thinking, who could you make as your chief secretary, and how do you manage this and all this kind of stuff. Then on the Monday, he asked me to go to the Treasury [for a meeting]. He says, 'It's too difficult. It's too difficult. I can't do it.' And he shows me the board and says, 'Which one do you want? Do you want to be home secretary?' And I said, 'You've already told Jacqui Smith she's going to be your home secretary.' And he said, 'Which one do you want?' And I said, 'Well, I'll do the education and children's job.' He says, 'Fine, that's it. That's the deal.' So that's how it happened.[8]

This fumbled attempt at installing Balls as chancellor, who incidentally had only been an MP for two years by this point, and then the reversal of the offer, showed a new indecisiveness – even nervousness – in Brown after he took on the top job. It was an indecisiveness that he had not displayed as chancellor but that would come to define the early part of his premiership.

Meanwhile David Miliband, whom Blair had described as 'my Wayne Rooney' was indeed made foreign secretary. His brother Ed was promoted to minister for the Cabinet Office and chancellor of the Duchy of Lancaster. 'It was a significantly younger Cabinet and included the first woman home secretary,' Nye recalls. 'One of Gordon's themes was that he wanted the government to be all the talents – they became known as GOATS – so had appointed outside experts to boost his cabinet.'

Sir Alan West, recently retired First Sea Lord, worked with Jacqui Smith on national and cyber security. Mark Malloch Brown, a former deputy secretary general at the UN, was made a minister of state in the Foreign Office. Professor Ara Darzi, a brilliant surgeon, worked with Alan Johnson, the new health secretary, on NHS reforms but insisted he would take the job only if he was still allowed to operate because he didn't want to get too far from the front line.

'Gordon was never London- or Westminster-centric so also decided to take the Cabinet outside of London to all corners of Britain,' Nye says. That had happened only twice in history before, under Lloyd George, who did not want to interrupt his holiday in Inverness, and when Wilson held a cabinet meeting during the Labour Party conference in Blackpool over prices and incomes policy. Brown held his first cabinet meeting outside Number Ten in the West Midlands on 8 September 2008, in a move spun as Brown being more in touch with the people. Hazel Blears, the communities secretary who had publicly backed the idea, said: 'I'm delighted that for the first time a cabinet will be meeting outside of London. We will be taking politics closer to the people and hearing their concerns first-hand.'[9]

Brown's in-tray included early signs of an economic slowdown; the question of whether to speed up troop withdrawal from Iraq and Afghanistan; attacks from the Tories over the development of a perceived European 'constitution'; and a fiery debate over how long police could hold terrorism suspects without charge after Blair's attempt to lengthen it from twenty-eight days to ninety days was defeated in the Commons in 2005. There was also the threat among some higher education institutions to increase top-up fees to more than the £3,000 maximum; a revolt among NHS staff over the use of private provision; a row over nuclear power and the extension of power stations; and major backbench rebellions over his repeated attempts to press ahead with an idea to sell off a 30 per cent stake in the Post Office, a move that national archive minutes show he had opposed while Blair was prime minister.[10] Brown pursuing a policy he had opposed under Blair demonstrates again how minor were the differences in political outlook between the pair in reality.

But of course unforeseen events soon took over. Brown was widely seen as having a successful 'honeymoon' period as prime minister, taking a hands-on approach to failed terrorist attacks in London and Glasgow in the first few days of his premiership. Jacqui Smith, who had chaired a meeting of COBRA, the cabinet's crisis response committee, on 29 June, after two unexploded bombs were discovered in London, has said of Brown: 'He showed not a jot of panic ... He was commanding in laying out what he expected to happen.'[11] Brown addressed the nation on television that evening.

This was followed by flooding across much of England. He abandoned a short-lived Dorset holiday and gripped the handling of a separate, limited outbreak of foot-and-mouth disease at the same time. Meanwhile, he pursued something of a 'moral crusade' that appealed to his on–off ally the *Daily Mail*, in which he banned 'super casinos' and 'twenty-four-hour drinking' – new flexible licensing laws introduced by Blair – and rejected upgrading cannabis from a grade C drug to a grade B one. Brown also introduced a neighbourhood policing unit in every area, 'where you know the name of the person that can help you', as he had promised during the general election campaign, and a legally enforceable right to early cancer screening and treatment within one week.

Having responded quickly to the flooding emergency and foot-and-mouth, what advisers saw as Brown's 'father of the nation' approach gave him his highest ever personal prime ministerial approval rating of 65 per cent in August. When Brown took over as prime minister in late June, Labour was trailing the Conservatives by 32 points to 34 in the ICM poll for the *Guardian*. By 16 September, the leads had reversed in the same polling and Labour was ahead by 40 to 32, enjoying its biggest lead since September 2005. This of course partly reflected the refreshing change after ten years of Blair, whose appeal had been tainted by Iraq, but Brown deserves credit for his own specific perceived solidity, his tireless work ethic which saw him through the series of mini crises, and his empathy with the working people of Britain. Brown's aides were briefing the press that a new type of voter, 'Brown's Tories', were switching from the Conservatives to Labour because of Brown's 'strong leadership'. In foreign policy meanwhile, Brown, together with France's Nicolas Sarkozy, pushed through a UN resolution in July establishing a 26,000-strong peacekeeping force in Darfur.

Late that summer, many in Brown's circle believed he should call a snap general election on 1 November to capitalise on the bounce and gain a mandate of his own. Brown was tempted and actually appointed Douglas Alexander, who was pushing for it, as election coordinator and Ed Miliband, who was more sceptical, as an emergency manifesto author.

The autumn annual Labour conference in Bournemouth in 2007 was dominated by speculation over whether Brown was about to go to the country. Behind the scenes the decision to go ahead was taken: journalists were briefed, the advertising agency Saatchi and Saatchi came up with the clever poster slogan 'Not flash. Just Gordon', early drafts of the manifesto were produced and the unions were given the green light. Amicus, the single biggest union, began to print election material. Union political officers were instructed to be ready to move into election headquarters. More than 200 computers were hired and 100 slots were booked at Battersea heliport.

For Brown's part, he was sceptical of the whole idea from the beginning. He knew the reason to go for it was to gain a personal mandate. He was popular at this point. But the question of whether he could lose the job he had coveted for so long played on his mind. And financially the party was arguably not ready to go into a general election. 'Douglas Alexander and I went off to investigate that. And you know, the finances were not strong,' says Bob Shrum. 'They were not what you would want going into a general election. But it still may be the case that yes, maybe we should have gone ahead.'[12]

Labour had enjoyed a good August in power. Cameron was seen to be faltering; the polls were strengthening for Brown's party. 'There's no conversation about going [for the] election. It's not part of anybody's plan,' Balls says. 'And then we all get asked to go over to Chequers in the middle of September, and on that day, we find out there is a sort of Spencer Livermore [Brown's director of strategy] plan, which Bob Shrum and he had been working on to go for an early election and maybe even to announce it in the conference speech. And this is genuinely the first time that Ed [Miliband] or I heard had about it. I'm not going to say if it's the first time Gordon had heard about it, but it was the first time there was a conversation with all of us. I thought it was going too quick – did you know what the Brown prime ministership was going to be about? And so as we then went into the week before party conference, we're not thinking we're going for early election, but the polls are really strong.'

Then on Saturday 22 September Douglas Alexander gave an interview with the *Guardian*, headlined 'PM's election chief: We are ready for poll', in which Alexander said: 'There have been significant donations in recent weeks, notwithstanding our financial difficulties in the past, we have been working hard and we will be ready whenever the prime minister decides to call the election.'[13] Balls then did an interview the following day for Radio 4's *World at One* in which, he says now, 'I'm calming things down a bit and saying, you know, in the coming weeks and months we will set out our stall.' Then, he adds, 'the Number 10 operation contradicted me. So by the time you get to the Wednesday, Thursday, big momentum.'

On Sunday 30 September, following the conference, the Browns gave lunch at Chequers to Alan Greenspan, the former chairman of the US Federal Reserve, and his wife, the NBC correspondent Andrea

Mitchell, along with Bob and Marylouise Shrum. After the meal, Brown met with his advisers including Ed Balls, Ed Miliband, Douglas Alexander, Livermore and Shrum to discuss an early general election as a group for the first time. Shrum reflects today: 'I was in favour of seeing if we could have an early election. Was the party prepared financially? Were we ready to go? I think my mistake there ... was to think that we could consider that without having a leak to the press, thereby setting up the expectation that we were going to have an early election, [and] by the time that exploration process was over, I was against having an early election.'

Balls played devil's advocate. 'Look, it's still not too late. Are you sure?' he told the gathering. But, he explains now, 'it's got this momentum, and it's in the media, and they're already talking to the unions and working out stuff. Gordon says to be sure, we should do some marginal polling. He then goes off and has this sort of messy trip to Iraq which was seen as trying to overshadow the Tories. George Osborne does his Monday inheritance tax thing, which was like a scam, because it was never an electorally appealing thing for the Tories but it was destabilising, and the marginal seat polling was also a little bit cautious.'

There was then a crunch meeting planned for the Friday, 5 October. 'I can't go to the meeting on the Friday,' Balls goes on,

> [B]ecause I'm in my constituency [Morley and Outwood] having all my election photos done, because we're having an election, but I spoke to Gordon at 6.30 on the Friday morning, and we were going for an election, and the reality was that Gordon had not decided in September, or all the way up to the conference, or at the conference, or even that weekend before we were not definitely going through with it. He hadn't made that decision, but he allowed the speculation to grow, and so it became self-fulfilling.
>
> So the marginal seat polling says it might be tighter. And then they changed their mind, and I actually had a call from [pollster] Deborah Mattinson and Ed Miliband, both of them [saying] he's been advised ... not to go for it, and he's about to change his mind. And by the time I spoke to him that afternoon, he was done. They decided. And so I then get summoned down into Downing Street

on Saturday morning, and it's all about, how the hell do you explain you're not going to have an election when you've allowed it to become clear you are?[14]

Balls says now that he took the view then, that Brown should either have decided by mid-September to go for an early general election and put every resource behind it, independent of the polls, or resisted and governed on that basis. The worst option was the one Brown took, which was to allow pressure and speculation to build, and then reverse it.

Things started to shift the other way the week after the Labour conference. At their own annual gathering the Conservatives pulled together like the ruthless electoral machine they still could be and their messaging was disciplined. Cameron put in a collected performance on BBC1's *Andrew Marr Show* on the Sunday morning, and on the Monday, the shadow chancellor George Osborne made a sudden, audacious but regressive commitment to increase the threshold for inheritance tax to £1 million.

Brown is open to criticism that he was unnecessarily thrown by that Tory announcement. Some insiders felt it caused him to 'bottle out' of calling an election. Michael Gove says: 'As it happens, I said to George that I didn't think it was the right thing to do, because I thought it reinforced the idea that we were the party of the rich, but I have to acknowledge that it was a very successful political move.'[15] Cameron at his conference speech on 3 October had declared 'let the people decide' and 'go ahead, call that election' while a hesitant Brown had until 9 October to call an election for 1 November. The conventional wisdom was that any later date would run the risk of asking voters to turn out in wintry weather – and Labour supporters might be less inclined to brave the cold.

Brown had travelled to Iraq during the Tory conference, announcing at Basra that 1,000 British troops would return home by Christmas, leaving a contingent of 4,000. It was hoped that the trip would be seen as statesmanlike. Instead, the move rebounded on the new prime minister and was widely condemned as a cynical 'stunt'. Even the respected former prime minister John Major chimed in: 'What is pretty unattractive is the nods, the winks, the hints, the cynicism, the belief that every decision is being taken because it is marching to the drumbeat of an election rather than to the drumbeat of solid, proper government. He has been letting the speculation run riot. It is clearly an attempt at destabilisation of the opposition parties.'

That weekend – as Brown and his inner circle agonised over whether to go to the country – a *News of the World* poll showed a lead for the Conservatives of six points in eighty-three key marginal constituencies, meaning that almost fifty Labour MPs would lose their seats. Brown used an interview with Andrew Marr on 6 October to end the speculation – which Downing Street had allowed to run out of control – and say there would be no autumn election.

He subsequently gave a press conference in which he claimed that he had not been fazed by the polls, but that he instead wanted more time to set out his agenda as prime minister. The inheritance tax move had plainly rattled him, along with polling suggesting Labour support was fragile. And although he continued to consider a spring 2008 election, as some say he always intended to go for, the damage was done. He was labelled an indecisive bottler – and the label stuck. David Cameron says today: '[Brown's] pretence that calling off the election was nothing to do with the polls was a big mistake. [It] was echoed by Theresa May when she said "nothing has changed" [over a social care cap U-turn] in the 2017 election. The public don't follow every dot and comma but when they are visibly taken for fools they sit up and notice big time.'[16]

The decision was arguably a political disaster for Brown. Up to now, he has maintained that his only error was allowing the speculation about an early election to run. Now, he says, 'I made a mistake … Well, I did.'[17] For as his friend and long-time media ally Piers Morgan says, it could have led to a premiership that was not only considerably prolonged, but also seen as more successful. 'I think history would have been very, very different if he called that election and won a thumping personal mandate … I think if Gordon had gone to the country, after four or five months, he would have had a powerful mandate from the electorate and that would have empowered him to do all the things he wanted to do as prime minister. Now then he really would have been one of our great prime ministers, I genuinely believe.'[18]

In fact, internal Labour polling had always shown that Labour would win – but with a slightly reduced majority. And at an encounter in Brussels, Peter Mandelson bluntly confronted Brown over his failure to call a snap election, according to a friend of Mandelson's. Mandelson told Brown that he assumed the new prime minister had declined in the end because he had feared he would get a smaller majority than Tony Blair. According to the source, Brown admitted this to Mandelson in Brussels.[19] In other words, Brown paid the price for his ego. There may be truth to this, but it was surely only part of the decision-making process.

Following the election debacle, Brown returned to work facing the challenge of rebuilding his credibility against the backdrop of an economic slowdown. Ominously across the Atlantic the 'subprime mortgage crisis' – as millions of Americans lost their homes when they failed to make repayments – was escalating. It was to spark the global financial crisis a year later which was to define Brown's premiership. In another foretaste of trouble ahead, reports about the financial problems at Northern Rock triggered panic among investors, who mobbed the bank's branches in September 2007 fearing they might lose their savings.

Towards the end of the year, Brown began to receive poll ratings that were among the worst on record for a serving British prime minister. According to a YouGov survey for the *Daily Telegraph*, in December some 60 per cent of the public were 'dissatisfied' with his performance, compared to just 27 per cent in July and 48 per cent in October. The poll gave the Conservatives a twelve-point lead on 43 per cent to Labour's 31 per cent. The ratings were seen as resulting from the snap election debacle as well as the run on Northern Rock. Rumours were also emerging about Brown's temper and 'flying Nokias', a reference to allegations that Brown threw mobile phones across rooms in Downing Street.

Brown's position was further undermined on 24 July 2008 when Labour lost the previously safe seat of Glasgow East to the SNP. Blairites were critical, and there was speculation about a leadership challenge from David Miliband. This mounted over the summer after the foreign secretary, in the *Guardian*, called for a 'radical new phase' without mentioning Gordon Brown and, when questioned, refused to rule out a leadership bid. Brown responded at the Labour conference in September with the famous line, which was later attributed to Ed Balls, that 'Everyone knows that I'm all in favour of apprenticeships, but let me tell you this is no time for a novice' – a jibe reportedly aimed not only at the young Tory leader David Cameron, but also at his own foreign secretary and younger leadership rivals within Labour. Balls revealed in July 2024 on his *Political Currency* podcast with George Osborne that the previous evening he had been at a dinner with the *Sun* team where he ran the line by the *Sun* editor and Murdoch executive Rebekah Brooks, who had said, 'That's the story: No time for a novice.'

The line demonstrated an ongoing alliance of sorts between the Brownites and the power-seeking Murdoch press at this stage, one that even helped see off allies of Tony Blair who might have been rivals to Brown, such as Charles Clarke, John Reid and Alan Milburn. In the same speech, Brown opened up more than he ever had during a conference, about his own background and his approach to politics. Also acknowledging the downturn in his popularity since the snap election fiasco, he said: 'I want to talk with you today about who I am, what I believe, what I am determined to lead this party and this great country to achieve … I didn't come into politics to be a celebrity or thinking I'd always be popular. Perhaps that's just as well. No, twenty-five years ago I asked the people of Fife to send me to Parliament to serve the country I love. And I didn't come to London because I wanted to join the establishment, but because I wanted and want to change it. So I'm not going to try to be something I'm not. And if people say I'm too serious, quite honestly there's a lot to be serious about – I'm serious about doing a serious job for all the people of this country. What angers me and inspires me to act is when people are treated unfairly.'

Brown made a rebuttal to a proposition his own aides had instigated to make more use of his wife and children to humanise his dour image. Derek Draper, the former Labour adviser and later husband of the TV presenter Kate Garraway, claimed privately that he had been asked by a Brown aide to write an article suggesting Brown use his family more in public appearances. Brown duly responded by telling that year's party conference: 'And so here I am – working for this incredible country, while trying as far as possible to give my children an ordinary childhood. Some people have been asking why I haven't served my children up for spreads in the papers. And my answer is simple. My children aren't props; they're people.'

Elsewhere at the conference, I interviewed Mandelson for the *New Statesman* and he told me he now backed Brown's premiership, which was a surprise.[20] I told Ed Miliband about Mandelson's endorsement ahead of the article's publication, and he reported it to Brown. The following week a rehabilitated Mandelson was elevated to the House of Lords and brought back to the cabinet as business secretary. In retrospect, the imaginative move – thanks to Mandelson's skills, the surprise factor, and the fact that Mandelson was a 'Blairite' who could quell criticism – nearly saved Brown's premiership.

Mandelson's appointment came after relations between him and Brown had slowly thawed during the first half of 2008. Brown had visited Brussels and had a long talk with Mandelson, then a European commissioner, about the domestic political scene. The two had once been very close and Brown, who still craved Mandelson's undeniable skill and guidance, had followed up by making regular phone calls to Mandelson and also sending him speeches.

Stewart Wood, the only Number Ten official then allowed to have contact with Mandelson, because of Brown's hesitation about trusting him, had given a dinner at his London home to which both Mandelson and Shriti Vadera, Brown's ministerial ally, were invited. Mandelson warmed to Vadera. Mandelson also had lunch with the veteran Downing Street official Jeremy Heywood. Brown had asked Heywood if he could attend that lunch but Heywood said no. However, the lunch was followed by another long face-to-face encounter between Brown and Mandelson at Number Ten. By the time Brown offered Mandelson the role in October 2008, Blair told Mandelson it was 'a no-brainer'. On the appointment, Brown declared: 'Serious people are needed for serious times.'

Towards the end of 2008, Brown also attempted to appoint the Blairite Alan Milburn to his cabinet, asking him what role Milburn wanted. Milburn says that Brown 'recognised he probably needed some New Labour cover', meaning, perhaps, distinctly Blairite cover at this stage. Milburn declined, and instead told Brown frankly that he should consider his position as leader and prime minister. 'I told him it isn't going to work – you don't trust me; I don't trust you. I was one of the few people who told him directly, "You need to consider your position. You're going to lead Labour to defeat." It was better to be honest and straightforward about it.' At this point Brown's cabinet role offer to Milburn was understandably withdrawn, though Milburn was appointed as a social mobility tsar in January 2009. Milburn reflects today that the irony of all their past arguments is that

Brown and he share a number of common values, including on the need for social mobility.

By this time, the economy was declining because of the banking crisis spreading from America, and governments around the world were faced with the daunting prospect of reacting to fears of a global financial meltdown.

The voters were little swayed by plaudits for Brown's leading role in confronting the emergency. In June 2009, a month after Brown hosted the G20 summit in London where world leaders pledged to make an additional $1.1 trillion available to help the world economy, he faced a fresh leadership crisis.

In the local elections, with the economy worsening, Labour had lost all of its councils, with some local authorities being cleared of any Labour councillors. Meanwhile the European elections were won by the Conservatives with twenty-seven seats and a vote share of 27.9 per cent of the national vote. Support for Labour – which came third – dropped significantly by 291 councillors, and the UK Independence Party (UKIP) finished second in a major election for the first time in its history, matching Labour in terms of seats and ahead of it in terms of votes. It was the first time in British electoral history that a governing party had been outpolled in a national election by a party with no representation in Parliament.

Hours after the polls closed in the local and European elections on 5 June 2009, James Purnell resigned as work and pensions secretary, urging Brown 'to stand aside to give Labour a fighting chance of winning the next election'. This was a moment of high jeopardy for Brown – probably the most vulnerable moment of his premiership – and the parliamentary party held its breath to see if any other cabinet heavyweights, such as David Miliband and Alan Johnson, would follow his lead.

At this point Mandelson rang wavering cabinet ministers, extracting oaths of loyalty. Ed Miliband also moved to prevent his elder brother David from following Purnell, urging him to remain in Brown's cabinet and allegedly assuring him that the leadership would be his after the next general election, though this is denied by the Miliband brothers. Meanwhile Alan Johnson was 'locked in' by Brown making him home secretary, and Darling was retained as chancellor though Brown had attempted to move him, just as Blair had tried with Brown himself. Plotters could not agree on a successor, and despite all the criticisms, Brown remained the towering Labour figure of his generation to whom there was no alternative. Nonetheless, the damage from Purnell's resignation was considerable, and the notion that Brown should step aside for someone more able to win the general election stuck for a while.

Less than two years after entering Downing Street on a high, Brown's stock had fallen so fast that he was dogged by dissent – in public as well as private – over his position amid growing alarm in Labour ranks that they were heading to inevitable defeat at the next election. It was little reward for the pivotal role he would play in rescuing the world economy from the brink in 2009.

15

Saving the World

It was on the evening of 2 April 2009, when G20 leaders, convened by Brown in London, agreed a framework for mitigating the crisis threatening the world's financial system and restoring growth. The crisis was a severe recession triggered by the collapse of important banks, resulting in falling earnings, rising unemployment and a sharp contraction in gross domestic product. The leaders were gathered in the grand old dining room at Number Ten, with no officials present except Tom Fletcher, Brown's highly rated private secretary for foreign affairs. Fletcher, who is now a senior UN official, recounts: 'That was where Sarkozy said, "The problem is, look around the table – compared to our predecessors we are nothing. Let's just be honest: in this room no one has a plan." And then Obama tapped the microphone, leaned forward and said, "Gordon's got a plan." And that did give Gordon real authority. He had it anyway, as the host, but from then on, it was very clear that [we were going to follow] his plan.'[1]

The summit demonstrated that, despite media attempts negatively to contrast the relationship with that of Tony Blair and George W. Bush, there was a genuine rapport between Obama and Brown.

Asked today if there was a conscious tactic by the Conservative Party to undermine Brown, Michael Gove admits: 'Yes. So, however unfair, the political temptation to tie his lengthy stewardship at the Treasury with a failure both to anticipate and properly to prepare for the crash was one that was reinforced. Hence the [failing to] "fix the roof when the sun was shining" [Tory] line.'[2] And it was David Cameron, the Tory leader, who in October 2008 had attacked Brown personally over the crash. After two weeks of cross-party support as the crash unfolded, Cameron had broken an uneasy truce, saying Brown's strategy had 'fundamentally failed' and accusing him of merely 'borrowing and borrowing and borrowing'.[3]

Brown, who reacted quickly to the crisis, puts the blame at the feet of capitalism, of self-regulation and rampant free marketeerism, saying, 'as the crisis revealed, market disciplines – particularly self-regulation and regulatory approaches that reinforced greed – were inadequate to deal with the problem. The market is a necessary but not sufficient mechanism for a continuously successful economy and society. And because we are agreed that markets depend on trust, which has to be underpinned by self-discipline (which failed) or imposed discipline, we have a duty to act in the public interest.'[4]

So what happened in the build-up to that summit, and to Brown's 'plan'? In order to answer, it's necessary to delve back into the modern history of the banking system.

The genesis of what would become a world financial crisis began in the American mortgage market and the financial experimentation that grew up around it in the 1970s. While Brown was moving from Edinburgh University into politics, America's financial institutions increasingly traded in what are called mortgage-backed securities (MBS), which effectively enabled mortgage lenders to resell their mortgages to other financial institutions. After MBS were launched by the US government national mortgage association Ginnie Mae in 1970, these experimental financial assets were first traded by a private bank, Salomon Brothers, in 1977, and quickly became a mainstream financial product for Wall Street firms.[5] Typically, MBS were segregated, based on how risky the underlying mortgages were, and pooled into collaterised mortgage obligations (CMO), before being sold on to investors.

The creation and sale of MBS and CMO formed part of a so-called 'originate and disseminate' model in which consumer debt of varying quality – mortgages, credit card debt, student loans and car payments – were traded between financial institutions. Instead of mortgage lenders continuing to hold their mortgages on their balance sheets for the length of their term, mortgage lenders sold on these liabilities. This meant that the risk from defaults or a fall in housing prices was spread across the financial industry. MBS and CMO typically passed through at least five separate institutions: the original lender, wholesalers of MBS and CMO, government-sponsored enterprises (GSE), servicers and institutional investors. In 1980, 67 per cent of American mortgages were held directly on the balance sheets of the originating bank.[6] This proportion collapsed from the 1980s until the 2000s, as American banks embraced 'originate and disseminate' and America's mortgage debt became stratified across its financial system.

Theoretically, spreading the risk across the financial system made it less likely that there would be a repeat of the 'savings and lending' crisis in the 1980s and 1990s, when housing-market turmoil had led some banks to fail. Some believed that this financial engineering enabled banks to significantly improve their profits from the otherwise low-yield mortgage market, which incentivised greater mortgage lending, thereby allowing lower-income or disadvantaged groups more ready access to credit, which in turn enabled them to gain a foothold in the booming American housing market.

Fatally, however, the 'originate and disseminate' model also distanced the mortgage lender from the risk of the mortgages they were issuing. Previously, the mortgage lender's financial performance had been directly tied to the quality of their mortgage lending because they bore the cost of any defaults or negative equity from the mortgages they created. Now, because of 'originate and disseminate', mortgage lenders were rewarded with a fee when they resold the mortgage, but were not penalised for any subsequent defaults. This incentivised them to issue more mortgages and, ultimately, increasingly to ignore the financial circumstances of those they were lending to.

It was this shift in the American mortgage market, from consisting predominantly of higher-quality conventional mortgages to the proliferation of subprime mortgages, which doomed the global financial system to another episode of volatility and crisis.

The march of the American financial system towards inevitable crisis did not begin in earnest until the early 2000s in the environment of low interest rates that followed 9/11. The Federal Reserve chair, Alan Greenspan, reduced interest rates to 1 per cent, wishing to enhance market liquidity and increase asset values in the face of major uncertainty. This led to a boom in the mortgage market with new mortgages issuance reaching $3.8 trillion in 2003 as falling borrowing costs encouraged more people to become homeowners, individuals to speculatively invest in their second, third and fourth properties, and existing mortgage holders to refinance on more favourable terms.[7]

After the initial boom, conventional mortgage borrowing began to lapse, and interest rates fell again in 2004. Further, investment banks aggressively seeking higher returns and bigger bonuses started to eye subprime mortgages – loans to borrowers with impaired credit ratings – as a way to prolong the booming trade in MBS and deliver greater margin. Conventional mortgage borrowing under the auspices of Fannie Mae and Freddie Mac, government-sponsored enterprises, topped out at 57 per cent of the total mortgage market in 2003.[8] From 2004 onwards, the subprime mortgage market exploded. By 2006, 70 per cent of new mortgage lending was unconventional.[9] In both 2005 and 2006, $1 trillion was loaned in subprime mortgages compared to only $100 billion in 2001.[10]

This explosion in subprime mortgages sharply increased the risk profile of America's mortgage debt. Trillions of dollars of subprime mortgage debt now filled the books of America's banks, tying their financial future and the future stability of America's financial system to the ability of thousands of individuals with untested credit histories and precarious financial circumstances to continue to repay their mortgages. In an environment of low interest rates and ever-increasing house prices, such risk was too easily ignored. In fact, 80 per cent of new CMO continued to get the top AAA credit rating from America's credit rating agencies.[11] But interest rates had to rise eventually, and the boom in subprime mortgages meant that when they did, thousands were likely to default, putting the value of trillions of dollars of securitised assets at risk.

To make matters worse, amid this boom in subprime mortgages, consolidation within the American financial sector meant that subprime mortgage debt was increasingly concentrated in the hands of a few, critically important banks. The 'originate and disseminate' model had initially worked to spread the America's mortgage markets' risk across its financial system. But from the early 2000s this process swung into reverse, as ambitious banks looked to capture more of the profits from the boom in mortgage securitisation by integrating more of the process under their own roof and holding on to MBS for longer. This was enabled by the Clinton administration's 1999 Financial

Services Modernization Act, which had removed the final New Deal-era regulatory barriers set after the Great Depression by Franklin D. Roosevelt, between retail and investment banking. Bear Stearns added the mortgage lender EMC to its portfolio while Lehman Brothers also acquired four small mortgage lenders.

By 2005, two-thirds of the mortgages in Lehman's securities portfolio originated from its own lenders.[12] As unsustainably low interest rates in the US eventually began to rise, from 1 per cent to 5 per cent between 2004 and 2006, some of America's most systemically important financial institutions held billions, and sometimes trillions, of dollars of high-risk mortgage debt tottering on the brink of default. To continue funding these portfolios of high-risk assets, investment banks and hedge funds had continuously to access short-term wholesale funding from the interbank lending markets. This funding model meant that the continued viability of many of America's banks relied on their ability to access short-term loans, or liquidity, from their fellow banks.

Unfortunately for the Brown government back in the UK, these issues were not confined to America's financial market. British banks trading heavily in MBS and CMO had not only exposed the British financial system directly to the risks inherent in subprime mortgage debt, but had also made themselves – like their American and European counterparts – reliant on being able continuously to access short-term dollar funding on the wholesale markets to fund their dollar-denominated securities portfolios. If those funds were to dry up, they would find themselves on the brink of collapse, unable to fund their liabilities, which could risk, through contagion, bringing down the wider UK financial system.

British banks, like their European peers, faced even more jeopardy than their American counterparts because they existed outside of the jurisdiction of the US Federal Reserve. British banks were reliant on access to dollars to fund their gigantic portfolios of US-based securities and retain viability. However, they could not rely on the Federal Reserve to act as a lender of last resort if they found themselves unable to access dollars through wholesale funding markets. The Bank of England – under-appreciating the exposure of the British banking sector to a shortfall in dollar funding – also had less than £200 billion in foreign currency reserves by the summer of 2006, a fraction of the value of the dollar-denominated assets swirling around the

British financial system.¹³ All this meant that while many of Britain's largest banks entered 2007 with a vast portfolio of high-risk dollar-denominated US assets, they lacked a clear dollar funding backstop in the eventuality that these assets suddenly lost value.

Even British banks which did not hold dollar-denominated portfolios, and were not directly exposed to high-risk American mortgage debt, had undermined their financial resilience by engaging in increasingly risky mortgage lending on the basis of inadequate capitalisation, leaving them overly leveraged and reliant on the wholesale funding market. No bank was more illustrative of this risk than Northern Rock. Based in Newcastle, Northern Rock had transformed itself in the 1990s onwards from a small, regional building society to the biggest proponent of the 'originate and disseminate' model within the UK. By 2007, it was responsible for 20 per cent of new mortgage issuances in Britain.¹⁴ The bank had loaned out more money than the value of the property (on the assumption that property prices would always rise) and had done this with people who couldn't really afford the interest in the first place – let alone if interest rates went up.

Northern Rock's balance sheet had grown fivefold between 1998 and 2007 but without a proportional growth in its capital pool, leaving it dangerously overleveraged and unlikely to be able to absorb the losses ensuing from any mortgage defaults. By the start of the crash, nearly 80 per cent of its funding came from wholesale funding, meaning it borrowed from other financial institutions rather than relying solely on deposits. While Northern Rock's position was particularly exposed, it was typical of many of the UK's central financial institutions that entered 2007 overleveraged and with a substantial portfolio of high-risk debt which would quickly lose its value in the face of disruption in the housing market, leaving them – and the wider financial system – on the verge of collapse.

Very few at the time were sounding the alarm bells about the risk of a financial crisis. One who did was the journalist Gillian Tett, who in the *Financial Times* on 18 January 2007 quoted an email she had received from a banker reader, saying: 'I don't think there has ever been a time in history when such a large proportion of the riskiest credit assets have been owned by such financially weak institutions ... with very limited capacity to withstand adverse credit events and market downturns.'¹⁵

It was on Brown's watch that this level of systemic risk had been allowed to build up more or less unchallenged. As we have seen, inadequate City regulation has been recognised, retrospectively, as regrettable by key figures in Brown's team, including by Brown himself, as well as by Treasury aides Ed Balls and Ed Miliband.

The approach to financial regulation by the Financial Services Authority – the new statutory regulator which Brown had established in 2001 during his tenure as chancellor – was widely seen as 'light touch' and was thought, even in the permissive environment of the early 2000s, to enforce some of the lowest regulatory constraints of any major financial centre. While American banks complying with US regulations had an average leverage ratio, comparing its potential debts to its equity, of 20:1, British banks complying with UK regulations had an average leverage of 40:1.82. After the crisis, banks were disciplined by a minimum leverage ratio, protecting the system from risks and uncertainties that are hard to measure. Ten years after the crash, in 2018, the average ratio of capital to risk-weighted assets had increased from 4.5 per cent to 14.3 per cent. In 2025, the rules required banks with retail deposits of £50 billion or more to meet a minimum leverage ratio requirement of 3.25 per cent.

In 2011, Brown would admit he made a 'big mistake' by setting up the FSA without realising the 'entanglements' of global institutions. 'We set up the FSA believing the problem would come from the failure of an individual institution,' he said. 'That was the big mistake. We didn't understand just how entangled things were.'[16]

Brown's 'light touch' regulation could even be argued to have indirectly contributed to overly loose financial regulations globally, including in the US. The US's 1999 Financial Services Modernization Act was critical in facilitating the concentration of high-risk mortgage debt on the balance sheets of America's most important banks, because it had removed the final regulatory barriers between retail and investment banking. The US Congress had passed the bill under intense lobbying from the financial sector, which aggressively argued that America's relatively strong regulations were disadvantaging New York as it competed with the City of London for dominance. This rationale was laid bare in the words of New York's Democratic Senator Chuck Schumer, who stated that 'the future of America's dominance as the financial center of the world' could only be secured by 'reforming' – i.e. loosening – America's financial regulations.[17] In other words, Brown's loose regulation may have caused the US to ease its own financial rules in order to compete.

In fairness, Brown and the governments he led did not always avoid confrontation with the City. On becoming chancellor a decade previously, Brown had risked friction with the City, despite his broad support, when he commissioned Don Cruickshank, the former telecoms regulator, to conduct a review into competition in the banking industry. According to Ed Balls, 'the banks definitely saw it as an unfriendly act'.[18] In May 2000, Cruickshank in his report 'Competition in UK Banking' concluded that the banks were overcharging and making excessive profits. Ultimately, though, Cruickshank's report would be largely ignored: its main recommendations were seen as impractical by many in the Treasury at a time in which the growth of the financial sector was a key driver of Britain's overall economic growth. Furthermore, the recommendations, like most of the UK government's regulatory impulses during the 2000s, had focused on addressing abuses within consumer banking rather than introducing more stringent requirements to ensure financial stability. However, it is still illustrative that even this relatively timid attempt to regulate the City was given what Iain Martin, the financial journalist and Brown critic, has described as a 'quiet burial'. Ed Balls himself would refer to his and Brown's response to the report as 'a bit of a damp squib'.[19]

Brown's 'light touch' approach to banking regulation wasn't a reflection of some personal admiration for the City or the influence of any close personal relationships with top City bankers. In fact, when in 2006 Ed Balls was appointed City minister, he described the relationship between the government and the banking industry as having become 'very antagonistic'.[20] Instead, the New Labour government had a Faustian pact with the City. In other words, although Brown had no personal interest in giving the City free rein and didn't profit by it, he thought it was a good idea for the economy as a whole to let the City rip.

The City of London had risen to become the world's largest financial centre by 2007. Of an annual turnover in interest rate derivatives of over $600 billion, London claimed 43 per cent to New York's 24 per cent.[21] The expansion of the UK's financial sector was a primary driver of the UK's economic growth throughout the 2000s, and the

UK Treasury was benefiting handsomely through increasing tax receipts. RBS had also become the world's largest bank, with a balance sheet of £1.9 trillion by 2008.[22] RBS was a historic bank dating back to 1726, famous for its role in making Edinburgh a financial powerhouse in the UK. Throughout the 1990s and 2000s, its global ambitions had been largely realised under the leadership of its now infamous chief executive Fred Goodwin, a Scot born and bred in Edinburgh.

Brown described their new offices: 'Their plush £350 million headquarters ... were the size of a small village, with shops, cafes, auditoriums, a swimming pool and even space at the rear for a proposed golf course.'[23] Such largesse, however, could be tolerated because RBS served to boost the UK's economic clout and delivered around £800 million of tax revenue in 2004. Overall, corporate receipts from the financial services industry accounted for up to 25 per cent of revenue into the UK Exchequer.[24] If you also include the increased stamp duty revenue, which rapidly rising house prices were delivering, then the UK government was profiting handsomely from the increase in high-risk mortgage lending and the exploding trade in high-risk assets that was hurtling Britain towards financial disaster. The expanding tax receipts from British banks were essential for funding spending on health, education and other social priorities, especially as Brown had opted against increasing income tax rates to fund them.

The international financial crisis actually began to unfold in 2006 when US house prices started to decline, bringing an end to a decade of unprecedented housing-price growth. The average price of American real estate had doubled in the decade leading up to 2006 which had added nearly $6.5 trillion to the size of the world economy.[25] However, as the Federal Reserve increased interest rates seventeen times, from a low of 1 per cent in June 2004 to 5.25 per cent in June 2006, the cost of mortgage borrowing increased substantially and the amount of new mortgage lending, which had exploded in a low-interest environment, plateaued and then began to fall, causing a period of stagnation and then a decline in house prices.

More ominously, the increasing cost of borrowing meant that many American households who held subprime mortgages and had been just about managing to make the minimum payments found themselves unable to keep up with increasing monthly costs and fell into default. This 'payment shock' led to a wave of defaults which affected a vast swathe of the housing market.

Over 2006, the more aware and astute investors began to appreciate the risks facing the market for MBS and CMO from the coming torrent of 'payment shocks', and started pulling back from purchasing securities and providing funding for these products. From the point of view of those holding or financing mortgage debt, the risk was twofold. The increasing rate of defaults decreased the value of the underlying mortgages behind the MBS and CMO. This in turn lowered the value of these assets and put the AAA credit rating of these products in jeopardy, which if adjusted would lead to a further fall in their value.

The increasing defaults and ensuing fall in house prices also meant that the value of the real-estate assets behind these mortgages was decreasing substantially. This meant that a significant amount of mortgage debt now represented negative equity on a bank's balance sheet: the value of the mortgage debt was larger than the value of its real-estate collateral. So banks would be unable to recoup their investment in the event of a default. Given the extent of mortgage borrowing and the fact that America's mortgage market was entering a period in which a constant stream of 'payment shocks' would lead to an avalanche of defaults, further lowering house prices, this dynamic represented an existential threat to the future value of America's mortgage debt as well as the value of the MBS and CMO built on top of it.

As awareness of this danger spread throughout the financial sector, banks on both sides of the Atlantic became increasingly reluctant to lend to each other through the short-term wholesale lending markets. The uncertainty about which institutions were most exposed to mortgage securities meant that fear about lending spread far more widely and affected far more borrowing than just the mortgage markets. Rates for short-term borrowing on the wholesale interbank lending markets spiked significantly and credit dried up not only for banks but also for business and consumers on 'main street', sending the UK and US economies down the road to recession and a further fall in house prices.

By 8 February 2007, HSBC in the UK announced it had made provisions for a $10.6 billion loss on its mortgage investments.[26] By May, UBS in America had closed its Dillon Read Capital Management hedge fund because of its MBS-related losses, and by July the small German regional bank IKB required a bailout from a consortium of banks in order to stave off its losses.

However, it wasn't until 9 August that the credit crisis began to have a major effect on the UK banking sector. On this day, BNP Paribas in Paris told investors they would not be able to take money out of two of its funds because it could not value the securities assets in them, owing to a 'complete evaporation of liquidity' in the market. This led to a collapse in the interbank lending markets as panic spread throughout the industry. In response, the European Central Bank moved to restore liquidity, and by the end of 9 August it had injected €95 billion into the European banking sector. Within a few days, over €200 billion had been injected.[27] The Federal Reserve, Bank of Canada and Bank of Japan also initiated massive interventions to restore liquidity and shore up confidence in their own financial markets.

The contagion was spreading across international borders. In the UK, the collapse of wholesale funding markets after BNP Paribas's announcement meant that Northern Rock found itself running out of liquidity quickly and unable to access wholesale funding. By 13 August, Northern Rock had informed the Bank of England that it faced a significant liquidity problem and was in impending need of help.[28] However, unlike its counterparts in North America and Europe, the Bank of England turned down the ailing bank's request, leaving Northern Rock at imminent risk of collapse. This was because of the Bank of England governor Mervyn King's concerns about 'moral hazard' – the notion that if you reward irresponsible behaviour you will encourage more irresponsible behaviour.

The crisis of Northern Rock would reach a peak just over a month later when news of its difficulties became public. On Thursday 13 September, the Bank of England reversed its position and began to negotiate a support package with Northern Rock in fulfilment of its role as a lender of last resort. The journalist Robert Peston reported this, saying there was 'no need to panic'. Brown compares Peston's comment to the famous 'don't panic' catchphrase of Corporal Jones in the BBC sitcom *Dad's Army*.

The ensuing scare created the first run on a bank since the 1930s and the television news led with images of anxious Northern Rock customers queuing on the streets to withdraw their cash. Northern

Rock, whose customers did much of their banking online, was particularly vulnerable, as it lacked the server capacity to deal with customers who wanted to transfer their money. Over the weekend of 15 and 16 September, shortly before he was to appear at his first Labour conference as leader, Brown was involved in detailed discussions with his minister and key adviser Shriti Vadera, on whom he would rely throughout the crisis. Now a peer, Vadera held the role of parliamentary under-secretary of state for competitiveness and small business, but in practice would help Brown navigate the scope of the challenges his government faced.

While the Bank of England's support had prevented the Northern Rock crisis from becoming a wider financial crisis, Brown was aware that severe problems within the financial system remained. He spent most of his first Christmas as prime minister engaged in talks with Vadera. Brown understood that the banking system effectively had two challenges that needed to be dealt with together: a lack of liquidity and a lack of capital.

Because interbank markets remained diminished, banks were increasingly forced to sell off their securitised assets, including MBS and CMO, in order to raise funds, which further diminished the value of these assets, leading to further entrenchment in the wholesale funding market. Critically, the reduction in lending also led the wider UK economy into recession and unemployment began to rise. From October 2007, UK house prices began to fall, demonstrating that a problem originating in the declining value of US house prices had now introduced the same problems into the UK.[29] As UK financial institutions entered 2008 they found themselves confronting the additional problem of rising defaults, negative equity and diminished access to interbank lending for their UK-based mortgage debt, while they continued to grapple with the fallout from the collapse in the value of US-based mortgage debt.

On the first day of trading in 2008, world stock markets suffered their largest losses in a day since 9/11. Having been stabilised briefly following the injection of liquidity from the Bank of England, Northern Rock's poor capitalisation meant that it continued to face liquidity struggles. In February, this came to a head and Northern Rock was temporarily nationalised by Brown's government in an attempt to restore consumer confidence in the banking system. On

13 March 2008, the crisis reached a new peak as Bear Stearns – one of Wall Street's biggest investment banks – collapsed following another round of mortgage failures, which left it unable to access short-term borrowing arrangements.

Brown's relationship with his chancellor had been tense for some months, but they hit a low point when in August 2008 Darling told the influential journalist Decca Aitkenhead that the economy was facing 'arguably the worst' downturn for sixty years. Darling was surely correct, but the Brown camp felt this would alarm people and in itself add to the crisis. The *Guardian*, for whom Aitkenhead worked at the time, rushed out the news story on 30 August ahead of her wider interview which was published in September.[30] The reaction among Brown's team, especially Damian McBride, was what led to Darling's description of the 'forces of hell' coming after him.

By September 2008, events were unfolding that were to prove the most challenging of Brown's premiership. On 7 September, the US mortgage firms Fannie Mae and Freddie Mac were nationalised because they held nearly $1.8 trillion in MBS which they were now unable to provide the liquidity for.[31] By the weekend of 13 and 14 September, almost exactly a year after Brown had first confronted the issues created by Northern Rock's collapse, Lehman Brothers was on the verge of meltdown. Having lost access to wholesale funding, Lehman had only $1.4 billion of liquidity available.[32] This was a shocking development for those within the financial system and for the general public at large, who sensed a real crisis was under way. But this time, under pressure from Republicans, Bush's Treasury secretary Ron Paulson was unwilling to offer the same kind of support to Lehman that it had for Bear Stearns. A possible buyer, the Bank of America, pulled out due to the US authorities' unwillingness to provide guarantees – especially in respect of exposure to bad assets and trades that might take place before finalisation of the sale.

Barclays, a key British bank, was another potential buyer, and they became Paulson's last hope that Lehman's could be saved without a bailout. Any chance of a purchase, however, was blocked by the chancellor, Alistair Darling, who said it would be 'like importing US cancer'. An emergency call was made by Paulson, pleading with Darling to change his mind. Darling would later say: 'I had kept Gordon in touch. We agreed that there was no way our government could effectively bankroll an American bank that was in trouble, when the US authorities wouldn't and when other US banks were running a mile.'

Paulson was angry, describing the decision as a 'very unpleasant surprise' and adding that 'the British ... fucked us', according to the US journalist Aaron Ross Sorki. Paulson, when faced with the reality of failing to find a buyer for Lehman's, suffered a panic attack, forcing him to leave his meeting with officials at the US Treasury. Without a buyer, Lehman filed for bankruptcy on Monday 15 September. This sent shockwaves throughout the world financial sector.

The fall of Lehman Brothers had increased fears of a wider contagion within the global banking system, and both Darling and Brown now believed the clock was ticking towards the next significant event. Brown – realising the scale of the problems facing the world economy at a time when domestic problems were piling up for him – was clear that the only way to tackle the threat of global meltdown was for international leaders to overcome their personal and political differences to pull together.

He flew to New York to attend the UN General Assembly on 25 September. Brown addressed delegates on one of his preferred projects, the Millennium Development Goals (MDGs), arguing that the financial crisis should not divert the UN from its plan to raise food production, eliminate malaria and improve education.

The next day, Brown met with George W. Bush at the White House. Bush accepted that the 'crisis had moved' from a 'liquidity problem' to a solvency problem, but still insisted that his administration's proposed solution, the Troubled Asset Relief Program, had to be the priority. Events back home were meanwhile moving rapidly. As Brown was leaving the White House, Darling phoned him to tell him of the collapse of Bradford & Bingley, which the Treasury had moved to nationalise.[33] Brown describes how on the flight home from Washington he wrote on a napkin 'RECAPITALISE NOW'. He also wrote 'NO LIQUIDITY WITHOUT RECAPITALISATION'. What followed over the next few days were discussions with Darling and the Treasury to turn the orthodoxy of the past thirty years on its head.

Events in Ireland the next day further renewed Brown's view that a coherent, coordinated international response was required to fully stem the flow of crisis. Facing the collapse of its three largest banks

(Anglo Irish Bank, Bank of Ireland and the Allied Irish Bank), the Irish government had announced that it would guarantee the entire liabilities of the six major Irish banks for a period of up to two years. This amounted to a forecast commitment of €440 billion and led to further panic in Europe as financial institutions and consumers assumed that such a large commitment meant that the crisis was even worse than they thought and questioned why their own governments were not offering a similar level of support.[34]

In response, Brown spearheaded an effort to coordinate with the governments of France, Germany and Italy in which they would create a combined bank rescue fund amounting to 3 per cent of GDP. However, these efforts were thwarted by German chancellor Angela Merkel's refusal to sign off on a blank cheque for bankers. Treasury reports at the time that Number Ten had been blindsided by Merkel's announcement underscored the uphill battle Brown faced in coordinating the international response he believed was essential.

At the G20 summit on 4 October, Brown again took a leading role. He tried to craft a coordinated European joint action but left disappointed. A European response failed to gain adequate support partly because of France and Germany's insistence that this was an 'Anglo-American' crisis for which their nations did not share equal responsibility. Instead, on 5 October, Merkel and her finance minister, Peer Steinbrück, announced that Germany was guaranteeing all savings deposits. Again, Merkel made this commitment without advising Number Ten.[35]

On 6 October, despite the unilateral improvisation of the US and German governments, among others, global equity markets suffered another significant shock and shed a further $2 trillion in value. Closer to home, the mighty RBS was in serious trouble. RBS's rise to global eminence was swift, in large part thanks to its takeover of the bigger NatWest in 1999, spearheaded by its then new deputy head, Fred Goodwin. As chief executive, a role he assumed in 2002, Goodwin's desire to grow RBS exponentially remained unabated, and, despite the warning signs that had been present throughout 2007, RBS pursued a risky takeover of ABN Amro, a Dutch bank riddled with subprime and other impaired assets. Overnight, this takeover made RBS the biggest bank in the world by balance sheet, with assets of over £1.9 trillion. The FSA would later report that the takeover of ABN was completed using just one lever-arch folder of documents and a single CD-ROM. Goodwin's knighthood, given in 2004 and later to be revoked in 2012, was given on the recommendation of Scottish first minister Jack McConnell, not Brown, and was approved without controversy at the time.

RBS had grown far too fast and was seen as too big for any one individual to manage effectively. Goodwin, as CEO, was not someone who liked to receive bad news and the culture of fear that he created, combined with a hubristic drive for growth at any cost, would be key ingredients in the bank's downfall. But the catalyst for its failure was that RBS, like Northern Rock, had on its balance sheet mortgage-backed assets that were becoming increasingly worthless. RBS had invested heavily in MBS and CMO, and had an American subsidiary, Greenwich Capital, dedicated to this business.

On the morning of 7 October, a tipping point was reached. Goodwin was giving a presentation about the bank's opportunities when, during questions and answers, an audience member asked why, during the course of his speech, the share price had plunged 35 per cent. Later that same day, Darling received a call from the RBS chair Tom McKillop, who anxiously told the chancellor that they were about to run out of money and asked bluntly, 'What are you going to do about it?' By the evening, RBS had suspended trading and it became clear another key British bank was on the verge of collapse.

That night, the heads of the major banks were summoned to the Treasury. The expectation was that they were not to leave until a solution was found. Fuelled by takeaway balti curry delivered by the Indian restaurant Gandhi's in Kennington, south London, Treasury officials worked through the night, eventually thrashing out an agreement which was concluded at around 5 a.m. The aim was to provide a combination of a massive injection of cash and government assurances. RBS, however, was troubled by the potential reputational damage from accepting the £50 billion offered, and tried to halve this figure. Darling and Brown, believing only such a large injection could stem market panic, insisted that the deal was 'take it or leave it'. As a compromise, though, Darling agreed to announce that £25 billion would be made immediately available, with a further £25 billion 'to follow'. But the key proposal – which would be accepted – was that the government would become the majority shareholder in RBS.

For the first time, the UK government would become effectively the owner of a global bank.

Before the markets opened on 8 October, Darling had announced the government-led recapitalisation plan to buy up to £50 billion of bank capital and equity together with a £250 billion credit guarantee for banks issuing debt and £200 billion of extra liquidity. In the end, the UK government provided RBS with £15 billion in capital in exchange for a 58 per cent stake.[36] This action quickly led to a stabilisation of the British banking sector.

At this point, even Brown was unsure his plan would work, and had considered resigning as prime minister. 'When I got up the next morning, I told Sarah that she would have to be ready to pack our things for a sudden move out of Downing Street,' he wrote in his memoir. 'If what I was about to do failed, with markets collapsing further and confidence ebbing away from Britain, I would have no choice but to resign. As I walked into the office, I didn't know if I'd still be there at the end of the day.'

The stakes had been incredibly high: Darling was to disclose three years later that the UK was just two or three hours away from the cashpoints drying up.

The Brown government's actions were heralded internationally as a major breakthrough. The government had boldly led the world in recapitalising the UK's banks and many governments now followed suit. On 13 October, Ron Paulson announced to the CEOs of America's nine major banks that they were to take slices of capital in exchange for preferred shares in their business. By the end of the day, all nine had agreed and accepted $125 billion from the US government. Many economists, such as Columbia University's Adam Tooze, argue that it was the fact the US followed the UK's example in implementing such an extensive capitalisation programme that enabled it to recover more effectively from the financial crisis than its European peers, who had avoided such an approach.[37]

The UK government attempted to make its own response the blueprint for other major economies at the meeting of the G7 finance ministers on 10 October. The meeting began with recriminations from the Italian, Japanese and German finance ministers about the failures of 'Anglo-American capitalism'. Against this backdrop, the US and UK governments attempted to argue that Lehman Brothers' collapse was the symptom rather than the cause of wider problems in global finance. The UK government as well as the Bank of England governor Mervyn King also attempted to push through a five-point plan which would have included a commitment by each nation that 'there would be no more failures of systemically important institutions, there would be measures to assist recapitalisation, they would work to unfreeze liquidity in interbank markets, they would provide adequate deposit insurance and they would rebuild the markets for securitised assets'.[38]

With the financial sector stabilised, Brown's focus now turned to addressing the ongoing recession which, if left to run its course unabated, risked dragging the world economy into another great depression. Arguably, the US government under Bush failed to recognise, and Obama's administration was late to see (when he took over in January 2009), the urgent need to coordinate an international response. It was Brown, alongside French president Sarkozy, who was instrumental in getting his fellow leaders of the G7 to agree that a bigger forum, including more major economies, was needed in order to create an international response to the global financial crash.

Accordingly, on 15 November 2008 the G20 met in Washington DC. The G20 included the G7 members of Canada, France, Germany, Italy, Japan, UK and US as well as the leaders of Argentina, Australia, Brazil, China, India, Indonesia, Mexico, Russia, Saudi Arabia, South Africa, South Korea and Turkey, plus the EU. The Netherlands and Spain were also invited to attend. While this summit failed to secure any substantial international agreement, Brown was successful in getting members to agree that there would be a subsequent G20 summit in London in spring 2009 which his government would host.

Brown worked tirelessly in the lead-up to the G20 summit to lay the groundwork for a successful international agreement. On 3 March, he addressed a joint session of the US Congress, in the country he had loved since childhood, giving Senator Ted Kennedy an honorary knighthood in a surprise announcement of the sort Brown loves to produce, and saying, 'Working together, there is no challenge to which we are not equal, no obstacle that we cannot overcome, no aspiration so high that it cannot be achieved.'

His speech was greeted with frequent standing ovations on both sides of the aisle. Brown and Darling also hosted a preliminary meeting of G20 finance ministers on 14 March. As with Brown's earlier attempts to coordinate an international response to the imminent collapse of the banking sector, this meeting underscored the deep divisions between the world's major governments and the scale of Brown's challenge in bringing them together. At this meeting, German chancellor Angela Merkel and French finance minister Christine Lagarde pushed back both on the size of the proposed stimulus package and on the notion that the G20 should focus on a coordinated stimulus package, rather than on addressing the root causes of the crisis, which they believed to be failures within the UK–US economic model. As Merkel would later state, 'the tendency is not to deal with the roots of the evil. We need to learn something from this crisis.'[39] The head of the Chinese Central Bank, Zhou Xiaochuan, also created difficulties by launching his own call for a new Bretton Woods on 23 March.

Despite this, Brown remained steadfast in his arguments that an unprecedentedly large, multilateral stimulus effort was needed in order to mitigate the effects of the global financial crisis. On 24 March, Brown addressed the European Parliament and called on European governments to do 'whatever it takes to create the growth and jobs we need'.[40]

However, in this effort, Brown also faced domestic opposition. The same day as he addressed the Treasury select committee, Mervyn King concurred with some elements of the German and French opposition to a large stimulus by stating: 'Given how big those deficits are, I think it would be sensible to be cautious about going further in using discretionary measures.'[41]

But Darling – who in May 2023 told me he became friendly again with Brown at a party for one of John Smith's daughters in an Edinburgh bar in late 2022 – helped Brown make the government bail out the major banks, which was effected in a move hailed in the *New York Times* by the Nobel Prize-winning economist Paul Krugman as Brown having 'saved the world financial system'.[42]

According to Darling's account, the breakdown in the relationship between himself and Brown began around the time of the April 2009 Budget. This was because of Darling's perceived firm 'austerity' measures, which clashed with Brown's desire to maintain fiscal support during the financial crisis. The prime minister, facing a sharp downturn in government popularity, was putting pressure on his chancellor to spend money the Treasury did not have. Darling wrote in his memoirs, *Back from the Brink*: 'It ... marked the moment when my friendship with Gordon, which had lasted more than twenty years, was driven to breaking point. Richard Crossman in his diaries observes that political friendships should be cool and detached. I am afraid he is probably right. By now ours was lacking in both qualities.'[43]

When Darling died in late 2023, Brown expressed regret about briefings against him from Brown's camp, telling the Radio 4 *Today* programme on 1 December: 'I personally don't know much about that, to be honest. One of the problems in government ... is you have lots of people said to be briefing on your behalf who you don't even know the names of, and so some of these things happen and you've got to apologise afterwards but you don't actually know who has done them ... If there had been a briefing against him that was attributed to me: yes, of course, it was completely unfair.'

Despite facing discord at home and abroad, Brown entered the G20 summit confident and determined, and was instrumental in creating a landmark international agreement which many credit with mitigating some of the long-term effects of the global financial crisis. At the G20, the wider summit took place at the Excel Centre in east London, a large venue that made it difficult to hold the informal discussions between leaders that Brown thought essential. 'I made a quick decision,' Brown says. 'I told staff that most of the work would now be done during the leaders' lunch, at which only leaders would be present. We started lunch as early as possible, and until I had an agreement on the issues that mattered, I refused to let the lunch finish.'[44]

By this stage, the outline of the plan for a $1.1 trillion injection of money from governments for stimulus had been agreed by the G20, involving extra money for the International Monetary Fund to lend to struggling economies, extra lending to the poorest nations and a boost to world trade. But the leaders needed to show that they were aligned and could present the package to the media, once the full agreement was in place. The day was derailed, however, by Sarkozy, who threatened to walk out over the granting of Chinese tax havens, complaining that tax was no issue for the G20. Meanwhile, the Chinese refused to turn up until the French issued a joint diplomatic statement moderating their position on Tibet. Eventually, it was agreed that all of the G20 countries had to put in place new rules on capital and liquidity by the end of the year. The Financial Stability Board – a means of providing global oversight and a coordinated response to global financial risks whenever they emerged – was created.

Following the final wrangling in a 'leaders' lounge', furnished with white and green sofas and artificial trees, Brown emerged to the global media and declared that the world's major powers had pulled together. Merkel herself praised the agreement: 'This is a victory for global co-operation', and Obama later reflected that 'the London summit was historic ... [the decisions we took] were bolder than any other response in living memory'.[45]

As Obama's comment suggests, the G20 agreement largely came about because of Brown's clarity of strategy. Its achievement was the result of many of Brown's qualities: his single-mindedness, his ambition and his unrelenting work ethic, which also, in different contexts, were his limitations. Tom Fletcher, a respected civil servant and diplomat and now the principal of Hertford College, Oxford, had worked for Tony Blair, and would serve David Cameron too, and he saw their contrasting styles close up.

Fletcher remains friends with Brown today, and praises him. But he says that Brown's team as a whole, regarding the broader premiership period, struggled to support the relentlessness with which Brown worked, often in the early hours, late at night and on weekends. 'We just weren't ready, as a system, for the pace at which he worked and the intensity,' he says. 'And I think that was what let him down. Actually, I think that's where we failed. It wasn't for him to work out. We should have worked that out for him. You know, it was for him to say, here's the stuff that matters to me, and we should have built a system around him.'[46] Brown's work ethic and his inability to delegate suited the chancellorship better than the premiership, where a multiplicity of issues and problems are continually crowding in. As Blair told him, prime ministers should stand above the fray and it isn't healthy for them to be workaholics.

Fletcher did witness Brown relax sometimes, however, mainly as he sipped champagne and made jokes on flights back from overseas trips, or when Brown impersonated the Foreign Office by toasting Fletcher's birthday in the style of an FCO memo, or when Brown performed impressions of himself, mocking his own more mechanical style compared to that of Barack Obama, who was seen as lighter in public. Once in late 2008, Brown agreed to spend a weekend at the British embassy residence in Paris with Sarah and the boys and their friend J. K. Rowling and her family, to celebrate Fraser's birthday. However, even then, the group went off to enjoy Disneyland Paris while Brown and Fletcher toiled away at the residence – the Hôtel de Charost, in rue du Faubourg Saint-Honoré, near the Élysée Palace – writing speeches.[47]

To prevent a financial crisis turning into a prolonged recession due to the fall in business lending, rise in unemployment and decline in consumer spending, Brown's government implemented significant stimulus measures. By 2009, the UK economy had contracted more than 6 per cent, the biggest contraction in economic output since the Second World War. The UK's unemployment figures had risen to close to 8 per cent – the highest figure since the 1990s – and sterling had lost close to 20 per cent of its value against the dollar amid optimism across the Atlantic over Obama's economic recovery plans.[48] The pound slid against a rising dollar as the Bank of England aggressively slashed interest rates from 5 per cent to 0.5 per cent. The IMF calculated that the UK had suffered a fall in household wealth from the decline in house prices and the decline in the stock market of $1.5 trillion between 2008 and 2009.[49] This was the equivalent of 50 per cent of its GDP.

Brown wanted the UK to spend its way out of the crash, and thought that it was appropriate for it to do so because this was a demand-side rather than a supply-side shock. Brown and Darling introduced a series of measures throughout 2008 and 2009 aimed at stimulating the economy, restoring growth and reducing unemployment. VAT was cut from 17.5 per cent to 15 per cent.[50] Capital spending was brought forward and stimulatory programmes such as a 'cash for clunkers' car-scrappage scheme were introduced. However, the largest part of the Brown government's stimulus initiative was the welfare systems which he had spent his decade as chancellor enhancing.

While Brown spent only 2.5 per cent of GDP directly on stimulus measures, the government deficit grew significantly from 2.9 per cent of GDP in 2006/7 to over 10 per cent for 2009/10 on the back of diminishing tax receipts and exploding welfare spending.[51] Such welfare spending provided an essential floor, which prevented UK consumer spending collapsing, and was instrumental in ensuring that the rise in poverty following the global financial crisis was much lower than many had feared. But these ballooning deficits proved to be a political liability for Brown. David Cameron had accused him in 2008 of a 'reckless' borrowing and 'spend now, forget the future' approach to the economy – it was a charge that was to stick at the general election two years later.

Concluding, Bob Shrum argues that Brown 'saved the world from going into a depression'. Ed Balls adds: 'The learning from history, the scale of the intervention in the autumn of 2008, the kind of global response to the depression threat was … hugely important, and only Gordon could have done that. If Gordon hadn't been prime minister, I'm not sure that there would have been a chancellor who'd done what Alistair Darling did. I certainly don't think Alistair Darling could have done it on his own … And I think the same thing is true for the kind of the whole global response.'[52]

It is as much over the financial crisis as anything else that Brown is in need of reassessment and rehabilitation. As the *Guardian* columnist Aditya Chakrabortty wrote in 2012: 'What sticks out about that period is how Brown and Alistair Darling were not only acting without a roadmap, they were driving with Cameron and Osborne right on their bumper telling them to do a U-turn … We can argue over the details of the Brown bailout, but the big lesson is: governments can stem mass joblessness and banking crises.'[53]

Brown today regrets that such international cooperation and international decision-making was not made permanent. But overall, it is uncontroversial to say that Brown emerges from this period with considerable credit. He used all his 'kit', to borrow Neil Kinnock's word: the quick and sound judgement of an alert historian, creativity, resilience, determination, persuasiveness, and the air of authority which even Barack Obama had both admired him for and, at that G20 dinner inside Number Ten, helped to give him.

David Cameron, Gordon Brown's successor as prime minister, reflects today that Brown 'did a great job in the crash', though he adds that 'I thought his failure to accept that spending would have to be cut was a mistake.'[54] But as Brown's predecessor Tony Blair says now: 'The job he did, bringing the world together in the financial crisis, that is … [his] most significant achievement.'[55]

16

Fighting Chance

Despite everything he had achieved tackling the financial crisis, there remained a lingering sense during 2009, in the media if not in the majority of his party, that Gordon Brown should give way to another leader. This situation had not been helped by the *Telegraph*'s coverage of the parliamentary expenses scandal in May that year, which damaged trust in all politicians, including or perhaps especially Brown as head of the executive in Parliament despite his own expenses being shown in the end to be innocent. The blow to the public trust in MPs from the scandal reverberates to this day.

The *Telegraph* had bought a disk held by a source of a leaked database of parliamentary expenses derived from a freedom of information request, which other papers had declined or couldn't afford, and proceeded to reveal hundreds of stories about what MPs charged the taxpayer for. Some of the more memorable claims included a 'duck island' by the Tory MP Sir Peter Viggers and an 88p bath plug by the home secretary Jacqui Smith.

At one point in the midst of the reporting of the scandal, Brown was hosting the Israeli prime minister Ehud Olmert, who walked up to the flat in 11 Downing Street where the Browns were residing, and found Sarah on her hands and knees going through expense claims to make sure the couple had not inadvertently left anything out or got anything wrong. Olmert, who would later face corruption charges back in Israel, was stunned at the way the level of scrutiny reflected on the British system. It echoed Barack Obama's amazement at how tough the British press was towards Brown, constantly portraying, falsely, the White House as 'snubbing' the prime minister during trips to Washington DC.

Brown paid back some £12,000 of his expenses for cleaning, gardening and decorating, and he urged all Labour MPs to follow his lead. He took the story personally, though, and according to some who worked for him it clouded his judgement and news sense. During the furore, Brown decided to give up his prime ministerial pension. 'He thought it was all about him,' says one Downing Street insider from the time. 'It was hard to get him to see it was a parliamentary scandal.' At the same time, however, the *Telegraph* focused on Brown and Labour for several days initially, before they turned to the Conservatives, giving Cameron time to prepare a more deft response.

On one train journey in the first days of the expenses scandal, to the horror of his aides, Brown seemed to read every word of the coverage in all the newspapers, and, despite the massive pressures of his job, penned articles explaining how he would crack down on abuse of MPs' allowances. Not for the first or last time, those who worked for the prime minister wished they had hidden the media from him. Brown could barely believe what he was reading because, as one longstanding Labour MP puts it, 'I have never met anyone less interested in money than Gordon Brown.'

Over the summer of 2009, Afghanistan became a major preoccupation in Downing Street. Domestically, Murdoch's *Sun* used increasing British casualties and claims by some military leaders about alleged lack of adequate equipment to blame Brown's premiership. But more importantly, the US, which had neglected Afghanistan in favour of Iraq in recent years, began focusing on the former. Barack Obama, who had become president in January, had ordered a strategic review before committing 17,000 further American troops to Afghanistan a month later. But as the situation worsened dramatically, he sent another 4,000 military personnel before ordering another strategic review. The Americans then pressured Brown, via his foreign policy adviser Tom Fletcher, into also committing more troops, against his instincts. Brown ended up announcing on 29 April to the Commons that troops would increase temporarily by 230 to 8,030. Privately, he was concerned that Britain was sinking deeper into a war of occupation potentially without an end, and all along he had wanted to limit British involvement to training and mentoring of native Afghan soldiers.[1]

On 24 September 2009, just before the annual Labour Party conference, I interviewed a somewhat tense Brown in Number Ten with my *New Statesman* colleague Mehdi Hasan. A brief excerpt of the transcript shows that Brown's leadership was indeed under pressure, but also demonstrates Brown's determination to get on with the job:

> JM: Prime Minister, if you believed that another candidate was better suited to lead the party to success in the election, would you stand aside?
> GB: That's not the issue at the moment. The issue at the moment is that the Labour Party has to take this country through a very difficult time. I think we'll be judged by results but I think we made the right choices. This is the time for us [to show] the party not really what we've done, but what we're going to do together for the future ...
> JM: But you haven't actually said explicitly that you will be leader until the election.
> GB: Of course I'm going on. I mean, for goodness' sake, I wouldn't be having this interview with you if I wasn't determined to get my message across to the British people.[2]

At the conference in Manchester, Brown's speech was seen as a success, not least because he finally agreed to champion the broader New Labour record in government – meaning Blair's as well as his own. Despite his previous refusal to use his family to soften his image, Sarah passionately introduced her husband. She said:

> I know he's not a saint – he's messy, he's noisy, he gets up at a terrible hour – but I know that he wakes up every morning and goes to bed every evening thinking about the things that matter. I know he loves our country and I know he will always, always put you first ... The first time I met him I was struck that someone so intense and so intelligent could be so gentle, could ask so many questions, could really care. He will always make the time for people, our family, for his friends and anyone who needs him – that's part of the reason I love him as much as I do. And you know, friends, that is what makes him the man for Britain too. Gordon has got a tough job and

I wouldn't want it for the world, but each time I am thankful that he's the one who has it; that he's the one choosing the policies and making the calls.

Brown then took to the stage, and in a passage that remains popular on social media, Brown listed the achievements of his government to a roaring standing ovation: 'Because if anyone says that to fight doesn't get you anywhere, that politics can't make a difference, that all parties are the same, then look what we've achieved together since 1997: the winter fuel allowance, the shortest waiting times in history, crime down by a third, the creation of Sure Start, the Cancer Guarantee, record results in schools, more students than ever, the Disability Discrimination Act, devolution, civil partnerships, peace in Northern Ireland, the social chapter, half a million children out of poverty, maternity pay, paternity leave, child benefit at record levels, the minimum wage, the ban on cluster bombs, the cancelling of debt, the trebling of aid, the first ever Climate Change Act; that's the Britain we've been building together, that's the change we choose.'[3] MPs from all sections of the party – including previously critical ultra-Blairites who believed Brown was failing to pursue a New Labour modernising agenda – were happy with the speech.

But the mood shifted quickly. Late the following night, on Wednesday 30 September 2009, Brown's inner circle was gathered amid half-empty wine bottles and loosened ties in an apartment suite at the Metropole Hotel in Brighton after their various dinners. 'It had been a rough day,' says one of those present. That morning, the *Sun* had backed David Cameron's Tories with a front page declaring 'LABOUR'S LOST IT'.

Twelve years after first endorsing Tony Blair, the *Sun*'s move had been calculated to inflict maximum damage on Brown's Labour and present maximum advantage to the Conservatives. All day, while Sky News interviewed *Sun* reporters in Brighton, the paper's editor, Rebekah Brooks, had been trying to reach Brown on the phone via his aides. Brown's view, and that of those around him, had been that Brooks should not be dignified with a pointless conversation about why the *Sun* had done this.

Eventually Peter Mandelson, who had been brought back into the heart of government as business secretary the previous year, had taken the call. Now he walked into the suite full of tired staffers and animatedly recounted the exchange, gently mocking Brooks and lightening the mood. 'What on earth is the matter, Rebekah?' Mandelson recalled asking her. Brooks had pointed out that she'd been trying to get hold of Brown. 'Why?' he'd asked. An incredulous Brooks mentioned the obvious, that the *Sun* had backed the Tories and she'd wanted to explain. 'Well, that's okay, isn't it?' Mandelson had replied, deflating the self-importance of it all. 'It wasn't exactly unexpected.' The team laughed and even cheered. Michael Dugher, Brown's chief political spokesperson at the time, says Mandelson 'was deliciously dismissive and more than a little patronising'.

As Dugher explains: 'There was quite a togetherness. It was basically us against them now. You have to understand that a big chunk of the inner circle were Kinnockites.'[4] They knew better than anyone what the *Sun* can do to Labour leaders. Sue Nye, who was there, had worked very closely with Neil Kinnock throughout his leadership. Kinnock's daughter Rachel was in charge of events for Brown. And of course Mandelson himself had been Kinnock's director of communications. 'They had seen it all before,' Dugher says. It was a rallying moment for the beleaguered Brown and his team. A bold decision was taken to keep the *Sun* out of political briefings from Number Ten, and to actively give stories to rival outlets such as the *Mirror* and the *Telegraph*.

Less than two months later, however, on Tuesday 10 November 2009, from 12.33 p.m. to 12.50 p.m., with the general election round the corner the following spring, Brown did take a phone call in Number Ten from Rupert Murdoch himself. Murdoch ostensibly wanted to apologise for the *Sun*'s undeniably iniquitous coverage in the days before, after its feigned uproar on the front page over a handwritten condolence letter Brown wrote with a large black felt-tip pen, due to his poor eyesight, and with apparent spelling mistakes, to Jacqui Janes, the mother of the twenty-year-old Afghanistan veteran Jamie Janes. Several newspapers had been offered the Janes letter story and declined to use it. Brown was so upset about the report that he had spent a plane journey back from Germany, where he had been marking the twentieth anniversary of the fall of the Berlin Wall, repeatedly rewriting the mother's name.[5]

Brown's eyesight was especially poor at this time. He recalls that he woke up in Downing Street one Monday in September 2009, and 'I knew something was very wrong. My vision was foggy.' That morning, his team had organised a visit to the City Academy in Hackney to speak about the government's education reform agenda. 'I kept the engagement, doing all I could to disguise the fact that I could see very little – discarding the prepared notes and speaking extemporaneously,' he says. 'Right afterwards, I was driven to the consulting room of a prominent eye surgeon at the Moorfields Eye Hospital in London.'

While examining Brown's right eye the surgeon discovered that the retina was torn in two places and said that Brown urgently needed an operation, which was arranged for that Sunday. On his way out of the consultation, Brown asked whether his old friend Hector Chawla, whom Brown had last seen briefly on the day he retired as a surgeon, could be invited to give his opinion too. Brown emailed Chawla, who was in France on holiday but offered to come to the hospital that Sunday morning on his way back home.

Brown was already prepared for surgery when Chawla examined him and said he was convinced that the tears had not happened in the previous few days – that they were long-standing. Chawla's advice was blunt: there was no point in operating unless the sight deteriorated further, and laser surgery in Brown's case was more of a risk than it was worth. Brown reflects that 'it was after losing the sight in my left eye and then some of the sight in my right one that I started to think more about my future. There were certain things I couldn't or shouldn't do – playing the sports I loved, and driving a car, despite having a licence – but I was not going to be deterred. Even if I felt fate had dealt me a bad hand, my time in and out of hospital – and the fight for my eyesight – gave me a perspective that I still feel helps me to be more understanding of difficulties facing others in a far worse position than me.'

Brown had subsequently called a hostile Mrs Janes and tried to say sorry. The conversation was recorded by a third-party news agency and sold to the *Sun*, and it too was duly exposed by the tabloid. 'They'd been weaponising Afghanistan,' says Dugher. 'It was fucking outrageous to be honest,' says another aide.

The campaign doggedly pursued by the *Sun*, which saw itself as the troops' newspaper and reported heavily on military matters, focused on the Brown government's funding for defence, seeking to exploit criticisms from both Charles Guthrie, the chief of the defence staff, and Richard Dannatt, the chief of the general staff (the army), over what the latter called 'insufficient' funds. Brown had visited Camp Bastion in Helmand, Afghanistan – his first trip to a war zone – in December 2008, committing upon his return in the Commons some £450 million in aid and the retention of 7,800 British troops. However, privately he felt the British war effort in Afghanistan should have ended by 2005, and disagreed with Tony Blair's belief that it was still going to be part of a necessary and wider long-term commitment to fighting Islamic extremism across the world.

The Australian media magnate, by now a US citizen, wanted to retain his influence on British prime ministers, despite the *Sun* having come out in support of the Conservatives after weeks of negative coverage over Brown's alleged faltering commitment to the Afghanistan military effort, which the right-wing tabloid strongly supported. During the 10 November phone call, Murdoch claimed, falsely in Brown's view, that he had passed all decision-making on politics to his son James. Murdoch also urged Brown to talk directly to Brooks who, as revealed by the Leveson Inquiry into the media and phone hacking, was regularly flirting politically by text message with Cameron in the run-up to the 2010 general election, saying, for example: 'I am so rooting for you, not just as a personal friend but because professionally we are in this together. Speech of your life? Yes he Cam!' And: 'Brilliant speech. I cried twice. Will love "working together".' Brown was duly unimpressed. He told Murdoch on the phone that he held Brooks responsible for the Afghanistan coverage.

Brown followed up that phone call with an email to Murdoch complaining that his efforts to drum up support internationally for more troops in Afghanistan were being undermined by the *Sun* 'constantly criticising us'. Tom Fletcher, though appalled by the *Sun*'s campaign, warned against sending messages directly. But, in the email seen here for the first time, Brown wrote:

Dear Rupert

I want to emphasise to you the point I made about Afghanistan, and the seriousness that has resulted from the consistent criticism.
    We are the only large country who in recent weeks proposed extra troops for Afghanistan, even while others refused the offer of extra troops before the election campaign.

I stress that to my knowledge no essential equipment needs of the MoD [Ministry of Defence] have been refused [a claim by the *Sun*], and while four years ago we spent £650m on Afghanistan this has risen more than fivefold to £3.5bn this year.

My job in the next few weeks is to persuade a number of European countries to offer real support with extra troops.

This I will do. But it is difficult when one of the newspapers which has consistently supported us in Afghanistan is constantly criticising us.

Yours, Gordon[6]

Murdoch did not reply and their conversation earlier that day would be the last time they spoke. Murdoch would later claim inaccurately to Leveson that the conversation had taken place in September, and that Brown had threatened to sue. Brown insists he did not say this.

From that autumn onwards, following the night of gallows humour after the *Sun* abandoned New Labour, it was as if the complicated relations at the heart of New Labour had largely reconciled. The consensus now was that Brown had saved his leadership, and a final attempt to replace him – led by ex-ministers Patricia Hewitt and Geoff Hoon – fizzled out in early January 2010.

Despite the hammering to his personal political standing with voters, Brown was also seen to have stabilised Labour's position. On 1 December, the *Independent* ran a ComRes poll with the party on 27 per cent, ten points behind the Conservatives, but because of the electoral system this would have resulted in a hung Parliament. Labour was in the running again and for a period the Tories appeared on the back foot.

Two months before the general election, on 5 March 2010, Brown, who had been encouraged not to believe the domestic polls by world leaders during the crash, spoke to Margaret Thatcher for the first time since she visited Number Ten under Brown on 13 September 2007. Back then, Brown had hailed her as 'a conviction politician' and laid on a special welcome in Downing Street soon after he formed his 'government of all the talents', but in this phone call, Thatcher 'showed her age', according to one official in on the call.[7]

Elsewhere, although Brown could not hope to match Tony Blair's achievement in Northern Ireland with the Good Friday Agreement of April 1998, the hard work there went on. Throughout his premiership, Brown and his Irish counterpart Brian Cowen cooperated to negotiate the devolution of policing and justice powers. An agreement was finally reached in February 2010, and the powers were officially passed to Northern Ireland's government in April. Brown says: 'People forget that during the financial crisis we were having to spend hours negotiating a Northern Ireland settlement and making sure that violence did not reoccur. I spent many nights at Hillsborough trying to get a deal and eventually we got it, thanks to the help of the Irish government.'[8]

On 6 April 2010, outside Number Ten, flanked by senior MPs, with Harriet Harman and Peter Mandelson prominently positioned behind him, Brown announced that he was calling a general election for 6 May. 'I come from an ordinary family, in an ordinary town,' he said, 'and I've never forgotten where I come from, or the values – hard work, duty, fairness, telling the truth – my parents instilled in me. And that's why during this world recession the team and I have fought so hard for families on middle and modest incomes. And from now until polling day I will travel the length and breadth of Britain with one clear message: Britain is now on the way to economic recovery.'

Earlier that day, Brown met his cabinet for the last time, for forty-five minutes. Then he was driven to Buckingham Palace to request the dissolution of Parliament, during a twenty-two-minute meeting with the Queen. Back at Number Ten, standing alongside Sarah in the Pillared Room, Brown addressed all Downing Street staff to thank them for their work over the past three years. In a witty speech, he recalled one of his first dates with Sarah when he tried to give her dinner at home and inadvertently placed a duvet cover on the table as opposed to a tablecloth. Brown then set off on the campaign trail with Sarah, walking through St Pancras Station and stopping to speak to shoppers before taking the train to Kent and touring marginal seats.[9]

During the campaign, which paved the way for the Tory–Liberal coalition after Nick Clegg thrived in the TV debates which began on 15 April, there were extraordinary highs and lows for Brown. On the one hand, anyone who was at his Methodist Central Hall speech to the charity Citizens UK on 4 May saw Brown at his best – it was one of the most electrifying speeches by any British politician for decades.[10] I was there, and have never seen anything like it first hand in British politics. The *Guardian* splash the following day concurred, as the journalist Patrick Wintour wrote under the headline 'Battered Gordon Brown finds his voice' that Brown 'dramatically threw off the shackles of his foundering campaign to deliver one of the most passionate speeches he has ever given, leaving even disillusioned cabinet members stunned by his sudden display of fervour. To several standing ovations, he told the Citizens UK conference: "As you fight for fairness, you will always find in me a friend, a partner and a brother."'[11] To anyone covering the campaign at the time, the speech underlined the unfairness of the majority of the media portrayals of Brown. But it was too late in the campaign to make a difference.

On 28 April the campaign had been dealt a potentially devastating blow when Sky News played an off-camera comment he made in his car with his microphone still on about a 'sort of bigoted woman', a Rochdale voter Gillian Duffy, who was complaining about immigration. The story, with images of Brown's head in his hands in a TV studio afterwards and even later returning to Duffy's house to try to apologise, featured on the front of every newspaper the following day. The excruciating exchange, caught because Brown had forgotten to remove his Sky News microphone, was symbolic of a wider problem, and played into the general perception that politicians were out of touch, a perception that would arguably help lead to Brexit six years later.

Brown told reporters by Duffy's home after the incident: 'I've just been talking to Gillian. I'm mortified by what's happened. I've given her my sincere apologies. I misunderstood what she said and she has accepted that there was a misunderstanding and she has accepted my apology. If you like, I'm a penitent sinner.' As a footnote to the Duffy story, according to the former BBC broadcaster Jon Sopel, on the *News Agents* podcast on 24 December 2024, Brown and his team got to the BBC Leeds studios and asked for a room in which to confer about the encounter, only to discover a CCTV camera in the room. Sopel claimed that one individual – presumably in Brown's team – apparently already traumatised by the Duffy incident, climbed onto a table and smashed the camera.[12] Alastair Campbell had to hold one-on-one conversations with Brown over the Duffy affair trying to reassure him it wasn't as bad as he thought.[13]

Today, Brown heavily blames himself for the 2010 general election defeat, despite the ruthlessness of the right-wing media narrative blaming him and Labour over the financial crash. Perhaps he is being hard on himself: after all, he went on to give the party a slim chance, at least, of forming a natural alliance with the Liberal Democrats who had demanded his political head as a condition of talks. He also saved Labour, suffering from inevitable weariness among voters after thirteen years in office, from electoral oblivion.

Brown always faced an uphill battle because of the grim state of the nation's finances following the global crisis. He also had the ill fortune compared with Blair, who faced William Hague in 2001 and Michael Howard in 2005, to be pitched against the smooth David Cameron, who successfully presented the Tories in a fresh, more appealing light.

There was no landslide against Labour as some commentators predicted. But he remains especially stung by his strained relationship with the Murdoch press, which saw the stable back Cameron. Even the normally reliable *Guardian* – along with the *Independent* – took the unusual step of supporting the Liberal Democrats, who ended up entering into a coalition with the Tories after a short-lived outbreak of 'Cleggmania'.

The *Guardian* was clear in its election leading article: '[If] the *Guardian* had a vote in the 2010 general election it would be cast enthusiastically for the Liberal Democrats.'[14] Dugher says: 'There were some in the policy team and elsewhere in Downing Street who were sympathetic to the *Guardian* and started every day with the *Guardian*. I was among those who were sceptical about the *Guardian* and didn't see it as Labour's natural friend anyway.'[15] Nonetheless, in 2010 Brown needed all the allies he could get, and his relationship with the media was, on the whole, an unhappy one.

Brown's aides were often zealous, perhaps even a little overzealous, when it came to protecting him from seeing the media. As an example, one day during a cabinet meeting, Sue Nye quickly left the room and turned off the televisions showing rolling news across the open-plan office. Then, stepping into the separate press office area, she told Michael Dugher to switch off the TV there too. 'Er, I'm watching the news,' replied Dugher, who is from Edlington in South Yorkshire. But Nye explained it had not been a good cabinet and she did not want the mood to get worse. 'But I'm a press officer,' said Dugher.

'Okay, change channels then,' said Nye. Dugher came back: 'Well, it's really going to lift the prime minister's spirits when he comes in and finds his spokesman watching *Bargain Hunt*.'

Nye got her way, and like the others across Number Ten, the screen went blank. Just as farcically, after strenuous attempts had been made to hide the newspapers from Brown on a flight back from Afghanistan, to the extent that British Airways staff were told to go around clearing them away, one aide had to sit on a stray copy of *The Times* with a negative front-page story for the whole flight, leading to newsprint staining his chinos.[16]

It should be said that when it comes to Brown and the media, there is a paradox. Despite appearances, he has always known how to play the press at their own game, as we have seen, or to get others to – he surrounded himself with advisers who showed no qualms about issuing brutal off-the-record briefings about political rivals. He has held a fascination with journalism since childhood, throughout university when he edited and contributed to the student paper, and later too when his elder brother John went into the trade after university. He himself wrote a weekly column for the *Daily Record* for decades before he became chancellor. And to this day he is a voracious reader of the media, one not adverse to courting populists within the trade, including his confidant Piers Morgan, the one-time *Sun* gossip columnist and then *Daily Mirror* editor who is now a star YouTuber.

Despite his interest, though, Brown does not have a great understanding of how the media works. However, one appearance certainly hit the mark. As we have seen, Morgan interviewed Brown on ITV in February 2010, including about the death of his prematurely born baby, with a tearful Sarah looking on. Such is the closeness of the Browns and Morgan that they discussed raising the subject of Jennifer before the broadcast. The interview was a success, with more than 4 million viewers.[17] Nonetheless, Brown was in a 'dark' mood the following morning, furious with the predictable newspaper coverage in the right-wing media, according to one aide who shared a car with him that day.

Brown and Morgan still watch football together. To Morgan's amusement, Brown tends to wear a suit while watching, and, 'when there's a half-time break, you basically get a fifteen-minute monologue about the world'. He lavishes praise on Brown, saying:

Honestly, I don't think there's any politician I've ever met with the possible exception of someone like Bill Clinton, who has a better grasp of global politics and a better, more eloquent and articulate way of explaining it. So I will see a time spent with Gordon, even when I first met him [through Sarah] to now, as almost like you're getting a masterclass in geopolitics. That just says to me that he just has this extraordinarily formidable brain. And honestly, I've never met anyone in British politics who's had a brain quite like Gordon's. And all this kind of insatiable hunger for information about what's going on in the world. And trying to make the world a better place. People can say what they like about Gordon, they can dislike his temperament, his personality, whatever. But they cannot ever dispute the fact that really his entire life has been devoted to trying to make Britain and the wider world a better place.[18]

On the one hand, like many political and media observers, Morgan blames Brown's decision not to call an early general election in late 2007 for the perceived failure of his premiership. But on the other, the TV presenter says the media treatment of Brown was so unfair as to be 'heartbreaking', and that the electorate, influenced by the media, got the 2010 general election verdict wrong.

As a friend of his with great admiration for him, I felt he could have been a really great, long-running prime minister for a few terms. It was pretty heartbreaking to watch how the media turned on him. And he didn't seem capable of being able to repel, to change that or to change the narrative.

He was hit by the financial crisis, but that should have been an incredibly powerful tool for him to be elected. Because he actually saved this country from financial disaster … So I felt at the time he never got the recognition he should have done. He still hasn't got the recognition he should have done. But what he did in that period, he was unbelievably bold and decisive. And he saved this country from an absolute financial Armageddon, probably helped save the world as well, with his actions in that period. And people never give him credit for that, [and] in my estimation, he should have won in that 2010 election. But by then, the narrative had set hold … And that all came from that [early] election issue.

What is also striking is that this view of Brown's media coverage is put forward by a journalist who is seen as anti-'woke' and anti-liberal. It helps to demonstrate Brown's own relative conservatism compared to the more liberal Tony Blair, and his occasional appeal to non-tribal and even Tory media.[19]

Indeed, Brown was grateful that Paul Dacre, the traditionally right-wing editor of the *Daily Mail*, attended Jennifer's funeral, a small affair. That fact caused as much shock in the *Mail* newsroom as it did in Labour circles. 'We were all appalled,' says a former Blair aide. Brown sought Dacre's support extensively, with some success, especially early on in his premiership. Even as late as 3 April 2009, the *Mail* was perhaps the most effusive of the papers over the G20 summit on the financial crash, with the headline, devised by Dacre, hailing 'BROWN'S NEW WORLD ORDER!'.

Before that, the *Mail* titles had been 'looked after' by Brown press aides over Budget leaks while Brown was chancellor, and used to help 'take down' Brown's perceived potential Blairite leadership rivals such as Charles Clarke, Alan Milburn and John Reid, according to a former spin doctor. One *Mail* insider goes so far as to claim that Brown would not have become prime minister without the *Mail*'s support, though that is probably fanciful. A source close to Brown says that he and Dacre bonded over Brown's 'moral' side with 'a touch of religion'. Also, of course, they shared a suspicion of Tony Blair and Alastair Campbell, who has long hated the *Daily Mail* and indeed Dacre. 'GB was the device with which Dacre could bash Blair,' says one individual familiar with the *Mail*.

Dacre's disdain for Blair is said to have gone back to the prime minister's 1999 autumn party conference speech against the 'forces of conservatism', which Dacre saw as an attack on himself, his readers and 'Middle England'. Soon after, Cherie Blair is said to have breastfed her baby during a meeting in front of Dacre, which the latter saw as 'an aggressively feminist act' according to a *Mail* insider. Brown, meanwhile, beyond doubt did develop a working relationship with Dacre, warm enough that he delivered a video message for a party to celebrate Dacre's twenty-five years as *Mail* editor in 2017.

The Browns also took Dacre and his wife Kathy to a production of Shakespeare's *Hamlet* at Stratford-upon-Avon during the premiership.[20] Brown confirms he went to see Dacre at the *Mail* offices several times, and tried to find agreement on certain areas, but that Dacre would insist that the *Daily Mail* was 'a Conservative newspaper and always will be'.[21] Dacre courteously declined to be interviewed for this book, on the grounds that he is still active in journalism and Brown is also still an active public figure.

And just as Charlie Whelan has now admitted being the source of the story which brought down Mandelson, Damian McBride, who was the controversial spin doctor to Brown during his premiership, wrote in his 2013 book *Power Trip* about briefing against Brown's perceived rivals and opponents – including those within the party such as the Blairite Charles Clarke. 'Labour, Conservative or Liberal Democrat; Ministers, MPs or advisers; if they'd ever shared their secrets with colleagues in Westminster, the chances were that I ended up being told about them, too. Drug use; spousal abuse; secret alcoholism; extra-marital affairs. I estimate I did nothing with 95 per cent of the stories I was told. But, yes, some of them ended up on the front pages of Sunday newspapers.'[22]

Loathed by some of his colleagues for his cynical tactics, McBride was also revered by others who worked with him, for his creativity and, according to one former colleague, his 'genius'. And McBride – who now works for the cabinet minister Yvette Cooper, the wife of Ed Balls – was not alone when it came to the notorious briefings from certain advisers and MPs supporting Brown. By the same token, some advisers were briefing against the prime minister.

But for all that Brown was the victim of the media, he was also capable of fighting his own corner, albeit crudely, and often against the Blairites, via his own spin doctors Whelan and McBride.

Tensions were running high at Labour's London headquarters when the clock struck ten on 6 May and the BBC broadcast its exit poll, projecting a hung Parliament and the Tories 19 seats short of the 326 parliamentary seats needed for an overall majority. Its projection was to prove almost spot on: the Conservatives ended up with 306 seats, Labour 258 and the Lib Dems 57.

Nearly 400 miles away, an exhausted Brown was asleep in his North Queensferry home when the poll was released. His team – including Sue Nye, speechwriter Kirsty McNeil, media aide Iain Bundred and policy adviser Stewart Wood – made their way from the local King Malcolm Hotel to the Browns' home at around 11 p.m. They found Sarah Brown watching a movie. 'I suppose we had better get moving,' she said as she went upstairs to wake her husband while the team set up the dining room to make calls and await the results.[23]

At around midnight on Thursday 6 May, they left for the Kirkcaldy count and Brown phoned a close adviser and Labour peer Andrew Adonis from the car, saying: 'It's all up in the air.' Adonis advised him to make clear he had no option but to allow talks between the parties. Nye outlines what happened that day from the inside: 'We knew by then that the Tories would probably be the largest party but were ... unsure about whether they could form a government. We were in hung Parliament territory. They hadn't made the gains they were looking for – such as Tooting [in south London] which was high on their list of marginals.'

Brown and his team flew at 3.30 a.m. to Stansted airport, with Brown telling reporters on the flight: 'I'm used to difficulty. Difficulty is not an excuse for failure. But difficulty does not set you back.' He got in to Labour's headquarters in Victoria Street around 5 a.m. and was met by the party staff. 'He gave an emotional, graceful speech thanking them,' Nye says. 'We went into a conference room where there were more sandwiches – all campaigns are run on sandwiches – and Gordon looked at the figures, and while it looked like a Conservative minority government that was by no means certain, would the final figures mean a Labour–Liberal coalition could be on the cards?'

Brown persuaded a reluctant Mandelson that it was a possibility, and Mandelson agreed to go on the airwaves to keep Brown in play, while the prime minister returned to Downing Street. 'Gordon always knew it was a long shot but also felt he had an obligation to make the effort for a Labour–Lib Dem agreement,' Nye says. 'The truth was that people hadn't voted for the Tory austerity programme and he felt he had a duty to try and stop that by default. No one knew better than Gordon that if the Tories formed a government they would use the economic crisis as an excuse to cut back the state.'

Constitutionally, Brown would remain as prime minister until a new government was formed with a majority, and three days after the election Alistair Darling, the chancellor, went ahead with plans to represent Britain at EU talks on problems facing the single currency. Kirsty McNeil's drafted 'immediate resignation' speech was left unused on her laptop. Brown was to find, however, that the Whitehall machine had expected him to be gone. As Nye recalls:

Although this was all new territory for everyone, he was still prime minister and there needed to be continuity while the uncertainty of the situation played out. So Gordon went back to Number Ten, which was not something we had envisaged doing. I went in the car with him and we went to the now deserted room in Number 12 that Gordon had occupied for the last year of his time in Number Ten. It was obvious that the civil service hadn't been expecting us to be back because our emails had been cut off and the furniture rearranged in the old den. That is the brutality of the British electoral system.

As Gordon had shown during the global economic crisis and in the lead-up to the G20, he had relentless resolve and he was determined to see if it was possible to form a progressive alliance with the Liberals, and it was his duty to seek to stop what he knew would be a terrible austerity programme from the Tories if they came to power ... In the call that took place later that day with Clegg, while discussing the similarities of the centre-left manifestos, the issue of personnel [whether Brown should stay on or not] did come up, but Gordon batted that away [saying] we can discuss that when we meet.[24]

When Cameron later spoke at his press conference, he offered a full coalition with the Lib Dems. 'He did not go down the Alex Salmond–SNP route of claiming victory after the Scottish Parliament election even though the numbers weren't there – which had been a worry for Gordon,' Nye explains. This had been one of Brown's biggest fears. On the Saturday, Brown attended the VE Day ceremony at the Cenotaph before flying back to Scotland with Sarah. The couple would return to London the following morning. Meanwhile, the first talks between Labour and the Liberal Democrats took place. On the Labour side were Ed Balls, Harriet Harman, Ed Miliband, Andrew Adonis and Peter Mandelson.

On 10 May, Brown met with Clegg at the Foreign Office. 'We were becoming increasingly worried about hanging around too long,' Nye says. 'This was never about Gordon wanting to stay on as prime minister. Gordon very early on recognised that his departure could be used as a negotiating tactic, but could only be used once and at the right time. I know people that were in Number Ten who thought he didn't understand that but I think he was very wary of [the tactic] being common knowledge and being used at the wrong time. He also felt an obligation to sort this out until a new leader was in situ.'

Next, Brown met Clegg again, this time in the Commons – and to avoid the press they walked through an underground tunnel to the Ministry of Defence. Personnel issues were raised by Clegg and Clegg's former chief of staff, Danny Alexander, a Lib Dem MP. 'If [Brown] resigned immediately that would have drawn the Queen into the situation which everyone was trying very hard to prevent,' Nye explains. The palace would then have had no choice but to invite the Tories as the largest party to form a minority government, which would have left the Liberal Democrats out of the equation. 'Gordon said he wanted to make sure the referendum [on electoral reform, which the Lib Dems insisted upon as part of any agreement for a coalition] worked and he felt he needed to be there for getting support for electoral reform from Labour. Gordon [said he] would announce he was leaving but if there was to be a coalition he couldn't leave the party rudderless at that critical point.'

At 5 p.m. on 10 May, Gordon made a statement from the steps of Number Ten in which he referred to Britain's 'progressive majority'. It is worth quoting parts of it at some length:

> Mr Clegg has just informed me that, while he intends to continue his dialogue that he has begun with the Conservatives, he now wishes also to take forward formal discussions with the Labour Party. I believe it is sensible and it is in the national interest to respond positively ...
>
> There is ... a progressive majority in Britain and I believe it could be in the interests of the whole country to form a progressive coalition government. In addition to the economic priorities, in my view, only such a progressive government could meet the demand for political and electoral change which the British people made last Thursday.
>
> Our commitments on a new voting system for the House of Commons and for the election of the House of Lords are clearly part of this. I would, however, like to say something also about my own position. If it becomes clear that the national interest, which is stable and principled government, can be best served by forming

a coalition between the Labour Party and the Liberal Democrats, then I believe I should discharge that duty to form that government which would, in my view, command a majority in the House of Commons in the Queen's speech and any other confidence votes. But I have no desire to stay in my position longer than is needed to ensure the path to economic growth is assured and the process of political reform we have agreed moves forward quickly.

For Brown, the move was – once again – self-sacrificial, not least because at that stage there was still an outside chance of a progressive coalition of sorts between Labour, the Liberal Democrats, the Greens (albeit with one seat) and others such as Plaid Cymru, the SDLP and the Alliance. With the five Sinn Fein MPs not taking their seats, that might have just been enough to form the tiniest of overall majorities. Charles Clarke claims now with hindsight that Brown's move effectively to set out a timetable for his resignation as Labour leader came three days too late, and that had he done so on the Friday before, a new leader – such as Alan Johnson – could have made it much more difficult for the Lib Dems to go into coalition with the Tories.[25]

Sue Nye recounts: 'It was a dignified and graceful exit and I was watching this from inside with Peter and it was a hugely emotional moment for both of us. Gordon tried to speak to Peter when he came back in but [Mandelson] had to move away – it was too emotional for him. Remember we had shared history – the Michael Foot years, the years we had worked with Neil Kinnock to transform the party, the modernisation project from the early nineties, the exhilaration of the election in 1997, and now we were all together at the end.'

Brown had been taking soundings all weekend from the cabinet, some linked in via a 'spider phone', a conference device on speaker. The meeting began with an update on the economy from Alistair Darling before Brown gave an update on Afghanistan. It then turned into a discussion about the politics of the situation – half wanted the coalition, with a similar number against. 'Some were doubtful or ambivalent – colleagues paid tribute to the way Gordon had been handling the negotiations,' recalls Nye. 'The calculations were all about fewer than a dozen votes and what the nationalist parties or the Northern Ireland parties would do. But the cabinet agreed that the attempt to form a progressive coalition should proceed.'[26]

Brown sent a hitherto unseen passionate letter to Clegg outlining how they could work together in a progressive, pro-European alliance. In a sign of what could have been, instead of the move towards Brexit that followed, Brown wrote: 'All decisions the new Government makes will be taken on the basis of a pro-European and outward-looking pro-global and non-protectionist agenda ... To achieve this – a new approach to the public life of our country, and then a new approach to economic management and objectives – all brought about by a new form of Government in which power is shared on an agreed basis between two parties, would in my judgement constitute real change: exciting, dynamic, innovative and long term and empowering.'[27] Brown describes phoning Clegg from Number Ten just before he resigned as prime minister, saying that Clegg had failed to get back to him by a certain deadline, which showed he had wanted to go in with the Tories all along and that Clegg was just using Brown and stringing him along while he gained concessions from the Tories.

Immediately after the poll, there were too few people, with notable exceptions such as Alastair Campbell and Andrew Adonis, both unelected, willing to fight wholeheartedly alongside Brown. Both Brown and Adonis believed this was possible, as the latter outlines in *5 Days in May*. Indeed, in that important book Adonis says that the 'possibility of a Lab–Lib partnership had been a preoccupation of Gordon's since becoming prime minister in 2007'.[28] Assuming all the small parties voted with Labour to form a 'rainbow coalition', or abstain, the thinking by Brown and Adonis was that the Queen's speech would command between 330 and 338 votes, with only the 306 Tories against, and this was enough to conduct basic government business.

But Clegg insists 'the maths' would never have worked. He says today:

> No one, despite whatever axe they have to grind, or narrative they want to tell, or history they want to retell, can escape the fundamental maths, and the fundamental maths was and remains and will immutably always be the following: Labour and the Liberal Democrats together fell well short of [an overall] majority. We simply didn't have a majority. And I said that publicly, I said that privately ...

And I really do think it's verging on the wilfully dishonest somehow to pretend that there was an off-the-shelf and easy-to-be-done deal there. If we had done what Gordon tried to propose to me – and I didn't really ever fully understand it as it was this contorted minority government of Labour, Lib Dems – then you're borrowing and stealing for every vote. This wouldn't last. It wouldn't last even probably a matter of weeks before it would collapse.

I was always very clear in my mind that in the end, the choice that the country faced, because that is the agonising set of cards that the voters dealt to us ... after that election [there] was either going to have to be another election within a few months, or a government composed of the only two parties that could actually create a parliamentary majority. I remember ... one of my last meetings with Gordon, when we were on our own in his parliamentary office behind the Speaker's chair in the House of Commons, and he took one of his favourite thick felt-tip pens and started sketching out on a little paper how you could put together some unworkable, ramshackle alignment of MPs with Plaid Cymru here, one Green there, and I literally remember interrupting him and saying, 'Gordon, it doesn't work. It does not add up.'[29]

Labour is also open to the criticism that it did not plan enough for meetings with the Liberal Democrats: there was no document prepared from which to work. Clegg feels that Balls and Mandelson did not have their hearts in a deal. Balls confirms today that 'none of us' on the Labour negotiating side believed a Labour–Liberal deal was possible. 'The only person who believed that we could somehow magically conjure up a governing arrangement was Gordon,' Clegg says. 'He was the outgoing prime minister. Generally, I try and be civil to people, even people who are my opponents. I had respect for him. I still do, but I do think it's really not worthy of him or the people around him to reinvent history. It's somewhat self-serving, almost somewhat self-pitying, to suggest that somehow I tricked them out of the government when ... their own side didn't believe it was possible, and the maths clearly made it impossible. I really think it's beneath Gordon.'

Balls responds: 'Of course, when given their opportunity to go into government, the Liberal Democrats were right to take it. I have no criticism of Nick Clegg for that ... We knew that the Liberal Democrats were game-playing. Gordon kept believing that political forces on Nick Clegg within the Lib Dems might persuade him that there was genuinely a Labour–Liberal alternative. But I don't think any of us in the coalition discussions ever thought that was possible ... Nick Clegg was a pro-European Tory, so I don't think he disagreed with George Osborne on austerity. So my view is that their enabling of Osborne austerity was the wrong moral choice ... Fundamentally, Nick Clegg enabled an austerity coalition.'[30]

Either way, while stringing Labour along, the Lib Dems were by now demanding Brown's political head as a price for entering into a deal with a party that historically at least, despite what Balls says, would and should have made for more natural bedfellows. Clegg's desire for a Tory alliance became clear on the morning of Tuesday 11 May, when negotiating teams from Labour and the Liberal Democrats met in private in room 319 of Portcullis House at Westminster. On the Labour side of the table were Andrew Adonis, Peter Mandelson, Ed Miliband, Ed Balls and Harriet Harman. Their plan, in the face of signs that Nick Clegg was on the verge of a deal to enter into coalition with the Conservatives, was to try to persuade the Lib Dems to switch sides. This would reunite the historically divided Labour and Liberal movements and, in the words of one source, 'smash the Tories into a thousand pieces'.[31]

But it was clear the Lib Dems were not interested, and that morning senior Labour figures, including John Reid and David Blunkett, spoke out publicly against the possibility of a coalition, urging Brown to respect the voters' verdict. Their intervention was widely seen as the final blow to his hopes of cobbling together an anti-Tory alliance. As Sue Nye says of that Tuesday: 'Mood changed – Gordon resolved that today was the day he would resign if there was no movement on the Liberal Democrat side. He was also very adamant that he wanted to leave in the daylight and Sarah wanted the family to leave together.'

As it became clear that Brown's time – and that of Labour in office – was coming to an end, old party hands including Alastair Campbell, Douglas Alexander, Ed Balls and Ed Miliband were called into Downing Street and the moments were captured in iconic images organised by Sue Nye. At the beginning of the general election campaign, Nye had mooted the idea of getting a newspaper to conduct a photo montage of the campaign on the basis that a photograph can sum up stories in an instant. The pros and cons were discussed but eventually Nye was given the green light. Nye had known Martin Argles from the *Guardian* for many years and she put the proposition to him to see if the *Guardian* would be interested. There were obviously issues about editorial independence, which were subsequently resolved.

'The mood in the office between the Nick Clegg calls had lightened, given the die was cast, and I had made sure that most of the old team were all in Number Ten,' says Nye. 'Gordon's mind had been made up from the moment he had come down to the office that morning. It was therefore quite light-hearted in Gordon's office overlooking the garden. There were reminiscences about elections, old favourite jokes, some bottles of whisky were signed for raffles – nothing in politics gets in the way of raffle prizes. It was also quite strange because it was obvious that [the permanent secretary] Jeremy Heywood was disappearing into private rooms to have talks with the other parties. Gordon took the last call from Nick Clegg at around 7 p.m., Nick Clegg wanted another night but Gordon was adamant that he was going to the palace that night.'[32]

Clegg had meanwhile vetoed a planned key meeting between Alistair Darling and Vincent Cable, the Lib Dem Treasury spokesperson. Cable was said to be more sympathetic to a deal with Labour, though Brown today doubts that. Eventually, after running out of patience with Clegg, who clearly did want to join forces with the Tories – despite characteristically principled opposition from Charles Kennedy, who similarly had been a somewhat lone voice even in his own party leadership over the Iraq war – Brown resigned with dignity the same day as the Portcullis House meeting, after phoning Clegg and telling him he was doing so. Sue Nye was beside Brown at the time and took a shorthand note of the call. As she says now: 'Clegg wanted to spin the talks ...'

Clegg does not deny this. He says, effectively, that's politics.

> That was my role at the time, to try to secure the maximum amount of Liberal Democrat influence in any government we're going to go into. And there was the all-important issue of the degree to which we could get a commitment – a meaningful commitment – to change

the electoral system through a referendum and in my negotiating team, I remember, particularly Chris Huhne was very adamant about this; [he] felt that it was more likely that we were going to extract something which the Conservatives were desperate not to concede, which was a referendum on changing the electoral system, unless they felt that there was some credible means by which we could secure something better from Labour.

So, of course, given that Gordon was so keen to talk to us, and was so keen to constantly propose these, what we knew to be implausible suggestions – the fact that the Conservatives thought that there might be some risk in that happening, we were not going to dispel that. Why should we? That wasn't my role. My role was not to look out for the Conservative Party, the Labour Party. My role was to look out for the Liberal Democrats. As the leader of the Liberal Democrats, my job was to judge what best served the things we believed in, and that was also a collective decision.

You've got to remember, unlike the other parties, I only acted within the negotiating remit that was granted to me both by the parliamentary party and then, finally, by a meeting of the wider party membership ... And we saw that they [the Conservatives] were anxious that somehow they were going to be outbid on that issue by Labour. I'm so mystified that they [Labour] level this moral accusation. Gordon and his people have this moralising tendency – it's as if they can't admit their own shortcomings, so they assume it has to be the fault of someone else's perfidy. I tried to do the best in the service of the things we believe in ... What did they expect us to do?

It was all over for the dream of a progressive alliance. Sue Nye describes the end: 'Sarah and the boys came down from the flat. Gordon thanked the team that had worked so hard. We organised for the cars to be moved further down the street so that the family could walk the short distance to get into the cars to head to the palace. We then went back in and packed up our desks again for the last time and left the building. I had left through the same door in 1979 after that election defeat by Mrs Thatcher, never dreaming that it would take eighteen years before Labour would win the biggest election landslide in history in 1997. It was then a privilege to be part of thirteen years of New Labour history with first Tony Blair and then Gordon Brown as prime ministers.'

The woman who was by Brown's side for more than twenty years reflects: 'There was much to be proud [of] in those thirteen years of government – a decade of solid economic growth and reform, the introduction of the minimum wage, the rebuilding of our health service and schools, the Good Friday Agreement, the fairer society that the party had spent so much time trying to achieve in the eighteen long years of opposition had finally begun to take shape in that period. There was obviously more to do and some things that should have been done differently, but at the end of the day it was still a Labour government to be proud of.'

As Brown left office in 2010, contrary to conventional wisdom, he had saved Labour from tearing itself apart amid recriminations, policy and personality clashes. Outside Number Ten, he said: 'Only those that have held the office of prime minister can understand the full weight of its responsibilities and its great capacity for good. I have been privileged to learn much about the very best in human nature and a fair amount too about its frailties, including my own. Above all, it was a privilege to serve. And yes, I loved the job, not for its prestige, its titles and its ceremony – which I do not love at all. No, I loved the job for its potential to make this country I love fairer, more tolerant, more green, more democratic, more prosperous and more just – truly a greater Britain.'

Gordon Brown's premiership began with goodwill from a public thirsty for the change and substance he had promised as he took over from Tony Blair. After a honeymoon with the electorate, it was damaged by dithering over the snap election that never was, an economic downturn, and even the subsequent global financial crash itself, the tackling of which most commentators now agree represents one of Brown's finest periods in public life. Most of the media, whose centre of gravity is to the right, gave Brown an especially hard time, returning to its anti-left instincts that had seen torrid coverage for Neil Kinnock before Brown. Brown tried to run his own aggressive media operation, largely positioned against what Brown's camp saw as his enemies among the Blairites, but it was too crude and ultimately failed. Brown should have showed his authentic self more in his campaign, which occasionally came to life as it did in his Citizens

UK speech, but was damaged by the Gillian Duffy 'bigoted woman' comments. Perhaps Westminster conventional wisdom is right for once, that Brown, having waited so long for the top job, was always going to be a better chancellor than he was a front man. After all, he was, as Roy Jenkins had said in 2002, a 'tail-end Charlie' – a reference to the perilous role of a rear gunner in war – coming after Tony Blair.[33]

Nonetheless, despite losing, in the end Brown kept the Labour Party together as an electoral force that would win again, when it could have been destroyed after thirteen years of tumultuous government which included the highly controversial Iraq war. To the party he has loyally served for five decades, Brown gave a fighting chance not just for a progressive alliance that never came about, but also for the future.

And in his departure from office and beyond, Brown was truly to come into his own.

PART FOUR

Moral Leadership (2010–)

17

After Downing Street: Referendum

For some months Brown was depressed back home at North Queensferry after the 2010 general election result, which he blamed harshly on himself. But he was never going to retire and play golf. As Tony Blair says today: 'He remains completely dedicated to public service and to making the world better. And that extraordinary energy, I don't notice it's lagging at all.'[1] Alastair Campbell adds: 'A former prime minister is entitled to go around the world and make speeches and get paid. That's not what motivates him at all.'[2]

Having resigned as prime minister and party leader, Gordon Brown, at fifty-nine and on the backbenches for the first time since 1987, still had boundless energy and things he wanted to achieve. Some predecessors, such as Margaret Thatcher and Tony Blair, had taken to the lecture circuit and made lots of money, as was their right, but Brown felt he still had more to offer, and with his status as a former PM set out to do what he could to help others.

First, Brown decided publicly to take personal responsibility – against the advice of his wife Sarah and his closest aide Sue Nye – for Labour's failure to retain office. He refused to nominate his preferred successor, but the suspicion remained that he privately opposed David Miliband and covertly favoured Ed Miliband, who narrowly beat his older brother to the post.

But Brown was dismayed when Ed Miliband, whose rise he had supported over the years, apologised for the invasion of Iraq. 'I criticise nobody faced with making the toughest of decisions and I honour our troops who fought and died there, but I do believe that we were wrong. Wrong to take Britain to war,' Miliband had told the Labour conference in Manchester, at which he had just been announced as the new leader, in September 2010. Along with many in New Labour, Brown felt it was seen as a denunciation of the party's broader record in government. In a sign of tensions at the top of the party, David, who had been Brown's foreign secretary, was caught on camera rebuking Harriet Harman for applauding the remarks, saying: 'You voted for it, why are you clapping?'

To be fair to Ed Miliband, he was not elected to Parliament until 2005, so there is no way of knowing for sure how he would have voted as an MP. He had phoned Brown from America, while he was lecturing on economics at Harvard on a sabbatical from being a Treasury special adviser in 2003, to suggest Brown oppose the Iraq invasion. And Brown would come to regret his failure to do so. But at this point, he disapproved of his protégé's words. In a sign that, after all, Brown truly is New Labour to his core, he described it to friends as the 'year zero' approach, as if the entire period of achievements from 1997 to 2010 was somehow an embarrassment to some in Labour afterwards.

Brown did make a handful of speeches in Parliament, on Scotland, on media phone hacking and, perhaps most powerfully, in a tribute to his old friend Nelson Mandela, who died in December 2013. Addressing MPs from the backbenches, Brown recalled unveiling the statue of Mandela in Parliament Square in the presence of the great man and his wife, Graça, in 2007, adding: 'Not only the greatest leader of our generation and across the generations [but] the most courageous man you could meet.' Nevertheless, after 2010, as a general rule, Brown decided to limit his trips to Westminster and stay mainly in his constituency. Apart from charity-related trips, he remains reluctant to visit London today.

However, it was from his home in Scotland where one of the most active of living former prime ministers would perform a further, dramatic act of public service. Brown was dragged back into action by a referendum on independence, promised in the 2011 Scottish elections by a victorious SNP – and given the go-ahead by David Cameron. On 21 March 2013 it was announced that the historic referendum would be held on 18 September 2014, triggering eighteen months of impassioned campaigning over Scotland's future.

Brown's old friend and Scottish Labour ally from the 1970s onwards, Alistair Moffat, had visited the Browns' home and found the former prime minister 'very down and very down on himself' following the 2010 result.³ But Moffat told him firmly, reverting to the term they have used for one another for fifty years, 'You've got to get involved, comrade.'

Initially, Brown was reluctant and said, 'They don't need me.' But eventually, after several months and when Moffat agreed to help him, Brown accepted he had to intervene, and was fired by his lifelong passion for the mutually beneficial relationship between Scotland and England, two nations that had proved since the Act of Union in 1707 that, despite their differences, they were culturally, economically and politically greater than the sum of their parts. Now this was all threatened. Bob Shrum, another friend, talked to Brown at that time and says: 'He finally decided that he had to go out and just wage a campaign on his own against it.'⁴

The stark political backdrop was the rise of the SNP and the fact they had won 69 out of 129 seats in the 2011 Scottish Parliament elections, with about 45 per cent of the vote, despite the system being created in such a way as supposedly to make outright one-party rule almost impossible. Suddenly, the party whose mission was independence was in complete control, and opinion polls suggested that what had once been a decent majority against independence was now much more narrow. The momentum was with the SNP under Alex Salmond – especially because the Tories were in charge in London and deeply unpopular in Scotland.

However, it was at Christmas 2013 when Brown was wrapping gifts for his two sons, John and Fraser, and staring out at the rough waters of the River Forth from his home in North Queensferry, that he first began to think seriously about emerging once more from the relatively quiet life he had finally got used to in Britain, and making the case for Scotland remaining within the United Kingdom – for the sake of his children. In the foreword of his 2014 book *My Scotland, Our Britain*,⁵ which argues Scotland and England should 'pool and share' their resources, and which is dedicated to his children including Jennifer, Brown explains: 'My boys had started to be aware that Scotland might leave Britain as a result of a referendum. Only one or two questions so far and the parcels under the Christmas tree were, unsurprisingly, still more of a discussion point for them. But, as my thoughts turned to events in Scotland, I kept asking myself the same question. What were the prospects for my children – and millions of children in Scotland and Britain? If we went for independence we were making an irreversible decision that, for good or ill, my children and their children would have to live with all their lives.' Alistair Moffat calls that book 'the frame' for the case against independence.

Brown had always advocated for the creation of a Scottish Parliament, which came in 1998, and today still wants to see further devolution to Scotland as well as the regions. Moffat – who points out that, uniquely among modern politicians, Brown has the judgement of a historian – is clear that this was the correct approach, and that had Labour ignored the desire for devolution in Scotland, the 2014 referendum would have been won by the nationalists.[6]

The background to Brown's perspective on the rise of nationalism and how best to tackle it is explained by deindustrialisation, and the weakening of traditional Scottish institutions. He has said: 'The economic roots of Scottish nationalism lay in the same long-term trends – industrial decline, insecurity and the squeezed middle class – that have bred anti-establishment rebellions across the West.' In the 1950s, 40 per cent of the British workforce was in manufacturing or mining, but by the second decade of the twenty-first century only 7 per cent was. In that time, a million skilled jobs had been lost in coal, textiles, steel and shipbuilding, and with it, the standard of living, status and prospects of many.

The Tories would have their own reasons for opposing devolution and independence, including in some cases a disdain for Scotland verging on English nationalism, surely based at least in part on the relative unpopularity of the Conservatives in Scotland, certainly beyond the borders with England. And in the first two years of Thatcher's administration, Scotland lost a fifth of its workforce, with an assault on the coal and textile industries and pit closures across the country. Following rising unemployment and cuts to tax and spending, while Scotland as a whole voted Labour and kept seeing the Conservatives elected, Thatcher would go on to use Scotland as a guinea pig, inflicting the poll tax on Scots before rolling out the policy that would be her undoing in November 1990.

As Brown explains, 'When the British state looked less able to reverse these trends, "London mismanagement" became a constant refrain of the nationalists, and "Westminster" an all-purpose adjective to sustain grudges, both real and imagined. There were cultural forces at work too: traditional Scottish institutions had ceased to be vehicles through which people could express their Scottishness in an apolitical way.' The Church of Scotland, meanwhile, had lost a million members since the 1950s and voluntary organisations no longer exerted the same influence. 'People were looking for new ways to express and assert their identity. With their "Scotland first" slogans – "it's Scotland's oil" being the prime example – the SNP were well placed to step into this vacuum.'

And the former prime minister who had given a speech about 'British jobs for British workers' also outlines how the rise of Scottish nationalism was boosted by the failure of politicians to forge a unifying British identity for half a century. 'Historically, countries like America and France have found common ground by consciously affirming shared ideals. Britain, especially England, has never felt the need to do the same. Partly because it has not been invaded, defeated in war or suffered a constitutional breakdown for three and a half centuries, it has never engaged in recent years in the kind of constitutional debates that could define the character of the country and bring people together as one. Unlike the French or Americans, Britain as a whole has shied away from a story we can tell about ourselves, a narrative that draws strength from our *past*, makes sense of our present and offers hope for the future.'[7]

My Scotland, Our Britain traces the origins of modern social provision to Scotland's demands for the abolition of the Scottish Poor Law and its replacement by a British welfare state. Contrary to conventional wisdom, Brown argues that the concept of 'sharing' across the UK was not an English imposition but in fact a Scottish invention. Brown's book provided the basis for his many speeches in those months following the announcement of the referendum, when Brown spoke at universities and in schools, at pensioner forums, to a range of faith and other groups, including Carmelite nuns and the Royal British Legion, across towns and villages the length of Scotland.

Yet he sensed that the message was not getting through, because it was overshadowed by a campaign that was effectively led by the Tory government which, Brown felt, was inadvertently playing into the hands of the nationalists who were pitching the argument as England against Scotland. 'What was getting through, loud and clear, was that the people of Scotland wanted change. And here was the irony: each pro-union party had a strong devolution programme, with detailed proposals about additional powers for the Scottish Parliament over taxation, employment, social policy and welfare. The problem was that nobody had heard about the proposals or had any idea that if they voted No, new powers would be delivered.'[8]

The cross-party, unionist Better Together campaign was often chaotic, which helps explain the dramatic narrowing of the polls, from a year before the vote, when the 'No' side was twenty points ahead, to the two sides being broadly neck and neck as the poll approached. Speeches were frequently composed at the last minute, the Liberal Democrats were accused of not pulling their weight and the press operation was weak, while the 'Yes' campaign was three times as active on social media compared to the 'No' team. Over the summer of 2014, however, the articulate shadow foreign secretary Douglas Alexander was called in to boost the unionist cause. The safe pair of hands that was Alistair Darling fronted the Better Together campaign, and helped to bring in funds – including from the revered authors J. K. Rowling, an Edinburgh neighbour of Darling, and C. J. Sansom – while the then political operator and now MP Blair McDougall helped to run it. Alexander scripted interviews and worked on general messaging and advertising designed to reach out to Scots still wavering over their momentous decision.

And after watching a YouTube video at 2 a.m. and spotting a 'Non merci' poster behind Pierre Trudeau, the prime minister of Canada, as he spoke against independence for Quebec during the 1980 referendum campaign, Alexander adopted the very Scottish – at once polite but dismissive – 'No thanks' for the campaign. The 'Love Scotland, vote No' posters which would later adorn the Maryhill Community Centre in central Glasgow for Brown's eve-of-poll speech had been Alexander's idea. Torsten Bell, now an MP, was brought in to hone the financial arguments, while Paul Sinclair, a former aide to Brown and political journalist, helped with the media. Eventually, the Labour-led machine was canvassing 200,000 homes per day.

However, as Moffat explains: 'One of the biggest problems we had was that David Cameron would not talk to us. I thought, he thinks that this is going to be won. I was absolutely certain that it was on a knife edge. And my son and my daughters were telling me that young people were moving towards the SNP. And Gordon shared that he was sure that this was going to be closer so he thought it was crucial to talk to David Cameron, but Cameron wasn't taking calls. He thought this was going to be fine.'

Eventually, through a contact organised by Moffat, Brown was able to persuade Cameron to prepare to make a political rather than merely economic intervention, pleading with Scotland to stay and not focusing on the financial case for the union. Douglas Alexander also spoke to Cameron on the phone from Edinburgh, explaining to him the need to intervene in a 'limited' and 'emotional' way.[9]

Then on the evening of Saturday 6 September, twelve days before the referendum vote, details emerged of the following morning's *Sunday Times* splash, featuring a YouGov poll which gave the 'Yes' side its first lead. The Tory pollster Andrew Cooper, working for the 'No' campaign, had predicted such a scenario, but there was panic nonetheless. Miliband sent more Labour staff to help with Better Together, and he met with Cameron on the Monday in the Commons where the pair agreed to cancel that week's Prime Minister's Questions and travel to Scotland to make last-ditch appeals. It was then that Cameron finally turned on the emotional appeal, arguing that a 'painful divorce' would be 'for good, forever' and pleaded with Scotland not to go. 'We want you to stay. Head and heart and soul, we want you to stay. Please don't mix up the temporary and the permanent. Please don't think: "I'm frustrated with politics right now, so I'll walk out the door and never come back." If you don't like me – I won't be here forever. If you don't like this government – it won't last forever. But if you leave the UK – that will be forever.'[10]

It was this same week that Brown decided, as he puts it, 'to move things forward' by publishing his own timetable, in the hope that all the unionist parties would follow it up. Now, just days before the vote, Brown spoke in Midlothian and called for legislation within a year, adding that proposals for enhanced devolution should be agreed by St Andrew's Day that November and legislation drafted and published by Burns Night the following January. With sign-off from the Conservatives and Liberal Democrats, this led to the Smith Commission on further powers for the Scottish Parliament cemented by the Scotland Act of 2016.

Brown had successfully convened the main parties, in a sign of his persuasiveness in a crisis and a sense of a turning point among the unionists. Brown's brainchild was 'the vow' under which the leaders of three main UK-wide parties would transfer more powers to Holyrood if Scots rejected independence. He hastily secured the backing of Cameron, Miliband and Clegg for the joint commitment, which appeared on the front page of the *Daily Record* on 14 September, four days before the referendum vote, and may have helped seal the deal of a No vote in 2014, to the fury of nationalists.

Brown had secured the paper's 'splash' and full support after persuading the *Daily Record*'s editor, Murray Foote, to run the front page. The creation of 'the vow' had been tense. Brown and his team were tired. At one point, Moffat and Brown had a lively argument over an adjective. Brown wanted to call it 'faster, fairer and friendlier change', but Moffat insisted 'friendlier' wasn't a proper word and it should be 'more friendly'. Swear words were exchanged. But 'the vow' did the trick because, as Moffat points out, it helped to show that voting 'No' would result in change.[11]

Brown arrived at the Maryhill Community Centre on Wednesday 17 September 2014 – the eve of the Scottish independence vote – to deliver the speech of his life. The intervention had only been finalised the day before, and Brown had been up writing it since 4 a.m. He was the one man in Scotland who – though controversial among Labour's opponents – was sufficiently respected, and armed with the skills of oration, to tip the balance.

Pausing outside the red-brick hall before the speech, Brown was alarmed to observe a striking number of 'Yes' posters in the shop and apartment windows opposite. This moment had been preceded by months of wrangling between Brown and the cross-party 'Better Together' campaign, which was hosting this event. Brown, who spoke at nearly a hundred rallies across Scotland, had wanted a distinct Labour pro-union campaign, and had privately asked David Cameron and George Osborne for half the 'No' funds to go to Labour for that purpose. The Tories had refused.

The difference of opinion over what Brown today still calls 'the ludicrous nature of the Better Together campaign' had even enhanced tension between Brown and his own former chancellor, Alistair Darling, who was seen as non-partisan enough by the

Conservatives to be running 'Better Together' after Ed Miliband persuaded him to do so. Osborne had stuck to the cynical and dry economic arguments based on keeping the pound sterling, insisting that Scots would be worse off on the outside. The lack of inspiring politics in the campaign had been part of what had frustrated Brown. He says today: 'I was always against project fear. You cannot say to Scottish people, you're too poor or too weak or too stupid to be independent.'[12] But now he had to forget all the internal arguments on the unionist side and issue a rallying call that would do no less than tilt a bitterly divided nation towards staying in the United Kingdom.

At the Maryhill Community Centre, Brown says, 'there was an altogether different atmosphere. The hall was packed to the rafters with noisy supporters of Better Together and the walls were adorned with the slogan "Love Scotland, vote No". It was the most positive poster message I had seen throughout the whole campaign. As I sat quietly in the corner of the upstairs green room, word came back of camera crews and journalists squeezed together, upstairs and downstairs, that it was hot, and that there was a real air of anticipation in the hall. The Maryhill speech had been organised by Better Together at short notice and would have to be word-perfect. While the stump speech that I had delivered to audiences across the country ran to forty-five minutes, this was to be just thirteen minutes.'[13]

Thirty seconds before Brown was due to be introduced onstage, waiting in a corridor and ready to go, he was startled as someone whispered, 'Your right shoe is covered in mud.' A Labour organiser, Annmarie Whyte, quickly had to clean the shoe with a paper towel while they could hear Eddie Izzard announcing Brown. But Brown had also been listening to the warm-up testimonies of pro-union members of the public talking about shipbuilding, the NHS, education and pensions, and he began spontaneously and to raucous applause, booming: 'At last, the world is hearing the voices of the real people of Scotland. The silent majority will be silent no more.'

Pacing the stage in his trademark dark suit, white shirt and red tie, his voice cracking with emotion, he made the case for taking pride in Scotland and in voting No. Powerfully reclaiming Scotland from the nationalist forces, he said: 'Scotland belongs to all of us. And tell the nationalists, it's not their flag, their culture, their country or their streets. Tell them it's everyone's flag, everyone's culture, everyone's country and everyone's streets.'

He concluded: 'So if you have any doubts about the future unresolved, any questions unanswered, any risks unexplained, if you don't know, then you have to vote "No"... If you, like me, believe the way forward is not separation but justice through cooperation, then I say to you today: Hold yourselves with dignity. Have confidence. Our values are the values of the people of Scotland. Have confidence. Our stronger Scottish Parliament meets the needs and aspirations of the Scottish people. Have confidence. Our future lies in cooperation and sharing, and not in separation and splitting apart. That unity is our strength. Have the confidence to stand up, be counted and say for Scotland's sake: not now, not this time, not the risks, no thanks. Have confidence to stand up and be counted and say, for Scotland's future, "No".'

Brown says today: 'The whole point was to make the Scottish people feel proud to vote "No".' The speech was widely accepted even by Conservatives to be one of the best any modern politician has given. As his fellow Scot but Tory opponent Michael Gove acknowledges: 'I think the single best speech, and the single most inspiring moment in the whole campaign, was the speech he gave in the final week in Glasgow. I still, from time to time, watch it on YouTube. And I marvel. It was quite brilliant, and I didn't think anyone else could have done it in that way or with such effect, because in crude terms, the Yes side had the better of the emotional arguments and the Better Together side the better intellectual arguments. But that was the moment when the speech touched people's emotions most effectively of any speech or any intervention in the campaign. And I didn't think anyone else could have done it as effectively as he did.'[14]

Brown says that throughout the tense campaign with its ups and downs – reflected by the fluctuating polls – he was never in doubt Scots would vote to stay in the union, but also that on the night the polls closed he was nervous over what would be the scale of the 'No' campaign's victory. However, once he heard the first result – a clear 'No' in Scotland's smallest local authority area, Clackmannanshire, by 53.8 per cent to 46.2 per cent with a turnout of 88.6 per cent – he was able to go to bed with some confidence and woke at around 6 a.m. on Friday 19 September, as the nationalist leaders conceded defeat. The 'No' campaign had won with 2,001,926 (55.3 per cent) votes, with

1,617,989 (44.7 per cent) voting in favour of breaking up the UK. The turnout – 84.6 per cent – was the highest recorded for an election or referendum in the UK since the general election back in January 1910, which had been held before the introduction of universal suffrage.

That morning, in an untimely concession to the party's right wing, Cameron called for 'English votes for English laws' – to the fury of Brown. From his North Queensferry home, at around 8 a.m. the former prime minister telephoned the cabinet secretary Jeremy Heywood, arguing that Cameron's move had been 'disastrous' and 'sectarian'. He said that by floating restrictions on the right of Scottish MPs to vote on the UK Budget, Cameron's words would only play into the divisive hands of the nationalists, who were claiming the moral high ground, maintaining that they had been stitched up by Westminster. Brown asked to speak to Cameron, who declined to take the call.

The following day, ahead of a service of reconciliation for the country, Brown gave a statesmanlike speech at his Fife constituency, in Dalgety Bay, Dunfermline, saying now was not the time for 'barnstorming speeches' but for a quiet recognition of Scotland's distinct thirst for social justice around which all parties could now unite. After paying tribute to the outgoing first minister Alex Salmond's 'lifetime of service to Scotland' (as well as Alistair Darling and the Better Together campaign 'for their two and a half years of advocacy, organisation and sheer hard work'), he went on: 'The Old Testament says that there is a time for everything and a season for every activity under the heavens. And we know from the psalms that there is a time to tear down and a time to build. A time to tear up and a time to mend. As they put it: "A time to kill and a time to heal." I would put it in modern language: there is a time to fight and a time to unite, and from today onwards this is the time to unite. Not just in words, but in deeds, and around what I know we can discover as a common purpose for our country.'

Brown ended by saying that for 'a confident Scotland, home rule in a more unified UK and in a more interdependent world is the next chapter of Scotland's story and the next stage of Scotland's journey'. It was a theme he echoed in the House of Commons a month later, leading a debate arguing that 'the vow' to the people of Scotland should be kept. But Brown still blames the cross-party

Better Together campaign for Labour's collapse in Scotland. His own website states that 'The Scotland Act that followed gave substantial new powers to the Scottish Parliament. However, unable to shake off the accusation that Labour had aligned with the Tories to deliver a negative message and could no longer speak for Scotland, they were virtually wiped out in the 2015 general election in Scotland. It would take until June 2017 for the party to mount the first stages of a recovery under Jeremy Corbyn and [former Scottish Labour leader] Kezia Dugdale.'[15]

Apart from anything else, the Scotland referendum showed that the idea Brown couldn't campaign successfully was a myth. Today, through his organisation Our Scottish Future, Brown is making the case for a 'people's constitutional convention' and a more federal approach to governing the UK, and for the replacement of the House of Lords by an elected 'senate of the nations and regions' – a proposal Keir Starmer has yet to implement. But what is clear is that the UK-wide 2024 Labour victory and the SNP implosion together appear to have settled the independence question for a generation. And not for the first time, Gordon Brown paved the way.

Though Brown tried to return to resting and recovering after the Scotland vote, another referendum – an electoral device Brown opposes – was around the corner. Cameron, his confidence boosted after being on the winning side in the 2014 vote in Scotland, committed himself to staging a poll on leaving the European Union if the Tories won the 2015 election.

Caving in to the constant pressure from the insatiably anti-European right wing of the Conservative Party and conscious that Nigel Farage's UKIP was surging in electoral popularity, he made the promise in the party's manifesto. However, it was one pledge Cameron reportedly felt he would not have to fulfil, expecting the Lib Dems to veto it in another coalition government. Instead, the Tories won a surprise overall majority and found themselves locked into staging the referendum in 2016.

As a result, in June 2015, Brown was filmed for a powerful video walking amid the bombed-out ruins of Coventry Cathedral, making the passionate, historical and political case for European togetherness. The video, produced by the film-makers Eddie Morgan and Mark Lucas, had 5.5 million views on Facebook.[16]

As Brown has said: 'At no time had the idea of "Little Britain" held any attraction for me ... I grew up in the shadow of the war and a Europe seized of the need for peace and preventing any return to conflict.'[17] In the video, he says: 'I'm walking through the ruins at Coventry Cathedral, bombed and destroyed by Nazi warplanes seventy years ago, and now painstakingly and lovingly maintained, as a monument to wars that we've left behind, and to the sanctuary of peace. And just think of it. For a thousand years and more, the nations of Europe at war with each other – murdering and maiming each other ... And what message would we send to the rest of the world if we, the British people, the most internationally minded of all, were to walk away from our nearest neighbours? We should be leading in Europe, and not leaving it.' Brown also wrote another book, *Britain: Leading, not Leaving*,[18] which expanded on the argument for remaining in the EU.

Brown was a major asset to the Remain campaign, not least because he was willing to inject some politics and emotion into the argument, instead of merely the dry economics of 'project fear' promoted by the Tory chancellor George Osborne in both the Scottish independence and Brexit referendums. He did, however, help bring about the last-minute cancellation of a plan first reported by me for all the then living former prime ministers – John Major, Tony Blair and Brown – to appear together alongside David Cameron making the case for staying in the EU.[19] Not for the first time, the tribal Brown was hostile to appearing alongside Cameron, though insiders such as Alastair Campbell and Andrew Adonis were also fearful that the event would appear to be an establishment stitch-up, as it was immediately portrayed by the conservative *Mail on Sunday* commentator Peter Hitchens.[20]

Brown was appalled by the UK's vote on 23 June 2016 to leave the EU – by 51.9 per cent to 48.1 per cent. His fellow Scots opposed the move by an overwhelming 68 per cent to 32 per cent, an outcome that gave fresh ammunition to the SNP as it pursued the argument for independence.

Elsewhere, Brown has worked closely with Keir Starmer, who became Labour leader in April 2020, on an increasingly influential policy agenda, focused on shifting power from Westminster to the community level. For Brown, this agenda must include the abolition of the House of Lords and its replacement with an elected senate of the nations and the regions. But despite repeated claims, again by Hitchens in both *Mail* titles, that Brown was masterminding a radical Starmer agenda,[21] Labour's manifesto going into the 2024 general election stopped well short of the former prime minister's proposals and merely moved to cap the age of peers at eighty and remove hereditary members, and there was no sign in 2025 of Labour in government expanding constitutional reform. Meanwhile, some around Starmer grumble about Brown's forceful style and the length of the constitution report, commissioned by Starmer, on 'the UK's future' entitled 'A New Britain: Renewing Our Democracy and Rebuilding our Economy'.[22] At one point, Brown is said to have suggested to Starmer that he would take his name off the proposals unless they were accepted in full.

Though conscious of the need not to give a running commentary, Brown remains full of ideas today, and undoubtedly frustrated he no longer has the direct power to make changes.

On relations between the current Labour prime minister and the last, a source close to Starmer says: 'Keir was talking to Gordon quite a lot when [he] got into Parliament [in 2015]. Keir admired him. They had more conversation when Keir was shadow Brexit secretary [2016–20]. In that stage [Starmer] didn't really talk to Blair. One of the reasons that Gordon could be trusted was that they were talking and Gordon was not putting it out in public domain. But the thinking was that Blair might have, or people around him.

'When Keir became leader he obviously commissioned GB to do a report on the constitution and so on, and that was in line with where Keir was at the time. His people found it quite frustrating dealing with Gordon – they asked for a draft to be cut down and GB sent a new one which was 5,000 words longer. It was also sent as a document which they couldn't change because it was a PDF. And the last-minute nature of everything Gordon does. There was agony going through it.

'Now, the more Keir appears with Tony, the more distant [Gordon] will be. Blair is useful because he thinks about government and solutions. It was telling at Glenys Kinnock's funeral [in December 2023] when Keir was sitting next to Gordon at one point and then suddenly, after Tony walked in, Keir was sitting next to Blair ... Morgan [McSweeney, Labour's former campaign director and now Starmer's chief of staff at Number Ten] once described this meeting that Gordon and Keir had up in Scotland in Gordon's house – and while Keir was there it was focused on change in Britain. Then when Keir left it was who's up and down in the Scottish Labour Party. GB is more political than Keir, and actually more into gossip.'

This may, or may well not, be fair. And just how influential Brown will be through this Parliament remains to be seen. In 2025, it certainly appeared that the leadership needed Brown's help. Labour had showed in 2024 that it could still be an election-winning machine but questions remained over the wisdom of backing Starmer as the front man for the party after an undeniably difficult start. However, that Starmer was willing to share a platform with Brown for the constitution commission's launch in December 2022 shows that Brown was in favour within the Labour leadership, but it also reflects the new and growing respect with which the public now regards Brown.

18

Charity Near and Far

At home today, Gordon Brown lives as normal a life as possible with Sarah and her rescue dog Winnie (her previous pet dog, Ethan, was sadly run over by a car), albeit with Brown's security detail constantly on hand. But he remains unusually active at seventy-five, and still gets up very early, at around 5 or 6 a.m., to bash away at his keyboard in the study upstairs on his latest projects. He keeps fit with regular walking, and has in recent years become keen on and even somewhat evangelical about regular online Pilates sessions, which have replaced his daily stints on the treadmill at Westminster. He likes traditional British foods but eats healthily, having replaced a KitKat habit with bananas during the 2010 campaign.

Brown is a constant reader – indeed a speed reader – of non-fiction and fiction in paper form and on Kindle, and always has several works on the go. He appreciates all genres, from detective stories to historical Scottish fiction to political biography. A letter he sent to a schoolgirl, Olivia Pring of All Souls' Church of England Primary School in Heywood, Lancashire, in 2005 explains that her request for him to write to her about his favourite book to mark World Book Day, was 'quite a difficult thing to do … I enjoy reading all kinds of books and have so many favourites that it is difficult to single out just one. When I was very young I always enjoyed the *Thomas the Tank Engine* books … The Harry Potter books that are written [by J. K. Rowling] in Edinburgh close to where I live are enjoyed by both children and adults. I think my favourite is the first one, *Harry Potter and the Philosopher's Stone*.'[1]

After much thinking, reading and writing after leaving office, Brown also pondered what he could do outside of domestic politics that could make a difference. And in July 2012 Brown concluded behind-the-scenes talks with the United Nations secretary general, Ban Ki-moon, and became his special envoy on global education. Having visited many countries as chancellor and prime minister, and having taken a keen interest in international development from childhood, Brown had seen at first hand how squalor, illiteracy, disease and abject poverty had destroyed the lives of so many of the world's children. He felt that one change that could help unlock the potential of millions, and free them from poverty, was what he sees as 'an educational revolution', in which every child in the world has the opportunity to learn. Yet it was education that was being neglected internationally in favour of what he calls 'more dramatic interventions on health and the environment'. As Brown says: 'Too few resources were being invested in teaching. Too many children remained out of school. Too many were still functionally illiterate at the age of eleven. And too many left school with no qualifications fit for the modern workplace.'

It was in this context that Brown agreed to the UN education role. Kevin Watkins, an international development sector veteran who had first worked with Brown at the Treasury on global debt alleviation, says:

> I was working at the time in UNESCO and got a call from the UK embassy in Paris asking if I would come over to have a quick meeting with Gordon. He had read a report we did on the state of education in developing countries and asked if I would work with him on developing some ideas. I remember asking him what he planned doing over the next few years, and he said he had three priorities: getting 50 million children into school in low-income countries; developing a plan for global job creation and fairer globalisation; and tackling local poverty in his constituency. He wanted to use his contacts and influence to drive those agenda[s]. I mention it because it illustrates what I've always thought about GB's motivations. He is the ultimate conviction politician and public servant. Political office for him was first and foremost a means of effecting change and improving lives, not a vehicle offering power for its own sake and means of personal aggrandisement. That was the ethos he took with him into his post-prime minister role in development.[2]

As he visited country after country in the first few months – Timor-Leste, India, Pakistan, South Sudan, Ethiopia and the Democratic Republic of Congo – Brown saw that 'the barriers to education were not just the critical shortage of resources, the untrained teaching staff, and the wilful neglect of curriculum reform ... I realised that many children could not attend school because they were subjected to modern slavery, discriminated against on the basis of gender, caught up in conflict zones or, having escaped war, denied access to education as refugees. I had to immediately adjust my focus, to take into account that the gateway to education for millions of children was being blocked through the violation of their fundamental human rights.' Brown authored reports on child labour and early marriage, outlining how national legislation and the application of international human rights provisions could make a difference for children 'locked out' of education.[3]

In Pakistan, Brown championed the cause of Malala Yousafzai and her two friends, Kainat Riaz and Shazia Ramzan, who had been shot on a school bus in the north of the country while defending the right of all girls to go to school free from discrimination. He travelled to India and worked with Kailash Satyarthi, the leader of the Indian movement against child labour, and talked to girls and boys who – having been rescued by Kailash from slavery – needed help to build a new life. He visited Nigeria and met the families of the Chibok schoolgirls – 276 students who were abducted by Boko Haram militants from their secondary school in the middle of the night. And when the Syrian war broke out, Brown worked with the Lebanese government to help deliver education to the millions of child refugees from that country, devising the 'double shift' school programme that enabled a crowded Lebanese school system to educate local children in the morning and Syrian children in the afternoon.

Brown reverted to his characteristic advocacy of a combination of funding and reform. 'Every troubled country demanded substantial additional financial resources to enable them to educate their children,' he says. '[But] they also needed interventions from international authorities that would help them to safeguard basic human rights. I sought to tackle the challenge of raising funds for education head on.' In 2016, Brown chaired the International Commission on Financing Global Education Opportunity, which aimed to secure inclusive and quality education by 2030 and promote lifelong learning for all. The report highlighted an urgent and ever-worsening learning and skills crisis that, if left unaddressed, would have left half of the world's 1.6 billion children and youth out of school or failing to learn by 2030.

Brown launched Christian Aid Week with a speech at Church House in central London on Sunday 12 May 2019, warning of the battle between 'globalists and nationalists' and saying: 'I've got a very personal interest in Christian Aid because I will always remember the mountain of red envelopes that my mother was responsible for.'[4] When an anxious Christian Aid staffer expressed fears backstage before the event started that people were 'still trickling in' because many supporters had been at church that Sunday morning, Brown reassured the employee and quipped back: 'It's when they're trickling out that you've got to worry.'

It's hard to find colleagues in his charity and international work today who aren't full of praise for Brown. Yasmine Sherif, the executive director of Education Cannot Wait, a global UN fund for education in crisis, has worked closely with him for eight years. She says: 'I believe the UK should be proud of having produced such an outstanding world leader. I have served in the UN system most of my life [for thirty-four years] … [and] Gordon Brown … stands out as the greatest of my close working relations. Very few leaders can speak without talking points and mesmerise the audience. Very few leaders can seek and provide advice with no ego but only in a search for truth and facts. Gordon Brown can and he does it with natural ease.' Contrary to conventional wisdom, Brown possesses 'the rare combination of both intellectual and emotional intelligence', she says. 'Today, his vision has been translated to action and impacted over 11 million children in the darkest corners of the world. This is one of his many legacies. He cares for people who suffer. And he acts.'

Similarly, Brown has campaigned tirelessly on global health, including on vaccine equity during the Covid-19 pandemic. He repeatedly called on wealthy nations as well as the private sector to ensure the fair distribution of Covid vaccines, advocating for a concerted global effort to tackle the pandemic and restore livelihoods the world over, in an echo of his handling of the 2008 global financial crash. It was a natural fit when, in September 2021, the World Health Organization (WHO) announced his appointment as the WHO ambassador for global health financing. Dr Tedros Adhanom Ghebreyesus, the WHO director general, said he was 'honoured' that Brown had taken on the role.

Brown's remit may officially be health financing, but he is proactive, and welcome to stray into the macroeconomic, the fiscal and more. Staff at the WHO say that Brown is a unique asset in the battle for multilateralism, against populist 'bad actors' such as Donald Trump, who withdrew the US from the organisation in July 2020 – and again on his first day as president for the second time in January 2025, saying 'world health ripped us off' – along with those closer to home such as Nigel Farage and even Boris Johnson. 'He realises who we're up against,' says one WHO staffer. Indeed, in January 2025 Brown devoted his *Guardian* column to urging Trump to rethink the decision, pointing out Trump 'got his facts wrong'.[5]

Dr Tedros says that what struck him about Brown was 'his humanity, deep interest, intelligence and practical way of thinking and working'. He goes on: 'Gordon is also a well-respected, connected, networked, influential and distinguished leader who is recognised globally for these traits. Yet, at the same time, he is so human, unpretentious and accessible. He truly walks the talk when it comes to doing what he says needs doing. He is also intensely serious about his time on earth and making the most of it to help people, especially the poorest in his own country and globally.'

Dr Tedros first met Brown in September 2007 at 10 Downing Street, where Brown convened leaders from government, donors and health agencies to forge a practical and urgent path towards equitable global health. 'That day in London, and in many encounters since, I witnessed Gordon's unwavering commitment to the well-being of all people, especially those facing significant economic, developmental and security challenges,' he says. 'What sets him apart is his ability to create strategic pathways and rally the right stakeholders around a common goal. The International Health Partnership he launched nearly twenty years ago exemplifies this. It identified crucial health indicators impeding progress in many African and Asian countries, particularly in child and maternal health, HIV/AIDS, malaria and tuberculosis … Gordon also recognised bureaucracy's barriers to effective healthcare delivery … Gordon has always understood the need to prioritise the interests of people in developing nations, where health outcomes lag behind those in wealthier countries. He recognised that only through pragmatic partnerships can we ensure health for all.'[6]

Brown's relentless work at home continues too. Throughout the middle 2010s, he worked with charities and the famous – and to some infamous – online retailer Amazon, persuading it to donate unused goods. This was done amid the cost-of-living crisis and what Brown calls 'austerity's children', caught in the type of poverty he frequently says he never thought he would see again following his youth. Brown created the concept of the multibank: a food bank, clothes bank, toiletries bank, bedding bank, baby bank, hygiene bank and furniture bank all rolled into one. Multibanks are stocked by the surplus goods of companies, including Amazon, and those goods are then passed on to experienced local charities who can distribute them to the families who need them most.

Opening the initiative in the capital in July 2024, with a project called the Felix multibank, Brown said: 'The London … multibank is opening at a time of transition from a Britain where child poverty has risen dramatically to one where we wish to see child poverty falling. As a new anti-poverty plan is being prepared, the multibanks still need to secure more supplies and more funds from generous donors so that, working with food banks, we can provide poverty relief.'[7] And John Boumphrey, the country manager for Amazon's business across the UK and Ireland, added: 'When we work hand in hand with local charities, community groups and other businesses to provide donations and support, we know we can make a huge difference for families in need.'

Brown was warning of a 'torn safety net' among charities, food banks and even churches in a report by the think tank Theos, with Rowan Williams, as early as November 2022.[8] That winter, Brown also launched the 'Warm Welcome' project, helping hundreds of thousands of people struggling to heat their homes – out of the 7 million who suffered fuel poverty at the turn of 2022 and 2023 – with around 4,000 warm spaces hosting 120,000 visitors a week. Brown was privately completely opposed to, and dismayed by, Keir Starmer and Rachel Reeves's decision to means-test the winter fuel allowance in 2024.

In May 2025, Brown gave a John Smith memorial lecture in central London on child poverty. Around his speech, Brown did several interviews suggesting the winter fuel allowance should be reinstated, and the same day Starmer signalled a U-turn. Brown said: 'Nobody who's working hard or nobody who's served the country well over their lifetime should be pushed into poverty if we can avoid it, and I believe that that's what [Starmer] is really thinking about, a fairness guarantee for pensioners.' Brown also reiterated his opposition to the two-child benefit cap. Intriguingly, that same week, Rowan Williams gave his own lecture at St Paul's Cathedral, on the German pastor and anti-Nazi dissident Dietrich Bonhoeffer: asked by an audience member who best represents Bonhoeffer's values today, Dr Williams's answer was Gordon Brown because of the former prime minister's defence of those under threat.

In August 2025, Brown launched a fresh campaign against the two-child benefit cap, introduced under the Conservatives by George Osborne in 2017, and maintained by Starmer's government. Brown did not want a direct confrontation with the governing party he had served loyally for five decades, but, as he told one ally privately, 'it may yet come to that'.

He decided before the launch of his latest campaign against child poverty to get faith leaders involved, given he was making it a moral issue by calling for new taxes on gambling profits to raise around £3 billion to fill the gap that would be left by abolishing the two-child cap.

'There is an urgent need to act,' Brown wrote in his *Guardian* column on 6 August. 'I have not seen such deep poverty since I grew up in a mining and textiles town where unemployment was starting to bite hard. Now, each night, 1 million children in the UK try to sleep without a bed of their own. Two million households live without cookers, fridges or washing machines, and many are without toothpaste, soap or shampoo. It is heartbreaking that 3 million children go without meals because their families run out of food.'[9]

Such was the power of Brown's interventions at that time, reflecting his enhanced reputation, that Reeves was forced to respond that same day as Brown also appeared on Radio 4's *Today* programme. 'I talk to Gordon regularly,' she said. 'Like Gordon, I am deeply concerned around the levels of child poverty in Britain ... We're a Labour government. Of course, we care about child poverty.' Reeves is an admirer of Brown, whose portrait she reportedly kept in her room at Oxford

University. Her chief of staff, Katie Martin, was the Number Ten civil service chief press officer under him. In August 2024, Reeves was reported to be studying Brown's conference speeches in the run-up to her own first speech as chancellor that autumn. And Brown visited Reeves at the Treasury before her first Budget in October 2024.

After corresponding with Brown, Dr Williams duly got behind the move, and on the day after Brown's article, 7 August, wrote in the *Financial Times*: 'Gordon Brown's recent [May 2025] report on *The Child Poverty Emergency* chronicles with detail and dispassion the effects on the well-being of British children of measures like the abolition of the Sure Start programme and the two-child benefit cap, showing beyond any doubt that the increase in child poverty, by any metric you can name, is dramatic and still accelerating ... Gordon Brown has also offered a major new proposal, worked through in some detail, for a new tax on the proceeds of the gambling industry, particularly online gambling, with the income from this hypothecated for tackling child poverty ... It is an absurdity that high-risk and socially corrosive behaviour should escape the demand to contribute to the care of the most vulnerable.'[10]

At the same time, Reverend Helen Cameron of the Methodist Church wrote in the *Church Times* that 'a fair levy on the unacceptably high profits from gambling would release considerable resource'. Richard Moth, the Catholic bishop who is chair of the Department for Social Justice for the Catholic Church in England and Wales, also told the *Tablet* in August 2025: 'The Catholic Church is well aware of the high and increasing levels of child poverty in England and Wales – and we are greatly concerned ... As such, we have consistently called for the two-child cap on universal credit to be removed. This policy directly pushes many families into poverty and creates anxiety for working families with more than two children who fear that even a temporary loss of income will be devastating.' Zia Salik, the interim director of Islamic Relief UK, added: 'Never in my life did I think that child poverty would reach the level it has in the UK, one of the wealthiest nations in the world ... The government's unfathomable decision to impose the two-child benefit cap has helped neither the reality of poverty on the ground for so many children nor stopped the false narratives being purveyed on this issue, all while failing to understand the utmost cruelty of this situation ... This is why we were grateful to see Gordon Brown's intervention ... Brown is right to call out the absolute epidemic of child poverty that is sweeping this country yet is not nearly being talked about enough.'

In January 2025, while Brown was in Washington for Jimmy Carter's funeral at the National Cathedral, Elon Musk, the world's second richest man and owner of the social media platform X, posted on it a series of attacks on Brown, building on his targeting of Starmer over the UK grooming gangs scandal. Posts alleging that a 2008 Home Office memo advised police not to intervene in child grooming cases because victims had 'made an informed choice about their sexual behaviour' were rebutted by Brown, whose team looked into the claims and who described them in a short statement sent swiftly to reporters as 'a complete fabrication'. One post, which was viewed 25 million times, saw Musk allege that 'Gordon Brown sold those little girls for votes' while reposting another user who talked about the alleged memo. In fact, the memo was not about the grooming gangs but about the 1989 Children's Act and its implementation.

The unfounded claim appeared to originate from an interview with Nazir Afzal, the former Crown Prosecution Service chief prosecutor for north-west England, on Radio 4's *PM* programme on 19 October 2018. 'You may not know this,' he told the presenter Carolyn Quinn, 'but back in 2008 the Home Office sent a circular to all police forces in the country saying "as far as these young girls who are being exploited in their towns and cities we believe they have made an informed choice about their sexual behaviour and therefore it's not for you police officers to get involved in".'

The first social media post to gain considerable traction was in July 2019 and the false allegation grew from there. Speaking to BBC Verify, Afzal clarified his position in January 2025, admitting that he has never seen any circular with the form of words he used in the 2018 interview. The words 'informed choice' do not appear anywhere in the text of the memo in question, and the circular is not about child grooming gangs. It does contain a section on how to judge significant harm to a child, saying: 'It is important always to take account of the child's reactions, and his or her perceptions, according to the child's age and understanding.' Afzal told BBC Verify that he was 'paraphrasing what I thought that meant to them' when he gave his interview to Quinn. 'You're right, it doesn't stack up. It doesn't give an excuse or explanation, but I can't give you any other circular.' By the time Brown sat down in the third row of pews for Carter's funeral on 9 January, the matter appeared to be settled and Brown had come out on top.[11]

Though Brown is open to criticism on his domestic political career, it is more challenging to fault the charitable and international work, which saw him awarded a Companion of Honour in June 2024. In a characteristic Brown quote, he said at the time: 'I feel slightly embarrassed as the opportunity to serve is an honour in itself and my preference has always been to recognise all those brilliant, unsung, local heroes who quietly and selflessly give their time to contribute to the vitality of our communities ... I want to thank those who put my name forward and thank too my family and all who have worked with me during the last fifty years in public life, to whom I owe everything.'

In a further sign of Brown's enhanced standing, including with the British establishment, he appeared alongside Prince William at an event in Sheffield on 1 July 2025 to mark the second anniversary of the launch of the prince's Homewards project against homelessness. The two men appeared relaxed and laughing, and Brown credited the prince's interest in social problems such as homelessness to the influence of his mother, Diana, Princess of Wales. Brown said that she had 'encouraged him to take an interest in why people were on the streets, and why people were homeless, and why people needed a better chance'. William added: 'The power of partnerships gives me hope. I feel less hopeful when I'm doing things by myself. I think we all as human beings want to feel connected and part of something.'

19
Joy in the Morning: Gordon Brown's Quiet Faith

Despite his reticence when it comes to talking about the subject, the effect of Brown's upbringing in the Church and indeed his faith throughout his life should not be underestimated. Previous biographers, authors and journalists have largely overlooked it.

After his marriage to Sarah and the births of their children, one of Brown's proudest personal moments came at the Vatican, on 8 February 2007 when, then chancellor, he met Pope Benedict XVI for the first time and invited him to the UK in the first papal visit since John Paul II in 1982. They would meet again in Rome when Brown was prime minister, on 19 February 2009, and again when Benedict made his visit on 16–19 September 2010. In the hour or so before that first encounter in 2007, Whitehall and Vatican diplomatic sources say Brown was nervous. He had brought with him his father John's book of sermons, *A Time to Serve*. The powerful collection starts with a lament over the decline of 'the vision of duty' and culminates in a final chapter entitled 'Today's Christian Duty', which advocates the need to do good works as well as to spread the Good News.

'All the sermons that spoke of social Christianity are what appealed to me,' says Brown of his father's book today.[1] He had previously given a copy to the Queen, but was it enough of a gift now, he asked one official as they made their way into the Vatican. Brown was reassured that it was indeed appropriate because it was personal and conveyed where he came from. 'His hesitancy was from humility,' says a source present at the time.

Brown need not have worried. When he emerged, he said to the same official with an element of awe that he wished his father could have seen him hand the book over. It was, the official says, a real insight into the man's soul. In the car driving away from the Vatican, Brown gazed out of the window and recalled how he and his brothers had persuaded their father to compile the book of sermons for them and for their own children, as something to be remembered by. 'Now it's in the hands of the pope,' he said.

It may have been one of those moments that some leaders experience, when their past and present collide. It was certainly, as a diplomat there observed privately, a deeply personal moment, connecting a chancellor and a pope, and a late father and a son. Brown reflects today: 'I didn't agree with all [Benedict's] views on certain issues. But I was actually bowled over by how kind he was to the kids, because they invited our children to come and they were very young. John had to be persuaded to wear a tie for the first time. But Benedict was very kind to them. Which you know, was something that … was very moving.'

The later visit on 19 February 2009, when Brown was prime minister, was similarly moving for Brown and for others present, and rather different from what followed in Italy on that same day. As Brown's former adviser Stewart Wood has recounted:

> On the way back to London, Gordon had been invited for a lunch with [Silvio] Berlusconi, who was in his third spell as Italian prime minister. Gordon was in the middle of the most important and energetic diplomatic offensive of his career, travelling the world to persuade leaders to back his plan to kick-start the world economy after the previous year's financial crash. Gordon was, to put it mildly, a Berlusconi sceptic. But as leader of one of the big four EU economies, the Italian PM's backing for the G20 plan was necessary, and a quick lunch with Silvio while we were in town was important to help secure his goodwill and support.
>
> It wasn't a quick lunch. We were ferried up to a wonderful palace on a hill overlooking Rome … Berlusconi, his team, some Italian military and photographers were waiting for us, and we were ushered into a stunning, grand dining room, with breath-taking views over the city.

Wood went on to recall that after prosecco, wines, brandy and cigars, Berlusconi delayed their joint press statement by regaling

Brown with a twenty-minute anecdote about a seventeen-year-old English girl he had romanced many years earlier and whom he had recently met again. 'The Presbyterian Team Brown was both embarrassed and quietly excited by the small dose of opulence we were enjoying.'[2]

What Wood left out was that before the lunch, and after a couple of glasses of fizz on the private balcony, Berlusconi bizarrely insisted on showing Brown a spacious bathroom off the main dining room. The bathroom contained a very large bath, which was obviously designed to accommodate more than one bather. The scene ushers in surreal images of an incongruous Brown, stalking indifferently through palatial opulence and murmurings of scandal. Was there ever a less Italian-style politician? According to Michael Dugher, Brown's chief spokesman at Number Ten and the one Catholic in the UK prime ministerial delegation that day: 'GB had a look on his face which unsurprisingly said, "Why is this guy showing me his bath?" but he said instead something banal like "Yes, nice bath".'[3] In marked contrast to their more spiritual morning with the Holy Father, Tom Fletcher whispered to Wood and Dugher in Berlusconi's bathroom: 'I suspect that bath has had more women in it than Berlusconi's cabinet.'[4]

Brown may frequently be ultra-serious, but he is not himself evangelical, and in the main his faith remains private – and ecumenical in its approach, as shown by his pride on meeting the pope despite belonging to the distinctly Protestant Church of Scotland, and indeed having been born to a family of 'dissenters' within that denomination. Brown's paternal ancestors had been against the patronage system and on the side of the Church of Scotland, not local landowners, choosing its ministers, in a major dispute which led to the 'great disruption' of 1843, in which some 450 evangelical ministers broke away and formed the Free Church of Scotland.

Religion features strongly in the earliest parts of Brown's memoirs. As he says: 'Kirkcaldy, to where my family moved in the spring of 1954, had such engrained religious traditions that I could step out my front door and in a few minutes' walk past nine churches that were within only a few hundred yards of each other. They claimed most of the population as adherents. Kirkcaldy was not alone: family life for millions of Scots and English was built around not just churches but religiously inspired organisations – like the Boys' Brigade and the Life Boys – and the sports teams they spawned.'⁵

In March 2009, a Downing Street spokesperson told Westminster reporters that Brown is 'not a regular churchgoer' but that he does believe in God, following a speech on the G20 at St Paul's Cathedral.⁶

As with his tribal Labour politics, Brown has never strayed from his faith, but up to now, he has hardly spoken publicly about it. A rare occasion when he did so was on the BBC's *Songs of Praise* filmed in Fife in November 2022, in which he recalled going to church twice every Sunday to listen to his father's sermons – adding that he regrets not having done so more often. He also echoed his father's preaching by rejecting the way politicians say 'God is on my side', and instead, he said, 'we should be on God's side'. In this as in many areas, his declaration is a window not only into the way Brown understands religion, but into the way he understands its place in politics more generally.

But Brown's reticence of style should never be mistaken for neutrality in matters of conscience. The former prime minister has sometimes held back from discussing faith issues, even after strongly considering making interventions. In February 2023, he was appalled by the way in which politicians and the media turned on Kate Forbes of the SNP, after her bid to succeed Nicola Sturgeon as nationalist party leader and first minister was damaged by her openly expressed evangelical – 'wee free' – Christian convictions on traditional marriage. The MSP for Skye, Lochaber and Badenoch lost at least half of her MP and MSP supporters, after she told Sky News that having children – and sex – outside marriage was 'wrong according to my faith'. Forbes's case can be compared to that of Tim Farron, the former Liberal Democrat leader whose undoing was his personal ethical convictions about sexuality coming into conflict with the socially progressive party he led.

In a tentative attempt to express himself in the area of faith, Brown drafted but didn't publish a nuanced but powerful article about Forbes's downfall, after consulting with his old friend Rowan Williams, the former archbishop of Canterbury and one of the world's leading living theologians. The two men share a long-standing mutual admiration, and Williams, who made only minor suggestions, thought the piece excellent.

Williams says of Brown today:

> Gordon is very unusual among contemporary politicians for all sorts of reasons, but not least in the way he approaches religious commitment in the public sphere. For some it's an embarrassment or irrelevance, for some it's a flag of convenience, for some it's a matter of defending traditional values or a battlefield in culture wars.
>
> Gordon's approach is very different. He is reticent about the details of his own convictions, though it is very clear that he sees the major moral problems of our world and society through the lens of Christian teaching and is not afraid to say so. But he also acknowledges that religious conviction has a really significant role in social debate – even when it does not follow the prevailing winds of social consensus. He genuinely believes in a society where diverse moral perspectives are free to contest issues in public – with patience and respect. Arguments are necessary for a healthy culture, and they need to draw in principles that are more than just pragmatic and utilitarian. One of his frustrations was the relative lack in our society of spaces where some of these fundamental arguments about the nature of human life and possibility might be exchanged and interrogated.
>
> He believes that it is important for political leadership to be held to account, and has spoken eloquently about the importance of religious communities keeping up the pressure on leaders and 'giving them permission' to act in morally courageous ways. I have vivid memories of talking with Gordon about the Jubilee 2000 campaign for international debt relief, and how the mobilisation of many faith communities around this issue helped to make it possible for government to move on this. He believed that this was an ideal model for how religious ethics could move a public and political consensus forward in creative ways. So he does not expect such communities to be either protected corners for licensed eccentrics (on condition they never open their mouths in public), or repositories of comforting traditions and cultural reassurance. So long as people of faith do not assume a right to dictate the outcome of an argument, they are welcome to join in robustly. When he addressed the assembled Anglican bishops at the 2008 Lambeth conference on global poverty and our response to it, he made an enormous

impression because of his clarity about this; several bishops said to me that they wished they had politicians like this at home.⁷

Brown told that conference:

Let me say first of all that I am privileged and I am humbled to be at a conference of so many men and women for whom I have got the utmost respect, the greatest admiration and the highest affection ... Let me tell you there are millions of people whom you may never meet who owe you a debt of gratitude for the work that you do in upholding the cause of the poor, and I want to thank every person from every country for what you do to remind the world of its responsibilities. This has been one of the greatest public demonstrations of faith that this great city has ever seen, and you have sent a simple and very clear message, with rising force, that poverty can be eradicated, that poverty must be eradicated, and if we can all work together for change poverty will be eradicated.⁸

Cormac Murphy-O'Connor, the Catholic former archbishop of Westminster, concurred with Dr Williams about Brown. He wrote in his memoir, *An English Spring*: 'Gordon Brown stands very high in my estimation. He was of course the son of a Church of Scotland minister. He was always gracious and eager to chat ... Brown's commitment to the poor both at home and in the developing world, is utterly genuine.'⁹

In February 2011, Dr Williams had invited Brown to give a lecture at Lambeth Palace. In his lecture, entitled 'Faith and politics?', Brown rejected both a firmly religious approach to politics and the liberal secularism that is frequently put forward as its alternative. In place of these, Brown called for a 'deliberative democratic politics, one in which the ethical basis of decisions is at its forefront, and in which we debate not only the "how" of policy but also the "why"', and a faith politics that is shaped by 'a framework which affirms the need for a debate on values but asserts the three responsibilities men and women of faith accept in politics – to seek common ground, to use our God-given right to reason, and to be prepared to accept the outcomes'.

The Forbes case is an interesting one, the last major example of strong faith being expressed in the largely secular UK political sphere.

But, as he had argued when he spoke at Lambeth Palace, Brown feels public decisions on the laws of a country cannot just be based on faith, but must involve a reasoned debate that subjects all views to scrutiny; and that in a democracy our laws have to be justified to the public on grounds other than simply religious ones if all those citizens who have no religious convictions are to be persuaded that the laws they have to uphold are just and reasonable.

For Brown believes that politics are 'the art of persuasion' and that as a leading politician you cannot merely impose your opinions on society. He wants more respect for religious values but he cautions against religious intolerance. Instead he calls for authenticity – honesty about your own views and values but respect for other people's truth, sometimes quoting Aneurin Bevan, who used to say, 'Here is my truth, now tell me yours.'

Brown is firm in his opposition to assisted dying, unlike Keir Starmer, who supported Kim Leadbeater's private members' bill in the House of Commons after promising time for a new vote on the issue. Brown has been influenced by the quality of end-of-life care in the local hospice where he quietly volunteered for a while during his premiership one summer holiday. He has said that he worries about legislation that requires a doctor, whose role has always been to preserve and extend life, to administer death as the final act of a bureaucratic procedure. And he worries too about older people feeling they have become a burden on their relatives and putting themselves under pressure to end their life.

Brown did intervene in the heated debate, in his monthly *Guardian* column in November 2024, which opened movingly with the tragic death of his and Sarah's baby daughter and was carefully thought through. 'The experience of sitting with a fatally ill baby girl did not convince me of the case for assisted dying; it convinced me of the value and imperative of good end-of-life care,' he wrote, before going on to call for a commission on improving palliative care instead of a law change.[10] The intervention was picked up across the media, and Brown followed up with an interview on Radio 4's religious *Sunday* programme, confirming that he had carefully avoided religious arguments to appeal primarily to an increasingly secular House of Commons. 'I see life as a gift,' he said. 'I do think that while religious views come into this for me and for other people, it is important to put the secular argument ... and I think that is more likely to appeal to MPs.'[11]

Assisted suicide isn't the only subject where Brown's outlook on faith impinges on the way he looks at moral questions. For example, in unpublished material, Brown has addressed homosexuality and makes it clear he has squarely changed his mind on that and on gay marriage. Brought up in a Christian faith and taught for years that gay predilections were illegal because they were wrong, he came to recognise the unjust persecution that had, over centuries, violated that very basic idea that no group should be discriminated against unfairly. He saw the damage that the ban on homosexuality was doing to good people who deserved to enjoy the same kind of love he and others enjoyed in getting married.

As prime minister he took the first steps towards apologising for the treatment meted out to the Bletchley Park decoder Alan Turing and others driven to suicide because of persecution and humiliation, and he equalised the rights of gay couples to transfer pensions to each other. He said that it was because he could no longer reconcile the way an oppressed minority was being demonised with the love and compassion that the Christian faith taught we should show to other people.

But was it the holding of strong religious convictions that made Forbes's position untenable, or the unfashionable issues that she dared to confront? She had taken on the prevailing consensus of a political establishment now firmly allied to a liberal agenda, and against that tide she had said something traditional about marriage. Had she expressed support for refugees, guided by a strong Christian impulse to charity, she would doubtless have seen off the wrath of her own base. But she was seeking to lead a political party dominated by a secular and progressive viewpoint. And, as he admits now, Brown himself did hold back from expressing his own faith. This could merely have been due to advice he was given, amid a culture in Downing Street overshadowed by Alastair Campbell's famous declaration to an American interviewer talking to Tony Blair in 2004 that 'We don't do God'.

Blair's and Brown's approaches to faith are different, with the latter less missionary, but engrained since youth. It is as if Tony Blair chose Christianity, and Gordon Brown was born into it. After all, Blair's family wasn't particularly religious, and he got confirmed at Oxford University. The brand of Christianity both men were attracted to – social Christianity – was arrived at via different routes. However, the two men have more in common on this than is widely assumed.

Despite his reticence, Brown did include a chapter entitled 'Faith in the public square?' in his own memoir. In that, he writes that his father taught him to 'treat everyone equally – subservient to no one and condescending to no one'. Brown writes: '[How] can a public figure who holds convictions that are religious in origin be authentic if we do not state what influences what we say and where we are coming from? A religious conviction cannot be equated with a private preference, such as a liking for sports or a taste in food or music: it is something that shapes your life, public as well as private.'

Brown wrestles with how far a politician should expose his faith. 'To expect those of us with strong beliefs to leave them at the door of the House of Commons or No 10 is to require us to bring an incomplete version of ourselves into the public arena. If the values that matter most to me are the values that I speak about least, then I am, at least in part, in denial of who I really am.'

Here Brown, not for the first time, is rueful about how he allowed others to shape how he was seen. 'This was, to my regret, a problem that I never really resolved. I suspect I was thought of as more like a technician lacking solid convictions. And, despite my strong personal religious beliefs, I never really countered that impression. Instead of defining myself, I gave my opponents room to define me.'

And Brown, who several times referred (controversially, from the media point of view) to his 'moral compass' while in office, says that politicians should not 'moralise, hector or sanctimoniously lecture people' but that they should appeal 'to an agreed morality that underpins our society'. He continues: 'But perhaps I did not get it quite right in repeating as a politician a phrase that my father had often used as a church minister – the need for a "moral compass". I was most definitely not seeking to claim a role for myself as an ethical arbiter: I was simply arguing the case for the role of ethics in politics. The distinction I should have made more clearly is between patently dogmatic attempts to impose your will on others – which are wrong – and focusing public attention on values we share.'

Brown condemns the binary and at times 'menacing' atmosphere created by social media such as Twitter, or X. 'Of course, the public square today is mediated not just by print and TV journalism, but also by Twitter, Facebook, Instagram and the explosion of social media. In both traditional and digital media, we have seen in my view a coarsening of public debate. All too often, the public square resounds with voices that are harsh and discordant, frivolous, or at times even menacing.'

And he concludes that he should have been 'more open' about his religious and moral beliefs. 'But while all my experience tells me that we have to be careful when we carry religious or even moral arguments into public decision-making, I believe, as I look back at the debates we had when I was an MP, chancellor and prime minister, that I should have been more open about my beliefs, more upfront in dealing with the difficulties of doing so, and more willing to take potential criticisms head-on. In the end, the choices in our public square should not be reduced to a theocratic and unacceptable dogmatism on the one hand and a joyless and barren secularism on the other.'

In an age of spin, Brown did ultimately appear, at least, unspun, despite his sometimes thuggish spin doctors. Like John Major before him, Brown stood for stability against the more animated and radical voices of his party. Like Theresa May and Angela Merkel, he was the faithful offspring of a Protestant minister. As he has conceded, Brown was in many ways not of the modern media age. But, with his background in 'social Christianity', he had substance. As the inspired Saatchi and Saatchi Labour poster put it early in his premiership, amid the beginnings of a campaign for the snap general election which Brown ultimately declined to hold: 'Not flash. Just Gordon'.

20

Supping with the Devil: Gordon Brown Versus the Murdoch Media

The decision by the Murdoch empire on 30 September 2009 to abandon New Labour under Brown, with the *Sun* coming out for the Conservatives the day after Brown's rousing party conference speech, appeared to be a major blow to the prime minister specifically, and it indicated that the shrewd businessman calculated that Brown would lose in 2010. It also marked the end of a close relationship with the party leadership forged by Blair and Alastair Campbell – and at times but to a lesser extent by Brown himself – from the mid-1990s onwards, after Rupert Murdoch had followed his support for Margaret Thatcher by abandoning the Conservatives under John Major.

It was the end of a dangerously mismatched political relationship between a principled centre-left politician and a right-wing gambling media mogul and the beginning of a spectacular falling-out, one that would reach the British courts, be handled at the top of the Metropolitan Police and, across the Atlantic, damage the once mighty *Washington Post*. It should be stressed that we are not talking merely about the media taking pops at their less favoured candidate: there are serious ethical questions around the campaign against Brown, including, for example, the *Sun* paying for access to family medical information, as well as alleged phone hacking.

As we shall see, Brown was undoubtedly targeted for intrusion. His continued determination to find out what happened and who was responsible is something that has opened up an avenue for others, such as Prince Harry, to exploit. At the time of writing, the Metropolitan Police are investigating Brown's case.

A generation of senior Labour figures had been preoccupied with the hostility they faced from the majority of the print media. Many blamed Neil Kinnock's unexpected defeat in 1992 on the unremitting antagonism of the *Sun*, culminating in its election-day headline showing his face in a light bulb with the words: 'If Kinnock wins today will the last person to leave Britain please turn out the lights.'

Two years later, when Blair travelled to southern France to join Campbell for walks around a rented family holiday home in order to persuade the journalist to work for him, Campbell made it a condition that the pair woo the *Sun* to the point where the tabloid supported the party at the next general election, which it did.[1] For better or worse, the *Sun* represented a major part of a powerful Fleet Street press with millions of readers, while social media was non-existent.

A year later in 1995, Blair flew to the Hayman Island off the Australian coast, to address Murdoch's top executives at News International's annual editorial conference.[2] Campbell's diaries disclose that potential revelations about contact between Blair and Murdoch deeply worried Blair. 'TB said he didn't fear them coming at him about me, but about the relationship with Murdoch. And he didn't fancy a question about whether Murdoch lobbied him.'[3] In retrospect there is no doubt that New Labour went too far in its courting of News International, especially if Murdoch is viewed not as a mythical arbiter of elections, but primarily as a business-minded gambler who follows his readers and backs the winner.

Brown was soon to discover that the Murdoch empire viewed him with much less sympathy than Blair. At first he tried to win over its papers but eventually realised in the latter days of his premiership that the enmity could not be overcome. To this day, he is seeking answers about the extent to which he was personally targeted by Murdoch journalists.

The intrusion started in earnest in early 2000, while Brown was chancellor and on at least six occasions in phone calls to his building society, the *Sunday Times* impersonated Brown to obtain information about his mortgage. An internal inquiry by the fraud department at Abbey National, Brown's bank, found that during January 2000 an individual acting on behalf of the *Sunday Times* contacted their Bradford call centre six times, posing as Brown, and succeeded in extracting details from his account.[4] Brown recalls that the *Sunday Times* alleged that he had bought his London flat at a knockdown price from the estate of the deceased and disgraced Robert Maxwell, through a company in which Brown's friend Geoffrey Robinson MP had a stake. The paper claimed the flat had been sold in a below-the-counter deal. In fact, Brown had bought it on the open market, knew nothing of any Maxwell connection and Robinson was not involved. For several weeks, the *Sunday Times* held to the story of a corrupt purchase.

Also in 2000, a mysterious character called Barry Beardall, working on behalf of the *Sunday Times*, obtained information from Brown's solicitors about the purchase of his London flat. Brown found that his phone was 'reverse-engineered' by the *Sunday Times* so the paper could trace his movements. In 2001 he was told that his tax returns had been stolen from the office of his accountants and ended up in the hands of another Sunday newspaper, which returned them to him. According to Brown, the UK's national police computer was unlawfully accessed by a police officer bribed by a private investigator to check whether police files contained information on him.

Ten years later, the former *Sunday Times* editor John Witherow confirmed that Beardall had 'blagged' information about Brown for the paper. Witherow's defence – that his pursuit of Brown was in the public interest, and that it was not a fishing expedition – did not hold water. There was no evidence Brown had done anything wrong. And the *Sunday Times*'s justification for pursuing him – that the flat was not advertised – was ironic because the flat had been advertised in their property columns.

Within days of becoming prime minister, Brown, who had promised 'a new kind of politics', released some details of Blair's calls and meetings with Murdoch – a move that risked annoying his predecessor and provoking the media magnate. Brown promised to respect 'the public right to know' and bring in 'new rights to access public information where previously it has been withheld'. In October 2007, he scrapped plans by Blair to make freedom of information requests more expensive to deter more frivolous requests.

Yet Brown, too, had – in the end fruitlessly – entertained the right-wing mogul. They met at Chequers, the prime minister's country residence, on the very weekend when Brown finally decided against calling a November snap election. But on 4 February 2008, the *Independent* reported that Brown's government was refusing to release information about his own contacts with Murdoch. A freedom of information request submitted by me for the newspaper asked for 'details of any meetings' between Murdoch and the prime minister. Nicholas Howard, a Downing Street official, replied to say that 'we do not hold any minutes of any meetings or other interactions' between the two men. This prompted Nick Clegg, the Liberal Democrat leader, to say: 'Gordon Brown must answer for this hypocrisy.'[5]

And in June 2008, Sarah Brown had reportedly hosted a 'slumber party' at Chequers with Rebekah Brooks and Murdoch's then wife Wendi Deng. It led Adam Boulton, the former political editor of Sky News, to tell the Leveson Inquiry, which was set up after the phone-hacking scandal: 'At the time I just thought this is completely bonkers that this sort of intimacy is being indulged in by the prime minister and his wife and a proprietor and his wife. I thought it would end in tears.'[6]

The Murdoch empire's opposition to Brown at the 2010 general election, which hurt him and allegedly went against past assurances of support, was legitimate in the rough-and-tumble of politics. But the personal elements, the hacking of Brown's mortgage account while he was chancellor and particularly the intrusion into his family's medical records in Fife, caused real ill-feeling between Brown and the Murdoch press.

In November 2017, seven years after Brown left the office of prime minister, he published his memoir. Not for the first or last time, Brown had taken an agonising decision to hold back. Late in the publishing process, he excluded a key chapter on his relations with the media and, in particular, the Murdoch outlets which he was convinced had been out to destroy him while he was chancellor and prime minister.

Brown says today that the stormiest political relationship he had was not with his political party opponents, Conservatives, Liberals or Scottish nationalists, but with the Murdoch media, and that for the time he was in government, the Murdoch group often seemed like the real opposition party, with Rupert Murdoch and his son, James, 'the leaders of the opposition'.

Brown has always hated talking about what happened to his family, but when giving evidence to the Leveson Inquiry about the decisions by Murdoch's *Sunday Times*, *Sun* and *News of the World* to invade his personal life, he revealed that he was the victim of surveillance by private detectives and, he alleges, almost certainly phone tapping. Brown understands that all politicians have to be subject to public scrutiny but believes that the Murdoch newspapers set no limits on how they were willing to invade the privacy of his family. Nothing prepared him for the interference when, in 2006, his second son was diagnosed with a health problem when just a few weeks old.

The *Sun*'s editor from January 2003 to September 2009, Rebekah Brooks, implied to the Leveson Inquiry into media intrusion that Brown had actually asked her to write about his son's condition. She said: 'I think the Browns' position at the time was very much that they had had the tests confirmed, and ... they felt that there were many, many people in the UK whose children suffered with cystic fibrosis.' But this was not the case, and in his report Leveson responded: 'The claim that the Browns were "absolutely committed to making this public" frankly defies belief: one hardly needs Mr Brown himself to point out that no parent in the land would have wanted information of this nature to be blazoned across the front page of a national newspaper.'

The *Sun* had in fact paid to expose the health condition of Brown's son, as the NHS Fife chief executive John Wilson later confirmed. '[We] now accept that it is highly likely that, sometime in 2006, a member of staff in NHS Fife spoke, without authorisation, about the medical condition of Mr Brown's son,' he said.

The *Sun* man behind procuring the story was David Dinsmore, who became editor of the *Scottish Sun* that same year, 2006, and went on to become editor of the *Sun* from 2013 to 2015. In July 2025, Keir Starmer appointed him permanent secretary for communications, making Dinsmore a senior civil servant. Starmer himself had interviewed Dinsmore and was impressed by him. Brown and other Labour figures were dismayed by the appointment, to put it mildly. Quite apart from the troubling connection with the highly personal story so clearly not in the national interest, Brown told friends at the time of the appointment: 'He is a well-known Conservative.' The question about Dinsmore's appointment is: who benefits? Rupert Murdoch's attendance at the Windsor Castle state banquet for Donald Trump in September 2025 appeared to provide a clue.

Unbeknown to Brown and most other people in the public eye, his premiership took place against the backdrop of the phone-hacking scandal. A private investigator, Glen Mulcaire, had discovered that it was relatively easy to hack into voicemails on mobile phones. Once the journalists at the *News of the World* found this out, they harvested a crop of scandals which won the editor Andy Coulson the award of Newspaper of the Year 2004/5. The England football manager Sven-Göran Eriksson was exposed as having had an affair with a secretary, Faria Alam; David Beckham was alleged to have had an affair with his personal assistant Rebecca Loos, which he denied; and home secretary David Blunkett, though himself single, was found to have had an affair with a married woman.

Then the royal correspondent, Clive Goodman, went too far. Not only did he hack Prince William's mobile, but he also printed information from a voicemail message made by the head of the Sandhurst military academy in 2006. The Palace and the army pounced. Goodman and Mulcaire were arrested and jailed. Andy Coulson claimed it was a one-off and the story fizzled out. However, there had been other victims, including Gordon Taylor, the boss of the Professional Footballers' Association. When the police contacted him, he decided to sue.

Taylor was one of hundreds, possibly thousands of victims, including the deputy prime minister John Prescott and the culture secretary Tessa Jowell. The *Guardian* investigative journalist Nick Davies had been working on revealing the scandal for a year. As the number of victims mounted, they were bought off and signed non-disclosure agreements, with the pay-offs amounting to millions of pounds, as Davies outlines in his book *Hack Attack*, elements of which are summarised briefly below.

As the hacking scandal slowly gathered momentum and more celebrities were pulled into the net, James Murdoch announced shortly after the 2010 general election that his company would buy the remaining 61 per cent of the broadcaster BSkyB that they did not already own, taking complete control of the richest broadcaster in Britain. Murdoch had wanted a Conservative victory with a compliant David Cameron and his pro-Murdoch ally, the culture secretary Jeremy Hunt – but there were two possible flies in the ointment: a Lib Dem business secretary – Vince Cable – and the regulator Ofcom.

Cable made it clear that he intended to block the bid, but unwittingly told two female reporters from the *Daily Telegraph* posing as ordinary mothers from his constituency that he had declared war on Murdoch. With his facade of neutrality removed, Cable now appeared unfit to handle the bid. The baton moved on to Hunt. All this time Hunt had been in communication with Murdoch aides, including his executive Rebekah Brooks, and they felt certain their bid would succeed while they waited for Ofcom to give the deal the green light. Meanwhile the *Guardian* continued to publish evidence of phone hacking of celebrities and government ministers.

Nick Davies was tipped off about Milly Dowler. She was a thirteen-year-old schoolgirl who had disappeared while walking home from school in Yateley in Hampshire in March 2002. Her body was found six months later. Davies discovered that the *News of the World* had hacked her phone.

On 4 July 2011, the *Guardian* published the story. There was national outrage. Newspapers called for heads to roll. Terrible evidence of hacking came to light: the parents of Jessica Chapman and Holly Wells, children who had been murdered in Soham in 2002, had been hacked; some of the bereaved families of the fifty-two victims killed by the July 2005 terrorist bombings had also been targeted.

The outcome was spectacular. Having dismissed the *Guardian* claims for years, the media got on board – and even the Murdoch-owned *Times* ran an editorial condemning the hacking. Parliament was in uproar. David Cameron announced two public inquiries: one into the press, the other into the police. And Hunt announced that he had decided to delay his decision on the BSkyB bid. The *News of the World* was forced to close. Andy Coulson, who had resigned as editor of the *News of the World* after the Clive Goodman scandal – going on to be the director of communications for David Cameron – and Rebekah Brooks, Coulson's successor, were charged with conspiring to pay public officials for information and sent to court.

The public inquiry, under Lord Justice Brian Leveson, took evidence from 337 individuals – ordinary people who found themselves in a media storm: film stars, chief constables, government officials, the then prime minister, three former prime ministers including Brown, and numerous current and former cabinet ministers. More than 300 others submitted written statements. Leveson provided a platform for dozens of media victims who variously told him of the blackmail, bullying, malicious invasion of privacy and toxic falsehoods which they had suffered. While the 2012 Leveson report detailed the media abuses, little changed. No regulatory media ethics were imposed. Andy Coulson went to prison, but Rebekah Brooks was found not guilty.

The Murdoch media remain a major preoccupation of Gordon Brown's to this day. In May 2024, he wrote to the head of the Metropolitan Police, Mark Rowley, to call for a new criminal investigation into News International over phone hacking, a decade after the police investigation which saw Brooks cleared. Brown's move came after new information in court documents alleged a massive cover-up by News International. News Group Newspapers (NGN) claimed that Brown's allegations were 'unfounded and wrong'.

Brown told the ITV journalist Robert Peston: 'We've known for some time that the News Group destroyed about 30 million emails. But what we didn't know was the explanation that they were giving to the police for why they'd done this. And it is totally shocking to think that what they should do is allege that I and [former Labour minister and Brown ally] Tom Watson should have been bribing one of their employees ... to try to get hold of their emails. And their pretext for destruction was that I was engaged in trying to get this information ... and of course, it's not true.'

Brown's move was sparked by statements in recent court documents showing that on 22 January 2011, a News International IT executive Paul Cheesbrough emailed Brooks and the then general manager, Will Lewis, saying Brown had a sympathiser inside News International who was stealing Brooks's emails. On 11 February that year, Cheesbrough asked for an investigation of the potential theft of data that was allegedly being passed to Watson. Then, on 8 July, months after the Met Police had been investigating phone hacking, Cheesebrough and Lewis claimed to the police there had been a suspected theft of Brooks's emails, that Watson had been handling this stolen data, and that he was working in a conspiracy with Brown. Peston asked Brown if he would be happy to swear on oath that the allegations against him were untrue. 'Absolutely,' was Brown's unhesitating reply.[7]

The context here is that the phone-hacking scandal re-emerged in 2024 following allegations that NGN hacked phones on an industrial scale to advance its business interests, as well as to obtain stories. Those accusations have been made in civil claims brought by the former Liberal Democrat politicians Chris Huhne, Vince Cable and Norman Lamb, as well as Labour's Tom Watson. NGN denies the accusations. Evidence offered to support allegations of phone hacking for corporate intent revolves around patterns of calls made to politicians' phones at points when NGN's business interests were apparently threatened.[8]

Incidentally, Rebekah Brooks previously sent a text message to Sarah Brown demanding that Tom Watson be sacked, a view that Brooks frequently expressed to Brown himself.[9] And as Watson told me in May 2012: 'I have a very clear recollection of a phone call with Gordon Brown where he says Rupert Murdoch has asked Tony Blair to ask me to ask you to pull back from your investigation [into hacking] – it was this Parliament, after the election, after the parliamentary report, when I'm getting up in Parliament. Now I have to be fair to all three of the people … Gordon Brown says he has no recollection of the phone call, Tony Blair denies making the phone call, and Rupert Murdoch denied making it to Leveson. But I simply restate that it's not a conversation you forget.'[10]

As Nick Davies reported in *Prospect* magazine, Will Lewis was accused in the High Court of 'perverting the course of justice'. Davies wrote:

> Documents deployed by claimants allege that Lewis and his close colleague Simon Greenberg played a key part in 'the scheme to destroy … as much of the [Murdoch] company's historic electronic data as possible, and were empowered … to complete this task and to conceal what had taken place.' The claimants infer that they would not have done this 'without the knowledge and approval of Rupert Murdoch and James Murdoch'. They also allege that after Rupert Murdoch, in summer 2011, set up a Management and Standards Committee (MSC) as 'an independent body' to liaise with the police, Lewis and Greenberg became its sole UK-based members and, having secured the trust of the Metropolitan Police's Operation Weeting, then undermined that investigation's effectiveness.[11]

Prospect published the following after Davies's piece appeared in May 2024: '... the Murdoch company wrote to *Prospect* to stress its denial that Brooks and Lewis authorised the alleged delay and suppression of evidence and the targeted deletions of the emails of senior executives; and that emails were deleted pursuant to a plan devised by Mr Lewis or other senior executives to conceal evidence.' In late July it emerged that a British police special inquiry team was examining allegations that Lewis presided over the deliberate destruction of emails for Murdoch's organisation. The Met told Brown in a letter that its standing unit responsible for high-profile cases was reviewing the complaint he submitted about Lewis after fresh disclosures emerged during civil actions. The letter was signed by the Met's most senior officer, Mark Rowley. It says: 'Please be assured that the contents of your letter, dated 2 May 2024, is being considered by the Met's special enquiry team.' It added: 'The issues you raise are complex and will take time to consider against investigations that have already taken place.'

At the time of writing, the publisher of the *Washington Post*, Lewis, and his old ally Robert Winnett, who was appointed by Lewis as editor of the *Washington Post* before swiftly resigning in June, are accused of benefiting from private investigators paid to break the law, allegations that Murdoch's companies deny. Brown is still finding out about the extent to which he was targeted by the Murdoch companies.

The senior police officer Sue Akers, who headed the initial investigation, has now said she finds Lewis's explanation to be unbelievable. According to Brown:

> The destroyed emails were likely to have revealed much more of News Group's intrusion into the private lives of thousands of innocent people, not least ordinary families hit by tragedy, and almost certainly would have added to what I have only recently discovered about what happened to me ... More recently, I have been given information alleging that the Murdoch group also paid investigators to break into other personal accounts of mine – including bank, gas and electricity – suggesting that nothing was out of bounds (in response, the *Sunday Times* said it 'cannot comment on the specifics of these new allegations' but 'rejects the accusation that it has in the past retained or commissioned any individual to act illegally'). The

Murdoch team has always claimed that the pursuit – not just of me but my family, too – was in the public interest, but it is now clear to me that these were 'fishing expeditions' to obtain personal and private information.[12]

Now, Brown is considering his next move when it comes to the Murdoch media. Some familiar with the case say that he has the power to bring key figures in the Murdoch empire, including Brooks, to justice, if he has the will. 'It's up to Gordon now,' says one. Alastair Campbell says: 'He's clearly going for it. All strength to his elbow.'[13]

In August 2024, the magazine *Vanity Fair* portrayed Brown's intervention as critical to the move by Prince Harry and others to seek justice over hacking. 'A former British prime minister has submitted new evidence in the hacking scandal, potentially dragging some of Rupert's high-profile former attack dogs back into the crosshairs,' it said.[14] And in December 2024, the Met confirmed they are still looking into Brown's case.

On 22 January 2025, NGN, publisher of the *Sun*, offered 'a full and unequivocal apology' to Prince Harry 'for the phone hacking, surveillance and misuse of private information by journalists and private investigators instructed by them' at the *News of the World*. Tom Watson, who settled with NGN along with Harry, demanded that the prime minister and the Met Police bring Murdoch executives, including Rebekah Brooks, to justice.

A statement from NGN reads:

> NGN also offers a full and unequivocal apology to Lord Watson for the unwarranted intrusion carried out into his private life during his time in government by the *News of the World* during the period 2009–2011. This includes him being placed under surveillance in 2009 by journalists at the *News of the World* and those instructed by them. NGN also acknowledges and apologises for the adverse impact this had on Lord Watson's family and has agreed to pay him substantial damages. In addition, in 2011 News International received information that information was being passed covertly to Lord Watson from within News International. We now understand that this information was false, and Lord Watson was not in receipt of any such confidential information. NGN apologises fully and unequivocally for this.

Tony Blair told Leveson that after Labour's eighteen years in opposition – and the ferocious hostility to Labour from the press – he had chosen to 'manage' the media rather than take them on. Brown, too, had first tried to manage a hostile right-wing media. All national editors and proprietors were invited to Chequers for either lunch or dinner and he was happy to meet them on a regular basis to put his case. But as the relationship between Murdoch and the Conservative Party deepened, Brown came to the conclusion that the Murdoch regime was never going to report him fairly and was working hand in glove with the Conservatives to get him out of office as quickly as possible.

Brown has never, from his days as a student newspaper editor, been in favour of heavy media regulation. He took the view that the press should speak truth to power. In 2006, the government had started to review section 55 of the Data Protection Act 1998 and its custodial penalties for hacking into data. Then as he looked into it as prime minister there were three public interest defences for breaching the Data Protection Act which seemed sufficiently broad to allow for investigative journalism: exposing criminal wrongdoing, threats to the security and safety of the realm, and uncovering deception. But, if arrested for behaviour which was not covered by these exemptions, reporters could face imprisonment.

Brown agreed to meet representatives of the newspaper industry, and then after further discussions with the Lord Chancellor Jack Straw and the relevant minister Michael Wills, they created a new defence available to the media of publishing information 'in the reasonable belief that the obtaining, disclosing or procuring was in the public interest'. In fact while the government had powers to trigger an order enforcing criminal penalties, it never did so. But he stopped short at condoning invasions of privacy that were just fishing expeditions and refused to support Murdoch when he engaged in an orchestrated attempt at taking a stake in ITV. And when, in his MacTaggart lecture at the 2009 Edinburgh TV Festival, James Murdoch revealed a breathtaking agenda that went far beyond buying BSkyB, Brown could see where this would lead: Britain would have a version of Fox News.

Of course, the media in Britain are subject to a confusing patchwork of regulations, unlike the internet. And while Brown believes there is no case for regulating what is in the news beyond what is deemed defamatory, fraudulent or incites hatred, he feels there is a compelling case to set rules for how the news is obtained to avoid the criminality of recent years.

As to Blair, despite his perceived closeness to the Murdoch empire, which had historically supported him, he reflects today: 'When the Murdoch press, particularly, turned against [Brown], it was absolutely vicious … completely unfair.'[15]

21

Conclusion: Power for a Purpose

During a one-to-one lunch of smoked salmon sandwiches and sparkling water in his kitchen at home in North Queensferry, Fife, in January 2025, Gordon Brown is reflecting on the 2010 general election result. 'It was my fault,' he says to me. When it's pointed out that he faced a very hostile media, and he denied the Conservatives a majority after thirteen years of Labour government, Brown insists: 'No, it was my fault.'[1]

But the reality is more complicated than conventional wisdom has allowed. The Conservative Party, immediately after the financial crisis for which Brown's premiership will be remembered, launched a ruthless campaign to blame it on Labour spending and Brown personally. This was in some ways standard political fare, but it was echoed by much of the media.

The Tories, who were to stay in office for fourteen years, had been handed a gift days after the 2010 election when Liam Byrne left a jokey message for his successor as chief secretary to the Treasury saying: 'I'm afraid there is no money.' The Conservatives harked back to the note throughout their time in office, cementing the message that Labour had been reckless with public money.

Initially Brown's reputation was also damaged by the next Labour leader, Ed Miliband, attempting to distance himself from the Blair and Brown governments. Many outgoing ministers believed that Miliband, who served in Brown's cabinet after all, should have repeatedly made the argument that Brown's leadership helped avert the worst global recession in living memory.

The Murdoch press had targeted Brown since at least as far back as the year 2000. Perhaps the right-wing outlets were prejudiced against the centre-leftist Scot. Perhaps they were threatened by what this powerful and strong-willed public figure – armed with what Michael Gove calls an 'intimidating presence' – could do. Either way, Brown lost control. Over lunch, he adds that 2010's was ironically the one general election campaign he had not been running because there was too much going on at Number Ten. As his friend Bob Shrum says: 'Gordon was the strategic heart of the Labour campaigns in 1997, 2001, [in the end] 2005 and was obviously a candidate in 2010 and could not run the strategy in quite the same way.'

What, then, is Gordon Brown's legacy, as a politician and as a man? Brown was of course a key architect of New Labour alongside Tony Blair. But more than that, as a learned historian, he provided much of its intellectual grounding. Brown is uniquely steeped in the history and culture of the Scottish and British left.

First, you have to take in the ten years he spent as chancellor amid what even opponents accept were great strides on alleviating poverty – including almost halving child poverty. This came after Brown almost single-handedly made Labour trusted on the economy in the late 1980s and early 1990s at a personal cost that helped steer him to an act of self-sacrifice in 1994 by stepping aside for Tony Blair to become leader.

Though he was reluctant to admit it at the time for fear of handing ammunition to the right, Brown's chancellorship was the most redistributive since the Second World War. This was – after two years of understandably sticking to Tory fiscal plans for credibility in the markets and the electorate – thanks to the introduction of the first ever national minimum wage in 1999, record levels of spending on public services from 2000, and the introduction and then the expansion of tax credits, especially the working tax credit and the child tax credit, designed to support low-income working families. And that's not to mention the creation of Sure Start and the winter fuel allowance.

During his three-year premiership, after a successful honeymoon, Brown damaged his reputation with the electorate by declining to call a snap election, and sometimes struggled to deal with the daily succession of events. But then he rose to the biggest challenge of his career with his response to the global financial crisis. Its domestic impact of worldwide turmoil – recession and heavy government borrowing to keep public services afloat – perhaps meant that winning a fourth term for New Labour would have been impossible for any party leader.

CONCLUSION: POWER FOR A PURPOSE 283

Yet he helped to save his party from heavy defeat in 2010, as the Tories failed to achieve an overall Commons majority. These achievements, as well his campaigning gifts, intellectual restlessness and creativity, combine to make him Labour's most comprehensively able all-rounder since Clement Attlee, prime minister from 1945–51. Asked for his assessment of Labour's greatest post-war figures, Alastair Campbell says: 'You've got to say Attlee. You've got to say Tony. You've got to say Wilson [prime minister 1964–70 and 1974–6] as a kind of electoral political figure, but I think Gordon's right, right up there in terms of contribution to change in Britain.'[2] As Neil Kinnock told me, Brown has 'all the kit'. And that was in the face of what Tony Blair said was 'absolutely vicious' and 'completely unfair' treatment from the media, especially the Murdoch press.

One individual who understands Brown and his place in history well is Ed Balls. Now a broadcast journalist, Balls is well aware of the flaws in Brown's – and his own – political legacy, as we have seen, for example, over light-touch banking regulation. But he reflects today on how Brown used power for a purpose: 'The thing which is distinctive about Gordon was that he didn't see being a politician or being a chancellor or prime minister as an end in itself, [but] as an opportunity to do things in government at the highest level, things which had been his purpose for all his life, for his dad and his childhood and growing up, and has continued to be his purpose in the fifteen years after office. And so when you think about tackling poverty, or investing in the NHS or being tough with the public finances, that was a moral purpose, which was there before he became a politician, an elected politician, and is there after he's left Parliament.'

That 'purpose' was social justice, and though Brown stands firmly on the social democratic side of the argument against the Thatcherite settlement, he and Blair were ultimately not so different politically. As Balls says: 'If you look back in those periods from 2001 through to 2010 at the people who popped up supposedly under a Tony Blair label, saying they were the reformers and Gordon Brown was a consolidator ... they were fools. They were minnows. And the reason why Tony Blair listened to Gordon Brown and not them was because he was a big guy with another big guy, and two of them together were delivering a New Labour legacy, and that is the truth.'[3]

It may well be unfair and overly combative to dismiss Brown's internal political opponents – especially Milburn – as 'minnows'. Balls's remarks are a reminder that the fissures within New Labour continue to this day. But he goes on: 'And I think that's an unusual thing, not to see politics and office as an end in itself, and not to see your achievements as things which deliver political goals, but to see the being in politics as a way to deliver ends which are bigger than your political career and bigger than you yourself.'

For all his personal foibles – including his inability to delegate and occasional volcanic temper – Brown was driven from his early days by a long-term moral purpose and deeply held ambition to transform the living conditions and life chances of Britons. As Balls says: 'The reason why people like me or Ed Miliband or Shriti Vadera and many others stayed with him – and we will have rolled our eyes and got frustrated with him lots of times – was because of the depth of that moral purpose and [political and social] ambition.'

Contradicting Peter Mandelson's claim that Blair was more 'New' and Brown was more 'Labour', Balls goes on: 'I think that Gordon was the person who made New Labour, New Labour.' Tony Blair and Gordon Brown were a partnership, and dependent upon one another. It remains inaccurate to ascribe easy labels, with Brown left and Blair right for example, and it was always a creative and sometimes highly successful team effort.

Instead, Brown can be compared now to John Major, who fell to heavy defeat following a torrid six and a half years as prime minister battling his party over Europe, albeit after a surprise general election win in 1992, only to emerge as a respected elder statesman. If anything, Brown is even more respected – and certainly more active at seventy-five – today.

Tony Blair, Balls claims,

> is the opposite: at the point where he left in 2007, he left to wild acclaim in the House of Commons, but obviously in the period through to Chilcot [the report into the 2003 invasion of Iraq] – other things too about his departure, but Chilcot really – that changed and I don't think he would have had the same cheers leaving the House of Commons today, twenty years on. That is not to say that he's not respected for great achievements and great successes and winning

elections and important reforms in Northern Ireland and in domestic policy. But if you take the *Blair & Brown* BBC documentary, and in particular both the foreign policy episode one and the last one, it is clear that there was a more equivocal judgement of Tony Blair, that the contextualisation of his legacy has not been good for him. And lots of things which we've seen from him since – around his institute, his comments on Covid and technology – those are Tony Blair trying to shift his legacy and how he's seen in history.

Again to be fair to Blair, he was very far from alone in supporting the 2003 invasion of Iraq, with many ministers, including Gordon Brown, plus MPs, advisers and indeed senior journalists doing so, too. Today, some of those recall their positions in a different light, with Blair blamed almost solely. And the view that Saddam Hussein was developing weapons of mass destruction (WMD) was widely held in Whitehall, though not by the weapons inspector, David Kelly. Blair, whose politics are arguably sometimes misunderstood in the Westminster village, as Balls himself has demonstrated, also of course deserves credit as obviously the most electorally successful Labour leader ever, apart from anything else.

Brown was not only the longest-serving chancellor of the modern era; he was a great and reforming chancellor. Perhaps it is true that, despite his quick and decisive handling of the 2008 financial crash, he was not a great prime minister. But after his premiership ended in 2010, he rebuilt his reputation with public service. At home, he tilted the balance in the 2014 Scottish independence referendum and helped save the union. He continued his mission to tackle and ultimately end child poverty by establishing the multibank across the UK. And overseas, he once again lived out the values instilled in him by his parents from his early youth, and focused on international development through his UN roles.

The polling company YouGov reported in its 2024 findings that Brown was the most popular of all Labour politicians, with a positive approval rating of 35 per cent. He was above, for example, Andy Burnham, David Blunkett, Rachel Reeves, Ed Miliband, Tony Blair and Keir Starmer.[3] He is also probably the most respected of the eight currently living former prime ministers – a dramatic turnaround since leaving the highest office at the start of the previous decade.

Personally, Brown, who was clearly gifted from early youth, is an unusually deep and complicated man. On the one hand, he can retain residual and sometimes needless resentment towards perceived opponents, as we have seen in the cases of Alastair Campbell, Peter Mandelson, Alan Milburn and, more complicatedly, Tony Blair. He has also displayed questionable judgement when it comes to one or two of those individuals he has included within his own circle in the past, allowing them to engage in the political 'dark arts' at odds with his own moral compass.

But on the other hand, Brown is capable of extraordinary and unpublicised acts of grace and generosity, from phoning Mandelson in February 2006 to offer his heartfelt condolences over the death of Mandelson's mother, Mary, at the height of one of the pair's feuds, to plying friends with unexpected books as gifts. He is frequently charming and funny in private despite being shy, and is exceptionally caring to those in need. This last quality may have been enhanced by the higher than average level of suffering and loss visited upon him over the decades, from his partial blindness to the death of his and Sarah's baby daughter, Jennifer.

Other analyses of Brown have focused on his alleged temper and 'bullying'. But what does the man who was supposedly the cause of this volcanic rage make of it? As Blair says today: 'I think when people talk about Gordon as a bully, he was immensely determined, and highly, highly able. So if he felt that a particular thing was important to do, he was pretty full on, but that's not the same as being personally unpleasant to people. I don't actually think he was like that at all. Actually I think personally he is a very generous person.'[4]

Looking forward, there are many lessons for the Labour leadership, including Keir Starmer, in the life and times in office of Brown, the conviction politician. One easy one is not to court the Murdoch media in a protracted, energy-sapping and ultimately doomed dance that will always end in tears. Quite apart from what should be the diametrically opposed values of the right-wing media and the Labour Party, newspapers as a whole undoubtedly anyway hold less influence today, in an age of social media, though that may be a phase, and – as with leading politicians of substance – a thirst for quality may return. But the *Sun* and *The Times* surely hold less sway in elections, as their last-minute and somewhat fudged editorials showed on election day in 2024 (in the end the *Sun* grudgingly backed Starmer but *The Times* did not). Yet in July 2025, as we have seen, Starmer hired as permanent secretary for communications the former *Sun* editor David Dinsmore, much to Brown's private fury and the dismay of many in Labour. The question they were asking was: who benefits?

The 'freebies' scandal, in which Starmer accepted thousands of pounds in gifts of suits and spectacles and more, was completely unacceptable in the eyes of Brown, who accepted no gifts while in office, declined his prime ministerial pension, paid his own way with suits, spectacles and decorating through his time in Downing Street and left office in considerable debt as a result. This may be partly because, as a son of the manse, Brown was used to personal sacrifice. But it also reflects a different approach to the purpose of politics. Indeed, Brown was worried early in the Starmer government that it would be dogged by problems over lobbyists with an agenda hovering too close to power.

More broadly, is Starmer's modernisation of the party more substantial than mere positioning for the benefit of the right-wing media, and a desire to 'crush the left' for effect? Does it reflect Brown's use of power for a purpose? Does Starmer have Brown's combination of intellect and political acumen? If not, perhaps he shouldn't seek to emulate Brown in times of crisis, and should instead rely more on those around him and delegate. Elsewhere, Brown's ongoing commitment to ending poverty, especially child poverty, at home and overseas is beyond doubt a lesson for Starmer, who at the time of writing was still committed to the two-child benefit cap.

In May 2025 Brown guest-edited an issue of the *New Statesman* dedicated to tackling child poverty and called for the 'cruel' cap to be scrapped, with the £3.5 billion cost funded by a banking or gambling levy. This alongside the early decision to abolish the winter fuel allowance points to Starmer and Rachel Reeves controversially adopting Treasury orthodoxy in a way recent previous chancellors have resisted. Worse, Reeves and Starmer showed every sign in early 2025 of getting it wrong on City deregulation, and failing to learn the lessons of the great economic crash. In July 2025, Reeves told delighted bankers at her Mansion House speech that regulation had 'gone too far'.

Brown's record as chancellor on poverty is outstanding. But perhaps Starmer needs to think about how best to entrench any comparable record into political orthodoxy to prevent a period of Tory austerity like the one that followed Brown's premiership. Will Starmer and Reeves ensure the City of London is properly regulated as Brown and Balls should have done? Reeves appears once again to be pursuing light-touch regulation. Is Starmer prepared for another financial crash, and ready to do whatever it takes to bail Britain out of one? Will he make a big, radical move in the way that Brown did with Bank of England independence, aside from the bold but relatively muted creation of GB Energy? Will he pursue meaningful constitutional reform in the way that Brown wants him to? Will he abolish and replace the anachronistic (and as the late Charles Kennedy used to point out, blasphemously named) House of 'Lords'?

Will he avoid major wars which are not in the national interest in a way that Brown wishes he had helped Britain to do? Is Starmer enough of a historian? Does he read enough political biography and history? Will he pursue proper, collegiate cabinet government? Will he ensure that the civil service provides support that enables 24/7 decisions in a way that the distinguished diplomat Tom Fletcher says it failed to do under Brown's premiership? Will he avoid negative briefings about party colleagues as Brown's team should have done? Brown showed the power of great oratory – does Starmer have the ability to make rousing speeches that mobilise Labour supporters as well as civil society? And perhaps finally, does Starmer understand, as Brown did, the contribution faith groups can make to the social justice ideal? In the summer of 2025, Brown was orchestrating behind the scenes a drive to get faith leaders in the media to encourage the government to go further to tackle child poverty. Brown was influential, on and off, like Tony Blair, when Starmer was in opposition. Now, for better or worse, as he himself concedes privately, he is less so when it comes to the current Labour government.

Brown, who is genuinely dismayed by corruption as well as people who go into politics for non-altruistic reasons, never pursued power for its own sake, and has set a lasting example to his party and to the country he loves.

As I walked with him after lunch on that quiet January afternoon in light rain up a hill behind his home, I reflected that Gordon Brown, infused by faith from birth as a son of the manse, is indeed a conviction politician from a seemingly lost age. He displays today the 'moral leadership' he attributed to the late Jimmy Carter. He will be judged as having delivered power with purpose for his beloved party, for Fife, Scotland, for Britain and, on international development, for the global south. Since the dishonest campaign for Brexit in 2016, the premiership of Boris Johnson from 2019 and, yes, the 2024 free gifts scandal, principle in British politics appears to many to have faded away. But hope is a duty, and we must believe it will return. If it does, not for the first time, Gordon Brown, for all his faults, will have set a most powerful example, not just for the future of the Labour Party which he helped to secure, but also for that of the country and indeed the wider world.

Acknowledgements

Halfway through this project I fell sick with acute pancreatitis, at one point receiving the last rites while in a five-week coma, and I must thank the medics of the Chelsea and Westminster Hospital, particularly those in the intensive care unit: it's no exaggeration to say they saved my life, and therefore also saved this book. As a result of that illness and my recovery, I've more people to thank than is conventional.

Professionally, my first thanks are to Gordon Brown himself for the unprecedented access he has generously given me for this new biography.

I'm especially indebted to Brown's brothers, John and Andrew, for their time, private notes and family photographs. Sue Nye, Brown's closest political aide for decades, has been incredibly helpful with conversations, private notes and the facilitation of other interviews.

Mary Bailey and Peter Tompkins in Brown's office were always helpful and efficient. I'm especially thankful to Gordon Brown's archivist, Ross Christie, for graciously allowing me to use some of his research into Bank of England independence and the Treasury, which is referenced. And Carmel Nolan, who helps Brown with media, was supportive and insightful.

I'm very grateful to my publisher, the wise, skilful and cool-headed Ian Marshall who 'gets' Gordon Brown, his excellent editorial assistant Amy Whitaker, and the rest of the team at Bloomsbury, including my quick-witted publicist, Jonny Coward, creative managing editor Francisco Vilhena, the brilliant Natasha Drewett and razor-sharp copy editor Katherine Fry. And I must thank my dynamic and resourceful literary agent, Gordon Wise of Curtis Brown. Any – all – mistakes are mine and mine alone.

ACKNOWLEDGEMENTS

This is not a comprehensive account, and in that sense, merely complements many other books: the 2017 memoir by Brown himself, and those of Tony Blair, Peter Mandelson, Jonathan Powell, Ed Balls, David Cameron and Nick Clegg, as well as Alastair Campbell's detailed series of diaries, and other relevant works by Robert Peston, Steve Richards, Paul Routledge, Tom Bower, Anthony Seldon, John Rentoul, Andrew Rawnsley and Donald Macintyre.

Elsewhere, heartfelt thanks to: my kind former boss, the seasoned *Independent* political commentator Andrew Grice, Matthew Parris, Scarlett McGwire, Tom Baldwin, Ed Thornton, Bénédicte Scholefield, Mark Scholefield and Roger Liddle, for reading early manuscript drafts and coming up with strings of astute and helpful suggestions; the parliamentary lobby veteran Nigel Morris for important help with political content; the academic and journalist Tom Clark for his input in the Treasury chapter; the Bank of England economist Jack Meaning for his expert comments on the Treasury and premiership chapters; Daniel Lewis, and funnily enough another Tom Clark, a university contemporary, for researching the financial crash material; Adam Minns, Stephen Khan, Jenny Khan-Hill, Gordon McKee and Lucie Rycott for reading early pieces of material and making observations at various points; and for the moral support of three exceptional clergymen during an occasionally testing time, my deep gratitude to Fr Steffan Matthias, Fr Ben Vertannes and Fr David Houghton. I'm deeply grateful to Olivia Beattie for her wisdom on publishing over many years, and to another senior publisher, Carole Welch, for her support.

Thanks too to Mehdi Hasan, Margaret Doherty, Francis Campbell, Chine McDonald, Patrick Watt, Lizzy Davies, Harry Farley, Jessica Benton, Joe Ware, Gloria de Piero, David Green, Tracey McIntyre, Rose O'Lone, Andrew Liddle, Shonagh Munro, Rachael McCaffrey, Mark Newby, Caroline Thomson, Ju Owens, Lindsay Thomas, Jon Speelman, Jill Coppin, Roger and Trish Foxwell, Simon and Sheila Launchbury, and Marta di Forti for being there when I was ill and beyond, alongside Anthea Eastoe, who also provided skilled early administrative work. Special thanks to Rachel Sigrist for her priceless counsel over this book and much else.

Last but not least, for long-suffering support, I want to thank my old friend Harriet Sherwood, my amazing sister Sophie Meyer, her father Ashley, her daughter – my niece – Sophie, and my inspiration and my 'moral compass', my father, Don Macintyre.

Finally, this is also written in loving memory of my late mother, Sue Freestone, a great publisher who died during this book's production and who, among so many other things, was a Gordon Brown fan.

Notes

PROLOGUE

1. Interview with author.
2. Interview with author.

1 SON OF THE MANSE

1. Gordon Brown and Alistair Moffat, *Fife: A history from earliest times to the present day*, Deerpark Press, 2019, p. 1.
2. Ibid.
3. Interview with author.
4. Letter provided by the Brown family.
5. Interview with author.
6. Interview with author.
7. See: https://www.mirror.co.uk/news/uk-news/prime-minister-gordon-brown-opens-202505
8. Interview with author.
9. Gordon Brown, *My Life, Our Times*, Vintage, 2017, p. 37.
10. See: https://www.heraldscotland.com/news/12020990.rev-dr-john-brown/
11. Brown, *My Life, Our Times*, p. 36.
12. Ibid.
13. Ibid., p. 37.
14. Ibid.
15. Interview with author.
16. From letters provided by the National Library of Scotland.
17. See: https://www.theguardian.com/politics/1998/sep/26/economy.uk
18. Brown, *My Life, Our Times*, p. 43.

19 Interview with author.
20 Brown, *My Life, Our Times*, p. 39.
21 Ibid., p. 44.

2 EDINBURGH

1 Brown, *My Life, Our Times*, p. 45.
2 Ibid., p. 46.
3 Interview with author.
4 Brown, *My Life, Our Times*, p. 48.
5 Letters provided by the Brown family.
6 Brown, *My Life, Our Times*, p. 50.
7 Interview with author.
8 Paul Routledge, *Gordon Brown: The Biography*, Pocket Books, 1998, p. 55.
9 Interview with author.
10 See: http://news.bbc.co.uk/1/hi/uk_politics/4683799.stm
11 Interview with author.
12 See: https://www.telegraph.co.uk/news/features/3632645/Romantic.-Beautiful.-I-fell-madly-in-love.html

3 TOWARDS WESTMINSTER

1 Robin Cook, *The Point of Departure*, Pocket Books, 2003, p. 11.
2 Brown, *My Life, Our Times*, p. 76.
3 Robert Peston, *Brown's Britain*, Short Books, 2005, p. 21.
4 See: https://bellacaledonia.org.uk/2022/05/16/reflections-on-revisiting-the-red-paper-on-scotland/
5 See: https://www.lrb.co.uk/the-paper/v20/n04/paul-foot/mr-straight-and-mr-good
6 Brown, *My Life, Our Times*, p. 53.
7 Interview with author.
8 Interview with author.
9 Interview with author.
10 Interview with author.
11 Interview with author.
12 Brown, *My Life, Our Times*, p. 61.
13 Ibid., p. 62.

4 WILDERNESS YEARS

1 Interview with author.

2 Brown, *My Life, Our Times*, p. 68.
3 Interview with author.
4 Interview with author.
5 Brown, *My Life, Our Times*, p. 67.
6 Ibid., p. 69.
7 Ibid., p. 70.
8 Interview with author.
9 Brown, *My Life, Our Times*, p. 71.
10 Ibid.
11 Ibid., p. 72.
12 Ibid., p. 73.
13 Interview with author.
14 Brown, *My Life, Our Times*, p. 74.
15 Interview with author.
16 Interview with author.
17 Donald Macintyre, *Mandelson and the Making of New Labour*, HarperCollins, 2000, p.218
18 Ibid., p. 217.
19 Brown, *My Life, Our Times*, p. 75.
20 Ibid.
21 Ibid.
22 Ibid., p. 76.
23 Interview with author.
24 Interview with author.
25 Brown, *My Life, Our Times*, p. 77.
26 Ibid., p. 78.
27 Ibid.
28 Ibid.
29 Interview with author.
30 Interview with author.
31 Brown, *My Life, Our Times*, p. 79.
32 Ibid., p. 80.
33 Ibid.
34 Interview with author.
35 Brown, *My Life, Our Times*, p. 81.

5 PAYING THE PRICE

1 Brown, *My Life, Our Times*, p. 81.
2 Ibid., p. 82.
3 Ibid.

4 Interview with author.
5 Interview with author.
6 Brown, *My Life, Our Times*, p. 82.
7 Ibid., p. 83.
8 Ibid.
9 Interview with author.
10 Brown, *My Life, Our Times*, p. 84.
11 Ibid.
12 Macintyre, *Mandelson and the Making of New Labour*, p. 263.
13 Brown, *My Life, Our Times*, p. 85.
14 Ibid.
15 Ibid.
16 Interview with author.
17 Brown, *My Life, Our Times*, p. 86.
18 Ibid., p. 88.
19 Ibid.
20 Ibid., p. 89.
21 Ibid.
22 Macintyre, *Mandelson and the Making of New Labour*, p. 290.
23 Brown, *My Life, Our Times*, p. 91.
24 Interview with author.
25 Interview with author.
26 Interview with author.
27 Macintyre, *Mandelson and the Making of New Labour*, p. 274.
28 See: https://www.independent.co.uk/news/uk/politics/parliament-politics-leftwing-challenge-to-brown-strategy-1409900.html
29 Brown, *My Life, Our Times*, p. 92.

6 TURNING POINT

1 Brown, *My Life, Our Times*, p. 93.
2 Ibid.
3 Ibid., p. 94.
4 Macintyre, *Mandelson and the Making of New Labour*, p. 286.
5 Ibid.
6 The book was Andy McSmith's *John Smith: A Life*, Mandarin, 1994.
7 Interview with author.
8 Andrew Brown's diary.
9 Interview with author.
10 Brown, *My Life, Our Times*, p. 98.
11 Interview with author.

12 Brown, *My Life, Our Times*, p. 98.
13 Ibid., p. 99.
14 Interview with author.
15 Macintyre, *Mandelson and the Making of New Labour*, pp. 294–5.
16 Interview with author.
17 Interview with author.
18 Brown, *My Life, Our Times*, p. 99.
19 Ibid., p. 100.
20 Ibid., p. 101.
21 Interview with author.
22 Interview with author.
23 Interview with author.
24 Interview with author.
25 Interview with author.
26 Interview with author.
27 Interview with author.
28 Jack Straw, *Last Man Standing*, Pan Books, 2013, p. 194.
29 Ibid., p. 193.
30 John Gray, 'Blair's Project in Retrospect', *International Affairs (Royal Institute of International Affairs 1944–)*, 80(1), 2004, pp. 39–48.
31 Interview with author.
32 Interview with author.
33 Interview with author.
34 Interview with author.

7 TRUCE

1 Interview with author.
2 Interview with author.
3 Brown, *My Life, Our Times*, p. 101.
4 Ibid., p. 102.
5 Ibid., p. 106.
6 Ibid., pp. 106–7.
7 Ibid., p. 107.
8 Ibid.
9 Letter provided by the Brown family.
10 Interview with author.
11 See: https://www.scotsman.com/news/opinion/columnists/how-john-prescott-and-i-were-proved-right-about-railway-privatisation-4879037

8 REVOLUTION

1. Ed Balls, *Speaking Out*, Hutchinson, 2016, p. 140.
2. From research by Ross Christie.
3. Interview with author.
4. From research by Ross Christie.
5. Ibid.
6. Ibid.
7. Ibid.
8. Ibid.

9 THE EURO DECISION

1. From the National Archives.
2. Alastair Campbell, *The Blair Years*, Hutchinson, 2007, p. 253.
3. Tony Blair, *A Journey*, Hutchinson, 2010, p. 537.
4. Interview with author.

10 TRAGEDY

1. See: https://www.shropshirestar.com/news/uk-news/2024/08/19/sarah-brown-reflects-on-life-at-no-10-downing-street/
2. Brown, *My Life, Our Times*, p.160.
3. Ibid., p. 161.
4. See: https://gordonandsarahbrown.com/2015/02/house-beautiful-speak-to-sarah-and-her-mother/
5. See: https://metro.co.uk/2022/06/08/after-my-daughter-died-at-10-days-old-i-was-desperate-for-answers-16790559/

11 REDISTRIBUTION, SPENDING AND DEREGULATION

1. Peston, *Brown's Britain*, pp. 246–7.
2. Cook, *The Point of Departure*, p. 120.
3. See: https://academic.oup.com/oxrep/article/29/1/178/402517
4. Interview with author.
5. Interview with author.
6. Interview with author.
7. See: https://www.bbc.co.uk/news/business-48177767
8. Interview with author.
9. Interview with author.
10. Interview with author.
11. Private information.

12 See: https://www.theguardian.com/politics/2011/sep/26/ed-balls-sorry-labour-failures
13 See: https://www.ukpol.co.uk/gordon-brown-1997-mansion-house-speech/
14 See: https://www.bbc.co.uk/news/business-13032013

12 IRAQ AND INTERNATIONAL DEVELOPMENT

1 See: https://nsarchive2.gwu.edu/NSAEBB/NSAEBB328/II-Doc05.pdf
2 Interview with author.
3 Interview with author.
4 Interview with author.
5 Interview with author.
6 See: https://www.theguardian.com/world/1999/sep/29/debtrelief.development
7 Interview with author.

13 DIVISION, CONSOLIDATION AND TRANSITION

1 See: https://www.ipsos.com/en-uk/brown-most-successful-chancellor-say-british-political-scientists
2 Interview with author.
3 Private information.
4 Peston, *Brown's Britain*, p. 304.
5 Interview with author.
6 Cook, *The Point of Departure*, p. 62.
7 Private information.
8 See: https://www.theguardian.com/politics/2004/jan/27/publicservices.uk5
9 Private information.
10 Chris Mullin, *A View from the Foothills*, Profile Books, 2010, p. 524.
11 Blair, *A Journey*, p. 616.
12 Interview with author.
13 Interview with author.
14 Private information.
15 Interview with author.
16 Interview with author.
17 For the most comprehensive account of this episode, see Macintyre, *Mandelson and the Making of New Labour*, including the lengthy footnote on p. 504.

18 See: https://www.thetimes.com/uk/scotland/article/charlie-whelan-interview-lying-just-seems-acceptable-now-i-can-honestly-say-i-never-lied-8dhz8v8rh
19 Private information.
20 Interview with author.
21 See: https://www.theguardian.com/politics/2006/sep/07/labourleadership.labour
22 See a series of Number Ten emails about the 'coup' here: https://www.theguardian.com/politics/2013/sep/19/tony-blair-gordon-brown
23 See: https://www.theguardian.com/politics/2006/sep/07/labourleadership.labour5
24 See: https://www.theguardian.com/politics/article/2024/sep/01/tony-blair-on-leadership-book-interview-starmer-ai-trump?CMP=share_btn_url
25 See: https://www.theguardian.com/politics/2007/may/10/tonyblair.labour
26 Interview with author.
27 See: https://www.theguardian.com/politics/2007/may/17/labourleadership.labour2
28 See: http://news.bbc.co.uk/1/hi/uk_politics/6235258.stm

14 HONEYMOON AND HESITATION

1 Private information.
2 Interview with author.
3 Interview with author.
4 See: https://www.theguardian.com/politics/2012/jun/27/browns-first-day-in-no-10
5 Interview with author.
6 Interview with author.
7 Anthony Seldon and Guy Lodge, *Brown at 10*, Biteback Publishing, 2011, p. 6.
8 Interview with author.
9 See: https://www.theguardian.com/politics/2008/aug/05/gordonbrown.labour
10 Minutes of a 10 Downing Street meeting on 5 November 1998 show Brown telling Blair, 'There was no need, on public finance grounds, to sell a minority stake – it would not raise much money and we did not need it anyway.'
11 Seldon and Lodge, *Brown at 10*, p. 20.
12 Interview with author.

13 See: https://www.theguardian.com/politics/2007/sep/22/labour conference.labour
14 Interview with author.
15 Interview with author.
16 Interview with author.
17 Interview with author.
18 Interview with author.
19 Private information.
20 See: https://www.newstatesman.com/long-reads/2008/10/labour-party-mandelson-brown

15 SAVING THE WORLD

1 Interview with author.
2 Interview with author, and see: http://news.bbc.co.uk/1/hi/uk_politics/7182612.stm
3 See: https://www.theguardian.com/politics/2008/oct/18/davidcameron-economy
4 Gordon Brown, *Beyond the Crash*, Simon & Schuster, 2011, p. 239.
5 Adam Tooze, *Crashed*, Viking Press, 2018, p. 48.
6 Ibid., p. 50.
7 Ibid., p. 55.
8 Ibid.
9 Ibid., p. 63.
10 Ibid.
11 Ibid., p. 49.
12 Ibid., p. 55.
13 Bank of England annual report.
14 Duncan Weldon, *Two Hundred Years of Muddling Through*, Little, Brown, 2021, p. 280.
15 See: https://www.ft.com/content/361be1d2-a71b-11db-83e4-0000779e2340
16 See: https://www.bbc.co.uk/news/business-13032013
17 Tooze, *Crashed*, p. 82.
18 Interview with author.
19 Interview with author.
20 Tooze, *Crashed*, p. 82.
21 Ibid., p. 81.
22 See: https://commonslibrary.parliament.uk/royal-bank-of-scotland-bailout-10-years-and-counting/

23 Brown, *My Life, Our Times*, p. 308.
24 Weldon, *Two Hundred Years of Muddling Through*, p. xx.
25 Tooze, *Crashed*, p. 43.
26 Ibid., p. 144.
27 See: https://www.ft.com/content/a8c5829a-466e-11dc-a3be-0000779fd2a
28 Tooze, *Crashed*, p. 146.
29 Ibid., p. 143.
30 See: https://www.theguardian.com/politics/2008/aug/30/economy.alistairdarling
31 Tooze, *Crashed*, p.172.
32 Ibid., p. 149.
33 Brown, *My Life, Our Times*, p. 313.
34 Ibid., p. 186.
35 Ibid., p. 189.
36 Ibid., p. 191.
37 Ibid., p. 197.
38 Ibid., p. 192.
39 Ibid., p. 269.
40 See: https://www.theguardian.com/politics/2009/mar/24/gordon-brown-eu-strasbourg-protectionsm
41 See: https://amp.theguardian.com/business/2009/mar/24/mervyn-king-financial-aid-recession
42 See: https://www.nytimes.com/2008/10/13/opinion/13krugman.html
43 Alistair Darling, *Back from the Brink*, Atlantic Books, 2012, p. 224.
44 Brown, *My Life, Our Times*, p. 333.
45 Tooze, *Crashed*, p. 271.
46 Interview with author.
47 Private information.
48 Weldon, *Two Hundred Years of Muddling Through*, p. 284.
49 Tooze, *Crashed*, p. 156.
50 Weldon, *Two Hundred Years of Muddling Through*, p. 281.
51 Ibid.
52 Interview with author.
53 See: https://www.theguardian.com/commentisfree/2012/feb/06/gordon-brown-save-world-uk
54 Interview with author.
55 Interview with author.

16 FIGHTING CHANCE

1. Seldon and Lodge, *Brown at 10*, p. 300.
2. See: https://www.newstatesman.com/uncategorized/2009/09/labour-party-election-prime
3. See: https://www.ukpol.co.uk/gordon-brown-2009-speech-to-labour-party-conference/#google_vignette
4. Interview with author.
5. Private information.
6. Private information.
7. Private information.
8. Interview with author.
9. See: https://www.theguardian.com/politics/2010/apr/06/gordon-brown-launches-election-campaign
10. See: https://www.youtube.com/watch?v=BFqrMP2HR1A&t=10s
11. See: https://www.theguardian.com/politics/2010/may/03/gordon-brown-plea-progressive-voters
12. See: https://x.com/TheNewsAgents/status/1871533785717559626
13. Private information.
14. See: https://www.theguardian.com/commentisfree/2010/apr/30/the-liberal-moment-has-come
15. Interview with author.
16. Private information.
17. See: https://www.theguardian.com/media/2010/feb/15/gordon-brown-interview-piers-morgan
18. Interview with author.
19. Several times during our encounters for this book, Brown made what could be described as relatively socially conservative remarks, about whether flights should or shouldn't be avoided because of their impact on climate change, about how Christmas was regrettably being turned into a 'winter festival', and about foreign foods – on one visit to a Japanese restaurant overseas, Brown complained to Tom Fletcher about the lack of simple steak on the menu.
20. Private information.
21. Interview with author.
22. Damian McBride, *Power Trip*, Biteback, 2014, p. 445.
23. Andrew Adonis, *5 Days in May*, Biteback, 2013, p. 10.
24. Interview with author.
25. See: https://www.bbc.co.uk/programmes/m0021bcr
26. Interview with author.

27 Private letter from Gordon Brown in Number Ten to Nick Clegg on 10 May 2010.
28 Adonis, *5 Days in May*, p. 1.
29 Interview with author.
30 Interview with author.
31 See: https://www.newstatesman.com/long-reads/2010/05/lib-dems-labour-clegg-tories
32 Interview with author.
33 See: https://www.independent.co.uk/news/uk/politics/roy-jenkins-the-statesman-who-never-became-prime-minister-but-excelled-in-being-a-european-138032.html

17 AFTER DOWNING STREET: REFERENDUM

1 Interview with author.
2 Interview with author.
3 Interview with author.
4 Interview with author.
5 Gordon Brown, *My Scotland, Our Britain*, Simon & Schuster, 2014, p. 2.
6 Interview with author.
7 Brown, *My Life, Our Times*, p. 395.
8 See: https://gordonandsarahbrown.com/campaign/scotland/
9 Private information.
10 See: https://www.theguardian.com/uk-news/2014/sep/15/david-cameron-emotional-plea-scotland-independence
11 Interview with author.
12 Interview with author.
13 Brown, *My Life, Our Times*, p. 404.
14 Interview with author.
15 See: https://gordonandsarahbrown.com/campaign/scotland/
16 See: https://www.youtube.com/watch?v=WLgwtfWYdTs
17 Brown, *My Life, Our Times*, p. 174.
18 Gordon Brown, *Britain: Leading, not Leaving*, Deerpark Press, 2016.
19 See: https://www.christiantoday.com/article/cameron.brown.blair.and.major.to.share.platform.in.last.ditch.bid.to.keep.britain.in.eu/88405.htm
20 See: https://hitchensblog.mailonsunday.co.uk/2016/06/this-ghastly-planned-exhibition-of-blairite-waxworks-should-ensure-british-exit-from-the-eu.html

21 https://www.dailymail.co.uk/debate/article-13522979/PETER-HITCHENS-Starmer-Gordon-Browns-Parliament-Left-wing-revolution.html
22 See: https://labour.org.uk/wp-content/uploads/2022/12/Commission-on-the-UKs-Future.pdf

18 CHARITY NEAR AND FAR

1 Seen in the Kew national archives.
2 Interview with author.
3 From Brown's introduction to the *Handbook on the UN Human Right System: The right to education*, Unesco and Right to Education Initiative, 2019.
4 See: https://mediacentre.christianaid.org.uk/gordon-brown-launches-christian-aid-week-making-moral-and-ethical-case-for-aid-and-development-says-britain-must-rediscover-its-internationalism/
5 See: https://www.theguardian.com/commentisfree/2025/jan/22/donald-trump-leave-who-world-health-organization-pandemic-coming-gordon-brown
6 Interview with author.
7 See: https://www.theguardian.com/society/article/2024/jul/21/gordon-brown-launches-londons-first-multibank-amid-uk-child-poverty-fears
8 See: https://www.theosthinktank.co.uk/research/2022/11/07/a-torn-safety-net-how-the-cost-of-living-crisis-threatens-its-own-last-line-of-defence
9 See: https://www.theguardian.com/commentisfree/2025/aug/06/gambling-industry-profitable-tax-fight-child-poverty
10 See: https://www.ft.com/content/3ea8e156-2da9-4caf-a2f7-394d57641232
11 https://www.bbc.co.uk/news/articles/c4g2g7qgl1eo

19 JOY IN THE MORNING: GORDON BROWN'S QUIET FAITH

1 Interview with author.
2 See: https://www.huffingtonpost.co.uk/entry/berlusconi-brown_uk_5a464acce4b0b0e5a7a5f7a3
3 Interview with author.
4 Private information.
5 Brown, *My Life, Our Times*, p. 34.
6 See: https://www.theguardian.com/politics/2009/mar/31/gordon-brown-churchgoer
7 Interview with author.

8   See: http://www.britishpoliticalspeech.org/speech-archive.htm?speech=337
9   Cardinal Cormac Murphy O'Connor, *An English Spring*, Bloomsbury Continuum, 2015, p. 188.
10 See: https://www.theguardian.com/society/2024/nov/22/gordon-brown-improve-end-of-life-care-rather-than-allow-assisted-dying
11 Listen: https://www.bbc.co.uk/sounds/play/m0025cx0

20 SUPPING WITH THE DEVIL: GORDON BROWN VERSUS THE MURDOCH MEDIA

1   See: https://www.independent.co.uk/voices/commentators/donald-macintyre/however-presented-alastair-campbell-s-departure-marks-the-end-of-new-labour-102437.html
2   See: https://www.independent.co.uk/news/uk/politics/how-labour-wooed-and-won-the-sun-1274590.html
3   Campbell, *The Blair Years*, p. 287.
4   See: https://www.theguardian.com/media/2011/jul/11/phone-hacking-news-international-gordon-brown
5   See: https://www.independent.co.uk/news/uk/politics/brown-refuses-to-reveal-contacts-with-murdoch-777681.html
6   See: https://www.theguardian.com/media/2012/may/15/leveson-inquiry-adam-boulton
7   See: https://www.itv.com/news/2024-05-02/gordon-brown-asks-met-for-new-probe-into-phone-hacking-amid-cover-up-claims
8   See: https://www.tortoisemedia.com/2024/08/14/rupert-murdoch-will-lewis-and-the-washington-post/
9   Private information.
10 See: https://www.prospectmagazine.co.uk/politics/50149/exclusive-james-macintyre-interviews-tom-watson
11 See: https://www.prospectmagazine.co.uk/ideas/media/phone-hacking/66047/did-washington-post-publisher-pervert-the-course-of-justice-under-murdoch
12 See: https://www.theguardian.com/commentisfree/article/2024/jul/31/gordon-brown-tom-watson-news-international-william-lewis-rupert-murdoch
13 Interview with author.
14 See: https://www.vanityfair.com/news/story/prince-harry-rupert-murdoch-gordon-brown-showdown
15 Interview with author.

21 CONCLUSION: POWER FOR A PURPOSE

1. Interview with author.
2. Interview with author.
3. See: https://yougov.co.uk/ratings/politics/popularity/labour-politicians/all
4. Interview with author.

Index

GB = Gordon Brown; q.v. = 'which see'

Abbey National Building Society 269–70
ABN Amro 196–7
Adam, Robert 19
Addison, Paul 24, 61; *The Road to 1945* 24
Adonis, Andrew 1, 220, 221, 224, 226, 245; *5 Days in May* 224
Afghanistan 144–5, 171, 206, 209, 210–12, 216, 223
Afzal, Nazir 256–7
Ahern, Bertie 119
Aitken, Jonathan 99
Aitkenhead, Decca 194
Akers, Sue 277
Alam, Faria 273
Alexander, Danny 222
Alexander, Douglas 61, 76, 172, 173, 174, 226, 238, 239
Allied Irish Bank 195–6
Allsop, Kenneth 23
al-Qaeda 141
Amazon 253
Amersham International 43–4
Amicus (union) 172
Ancram, Michael 37
Anglo Irish Bank 195–6

Argles, Martin 227
assisted dying 264–5
Attlee, Clement 283
Aznar, José Maria 119

BAA 93
Bailey, Andrew 109
Baldwin, Tom 92
Balls, Ed: as leader writer for *Financial Times* 72–3; works with GB 72, 73; discusses leadership with Blair and GB 79; at Granita dinner 83; on Blair and GB 85–6, 88–9, 151, 155, 157, 158, 159, 283–5; and Blair's fiscal policy 93; and Bank of England independence 95, 106, 107, 108, 109, 110; witnesses GB's reception at the Treasury 104–5; and euro membership 113, 114, 115, 116, 118–20; on level of redistribution under GB 128, 130; at GB/Kavanagh meeting on NHS 135; on New Labour economic reforms 136, 137–8; and City banking regulation 138–9, 188, 189, 288; becomes MP 139; tasked by GB to improve relations between government and banks 140; on 2005 election campaign

Balls, Ed (*cont'd*)
154–5; offered chancellorship by GB 169–70; and a possible early election 173, 174–5; as author of GB's 'no time for a novice' jibe 177–8; on the financial crisis (2008) 204; and Labour/Lib Dem alliance (2010) 221, 225–6
Ban Ki-moon 249
Bank of Canada 192
Bank of England: and bank regulation 139; given independence by GB 57, 95, 105, 106–7, 108–10, 126, 136, 150, 288; and financial crisis (2008) 186–7, 192, 193, 199, 203
Bank of Ireland 195–6
Bank of Japan 192
banking crisis *see* financial crisis
Barclays Bank 194
Barry, Ostlere and Shepherd 14
BBC 145; *Andrew Marr Show* 175; BBC Verify Live 256; *Blair and Brown* 85, 128, 285; *Breakfast With Frost* 134; *Desert Island Discs* 80; *Newsnight* 92; *PM* programme 256; *Songs of Praise* 261; *Sunday* 264; *Today* programme 98, 130, 201, 254; *World at One* 173
Bear Stearns 186, 194
Beardall, Barry 270
Beckett, Margaret 67, 77, 89
Beckham, David 273
Begala, Paul 73
Beith, Alan 65
Bell, Torsten 238
Benedict XVI, Pope 258, 259
Benn, Tony 40, 45, 56, 68, 89, 111
Berlin Wall, fall of the (1989) 62, 209
Berlusconi, Silvio 259–60
Best, Geoffrey 24
Better Together campaign 238, 239, 240–41, 242, 243–4
Bevan, Aneurin 30, 264
Bevins, Tony 115

bin Laden, Osama 141
Blair, Cherie 218
Blair, Tony: and CND 40; relationship with GB 4, 5, 44–5, 61–2, 63, 70, 71–2, 89, 91–2, 110, 159, 162, 282, 284; on GB 58, 156, 202, 204, 233; religious views 265–6; frustrated at state of Labour Party 46; a powerful speaker 53; as shadow secretary of state for energy 54; pilloried for comment on Mrs Thatcher 55; in Australia with GB (1991) 61; plans for party policy reform 61–2, 65, 66; and John Smith 35, 66–7, 74; fails to win deputy leadership 67; becomes shadow home secretary 68; and Clause IV of Labour's constitution 68, 94; elected onto national executive committee 68; backs 'one member, one vote' 68; his profile increases rapidly 70; and Ed Balls 73, 159, 284–5; in USA 73–4; and Labour leadership struggle with GB 3, 66–7, 75–90, 99, 153–4, 155–6; early days as leader 93, 94, 96, 98, 130; and Labour victory (1997) 99, 103, 104, 228–9; and its 'business manifesto' 138; agrees to Bank of England independence 106, 107–8; and the euro decision 112, 113, 114, 115–20; increases universal pensions 132–3; clashes with GB over NHS funding 134; and Murdoch/Murdoch press 135, 178, 208, 268, 269, 270, 276, 279, 280; and Iraq war 119, 141, 142–3, 144, 145–6, 154, 155, 162, 172; at G8 summit (2005) 147; policy differences with GB 149–54, 158, 171, 211, 218, 283; and 2005 election 154–5, 215; tries to sack GB as chancellor 155; supports Israel's war with Lebanon 160; resigns as prime minister 155–6, 157, 159–62, 163–4, 167, 168; and David Miliband

170; and Dacre and *Daily Mail* 218; makes money on the lecture circuit 233; and Brexit 245; and Keir Starmer 246
Blears, Hazel 171
Blunkett, David 68, 74, 226, 273, 285
BNP Paribas 192
Bonhoeffer, Dietrich 254
Boulton, Adam 271
Boumphrey, John 253
Boyson, Rhodes 47
Bradford & Bingley Building Society 195
Brexit 119, 214, 224, 244, 245, 246, 289
British Aerospace 44
British Airways 44, 118, 216
British Gas 44, 95–6
British Telecom 44, 93, 96, 97
Brooks, Rebekah 178, 208, 209, 211, 271, 272, 274, 275, 276, 277, 278
Brown, Andrew 10; on GB 11, 17, 18, 77; childhood 14–15, 16, 19, 259; works for GB 50–51; on GB/Blair leadership struggle 78–80, 87–8, 89
Brown, Cedric 95–6
Brown, Clare 88
Brown, Elizabeth 9, 10–11, 15, 16, 20, 97–8
Brown, Fraser 123, 124, 168, 178, 203, 228, 235, 259, 272
Brown, George 33–4
Brown, Gordon: birth 9; name 10–11; childhood 12–13, 14–17, 18–19, 20–21; education 17–18, 19, 24–5; blindness 21–2, 24; character and personality 34, 51, 177, 202–3, 249, 251, 284, 286; religious views 258, 260–64, 265–6; interest in politics grows 22–4, 25; as student rector at Edinburgh University 25–7, 28, 29, 31–2; and royalty 27–8; and 1974 general elections 29, 30, 33; feud with Robin Cook (q.v.) 29–30; his PhD on James Maxton 30–31; becomes chair of university Labour club 32–3; fails as Edinburgh North Labour candidate (1974) 33; selected for Edinburgh South (1976) 33; loses to Tories (1979) 33–4; at Labour conference 34; and Scottish devolution 34–6, 66; works for STV 37, 38–9, and as tutor and lecturer 37–8; works for Edinburgh Festival Fringe programme with Moffat 39–40; as Labour Party moderniser 40–41, 43, 53, 56; wins Fife seat (1983) 41–2; meets Blair (q.v.) 44–5; supports Kinnock (q.v.) 43, 45–6; gives maiden speech 46–7; has good relations with civil service sources 47, 50; and miners' strike 48–50; first shadow ministerial role 51; and Mandelson (q.v.) 53–4; and 1987 election 54–5; recruits trade unionists to Labour Party 55; appointed shadow chief secretary to the Treasury under John Smith (q.v.) 56; and the economy 56–7; becomes shadow chancellor 57–8, and shadow trade and industry secretary 59–60; and Douglas Alexander 61; and 1992 election 62–5, 66; and Labour leadership rivalry 66–7, *see under* Blair, Tony; in shadow cabinet under John Smith 68; elected onto national executive committee 68; focuses on changing Labour's economic agenda 69, 70, 72, 93, 98, 99; brings in Sue Nye (q.v.) 70–71; consults with Ed Balls (q.v.) 72; in Washington with Blair 73–4; publishes *How We Can Conquer Unemployment* and *Fair is Efficient* 74; and John Smith's death 75, 76, 77, 82; relations with Alastair Campbell (q.v.) 92–3; ignorant of Blair's plan to abolish Clause IV 94; opposes VAT increases 95, 98; supports PPPs 95, 135–6; his plans for windfall tax

Brown, Gordon (cont'd)
opposed by Blair 96–7; and press attack on his mother 97–8; and 1997 election 98–9, 103, 104; becomes Chancellor of the Exchequer 104–5; plans independence for Bank of England (q.v.) 105–10; and British euro membership 113–16, 117–20; proposes to Sarah Macaulay 121; marriage 122; and death of daughter 122–5; success as chancellor 126–33, 149, 156–7; his critics 133–40; and Iraq war 141, 142–4, 145; triples international aid budget 146–8; policy differences with Blair 149–54; and 2005 election campaign 154–5, 158, 159; invites Pope Benedict XVI to Britain 258; presents him with his father's book of sermons 258–9; accused of plotting coup against Blair 160, 161; becomes Labour leader and prime minister 162–4, 167, 168–9; considers Ed Balls for chancellor 169–70; first cabinet meeting 170–71; has successful 'honeymoon' period 171–2; fails to call snap election 172–5, 176–7, 282; trip to Iraq condemned as 'stunt' 175–6; poll ratings plummet 177, 181; and Murdoch press 178, 209, 211–12, 268, 269–72, 275, 277–80, 281; refuses to use family in public appearances 178; and Mandelson's rehabilitation 178–9; and Alan Milburn 179–80, 284; and global financial crisis (2008) 180, 182–3, 186, 188–90, 192–9, 200–1, 203–4, 282, 285; at G20 summit 199–200, 201–2; and parliamentary expenses scandal 205–6; meets Pope Benedict again 258; lunches with Berlusconi 259–60; blamed by *Sun* for British casualties in Afghanistan 206; interviewed by author 207; Manchester conference speech receives standing ovation 207–8; his eyesight deteriorates 209–10; speaks to Mrs Thatcher 212; calls general election 213; gives electrifying speech 213–14; and the Duffy affair 214; blames himself for election defeat 215, 233, 281; and the media 215–16, 217, 218, 219; and Piers Morgan 216–18; last days as prime minister 220–30; and Ed Miliband as his successor 233–4, 281; speaks in tribute to Mandela 234; gives lecture at Lambeth Palace 263–4; and referendum on Scottish independence 234–44, 285; and Brexit 244–5; works with Keir Starmer 245–7; a constant reader 248; concludes talks with Ban Ki-moon 249; becomes his special envoy on global education 249, 250–51; launches Christian Aid Week 251; campaigns on global health 251–3; his relentless charity work at home 253, 257; campaigns against child and pensioner poverty 253–4, 255–6; awarded Companion of Honour 257; and Rachel Reeves 254–5; attacked by Elon Musk on X 256; at Jimmy Carter's funeral 256, 257; gives 2025 John Smith memorial lecture 253; at launch of Prince William's Homewards project 257; legacy 282–3, 284, 285, 288–9

Brown, Jack 10, 14

Brown, Jennifer Jane 9, 122–5, 216, 235, 264, 286

Brown, Reverend Dr John (father): birth 11; marriage 10; his ministries 11, 12, 13, 14; his politics 11; GB on 12–13, 15; and his sons 16–17; visits Israel 18; his book of sermons 258–9; traces ancestors 9; death 9

Brown, John (brother) 10; on his grandfather and father 11; childhood

12, 14–15, 16–17; influences GB 12, 18, 19, 24; on GB 22; at university 18, 26; as journalist 18, 216; works for STV 37, 59, 65; joins GB in Madrid 39; helps GB's campaign 85; writes eulogy for GB's daughter 123; and Murdoch press attack on his mother 97, 98
Brown, John (son) 123, 124, 168, 178, 203, 228, 235, 259
Brown, Maureen 10, 14
Brown, Nick 54, 67, 76, 153
Brown, Sarah (*née* Macaulay) 121–2; on her mother's influence 124; on GB 29; early dates with GB 88, 121, 213; engagement and marriage 121, 122; and death of their daughter 122–5, 216, 264, 286; and GB's entry to Number Ten 168; and Rebekah Brooks 271, 276; in Paris with family and J. K. Rowling 203; and parliamentary expenses scandal 205; introduces GB at Manchester conference 207–8; and Piers Morgan 216, 217; and Paul and Kathy Dacre 218; on announcement of hung parliament 219–20; and the move from Number Ten 226, 228; and GB's decision to take responsibility for Labour's failure 233; with GB in North Queensferry house 9, 15, 248
Brown, William 'Bill' 39
Brunson, Michael 55
BSkyB 273, 274, 279
Bulger, James 70
Bundesbank, the 115
Bundred, Iain 219
Burnham, Andy 285
Burns, Sir Terry 108, 109
Bush, President George W. 141, 142, 162, 163, 169, 182, 194, 195, 199
Butler, Robin 108
Byers, Stephen 151
Byrne, Liam 281

Cable, Vincent 227, 273, 274, 276
Cable & Wireless 44, 96
Callaghan, James (Jim) 4, 36, 37, 45, 71, 168
Cameron, David: elected Tory leader (2005) 157; policies 136, 137, 148; instigates standing ovation for Blair 167; as Tory leader 173, 175, 178; on GB's mistake in calling off election 176; attacks GB over financial crisis 182–3, 204; and Tom Fletcher 202; and expenses scandal 206; becomes prime minister (2010) 1, 215; and Scottish independence 234, 238–9, 240, 243; and Brexit 244, 245; and Murdoch 273; and hacking scandal 274
Cameron, Reverend Helen 255
Campbell, Alastair: works for Blair 75, 269; and John Smith's death 75–6; on GB/Blair relations 77–8, 91, 92–3; and Bank of England independence 110; and euro decision 116; and Iraq war 142, 144; and NHS reforms 151; 'We don't do God' 265; and 2005 election campaign 155, 157, 158, 159; and Duffy affair 214; hatred of Dacre and *Daily Mail* 218; and end of GB's premiership 3, 224, 226, 233, 268; and Brexit Remain campaign 245; on GB and hacking scandal 278; on Labour's greatest post-war figures 283
Cancer Guarantee 172, 208
Carter, Jimmy 4, 73, 148, 256, 257, 288
'cash for questions' 99
Catherwood, Sir Fred 25
Catholic Church 146, 255, 263
CBI *see* Confederation of British Industry
Chakrabortty, Aditya 204
Channel 4 News 153
Chapman, Jessica 274

Chawla, Hector 24, 210
Cheesbrough, Paul 275
Cheney, Dick 141
Chibok schoolgirls 250
child poverty 128–30, 131–2, 136, 138, 164, 249, 253, 254, 255–6, 282, 285, 287, 288
Children's Act (1989) 256
Chinese Central Bank 200
Chirac, Jacques 119, 143
Christian Aid 13, 146, 147, 251
Church of Scotland 10, 18, 237, 260, 263
Church Times 255
Churchill, Winston 30, 136–7
Citizens UK 213–14, 229–30
City of London 138–40, 163, 188–9, 287, 288
Clark, Tom 131–2, 133
Clarke, Charles 53, 77, 153, 178, 218, 219, 223
Clarke, Kenneth 65, 75, 95, 98, 106–7, 109, 110, 112, 126, 147, 149
Clegg, Nick 1, 2, 213, 215, 221, 222, 224–5, 226, 227–8, 240, 271
Climate Change Act (2008) 208
Clinton, Bill 63, 73, 74, 85, 217; administration 133, 185–6
CMOs *see* collaterised mortgage obligations
COBRA 171
Coffman, Hillary 76
collaterised mortgage obligations (CMOs) 183–4, 185, 186, 191, 193, 197
Confederation of British Industry (CBI) 97, 118
Conservative (Tory) Party 2, 12, 110, 115, 146, 172, 175, 176, 177, 180, 254; in Scotland 32, 34, 41; under Mrs Thatcher 43–4, 47, 105, 268; under Major 60, 63, 64, 65, 95, 268; under Cameron 182–3, 208, 244, 245
Cook, Robin 29; relations with GB 29–30, 33, 104, 142, 146; against Scottish devolution 35, 36; supports Kinnock 46; advises GB on his maiden speech 46; against ERM membership 70; and Labour leadership 77; at post-election celebrations 104; warms to single currency 112, 117; in praise of GB 127, 152; resigns over Iraq war 142–3; *The Point of Departure* 29–30; *Poverty and Deprivation in Scotland: The Real Divide* (with GB) 104
Cooper, Andrew 239
Cooper, Yvette 219
Corbyn, Jeremy 40, 92, 163, 244
Coulson, Andy 273, 274, 275
Coventry Cathedral 244, 245
Covid-19 pandemic 251, 285
Cowen, Brian 213
Cripps, Stafford 149
Cromer, Lord 107
Crosland, Anthony 3, 4, 31; *The Future of Socialism* 31
Crossman, Richard 201
Cruikshank, Don 189
Cunningham, Jack 92
Currie, David 115, 117
'curry house conspiracy' 160

Dacre, Kathy 123, 218
Dacre, Paul 123, 218–19
Daily Express 97
Daily Mail 123, 158, 159, 171, 218, 219, 246
Daily Mirror 92, 123, 209, 216
Daily Record 76, 216, 240
Daily Telegraph 133–4, 177, 205, 206, 209, 274
Dalton, Hugh 132
Dalyell, Tam 34, 35; *Devolution: The End of Britain?* 35
Dannatt, Richard 210–11
Darling, Alistair: becomes Chancellor of the Exchequer 169; GB tries to

move 180–81; relations with GB 194; blocks Barclays' purchase of Lehman's 194–5; recapitalises Royal Bank of Scotland 197–8; hosts G20 finance ministers 200; and financial crisis 200, 203, 204; relations with GB 200–1; represents Britain at EU talks on single currency 220; in last days of Labour government 223, 227; and J. K Rowling 238; runs Better Together campaign 240–41, 243; death 201; *Back from the Brink* 201
Darzi, Professor Ara 170
Davies, Gavyn 72, 105
Davies, Howard 109
Davies, Nick 273, 274, 176–7; *Hack Attack* 135, 273
Dearlove, Richard 144
Dempster, Archie 37–8
Deng, Wendi 271
Dewar, Donald 35, 45, 48, 60, 76, 81, 82
Diana, Princess of Wales 257
Dinsmore, David 272, 287
Douglas, Dick 38
Dowler, Milly 274
Draper, Derek 178
Drummond, Allan 27
Duffy, Gillian 214, 230
Dugdale, Kezia 244
Dugher, Michael 209, 210, 215–16, 260
Dunn, Tom 19

Eagle, Angela 154
Economic and Monetary Union (EMU) 112, 113, 116, 117
Edinburgh University 14, 17, 19, 20, 22–3, 39; *Student* magazine 22, 23–4, 26; Labour club 32
Edmonds, John 68
Education Cannot Wait 251
EEC *see* European Economic Community

Elder, Murray (Lord) 17, 26, 46, 68, 75, 76, 78
Elizabeth II, Queen 163, 168, 169, 213, 222, 258
EMC (mortgage lender) 186
EMU *see* Economic and Monetary Union
Eriksson, Sven-Göran 273
ERM *see* Exchange Rate Mechanism
euro, the 111, 112–13, 114–15–20
European Central Bank 112, 192
European Economic Community (EEC) 111, 113
European Union (EU) 111, 112, 113, 119
Evening Standard 142
Excel Centre, London 201
Exchange Rate Mechanism, European (ERM) 70, 87, 105, 106, 113, 115
expenses, MPs' *see* parliamentary expenses scandal

Fabian Society 106
Fallon, Michael 139
Fannie Mae 185 194
Farage, Nigel 244, 252
Farron, Tim 261
Felix multibank 253
Ferguson, Mrs 34
financial crisis, global (2008) 177, 180, 181, 182–204
Financial Services Authority (FSA) 109, 139, 188, 196–7
Financial Services Modernization Act, US (1999) 185–6, 188
Financial Stability Board 202
Financial Times 72, 115, 128, 187, 255
Fitzgerald, Niall 118
Fletcher, Tom 3, 22, 182, 202–3, 206, 211, 260, 288
flooding emergency 171, 172
Foot, Michael 40, 43, 44, 71, 223
foot and mouth 171, 172
Foote, Murray 240

Forbes, Kate 261, 263, 265
Forde, Matt 121
Fowler, Norman 96
Freddie Mac 185, 194
free gifts scandal 289
FSA *see* Financial Services Authority

G7 summits 146, 147, 148, 198, 199–200, 201,
G20 summits 180, 182, 196, 201–2, 204, 218, 221, 259, 261
Gaitskell, Hugh 11
Galbraith, Russell 39
Galloway, George 40–41
gambling industry 254, 255, 287
Garraway, Kate 178
GB Energy 288
Geddes, Jenny 23
Geldof, Bob 147
George, Eddie 106–7, 108–9, 118
Ginnie Mae 183
Gladstone, William 149
Glasgow College of Technology (*now* Glasgow Caledonian University) 37–8
gold reserves 134
Good Friday Agreement (1998) 213, 229
Goodman, Clive 273, 274
Goodwin, Fred 190, 196, 197
Gould, Bryan 53, 57, 66, 67
Gould, Philip 93, 155, 157, 159
Gove, Michael 59–60, 135, 157, 175, 182, 282
government-sponsored enterprises (GSEs) 184, 185
Gramsci, Antonio 32
Granita restaurant, Islington 79, 83
Greenberg, Simon 276
Greenspan, Alan 173, 184
Greenwich Capital 197
GSEs *see* government-sponsored enterprises

Guardian 146, 158, 159, 172, 173, 177, 194, 204, 214, 215, 227, 274; GB's column 252, 254, 264
Guthrie, Charles 210

Hague, William 118, 215
Hämäläinen, Sirkka 112
Hammersley, Dr George 25
Hammond, Eric 48
Hardie, Keir 30
Harman, Harriet 68, 73, 163, 213, 221, 226, 234
Harry, Prince 268, 278
Hasan, Mehdi 207
Haskins, Christopher 118
Hattersley, Roy 45, 46, 65
Hawke, Bob 61
Hayman Island, Australia 269
Healey, Denis 3, 4, 37, 105
Heffer, Eric 52
Heseltine, Michael 50, 51, 60
Hewitt, Patricia 212
Heywood, Jeremy 132, 179, 227, 243
Hill, David 161
Hitchens, Peter 245, 246
Homewards project 257
homosexuality 265
Hoon, Geoff 144, 212
Hopkinson, David 97–8
House of Lords 245–6, 288
HouseBeautiful (magazine) 124
Howard, Michael 119, 157, 215, 271
Howe, Geoffrey 60
HSBC (bank) 191
Huhne, Chris 228, 276
Hunt, Jeremy 273, 274
Hunter, Anji 67, 71–2, 91, 161
Hussein, Saddam 141–2, 285
Hutton Inquiry 153
Hyman, Peter 132

IFS *see* Institute for Fiscal Studies
IMF *see* International Monetary Fund

Independent 76, 85, 115, 212, 215, 271
Independent Labour Party (ILP) 30, 31
inheritance tax 174, 175, 176
Institute for Fiscal Studies (IFS) 127, 128–9
Institute for New Economic Thinking 139
International Commission on Financing Global Education Opportunity 250–51
International Health Partnership 252
International Monetary Fund (IMF) 146, 147, 201, 203; Interim Committee 133
Iraq invasion/war 119, 141–6, 148, 154, 155, 162, 163, 171, 172, 175, 230, 233, 285
Ireland: bank crisis 195–6
Islamic Relief UK 255
ITV 123, 124, 216, 275, 279
Izzard, Eddie 241

Janes, Jacqui 209, 210
Janes, Jamie 209
Jenkins, Roy 3, 4, 40, 104, 230
Johnson, Alan 170, 180
Johnson, Boris 252, 289

Kaufman, Gerald 44
Kavanagh, Trevor 135
Keating, Paul 61
Kelly, Dr David 153, 285
Kennedy, Charles 157, 227, 288
Kennedy, John F. 73
Kennedy, Senator Ted 199
Kilroy Silk, Robert 46
King, Mervyn 192, 199, 200
Kingskettle, Fife 9
Kinnock, Glenys 82, 246
Kinnock, Neil: as Labour leader 4, 41, 43, 45, 46, 51–3, 54–5, 56, 65–6; and Sue Nye 52–3, 71, 82, 209, 223; and GB 36–7, 43, 45–6, 48, 53, 54, 56, 57–8, 59, 62, 63, 64, 66, 204, 283; and Scottish devolution 34, 36; and miners' strike 48; and the media 209, 229, 269; 'torn' between Blair and GB as his successor 77–8, 80–81, 86; and EEC 113
Kinnock, Rachel 209
Kirkcaldy, Fife 9, 12, 13–14, 16, 220, 260; High School 12, 17, 168; Forth Park Hospital 122–3
Krugman, Paul 200
Kwarteng, Kwasi 133

Labour Party 30, 37, 43, 55, 176, 177, 180, 215, 219, 230, 244–7, 279, 288; Militant tendency 37, 40, 44, 45, 48, 52, 53, 65, 66; manifesto (*A New Hope for Britain*) 44; in coalition *see* Liberal Democrats; *see also* New Labour; Scottish Labour Party
Lagarde, Christine 200
Laing, Ian 60
Lamb, Larry 37
Lamb, Norman 276
Lambert, Richard 72
Lambeth conference (2008) 262–3
Lamont, Norman 63–4
Lawley, Sue 80
Lawson, Nigel 56, 57, 58, 60, 105–6, 110; *Memoirs of a Tory Radical* 110
Leadbeater, Kim 264
Lehman Brothers 186, 194, 195, 198–9
Leighton, Ron 49
Lennox, Annie 147
Leslie, Chris 95
Leveson, Lord Justice Brian 274
Leveson Inquiry 211, 212, 271–2, 274–5, 276, 279
Levitt, Ian 33
Lewis, Will 275, 276, 277
Liberal Democrats 64–5, 145, 146, 157, 215, 219, 244, 261; possible coalition with Labour 1, 2, 3, 220,

Liberal Democrats (*cont'd*)
221–3, 224–6, 227–8; coalition with Conservatives 213, 215, 221, 223, 226; and Scottish independence referendum 238
Liberal Party 43, 55, 145
Liddle, Roger 107; (with Mandelson) *The Blair Revolution* 107
Livermore, Spencer 173, 174
Livingstone, Ken 94, 135
Lloyd George, David 170
London Underground 135
Loos, Rebecca 273
Lucas, Mark 244

Maastricht Treaty (1992) 111, 113
Macaulay, Pauline 124
McBride, Damian 85, 159, 160, 161, 167, 194, 219; *Power Trip* 219
McConnell, Jack 197
MacDonald, James Ramsay 31
MacDonald, Murdo 10
MacDonald, Sadie 10
McDonnell, John 163
McDougall, Blair 238
McGahey, Michael 33–4
MacGregor, Ian 49
McKechnie, Sheila 26
McKillop, Tom 197
McLeish, Reverend Robert 13
McLeod, Rory 25
Macmillan, Harold 11, 48, 136–7
McNeil, Kirsty 219, 220
McSweeney, Morgan 246–7
Mahmood, Khalid 160
Mahmood, Tahir 123
Mail on Sunday 245, 246
Major, John: 'a rising star' 56; as prime minister 60, 65, 70, 86–7, 99, 103, 111, 112, 267, 284; and Murdoch 268; critical of GB 175–6; and Brexit 245
Make Poverty History movement 147
Malloch Brown, Mark 170
Mandela, Graça 234

Mandela, Nelson 234
Mandelson, Mary 286
Mandelson, Peter 53; wins Hartlepool 73; and New Labour 40, 52, 53, 55, 74, 93–4; and GB 53, 54, 66, 284, 286; and Charlie Whelan 73; and John Smith's death 76; and Blair/GB leadership dispute 79, 81–2, 84, 85, 90, 94; and election campaign 103; backs Bank of England independence 107; and inequality between rich and poor 128; and Blair 151; brought down by Whelan 158–9, 219; and Wegg-Prosser 160, 161; and GB's failure to call a snap election 176–7; backs GB's premiership 178–9; elevated to House of Lords 179; back in GB's cabinet as business secretary 179; and Rebekah Brooks 208–9; and the end of GB's premiership (2010) 2, 213, 220, 223; at talks with Lib Dems 221, 225, 226; (with Liddle) *The Blair Revolution* 107
Manning, David 142
Margareta, Crown Princess of Romania 28, 38
Marr, Andrew 175, 176
Marshall, Colin 118
Martin, Iain 189
Martin, Katie 255
Maryhill Community Centre, Scotland 240, 241
Mattinson, Deborah 174
Maxton, James 30–31, 50
Maxwell, Robert 270
May, Theresa 176, 267
MBSs *see* mortgage-backed securities
Merkel, Angela 196, 200, 202, 267
Metropolitan Police 268, 275, 276, 277, 278
MI6 144
Milburn, Alan 150, 151–2, 154–5, 178, 179–80, 218, 284, 286

Miliband, David 142, 169, 170, 177, 180, 233, 234
Miliband, Ed; hired by GB 73, 95; on New Labour 139; and Ed Balls 159, 169, 284; promotion 170; sceptical regarding snap election 172, 173, 174; and Mandelson's support for GB 178–9; urges David Miliband to remain in GB's cabinet 180; regrets inadequate City regulation 188; at talks with Lib Dems 221, 226; and the end of GB's premiership 226; as GB's successor 233, 285; apologises at Manchester conference for Iraq invasion 233–4; appeals against Scottish devolution 239, 240, 241; attempts to distance himself from Blair and GB governments 281
Militant (newspaper) 52
Millbank Tower, London 103
Millennium Development Goals (MDGs) 195
Mitchell, Andrea 173–4
Moffat, Alistair 9, 33, 34, 36, 39–40, 63, 234–5, 236, 238–9, 240
Monks, John 115, 117, 118
Moorfields Eye Hospital, London 210
Morgan, Eddie 244
Morgan, Piers 123, 176, 216–17
Morrison, Herbert 53
mortgage-backed securities (MBS) 183–4, 185, 186, 191, 193, 194, 197
Moth, Bishop Richard 255
Mowlam, Mo 68
MPs' allowances 206
Muggeridge, Malcolm 22–3
Mulcaire, Glen 273
Mulgan, Geoff 72
Mullin, Chris 77, 154
multibanks 253
Murdoch, James 211, 271, 273, 276, 279
Murdoch, Rupert 113, 209, 211–12, 268, 269, 270–71, 272, 273, 274, 276, 279; press 67–8, 77, 83, 97, 135, 215, 268, 271–2, 274, 275, 276–80, 281–2, *see also Sun*; *Sunday Times*; *Times, The*
Murphy-O'Connor, Cormac 263; *An English Spring* 263
Musk, Elon 256

National Coal Board 41, 49
National Freight 96
National Health Service (NHS) 21, 47, 64, 74, 93, 128, 130, 132, 134, 137, 138, 150, 164, 170, 241, 283; and privatisation 95, 135, 151, 171; waiting lists 103; and foundation trusts 150–51
National Union of Mineworkers 48–9
NatWest Bank 196
Naughtie, James 98
Nellist, David 44
New Deal, the 127
New Labour 35, 90, 93–4, 98–9, 129, 130, 131, 137, 150, 157, 281, 282–3; slogans 70, 103; 1997 election victory 104; and the City 189; and Brexit 119; and Murdoch press 212, 268, 269
New Statesman 178–9, 207, 287
New York Times 200
News Agents podcast 214
News Group Newspapers (NGN) 275, 276, 277, 278
News International 269, 275, 278
News of the World 176, 272, 273, 274, 278
NGN *see* News Group Newspapers
NHS *see* National Health Service
North Queensferry: GB's home 9, 15, 79, 122, 219, 233, 235, 243, 281
Northern Foods 118
Northern Ireland 213, 223
Northern Rock (bank) 177, 187, 192–3
Nuffield Foundation 128
Nye, Sue 70–71, 72, 88, 163, 209, 215–16, 219, 223, 226–7, 233; on Kinnock 52–3; on John Smith 71, 76;

Nye, Sue (cont'd)
    on GB 71–2, 76–7, 82–3, 84, 89–90, 91, 163, 167, 168–9, 170, 220–22, 226, 227; and end of GB's premiership 1, 2, 228–9

Obama, Barack 3, 182, 199, 202, 203, 204, 205, 206
Observer 162
Ofcom 273
Olmert, Ehud 205
O'Neill, Martin 33
Orr, Lesley 31–2
Osborne, George 136, 137, 157, 174, 175, 178, 204, 226, 240, 241, 245, 254
Owen, David 40
Oxfam 146, 147

parliamentary expenses and 'freebies' scandals 205–6, 287
Parris, Matthew 46
Patten, Chris 98
Paulson, Ron 194–5, 198
pensioner poverty 129, 131–2, 136, 164
Peston, Robert 115, 127, 153, 192, 275
PFI *see* private finance initiative
Philip, Prince 27–8
Picasso, Pablo: *Guernica* 39
Pierce, Andrew 97
Pink Floyd 147
Plaid Cymru 223, 225
Political Studies Association 149
Post Office 171
Powell, Jonathan 161
PPP *see* public-private partnerships
Prentis, Dave 150–51
Prescott, John 51, 67, 68, 69, 77, 89, 98, 103, 143, 154, 273
Press Association 87, 97, 159
PricewaterhouseCoopers 135
Pring, Olivia 248
private finance initiative (PFI) 135
Professional Footballers' Association 273

Progress 72
Prospect magazine 276–7
public private partnerships (PPPs) 95, 127, 135
Purnell, James 180, 181

Quinn, Carolyn 256
Quintin Kynaston School (*now* Harris Academy), London 159

Radice, Giles 4; *Friends and Rivals* 4
Raffarin, Jean-Pierre 119
Raith Rovers Football Club 16, 18
Ramzan, Shazia 250
RBS *see* Royal Bank of Scotland
Reeves, Rachel 253, 254–5, 285, 287, 288
Reich, Robert 73
Reid, John 178, 218, 226
Rice, Condoleezza 142
Riddell, Peter 79
Rifkind, Malcolm 60
Robertson, George 35, 45
Robinson, Geoffrey 96, 158, 270
Rodgers, Bill 40
Rolls-Royce 44
Roosevelt, Franklin D. 186
Rosyth Naval Base 50
Routledge, Paul 158
Rowley, Mark 275, 277
Rowling, J. K. 203, 238; Harry Potter books 248
Royal Bank of Scotland (RBS) 190, 196–8
Rumsfeld, Donald 141
Ryden, Nick 78

Saatchi and Saatchi 172
Salik, Zia 255–6
Salmond, Alex 36, 221, 235, 243
Salomon Brothers 183
Sansom, C. J. 238
Sarkozy, Nicolas 172, 182, 199, 201
Satyarthi, Kailash 250
Save the Children 147

Scargill, Arthur 48, 49
Scarlett, John 142
Scholar, Tom 108
Schröder, Gerhard 119
Schumer, Senator Chuck 188—9
Scotland Act (2016) 239, 244
Scottish Daily Express 22
Scottish Daily Mail 19
Scottish devolution 34–6, 51, 59, 66, 104, 208, 236, 238, 239
Scottish independence referendum (2014) 234–44, 285
Scottish Labour Party (SLP) 36, 37, 61, 71, 98, 104, 234, 244, 247
Scottish National Party (SNP) 32, 35–6, 38, 56, 177, 221, 234, 235, 236, 237, 239, 244, 245, 261
Scottish Poor Law 237
Scottish Sun 272
Scottish Television (STV) 37, 38, 39, 40, 59
SDP *see* Social Democratic Party
Seyd, Patrick 55
Sherif, Yasmine 251
Short, Clare 98, 142–3
Shrum, Bob 138, 173, 174, 204, 235, 282
Shrum, Marylouise 174
Simon, David, Baron Simon of Highbury 117–18
Simon, Siôn 160
Sinclair, Paul 238
Sinn Fein 223
Sky News 208, 214, 261, 71
Sloboda, John 145
SLP *see* Scottish Labour Party
Smith Adam 13; *The Theory of Moral Sentiments* 13; *The Wealth of Nations* 13
Smith, Catherine 75, 76
Smith, Elizabeth 75, 76, 78
Smith, Ian 18
Smith, Jacqui 170, 171, 205
Smith, Jane 75, 76

Smith, John 44; pro Scottish devolution 35; introduces GB to Blair 44; and Murray Elder 17, 68; supports Hattersley for Labour leader 45; and Andrew Brown 51; GB works under 51, 56; keen to transform Labour 56; has heart attack 57–8; launches 'shadow budget' 64; and Blair 66–7; wins Labour Party leadership 45, 67, 71; makes Blair shadow home secretary 68; and the unions 68–9; persuaded by GB to ditch 'shadow budget' 69; and ERM membership 70; angry at Blair and GB's Washington trip 74; his death and afterwards 75–6, 77, 78, 82, 85, 86, 87, 92, 158
Smith, Sarah 75, 76
Smith, Sid 19
Smith Commission 239
SNP *see* Scottish National Party
Social Democratic Party (SDP) 40, 43
social media 208, 238, 256, 266–7, 269, 286
Soley, Clive 154
Sopel, Jon 214
Sorki, Aaron Ross 195
Spectator 135
Sporting Post 16
Starmer, Keir 92, 150, 244, 245–7, 253, 254, 256, 264, 272, 285, 286–8
Steinbrück, Peer 196
Sting 147
Stoddart, David 41
Straw, Jack 89, 279
student tuition fees 152–3, 159, 171
Sturgeon, Nicola 261
STV *see* Scottish Television
Summers, Larry 73
Sun 37, 216; attacks Kinnock 269; Blair's pre-election article 114; attacks GB 134–5; and Whelan's leaks 158; and Ed Balls 178; blames GB for British casualties in

Sun (cont'd)
  Afghanistan 206, 210–12; backs the Tories 208–9, 211, 268; wooed by Blair and Campbell 269; invades GB's personal life 271–2; and the 2014 election 286–7
Sunday Express 16
Sunday Times 77, 160, 239, 269–70, 272, 277; magazine 45, 67
Sure Start 128, 129, 208, 255, 282
Swann, Professor Michael 19

Tablet 255
Taylor, Gordon 273
Tebbit, Norman 47, 96
Tedros Adhanom Ghebreyesus, Dr 252
Tett, Gillian 187
Thatcher, Margaret: wins 1979 election 37, 105, 168, 228; and Falklands War 43, 154; and 'Watergate-style cover-up' 41; and miners' strike 45, 48; and Conservatives' drift to the right 47; and Westland affair 51; supported by Murdoch 268; her policies attacked by Blair 55; and Nigel Lawson's views on Bank of England 110; opposed to single European currency 111; and pensions 133; and poll tax 60, 65, 236; resigns as Tory leader 60; her legacy 137, 148; and GB 212; on lecture circuit 233
Theos 253
Tietmeyer, Hans 115
Times, The 26, 46, 59, 83, 97, 116, 117, 154, 158, 216, 274, 286–7
Tooze, Adam 198
Tory Party see Conservative Party
Treasury, the: GB's welcome 104–5; and Bank of England independence 106, 107, 108, 110, 126; and euro membership 114, 115, 117, 118; and GB 126–7, 135–6, 139–40, 149, 150, 155, 188, 190, 195; and stabilisation of banking sector 197–8

Tribune group 68
Trimdon Labour Club, County Durham 161–2
'triple lock', the 133
Troubled Asset Relief Program (US) 195
Trudeau, Pierre 238
Trump, President Donald 252, 272
Truss, Liz 133
Turing, Alan 265
Turner, Adair 118, 132
two-child benefit cap 254

UBS Bank USA 191–2
UK Independence Party (UKIP) 180, 244
unemployment 14, 25, 31, 47, 58, 63, 64–5, 69, 74, 95, 127, 129, 182, 193, 203, 236, 254
Unilever 118
Unison 150
United States: and Iraq War 145; subprime mortgage crisis 177, 180, 183–7, 188–9, 190–91, 193, 194–5, 198–9
US Federal Reserve 173, 184, 186, 190, 192

Vadera, Shriti 179, 193, 284
Vallance, Iain 96, 97
Vanity Fair 278
Vansittart, Nicholas 149
VAT (value added tax) 65, 95, 98, 203
Viggers, Sir Peter 205

Walden, Brian 46
Walker, Peter 96
Wallace, Moira 107–8
Walters, Alan 60
Wanless, Derek 134; Wanless review (2002) 152
'Warm Welcome' project 253
Washington Post 268, 277

Watkins, Kevin 147–8, 249
Watson, Tom, Baron Watson of Wyre Forest 160, 161, 275, 276, 278
Webster, Philip 116, 157
Wegg-Prosser, Benjamin 160–61
Wells, Holly 274
West, Sir Alan 170
'West Lothian question, the' 35
Westland affair 51
Whelan, Charlie 73, 77, 85, 88, 98, 104, 116, 158–9, 219
Who, the 147
Whyte, Annmarie 241
Wicks, Nigel 115
William, Prince 257, 273
Williams, Dr Rowan 253, 254, 255, 261–2, 263
Williams, Shirley 40
Wills, Jonathan 26
Wills, Michael 94, 279
Wilson, Brian 92, 98
Wilson, Harold 3, 12, 18, 38, 107, 142, 170–71
Wilson, John 272
windfall taxes 59, 69, 93, 96–7, 108, 127
Winnett, Robert 277
winter fuel allowance 133, 208, 253, 254, 282, 287
Wintour, Patrick 214
Witherow, John 270
Wolfensohn, James 143
Wood, Stewart 179, 219, 259–60
World Bank 143, 146, 147
World Health Organization (WHO) 251–2
Wright, David 160

Young, David 96
Yousafzai, Malala 250

Zhou Xiaochuan 200

Image Credits

Gordon, his parents and brother, John: Andrew Brown; Gordon and John, 1953: Andrew Brown; Gordon, aged 6: Andrew Brown; Gordon and Andrew in garden: Andrew Brown; Gordon, 1972: Andrew Brown; Gordon graduating from university: Andrew Brown; Gordon as a journalist for Scottish Television: STV; Gordon playing tennis: Andrew Brown; Gordon Brown and Ed Balls: PA Images via Alamy; Gordon Brown and Neil Kinnock: PA Images via Alamy; Gordon Brown with John Smith, Tony Blair and Margaret Beckett: Mathieu Polak/Sygma/Sygma via Getty Images; Blair 1997 Campaign team: Tom Stoddart/Getty Images; Gordon Brown Mansion House speech: Peter Macdiarmid/Getty Images; Gordon Brown and Tony Blair election night win: Mathieu Polak/Sygma/ Sygma via Getty Image; Gordon Brown and Tony Blair: Jeff Overs/BBC News & Current Affairs via Getty Images; Gordon Brown and Robin Cook: Allstar Picture Library Ltd via Alamy; 2006 Party Conference: Jeff Overs/BBC News & Current Affairs via Getty Images; Gordon Brown at Raith Rovers match: Danny Lawson / PA via Alamy; Gordon Brown school visit: Jeff Overs/ BBC News & Current Affairs via Getty Images; Gordon Brown with his newborn child: Ross Gilmore/WireImage; Prime Minister Gordon Brown and his wife, Sarah outside Downing Street: Jeff J Mitchell/Getty Images; Gordon Brown in Iraq: Daniel Berehulak / Getty Images; Gordon Brown with world leaders: Jean-Francois DEROUBAIX/Gamma-Rapho via Getty Images; Gordon Brown with Berlusconi: Eric VANDEVILLE/Gamma-Rapho via Getty Images; Gordon Brown calling for an election: Chris Ratcliffe/Bloomberg via Getty Images; Leader's debate: Ken McKay/ITV via Getty Images; Gordon Brown Citizens UK speech: LEON NEAL/AFP via Getty Images; Gordon Brown classroom visit during 2010 campaign: Lefteris Pitarakis/WPA Pool/Getty Images; Gordon Brown and Gillian Duffy: Jeff J Mitchell/Getty Images; Gordon Brown resigning from office:

Dan Kitwood/Getty Images; Gordon Brown's final moments in office: Martin Argles/Guardian; Gordon Brown Scottish Referendum speech: Jeff J Mitchell/Getty Images; Gordon Brown Scottish Referendum outdoor campaign: AP Photo/Matt Dunham; Gordon Brown Brexit speech: OLI SCARFF/AFP via Getty Images; Gordon Brown, Levenson inquiry arrival: MIGUEL MEDINA/AFP via Getty Images; Gordon Brown with brothers Andrew and John: Andrew Brown; Gordon Brown at the United Nations: Li Muzi/Xinhua/Alamy Live News

A Note on the Author

James Macintyre is a British journalist and author. He was senior producer of BBC1's *Question Time*, political correspondent for the *Independent* and *New Statesman* – where he covered Brown's premiership close up – and politics editor of *Prospect* magazine. He is co-author of *Ed: The Milibands and the Making of a Labour Leader*, and has written for a range of publications including the *New York Times*, *Guardian* and *Mail on Sunday*. He has appeared on Sky News, BBC News and LBC.

A Note on the Type

The text of this book is set in Linotype Stempel Garamond, a version of Garamond adapted and first used by the Stempel foundry in 1924. It is one of several versions of Garamond based on the designs of Claude Garamond. It is thought that Garamond based his font on Bembo, cut in 1495 by Francesco Griffo in collaboration with the Italian printer Aldus Manutius. Garamond types were first used in books printed in Paris around 1532. Many of the present-day versions of this type are based on the *Typi Academiae* of Jean Jannon cut in Sedan in 1615.

Claude Garamond was born in Paris in 1480. He learned how to cut type from his father and by the age of fifteen he was able to fashion steel punches the size of a pica with great precision. At the age of sixty he was commissioned by King Francis I to design a Greek alphabet, and for this he was given the honourable title of royal type founder. He died in 1561.